SUCH RARE CITINGS

SUCH RARE CITINGS

The Prose Poem in English Literature

N. Santilli

Madison • Teaneck
Fairleigh Dickinson University Press
London: Associated University Presses

©2002 by Rosemont Publishing & Printing Corp.

All rights reserved. Authorization to photocopy items for internal or personal use, or the internal or personal use of specific clients, is granted by the copyright owner, provided that a base fee of $10.00, plus eight cents per page, per copy is paid directly to the Copyright Clearance Center, 222 Rosewood Drive, Danvers, Massachusetts 01923. [0-8386-3951-8/02 $10.00 + 8¢ pp, pc.]

Associated University Presses
2010 Eastpark Boulevard
Cranbury, NJ 08512

Associated University Presses
16 Barter Street
London WC1A 2AH, England

Associated University Presses
P.O. Box 338, Port Credit
Mississauga, Ontario
Canada L5G 4L8

The paper used in this publication meets the requirements of the American National Standard for Permanence of Paper for Printed Library Materials Z39.48-1984.

Library of Congress Cataloging-in-Publication Data

Santilli, N. (Nikki), 1970-
  Such rare citings : the prose poem in English literature / N. Santilli.
    p. cm.
  Includes bibliographical references (p.) and index.
  ISBN 0-8386-3951-8 (alk. paper)
  1. Prose poems, English—History and criticism. 2. English drama—History and criticism. I. Title.

PR509æP7 S36 2002
821.009—dc21

2002023039

PRINTED IN THE UNITED STATES OF AMERICA

In Memory of
Anita Santilli

Contents

Preface	9
Acknowledgments	11
Introduction	13
Abbreviations	27
1. The Prose Poem and the Romantic Fragment	31
2. De Quincey and Baudelaire	71
3. Contexts I: *The English Mail-Coach*	98
4. Contexts II: *Mercian Hymns*	118
5. Parallelism: Blake, Wilde, Beckett	137
6. Beckett's Late Prose	161
7. The Prose Poem and the City	181
Notes	207
Works Cited	259
Index	277

Preface

I WOULD LIKE TO THANK THE FOLLOWING INDIVIDUALS AND INSTITUTIONS for their generous assistance at various stages of this project.

I have benefited from research awards granted by King's College London and the British Academy. I would like to thank the staff at King's, in particular, Janet Bately and Max Saunders. I am very grateful to Jacques Berthoud and Steven Connor for their spirited response to the work. To Michel Delville I am indebted for his informed comments and suggestions as much as for his generously expressed support. My thanks also to Ronald Corthell, Leonee Ormond, Christine Rees and Amanda Rigali for their comments on various chapters. The library staff at King's, the University of London Library and the British Library have been very helpful in my perennial burrowing for specific material. Christopher Ricks, John Beer and Rupert Loydell were very kind to reply to my detailed enquiries. John Pilling and Michael Bott welcomed me to the Beckett archive at Reading and generously took time to discuss my ideas with me. Richard Salmon, Joseph Roth, and Steven Whalen gave me their invaluable technical assistance. Many thanks to Harry Keyishian at Fairleigh Dickinson University Press and Julien Yoseloff at Associated University Presses. Special thanks to Tamsin Black for her advice on the translations and for discussing all things French with me. Also to Christine Retz who wisely kept me occupied with other thoughts while she carefully managed my manuscript through the press.

This project simply would not have been realized without the lively support of my family: Ron, Anita, and Marina Santilli. It is lovingly dedicated to the memory of my mother, who took into her hands each chapter that I wrote. Her touch imbues these pages.

Finally, to John Woolford, who first taught me the art of thought, and who continues to be an inspiring maestro, I shall always be grateful in my debt.

Acknowledgments

Photographs of MS Egerton 2800 f1–f1v by Samuel Taylor Coleridge, reproduced by permission of The British Library.

Excerpts taken from *Baudelaire: Poems in Prose and La Fanfarlo. Volume II*, translated by Francis Scarfe. Published by Anvil Press Poetry in 1989.

Excerpts taken from *Collected Shorter Prose 1945–1980* by Samuel Beckett, published by John Calder in 1984, reprinted by permission.

Excerpts taken from *Poems 1955–1980* by Roy Fisher, originally published in *Stopped Frames and Set Pieces*; reprinted in *Poems 1955–1980*, © Roy Fisher. And from *Poems 1955–1987* by Roy Fisher, originally published in *City*, selections of which were reprinted in *The Dow Low Drop: New and Selected Poems* © Roy Fisher.

Excerpts taken from *Philosophical Fragments* by Friedrich Schlegel et al., translated by Peter Firchow. Copyright © 1991 by the Regents of the University of Minnesota. *Philosophical Fragments* originally appeared in *Friedrich Schlegel's "Lucinde" and the Fragments*. Copyright © 1971 by the University of Minnesota.

Excerpts taken from *Collected Poems* by Charles Tomlinson, published in 1985, reprinted by permission of Carcanet Press Ltd.

Excerpts taken from *Mercian Hymns* by Geoffrey Hill, reprinted by permission of Andre Deutsch Ltd.

A version of Chapter 7 first appeared in *Prose Studies* 20: 1 (April 1997), 77–89. It is reprinted here by permission of Frank Cass Publishers.

Introduction

FOR JONATHAN MONROE, THE PROSE POEM IS A DIMINUTIVE POLITICAL champion that restores lost and oppressed voices.[1] In its one hundred and fifty year existence, the genre has never advanced beyond its minor classification and so by its own history it reenacts the muted voice of those it champions. The prose poem designates the literary space of battle, which it announces by its oxymoronic name. Fittingly, for a genre dedicated to individualism, this title corresponds to the single prose piece rather than to the collection within which it operates (for which the term becomes "prose poetry").

Implicit as it is in Monroe's discussion of restored voices, the concept of a genre that is actually founded on subversion is compelling and appears at varying degrees in most accounts, including mine. Margueritte Murphy, in *A Tradition of Subversion*, undertakes a basic reading in which a network of different discourses (Bakhtin's dialogism) appropriates a recognizable genre and subverts it in each text.[2] The prose poem, it is suggested, exposes the extent to which our understanding of language is driven by our recognition of types of discourse. The problem with this approach is that it presupposes a stability of genres: an unevolving standardization of form against which the prose poem can always be recognized as other. Stamos Metzidakis shares the aestheticism of Murphy's approach but offers a closer look at the dynamics of subversion. He deconstructs the subversive act into "good" and "bad" repetition: that which may engender future repetitions and that which is already present. The prose poem participates in both these types by, on one hand, establishing a model that can be repeated, but on the other, revealing the already written (which exposes the former as an ideal). This latter, or "bad" repetition prevents the text from fully unifying its separate parts, meaning that the prose poem may be read semiotically but not interpreted as a whole.³ However, Metzidakis ultimately defers to Jakobson's referential and poetic functions as analogous to his "inter-" and "intra-" textual forms of repetition. Moreover, he emphasizes the importance of the poetic or self-referential. Metzidakis never quite resolves the incompatibility between Jakobson's self-referential poetic and the outwardly referential acts of subversion together with the prose medium that the genre employs.

In *Discourse/Counter-Discourse,* Richard Terdiman sets out the strongest argument for a theory of subversion because he solves the problem to which Murphy falls prey: the apparent necessity in a theory of subversion to assume a stable model (for example, a static and universally recognized genre). Instead, he emphasizes the active element of time as crucial in sustaining a subversive system. The subverted object does not passively suffer its own parody but actually controls the times when such a reaction is possible by constantly shifting itself in order to contain anything deemed other. Terdiman's terms are not aesthetic (Metzidakis's repetitions, Murphy's self-evident genres) but political. The subversive counter-discourse (the prose poem) is subject to change when the idiolect of the dominant discourse (the French bourgeoisie, for example) itself changes or shifts to internalize anything discovered beyond its own limits in its continuing power struggle.⁴ The prose poem is a genre of the moment and Terdiman acknowledges that other theories (such as Derrida's deconstruction) treat the same battle for domination in different ways. What emerges from these accounts is that struggle, formalized by paradox, characterizes the genre as well as writings about it.

Within this international debate, Stephen Fredman states that American and French prose poetry are not the same and he renames the American genre "poet's prose" in an attempt to begin unraveling the hitherto tangled strands of cooperative scholarship. He is scolded by Murphy who insists on the title, "prose poem" and fears that "this French form seems to fall prey to an isolationist aesthetic that American poetry would construct to lay claim to its own turf as an independent and 'new' tradition."⁵ Fredman's argument, however, is strong. He argues that American poets' prose, in a crisis of identity, fights the international literary tradition itself (and "the tyranny of British verse" in particular), which it posits as the locus of its artistic oppression. It is, he argues, the very lack of tradition in American literature that makes it so self-conscious and therefore in crisis: "American poets characteristically feel themselves called upon to make these decisions, ['will there be an American poetry? How will it differ from, or develop from, European poetry?'] to affirm anew the very vocation of poetry—an act unthinkable (because unnecessary) in Europe."[6] Fredman articulates the fundamental difference between American and French prose poetry by distinguishing between the aesthetically determined French practice and the substitution of meter in America by the amorphous intellect. This distinction is marked by the introduction of factual matter into the American text with the result that intellect and imagination become inextricable.

Finally, Thomas O'Beebee, in his discussion of genre, identifies, somewhat curiously, Roland Barthes's *L'Empire des Signes* as a prose poem. O'Beebee's thesis becomes increasingly interesting (in the light of Fredman's argument) as he compares Barthes's objectives concerning cultural translation with the concept of the prose poem itself. In *L'Empire des Signes*, Barthes attempts to construct a semiotics of Japanese culture. However, his failure to adequately formulate Western equivalents for Japanese genres "is his way of expressing the ideology of genre, its use-value, which cannot be translated from one culture to another—nor from one historical epoch to another, even if the same name is preserved."[7]

The prose poem, symbolized by Barthes's text, becomes, for O'Beebee, a form that is neither prose nor poetry but a lack, "an artificial paradise, and ideological vacuum located *là-bas*, between disillusionment and belief."[8] The genre eludes capture, constantly self-transforming and as unattainable as its Oriental ideal.

The unusual dynamic established by the incomplete assimilation of a foreign literature that comes to inhabit the least-known point of its host's culture is, perhaps, one way of looking at the English prose poetic tradition within both a European and American context. English literature shares geographic and historic proximity with the European tradition and a common language with the American. However, when an English translation of Japanese prose poems appeared in 1980, the translator felt the need to write an introduction on the history of French as well as Japanese prose poetry:

> The lack of prose poems in English literature (there are some, but there is nothing like the French tradition I have outlined) indicates how little the literatures written in that language have truly responded to modernist poetics. This point needs to be stressed because a reader of English may well by unsympathetic to much modern Japanese poetry because it is in that tradition his own literature has never fully accepted.[9]

Although my own reading of the prose poem is guilty by being Romantically—rather than Modernist—based (taking, as Monroe does, the prose poem as a critical fragment), it may well be that the English prose poem will always appear somewhat odd, even foreign, within the context of the generic canon.

John Simon, on the subject of English prose poetry, has pronounced that "despite occasional practitioners . . . the prose poem is now dead." However, whether this was written originally in 1959 or during the thesis's 1987 revision, it is erroneous. Simon makes no mention of the work of Samuel Beckett, Geoffrey Hill, Roy Fisher, or any other mid- to late-twentieth-century prose poetic writers.[10] Similarly, Murphy opens her discussion "from Wilde to Ashbery" with Pater and Wordsworth but soon confines the English tradition to Wilde, Dowson, and Eliot. She blames the adverse publicity of Wilde's trial for the failure of the genre in Britain and does not risk the tidiness of her argument by looking to see if the genre was ever practiced again in this country.[11] Writers themselves collude with this convenient misreading: William Sharp (as "Fiona Macleod") rejected the designation "prose poems" awarded by his reviewers for his "prose rhythms," *The Silence of Amor* (1896); T. S. Eliot suppressed his own prose poems (except "Hysteria") and wrote against the genre in his article, "The borderline of prose," he also disuaded Richard Aldington from continuing to write in the genre; Geoffrey Hill has denied that *Mercian Hymns* are a collection of prose poems, preferring to call them instead "versets of rhythmical prose"; Beckett too once said that writers ought to be able to keep genres separate.[12]

The earliest use of the term, "prose poem," occurs in *Blackwood's Magazine*, 1831, in an essay by Christopher North (the pseudonym of John Wilson) entitled "Winter Rhapsody." Here, he welcomes the genre that, from his own example, appears as a set piece of prose verging at times on the impassioned. North regards this form of writing as the successor to the "lofty rhyme" of the previous century, although he will not claim for it the technical equality of its verse forefathers. Instead, he places the merit of prose poems in the fact that they are "breathed from inspiration" and, in typical Romantic expression, "obey the bidding of that Sense of Beauty which is born with every creature 'endowed with discourse of reason.'"[13]

Yet, as recently as 1985, the British poet George Barker published an essay on the prose poem, in which he characterizes the genre as a mythical beast that only certain poets and critics believe they have seen:

> Like the Loch Ness monster the prose poem is a creature of whose existence we have only very uncertain evidence. Sometimes it seems to appear, like a series of undulating coils, out of the dithyrambs of Walt Whitman; several French critics claim to have taken photographs of this extraordinary beast, and a great many American poets possess tape recordings of the rhapsodies it chants up from the depths of the liberated imagination.[14]

Barker argues that, like Voltaire's God, "the prose poem got itself invented simply because it did not exist." The term filled the gap demanded by the logical reasoning that runs: "Verse at its best ascends into the superior condition of Poetry, therefore Prose must at its best ascend into the condition of—what? The answer is the Prose Poem." Barker identifies heightened prose passages as prose poems and either willfully ignores or has not seen any of the *actual* prose poems in France, America, the United Kingdom, or elsewhere in the world, since T. S. Eliot. Nevertheless, his humorous, patronizing tone in this essay has had enough negative impact in Britain to prompt a retraction from even the Francophile surrealist poet, David Gascoyne, in the introduction to his *Collected Poems, 1988*: "A similarly convenient grouping together is that of all the items in prose. I hesitate to designate them 'prose poems' since this category has been denounced cogently and with wit by George Barker as representing a 'Jubjub Bird.' The sequence now retitled 'Automatic Album Leaves' is no more than early exercises in uncontrolled word-play."[15]

Yet, other writers who are open to American and French influence such as Roy Fisher and Charles Tomlinson remain comfortable with the prose poem genre. The title of this book, *Such Rare Citings*, is a refutation of Barker's "mythical beast" and offers concrete evidence for what is still so often considered to be one of the more exotic literary genres. My aim is to examine the British prose poem in particular, which has so far been neglected in anthologies and commentaries. Not only does it continue to exist beyond the few pieces written by Oscar Wilde, but it was actually instrumental in the initial development of the genre in France.

Ideally, I would have used this introduction to describe a typical prose poem and to give a précis of the international debate that has grown up around the genre. However, "typical" is not a helpful term in the field of prose poetry. Problematically for me, even critical accounts of the genre are all unusually distinctive and tend to redraw the subject rather than engage directly with each other. Yet the difficulty belongs only to my own attempts to summarize and engage with these discussions as recognizable and manageable sets. In fact, their difference is appropriate. In the paradoxical and unorthodox world of the prose poem, and despite being the literary genre most accommodating to the field of its own theorization, there can be no seminal text—of either a primary or secondary source. I have chosen to work in a similar way and have produced a singular and independent account of the genre referring to other sources where they directly intersect my argument.

In *Le Poème en Prose de Baudelaire jusqu'à nos Jours* (1959), Suzanne Bernard attempted an encyclopedic project for the genre by recording its chronological appearances and analyzing its developing aesthetic. This was a brave, useful, but ultimately misguided exercise as the tradition of the prose poem is as interrupted and discontinuous as the form itself. Accordingly, much criticism tends, sensibly, to eschew the hunt for an all-encompassing definition in favor of constructing models of its most characteristic elements.[16] These interpretations elucidate specific points, values or paradoxes in which this deceptively miniature literary form abounds. But this is not to say that criticism on the prose poem appears solely as articles, essays, or single chapters. There are several full-length works devoted to the genre. However, these remain extremely specific in their discussion and do not approach the all-embracing overview achieved to some extent by Bernard. I concur with these approaches and have concentrated on certain key areas while merely sketching what I believe lies beyond the immediate subjects of my inquiry. This seems to me to be the best way to conserve not just the fragmentary nature of prose poetic texts but also the sense of discontinuity when engaging with them.

In this book, I identify the English prose poem and locate it within the international critical debate on the genre. As there is not a comprehensive British anthology to which I can refer as a primary source, I have, from the works that I have uncovered, selected those that either look like "genuine" prose poems or exhibit movements towards or away from a prose poetic form.[17] If I dwell on texts that lie on the borderline of prose poetry, it is to show that, as a form of distortion (prose fiction tends to be of considerable length), the peculiarly brief prose piece is possible because of characteristics already present in literary prose. In my selection of texts, I concur with Yves Vadé, who states that the problem with defining and theorizing the prose poem is compounded by the fact that not all texts can equally justify the appellation. In addition, some works that do not lay claim to the genre, are arguably more suited to do so.[18]

This approach inevitably affects my choice of texts. For example, De Quincey figures prominently because his work progressively and self-consciously strives to achieve the form of contained, brief, independent units.[19] Although he cannot be said to produce prose poems, his style of writing, which is simultaneously discursive and self-analytical, offers the ideal texts against which to place the prose poem in order to understand the latter in greater detail. The form of the dream visions in the *Suspiria de Profundis* verge on that of the prose poem collection (represented here by Baudelaire's *Le Spleen de Paris*) and yet the two are almost undefinable. A parallel analysis should produce some essential differences. Furthermore, the fact that Baudelaire was translating the *Suspiria* at the same time that he composed his prose poems strengthens De Quincey's position within a prose poetry debate.

On the other hand, my appropriation of Geoffrey Hill's *Mercian Hymns,* as a collection of prose poems (Chapter 4) may be in direct contradiction to the poet's own statement on the subject but both Wesling and Fredman have concluded as I have in favor of the attribution—in fact, Wesling sees no need to defend his classification. I have tried to explain in this chapter why and how *Mercian Hymns* accords with the prose poetic (namely its form as a collection of fragments and its treatment of context).

My presentation of the works I have selected is both chronological and comparative: I take as my starting point the Romantic critical fragment and end with the prose pieces of Samuel Beckett, Charles Tomlinson, and Roy Fisher. At the same time, I juxtapose works by Thomas De Quincey and Geoffrey Hill to compare their formal structure; I examine the biblical styles of Wilde and Beckett; and I end on a discussion of the mechanics of the prose poem's urban theme, in works by Baudelaire and Fisher, among others. In this way I hope to achieve two things. Firstly, to give an idea of the covert development of prose poetic texts in English literature from the Romantic period to the present day. Secondly, and concurrently, my juxtaposition of texts is aimed at revealing the often subtle differences that distinguish a prose poem from a passage of prose or between English and French prose poems.

The theoretical complexity of the prose piece is supplemented by the fact that the genre's objective is not easily discernible. In fact, viewed historically, the avatars of the prose poem appear somewhat disjunctive: the tableaux of Bertrand and Baudelaire are replaced by the dense mass of words in Mallarmé that then reappear in the surrealist concoction of André Breton, and so it continues. What is the logic of this succession other than an engagement with canonical literary movements? It would appear that the prose poem acts as a kind of transparent container that, while it possesses certain constant attributes (prose sentences, brevity, and collective presentation, let's say), acquires its immediate effects from current literary moods that it absorbs or subverts. Wesling goes so far as to say that the prose poem is more of a challenge to its theorists than its practitioners, forcing "the most painful revisions of our literary beliefs."[20]

There is not, currently, a full-length critical study of the British prose poem so my work is fairly isolated in this sense. For this reason, I have used French and American scholarship through which to discuss the English texts and against which to distinguish them. However, the principal critical approach that I have tried to avoid is the development of a definition based on counter claims by "prose" and "poetry." I perceive too many problems with this method. Firstly, such an approach presupposes that the name given to the genre is a literal one. Actually, Baudelaire's publisher chose the title, *Petits Poèmes en Prose*, for the prose pieces, *Le Spleen de Paris*, when he printed them after Baudelaire's death. If we are to accept it at all, we must admit the possibility that "prose poem" is an impressionistic rather than a prescriptive appellation. Certainly, the title alerts us to the role of paradox that permeates the genre.[21] Secondly, the terms "prose" and "poetry" are themselves contentious issues and my need to place them inside inverted commas here testifies to this fact. Trying to define a third genre from two existing forms that are, in truth, no closer to standardization is to avoid or miss the actual issues, altogether. Vadé warns against any confusion between prose poetry and poetic prose but he continues the prose/poetry dialectic. Like others before him, he defines the prose element thematically as urbanity (the depiction of the 'prosaic') and poetry as a term of restriction and closure.[22] These combinative approaches to the prose poem offer tidy but misguided interpretations, which Tzvetan Todorov has preempted: "A and *not*—A divide up the universe exhaustively, so that to say of an object that it is characterized either by A or by *not*-A is to say nothing at all."[23]

In place of this dialectical method, I discuss particular attributes that, I will argue, are fundamental to the creation or continuation of the genre. These aspects may be classified under three headings: aesthetics, structure, and style. In Chapter 1, I discuss the first of these, the *idea* of prose poetry and its artistic necessity—why should the genre reappear if it had never fully established itself and which questions of thought, composition, and presentation does it answer? In England, the genre can be traced back to early nineteenth-century Romanticism and it is there, in the concept of the fragment, that the prose poem collection can be seen to be responding to specific literary needs. In the second half of this chapter, I collect together the fragmentary prose pieces that Coleridge wrote toward his projected work, *The Wanderings of Cain*, to show how the ideology behind the literary fragment, namely the re-presentation of the text, is essential to the aesthetics of the prose poem collection.

Bridging the Romantic and Victorian periods, De Quincey is a prominent figure in this book. I analyze his attempts to structure his own autobiographical prose as independent prose pieces and the reasons for his failure to do so. Secondly, De Quincey is important because of his influence on Baudelaire during the time the latter was composing *Le Spleen de Paris*, the brief texts that came to be considered as the first legitimate prose poems. The fact that Baudelaire was translating De Quincey's *Confessions of an English Opium-Eater* and *Suspiria de Profundis* at the same time that he was composing his prose poems is rarely recorded and has never, to my knowledge, been fully investigated in connection with the prose poem. Baudelaire claims in his Preface to be attempting an imitation of Aloysius Bertrand's *Gaspard de la Nuit*, but it is his subsequent apology for failing in this task that has allowed critics to name him as the prose poem's originator. I argue that it was De Quincey's influence on Baudelaire that resulted in a form of composition that he could no longer attribute to Bertrand.

Structure is examined closely in Chapters 3 and 4. I address the crucial problem of how the prose poem manages to be consistently lucid but strictly brief. I have already referred to the structure of the prose poem as a distortion of the extended prose norm. In fact, prose poetry is often confused with "purple" or poetic prose. Bernard, for example, makes the dubious but not isolated case of relating the emergence of the prose poem to the history of poetic prose. Simon too, defines the prose poem as a short passage of poetic prose. In fact, prose poetry and poetic prose exist at opposite ends of the prose scale and are mutually exclusive (thus De Quincey's rhetorical arabesques are precisely what prevents the dream visions from being independently realised). In addition, while prose poetry is a genre or form, poetic prose describes a prose *style*. It is precisely this style that cannot be contained inside the severe perimeters of the prose poem. Prose enacts a continuum, a process that moves the reader and itself inexorably onward (not necessarily forward). Poetic prose facilitates this movement by its characteristically florid verbosity. The style of the prose poem, on the other hand, is constrained by a relatively unnatural brevity.

Despite commentaries that classify the prose poem as an experimental branch of free verse, the form of the genre is unequivocally prose, making its strictly concise structure and visible appearance the first and most striking mark of paradox that clearly characterizes it. The way in which the prose poem achieves a high level of intelligibility within a minimal number of sentences is, I believe, made possible by the absences that it accommodates. As a fragment, the individual prose piece is an inevitably elliptical text and always stands in relation to a larger absent whole that represents the sum of its unselected contexts. I give the term "implied context" to this active space of signification. The place of the implied context is "marked" by the blank space that defines the text as brief (each piece is immediately identifiable as a discrete unit). This blank space is inherent to the experience of reading a prose poem collection as it both identifies the individual texts and indicates the contextual area in which the interpretative reading takes place. Chapter 4 illustrates this point by tracing the reduction of De Quincey's prose to the threshold of prose poetry in *The English Mail-Coach* and comparing it to the achieved prose poem, *Mercian Hymns*, by Geoffrey Hill, where the context is manipulated at each stage and at different levels in order to sustain a collection of such tightly controlled yet fragmented prose pieces.

Chapter 5 moves to the third category in a discussion of the biblical style that is used in many of these texts and which, I argue, is exclusive to British prose poetry. Blake, Coleridge, Wilde, and Beckett use the tighter parallelisms of the *Authorized Version* as formulated by Robert Lowth in the eighteenth century. These self-referential parallels actually lend themselves to the structural requirement of highly controlled prose. I show how the sense-parallel (as opposed to the poetic parallel of metrical symmetry) in prose closely resembles Jakobson's principle of the poetic function but moves beyond it to conserve its prose medium. This is achieved by a technique called "furtherance" that the biblical scholar, James Kugel, has identified as the motivation behind the apparently redundant repetition in biblical parallelism. Furtherance is the return to continuity after a poetic doubling or self-referential parallel; it pushes the parallel onward so that however self-reflexive the style it never dominates the referentiality of the prose medium. This crucial difference between the poetic and the biblical prose style (the latter understood as a literary model) produces a style that inches forward, keeping the extension of the text under control while offering strong closure.

Chapter 6 describes how Beckett's work is fragmented by the impasse created by the problem of causality, the most common form of narrative contiguity. Unable to develop a formula by which to advance his prose fiction, Beckett is obliged to write until the moment of change or else to witness solely the moment of change itself. He leaves a broken text that strives for stillness but whose implied context reminds us that this is not possible in prose. In terms of European influence, this chapter inverts the De Quincey/Baudelaire, English/French relationship and shows how Beckett took Proust's memory-driven *A la Recherche du Temps Perdu* and reduced it to the minimalist utterances which stain the pages in his late prose poetic work such as *Fizzles* and the *Still* trilogy.

Chapter 7 closes the book by taking a major theme of the genre, the city. I read the city in relation to the three fundamental categories of aesthetics, structure, and style through which I hope to have evolved a sense of identification for the prose poem. While not offering a concluding formula, this chapter comes closest to a portrait of the genre. The city is a concept that articulates agreements and disagreements that the English prose poem holds in relation to the French tradition. Unlike Baudelaire, British writers often feel ill at ease in the city. The urban image allows us to paint a picture of the British prose poem whose structure mirrors the crumbling city walls not quite enclosing private rooms (the block of text as privileged fragment). The form that the prose poem commonly takes, the anthology or collection, reinforces this clashing juxtaposition of private and public, given voice by the text and its implied context. Paradoxically, as we may now expect, the single prose poem, the fragment in isolation, appears to be deformed and disproportioned. To avoid such violence we return the piece to the collection, only to find that it too is defined, like the prose itself, as being in a state of continuous flux.

Ultimately, it may be that English literature will simply not yet tolerate the prose poem. As one reviewer has stated: "The boundary line of verse may be to some extent arbitrary, but that boundary represents a sensible distinction, and a kind of chaos lies outside it."[24] Or, British writers will continue to some extent to avoid the genre because, however subversively it is defined, subscribing to the cult of the prose poem introduces a dialectic of orthodox/unorthodox with a political and/or aesthetic choice that most have so far refused to take in the matter of form. Even for those who have chosen, Fredman has already indicated the exit from the room into which they may have inadvertently or unwillingly stepped. He names Beckett, Hill, and Tomlinson among a list of "modern European poets who have taken their prose beyond the confines of the genre we call the prose poem." This, he continues, "is not to deny that their texts often confront the issue of genre in the form of echoes, allusions, parodies, or other investigative devices but to allege that the writers do not situate themselves wholly within the sphere of a genre: From the standpoint of genre, they write into the open."[25]

To our disadvantage, these constant assurances, that British writing transcends European and American aesthetic problems by its liberal approach, not only sustains confusion and suspicion about the prose poem in the minds of the reading public, it also excludes us from a whole area of debate held on both sides of the Atlantic.[26] Besides, our lack of critical apparatus in this field means that we are ill-equipped to discuss and evaluate texts that do take on this question of form. One critic's response to the work of Roy Fisher is symptomatic of this confusion: "Writers will probably continue doing each as he thinks best and as occasion demands, while the most anyone can do is take a look now and again to see how things are going."[27] In the midst of averted eyes and towards an expansive terra incognita, this book performs one such peek.

A Note on Sources

As I have taken quite a broad chronological sweep and been somewhat eclectic in my choice of subjects, I think a brief moment to explain my methods and sources would be appropriate here.

Aware of Fredman's decisive separation of American from French prose poetry and also of the complexity of the subject as it stands, I have limited my discussion of non-British primary texts to French works only. I regret the lack of space and time that has prevented the inclusion of American poets' prose texts, but I felt that the importance of French prose poetry in the history of the genre and the crossover influence with De Quincey on British practice (of Baudelaire and the French tradition generally on figures such as Wilde and Beckett) were of particular significance and deserved priority. However, I have taken into account American scholarship on the genre as a whole and within the French tradition.

In the case of Beckett's bilingual output, I have used his English texts as primary sources. All non-English texts are presented in translation, except where matters of style are concerned. In discussing Baudelaire's translation of De Quincey, I have used Baudelaire's text where he paraphrases or deviates in some way from direct translation, but otherwise I present the appropriate passage from De Quincey. All translations that appear without acknowledgment are my own.

Owing to difficulties with Masson's disordered and unsatisfactory edition of De Quincey's collected writings, I have used the author's own *Selections* as a source-text. For the *Suspiria de Profundis*, which does not appear there, I have used the original 1821 edition in *Blackwood's Edinburgh Magazine*. However, I have included page references to Masson, which remains the most widely available source, although this will surely be superseded by Professor Lindop's authoritative edition.

In addition, I have found Michèle Stäuble-Lipman Wulf's parallel edition of Baudelaire's *Un Mangeur d'Opium* and De Quincey's *Confessions* invaluable for offering an immediate and precise comparison between the texts. However, I have again supported my own use of this edition with references to Baudelaire's *Oeuvres Complètes* and the appropriate source for De Quincey, as above.

Abbreviations

CL	*Collected Letters of Samuel Taylor Coleridge* (6 vols.), ed. Earl Leslie Griggs. Oxford: Oxford University Press, 1956–71.
CN	*The Notebooks of Samuel Taylor Coleridge* (4 vols.), ed. Kathleen Coburn. London: Routledge & Kegan Paul, 1962. [References are to the volume and entry number.]
CSP	Samuel Beckett, *Collected Shorter Prose 1945–1980*. London: John Calder, 1984.
CW	*The Collected Works of Samuel Taylor Coleridge*, ed. Kathleen Coburn and Bart Winer, Bollingen Series LXXV. Princeton: Princeton University Press; London: Routledge & Kegan Paul, 1969–.
M.	*The Collected Writings of Thomas De Quincey* (14 vols.), ed. David Masson. Edinburgh: A. & C. Black, 1889-90.
Mangeur	Charles Baudelaire, *Un mangeur d'opium, avec le texte parallèle des Confessions of an English Opium-Eater et Suspiria de Profundis de Thomas De Quincey*. Édition critique et commentée par Michèle Stäuble-Lipman Wulf, Études Baudelairiennes VI–VII. Neuchâtel: les Éditions de la Baconnière, 1976.
Oeuvres	Charles Baudelaire, *Oeuvres complètes* (2 vols.), texte établi, présenté et annoté par Claude Pichois. Paris: Éditions de Gallimard, 1975.
P.	Marcel Proust, *Remembrance of Things Past* (3 vols.), trans. C. K. Scott Moncrieff, Terence Kilmartin, and Andreas Mayor. London: Penguin Books, 1983. Reprinted 1989.
Pl.	Marcel Proust, *A la recherche du temps perdu* (3 vols.), ed. Pierre Clarac and André Ferre. Paris: Gallimard, 1954.

Prose Poems	*The Poems in Prose and La Fanfarlo,* ed. Francis Scarfe. London: Anvil Press Poetry, 1989.
PW	*The Poetical Works of Samuel Taylor Coleridge.* London: William Pickering, 1834.
Sel.	Thomas De Quincey, *Selections Grave and Gay, from Writings Published and Unpublished* (14 vols.). Edinburgh: James Hogg & Sons; London: R. Groombridge & Sons, 1853–60.

SUCH RARE CITINGS

1
The Prose Poem and the Romantic Fragment

I

THE FIRST SUBSTANTIAL PROSE POETIC FORMS EMERGE IN THE ROMANTIC period with the appearance of the German critical fragment. These fragments raise specific questions, such as the possibility of full artistic representation and the role of the individual prose piece inside a collection—the form of presentation common to both the prose poem and the fragment itself. Jonathan Monroe, who also began his investigation into the prose poem form, *A Poverty of Objects*, with a comparison between the prose poem and the Romantic fragment, insists that the prose poem be considered solely in its collective status. While I agree in principle, I do believe it is important to retain the distinction between the twin roles played by individual pieces as at once autonomous and interdependent. In fact, I will go further and propose that this duality lies at the very center of the genre's dynamic.

For the German Romantics (Friedrich and Wilhelm Schlegel, Novalis, and other contributors to the *Athenaeum*, in particular), the fragment form represented the *darstellung* (presentation) of Ideas in the world of experience. Art was to be the focal point of the embodied transcendent truth and the contracted sphere of the fragment was to provide the conditions for its appearance. In this opening section, I will argue that the physical resemblance of the prose poem to the critical fragment corresponds to their similar concerns with the extent to which literature can present a preconceived truth. The Romantic system was constructed after Kantian theories, yet Kant himself based the initial assumption of transcendental truth (Ideas) on a Platonic aesthetic that effectively divorced art from the sphere of truth. The problem of whether the work of art can be said to represent the Idea in any way, or whether, as Plato proposed, the artist is distanced from "the king and the truth" is the question that unites Plato and Kant, the Idea and the fragment, Romanticism and the prose poem.[1]

In section II, I explain the transition from German critical thought to British poetic practice through Coleridge's exposition of symbol and allegory. In terms of the prose poem, I situate the emerging genre at the intersection of these concepts in a step toward an understanding of one of the paradoxes on which it stands—that is, the poetics of prose and the prose of poetry. Finally in section III, I take two compositions by Coleridge to illustrate the metatext made possible by the critical fragment. My discussion here centers on the several fragmented versions of *The Wanderings of Cain*. Coleridge's compositional practice reveals a belief that poetry can be extracted from prose. Thus, the extant prose pieces of *Cain* are, finally, a collection of fragments that imply repeated failure to represent a subject that remains trapped within the texts. My examination of these works is directed toward revealing the extent to which Coleridge advances toward a prose poetic genre and the reasons for his failure to achieve it. Coleridge's place in the history of the prose poem is a familiar one. A key figure in the debate of much European Romanticism, his own abortive attempts to implement its concepts nevertheless mark an engagement with its most problematic areas.

Plato, Plotinus and the Status of Art

Plato's theory of art, in Book X of the *Republic*, famously sets the artistic work at three removes from the Idea or truth of its object. The Idea finds a copy of itself existing as phenomenon (in nature or as a man-made product) and, again, as an imitation of this sense object in the artistic work. The craftsman's products may exist in several variations but always share common properties that associate them with their corresponding Idea. In other words, after duplication, the particular object only "appears other but differs not at all" from its many manifestations.[2] Art, on the other hand, takes this illusion of change as the very object of its own imitation. Plato's hierarchical organization holds that truth is the essence of phenomena but is masked in the latter's manifestations. Art, as an extension of this principle, is not identified with the Idea because it cannot support essence but only appearance; it is founded on the illusion that replication involves difference with the loss of original truth. Moreover, art is deemed to be potentially corrupting because it makes one man release his unrestrained emotions such as ridicule and grief on the sufferings of others. Despite the fact that Homer's heroes are charged with not actually displaying the entire complexity of any single human emotion, the artist is exiled from Plato's Republic. Clearly, art can neither serve the Ideas (as the craftsman who makes his copy useful) nor adequately represent them.

The sustained evolution of Neo-Platonism, especially through Plotinus, bears witness to the attraction that the notion of Ideas and truth holds for the artist. Plotinus was responsible for reconciling Plato's theories with an acceptance of the artist, which he effected by claiming that the artist was, in fact, more capable than nature of presenting Ideas. His claim was possible after he reorganized Plato's system. In the fifth Ennead, Plotinus asserts that in constructing an object after a model, identity must include difference. In contrast to Plato's concept of difference as proof of falsity and deception, Plotinus claims it to be an inherent part of imitative reproduction (his exemplum is the staggering variety of human beings). He concludes that not only is difference often "beautiful," but goes as far as to say that it must also (however inconspicuously) actually inhabit the "archetypal idea." This is a radical thesis because it identifies truth as difference and imitation as truth by its association with difference.

Plotinus also removed the Ideas from their transcendent, pure medium of existence in order that they fulfil a new role as a vital presence within the actual mind of the artist.

> It is a principle with us that one who has attained to the vision of the Intellectual Cosmos and grasped the beauty of the Authentic Intellect will be able also to come to understand the Father and Transcendent of that Divine Being. It concerns us, then, to try to see and say, for ourselves and as far as such matters may be told, how the Beauty of the divine Intellect and of the Intellectual Cosmos may be revealed to contemplation.[3]

This passage is interesting for a number of reasons. The terminology is suggestive of Romanticism in its notions of "Intellectual Cosmos" (also translated as "Beauty") as a reflection of "the Father and Transcendent of that Divine Being" where the role of the artist as creator is clearly emerging. Furthermore, Plotinus initiates a move away from art as purely an imitative process by proposing that privileged vision recognizes truth and the transcendent divinity by its beauty through active contemplation. That is, truth is now *identified* as

Beauty—a clear victory for art.[4] However, the problem of the existence of Ideas whether believed or intuited and of their presentation, remains, so far, unresolved.

Kant, Schlegel, and the Romantic Fragment

Kant's investigation into the possibility of a priori knowledge is an articulation of the same problem of the existence of Ideas some centuries later. While empirical observations are contingent and therefore inconstant, universal truths, according to Kant, can be sought through a priori conditions. Reformulated by Kant as the concept of "pure cognition," the Platonic Idea is confirmed to exist but rendered as *"noumenon"* or "a thing in itself," knowledge of which is impossible for the human mind, which is bound to experience.[5] *Noumena* are necessarily unconditioned but cognition requires conditions in order to represent them. Thus, *"the unconditioned cannot be thought without contradiction"* since to represent it to the mind requires that it conform to subjective a priori principles to which it bears no relation, such as space and time.[6] *Noumena* are now presupposed in all experience although experience itself is unable to represent them. At the same time, all intuitions must become representation in order to be understood as concepts. Kant follows Plotinus and internalizes Plato's Ideas in the subjective mind where they are intuited and presented by the privileged subject in the Romantic age. The crisis for literature that occurs in the Romantic age, then, is not its divorce from truth, as taught by Plato, but a need to legitimize its claim to represent the truth that it has intuited. What sets the subjective mind apart as "privileged" is one's self-consciousness: an acknowledgment of oneself as the vessel of truths that resist verbalization. Hence, Romantic irony centers on the paradox between the human mind as the origin of truth (the infinite, the sublime) and the nature of that truth as noncommunicable intuition.[7] The mental activity that achieves enlightenment for the artist, therefore, occurs before the creation of the work and bears the same relation to it as truth itself. That is, the essence of the work is seen to exist in the self-consciousness of the artist while the implication is that the realized work is already in a state of decay.[8]

This paradox, truth being at once accessible and unrepresentable, poses a problem for literary Romantics whose claim to a visionary perception implies an ability to access truth coupled with an imposed inability to render it manifest in a work of art: "The issue is no longer how to depict, articulate, or illustrate something already present yet resisting adequate discursive or figural expression, but of how something acquires presence—reality, actuality, effectiveness—in the first place. The question of *Darstellung* centers on the coming into presence, or occurring, of the ideas."[9] This "coming into being" of the Idea affects both the question of literary representation in general and the parameters of form in particular (starting points, endings and the relation of the text to its frame or context). Beauty, engendered in this way, is both the agent of artistic presentation and the work as art.

The act of *darstellung* coincident with the author's ironical scepticism concerning the very possibility of presentation provided the main ingredients for the literary fragment, the predominant form arising from the Romantic dilemma of artistic production. At the moment of its appearance on the page, an overwhelming consciousness of its inevitable failure causes it to cut off almost immediately. Paul de Man registers a link between irony and brief prose pieces which has a clear application to the prose poem:

> It could be argued that the greatest ironists of the nineteenth century generally are not novelists: they often tend toward novelistic forms and devices—one thinks of Kierkegaard, Hoffmann, Baudelaire, Mallarmé, or Nietzsche—but they show a prevalent tendency toward aphoristic, rapid, and brief texts (which are incompatible with the duration that is the basis of the novel), as if there were something in the nature of irony that did not allow for sustained movements.[10]

However, this self-censorship is not a self-annihilation. One fragment does not cancel out another. Instead, totality is presented in the copresence of all writing that, in its collectivity, mimics rather than copies it, illustrating Plotinus's theory that truth must contain difference as seeds of its myriad manifestations. In contrast to the craftsman's beds, which may be multiple in quantity but at the same time share common properties, the work of art is always singular and its *real* difference now guarantees its place in the sphere of truth. However, it is as a result of its overtly cooperative status that these works of art become fragmentary in their singularity: "fragmentation constitutes the properly Romantic vision of the system. It conceives of the absolute under the form of the individual, of totality as being at the same time finite and plural."[11] As the system of collective fragmentation shows, plurality, rather than risking fidelity to a sustained constant, is actually necessary to any representation of truth at all. Re-presentation also supports fragmentation in the latter's inherently unfulfilled potential. In other words, the realm of art must comprise repeated attempts to capture the intuited essence.[12] And yet, preordained to be unsuccessful in this objective, the work of art is doomed to repeat itself: to be regenerative in its failure as inscribed in the *darstellung* of the text.

What is striking in the practice of fragmentation is not the "coming in to presence" of the unrepresentable, but the emphasis on its contradictory aspects: individuality and plurality. Friedrich Schlegel insists on their coexistence:

> Romantic poetry is a progressive, universal poetry. Its aim isn't merely to reunite all the separate species of poetry and put poetry in touch with philosophy and rhetoric. It tries to and should mix and fuse poetry and prose, inspiration and criticism . . . Other kinds of poetry are finished and are now capable of being fully analyzed. The romantic kind of poetry is still in the state of becoming; that, in fact, is its real essence: that it should forever be becoming and never be perfected. (*Athenaeum Fragment*, 116)

> A fragment, like a miniature work of art, has to be entirely isolated from the surrounding world and be complete in itself like a porcupine. (*Athenaeum Fragment*, 206)[13]

It seems that while the cryptic fragment 116 has been generally accepted as the key declaration of Romantic poetry, it is the "logic of the hedgehog" (the term coined by Lacoue-Labarthe and Nancy) that has provoked critical debate and unease. Monroe, who specifically equates the literary Romantic fragment with prose poetry, rejects the concept of the isolated piece. For him, Schlegel's fragments (and Baudelaire's prose poems) offer "not so much an illumination of the self *by itself* (alone and self-sufficient) as an illumination of the self by the discourses that surround, traverse, and overdetermine it and from which it cannot finally retreat—as Baudelaire's "A une heure du matin" trenchantly suggests—into sublime isolation."[14] Even Maurice Blanchot, in a penetrating article on *The Athenaeum* as a literary text, criticizes the emphasis on isolation without addressing the fragment that contradicts this, fragment 116. It is the authors of *The Literary Absolute* who manage a coherent account that embraces both the idea of hermeticism and the state of becoming. "Totality" they argue "is the fragment itself in its completed individuality" where 'individuality' is identified as a multiplicity.[15] This miniaturizing of the Whole creates a continuing process that corresponds to the incompletion in fragment 116. That is, the ideal fragment is a collection of all fragments and does not have closure in the traditional sense but performs a kind of closure at every point in its "state of becoming," which are the prose pieces themselves.

This is also the paradox of prose poetry: completed prose pieces that nevertheless appear to resist closure by the very irreconcilable differences on which they are based. However, it is Blanchot's perspective on the fragment as a collection that approaches the concerns of prose poetry in its relationship to Romanticism. His criticism of the hedgehog analogy is directed at its implication for the aesthetics of the fragment. Focusing on the isolation of the text, he argues, neglects "the interval (a wait and a pause) that separates the fragments." This fracture is what he regards as "the rhythmic principle of the work and its structure."[16] The properties that he mentions—the relationship of the text to its context and the musical dimension of the reading experience—are precisely the formal attributes that the English prose poem takes from its German ancestor.[17] At this juncture, however, I wish merely to present the closure/anticlosure contradiction as a central Romantic concern sustaining the fragmentary form and to suggest that the problem is somehow related to the latent tendency of the fragment to reiteration.

The "Absent Work"

Reflecting Plato's system where the Idea is absent from its material manifestations, the truth that the Romantic writer perceives through meditation is equally missing from the literary work. The integrity of the *principle* of *darstellung* becomes questionable under the problematic conditions of representation and, moreover, communication. In fact, *darstellung* never actually takes place or comes into being itself. What occurs as the literary work is only the principle of *darstellung*: the announcement of self-consciousness.

Athenaeum fragment 22 attempts to describe the experience of the "project," a stage of subjective intuition that precedes its artistic realization: "The feeling for projects—which one might call fragments of the future—is distinguishable from the feeling for fragments of the past only by its direction: progressive in the former, regressive in the latter."[18] The implication is that a fragment refers either to something anterior or something to come: about to be completed or already finished but not currently in existence. The work as fragment does not exist, in this sense, in the immediate moment, instead it is substituted for this period by the "project." However, the project, which is defined as "the subjective embryo of a developing object," while posited in the present moment, is not identified with it because its object is still in the (infinite) process of completion.[19] This inability to define a present work is also an inability to define a work of presence. As Lacoue-Labarthe and Nancy point out, if the fragment / project is not the work itself but only refers to the work, and that work exists only in the past, the future, or is misplaced in the present then it can only be said to be absent. Over and above Monroe's list of similarities this is the strongest point of resemblance between Romantic fragmentation and the prose poem.[20] Both forms project an event beyond themselves as the locus of their own sublimation into a unifying synthesis. Yet, while the principles of this composition are forever becoming, the piece itself is never begun. Schlegel's master plan for Romanticism never came to be and Novalis's encyclopedic attempt to set down all knowledge was abandoned. Romanticism is characterized not only by the Romantic failure of the text, where the work breaks off in despair of true representation, but also and more fundamentally by its distinguishing philosophy that investigates the theory of the work. At the very core of this quest the work is abandoned or excised.[21] Philosophy thus embedded in Romantic literature suppresses the raison d'être of this sphere: the work of art. Only by its silhouette, traced by the surrounding garland of fragments, can the work be identified and defined by this gap, which it leaves but in which it is immanent.[22]

If the work is defined in this way, then the formal structure, the parameters of the fragment take on extra significance. Once more, this is a question that is taken up by the practitioners of the prose poem rather than those of the theoretical fragment but it is because of this concept of the "Absent Work" that the prose poem concentrates on its starting points, its endings and how it fits into its surrounding circumstances. The nature of the garland, described in fragment 77, will itself become the collection of prose poems.

In conclusion, the literary work may be said to owe its creation to something outside itself and, in this way, an objective source, while the expression is necessarily tied to the experience of the artist and thereby remains subjective. Schlegel writes in the same fragment that as yet no genre exists that is "fragmentary both in form and content" but the expression "as yet" is redundant because *darstellung* is permanently postponed and the work can never be written but (like God and truth) only pointed at vaguely in the multitude of the representation of texts. By extension, the Romantic fragment provides the ideological basis for the prose poem form. Its concern with the nature of truth; a desire to represent totality as the only possible approximation to this Idea and the fragmentary way in which this is achieved; the principles guiding the parameters of the form and the absence of the work itself are all common properties of both types of composition. However, it is the character of both forms to preface a (missing) work that ensures their continuing marginal status in literary history.

II

Symbol and Allegory

The outline of the text and the nature of the fragment repeatedly come into question. Is the fragment conceived as such (a condensed work), or as a residue of a larger, lost or abandoned, work? If, as we have seen, the Idea is made manifest through the fragment, then totality is present in the piece and no larger work exists or is significant in its existence.[23] Such a perspective on totality explains why the fragment is considered to be both a part and a whole (Schlegel, *Critical Fragment*, 14). This contains implications for the prose poem as fragmented form in terms of the size and scope of its individual pieces. Fragmentation is more than the physical appearance of the text. The term implies that a related larger whole exists and describes the nature of their relationship. Symbol and allegory as literary forms denote attempts to schematize the fragment by distinguishing types of connections that it may hold to the larger work from which it is separated. The text either imitates its perceived whole or participates in it as a part to indicate the entirety surrounding it.

According to Kathleen Wheeler, the distinction between allegory and symbol, as it was pursued by Schelling, Solger, and Friedrich Schlegel, "further elaborated the purpose of this calculated and deliberate 'incomprehension' typical of the fragment as a dense and compressed form."[24] German thinkers accepted the fragment (as symbol) as an adequate representation of the unpresentable. The work embodied its own negative aspect of being separated from its source and absorbed the impossibility of its task in its own peculiar merits that, aesthetically appreciated, eclipsed the subliminal disparity. The symbol was posited at the intersection of the universal and the particular, that is, the meeting point of the transcendental Idea and its *darstellung* in the form of the work of art. In writing, this duality was effected by the interrelation of *langue* and *parole:* the individual work representing one part of the concept. The symbol therefore accorded with that other essentially Romantic principle of "becoming" by existing in a state of incompletion, and fragments, in this sense, were clearly regarded as symbols of varying success.

Coleridge's approach is slightly different in that he sees the symbol as a figure of elucidation in contradistinction to allegory which, as a translation of concepts into "picture-language" is "more worthless even than its phantom proxy," "unsubstantial" and "shapeless to boot."[25] Allegory moves back toward Plato's concept of artistic imitation that lies parallel to its object, neither enhancing it nor receiving effects from it. Elsewhere, Coleridge states that "a metaphor is a fragment of an allegory."[26] It is a closed system despite this use of the term "fragment" since the simile on which the metaphor is based is complete as an independent image and relies on an active participation by the reader to surpass the differences that are "everywhere presented to the eye" in order to achieve the likeness "suggested to the mind."[27] Coleridge's own "Allegoric Vision" best illustrates this essential divorce of the rhetorical device from its referent. The "Vision" originally formed a preface to his first theological lecture on "The Origin of Evil" but was subsequently adapted for use in different contexts where the target of criticism also differed, ranging from the Church of England to the Catholic church, to extreme views of any kind. At each reading, a different meaning could be extracted from the allegory and applied to the text proper, indicating that the pertinence of the text (as whole) was not intrinsically contained in the preface (as symbolic part). In effect, the allegorical text holds no larger meaning independently but requires a specific context and an active reader-participation through which to discover one by means of comparison. Ironically, the narrator reflects on this in the "Allegoric Vision": "but though each of the words taken separately I seemed to understand, yet when I took them in sentences, they were riddles and incomprehensible."[28] In other words, the vision, as allegory, does not operate on the same planes as the symbol (the universal and the particular), but on the singular only. This allows us to conclude that allegory owes more to Coleridge's Fancy than to his Imagination.[29] In addition, the "Allegoric Vision" has closure as a dream sequence where "—and in the terror I awoke" effectively stops the text and forcibly separates the sympathetic reader from the "I" of the narrative thereby precluding the continuation of any shared experience and creating a hermeticism. The prose poem will borrow from allegory the larger principle of dependence on different possible contexts. However, self-enclosure against contexts other than a specific current analogy is antagonistic to this very concern. As it stands, however, the "Allegoric Vision" does resemble Baudelaire's prose poems, which tend mostly to the metaphorical pole.[30]

The symbol, instead, elucidates, for Coleridge, because it actively participates in the whole that it represents. In fact, the image of illumination is central to his understanding of it:

> a Symbol . . . is characterized by a translucence of the Special in the Individual or of the General in the Especial or of the Universal in the General. Above all by the translucence of the Eternal through and in the Temporal. It always partakes of the Reality which it renders intelligible; and while it enunciates the whole, abides itself as a living part in that Unity, of which it is the representative. (*Lay Sermons*, 30)

Coleridge's definition of the symbol is organically based: the symbol can be defended as the highest literary form because—in a unique twist to the imitative nature of language—it can be said to be a part of its referent. In fact, to extend Coleridge's own formulation, if metaphor is a fragment of allegory, then synecdoche is a fragment of symbol.

I have made a choice here between metonymy and synecdoche that should help to elucidate the relationship that the prose poem holds to both allegory and symbol in the Romantic period. Synecdoche, as a part named for the whole, holds an integral relation to its whole, lending the symbol a closed aspect in its obvious restrictions (for example, it does not support a variety of contexts as does allegory). Metonymy, on the other hand, is the substitution of an *attribute* of the object for the object itself. David Lodge has described metonymy as "a figure of *nonlogical* deletion."[31] When it is restricted to the level of a single image, metonymy is difficult to distinguish from synecdoche. The figure is best exemplified when it accumulates over several sentences or in a passage of prose. In its larger form, metonymy is clearly related to the prose poem as fragment. Just as the single figure is logically related to its elliptical whole, so the prose poem projects a text of which it is an attributive (rather than imitative) part.[32] Thus, the prose poem situates itself ontologically at the intersection of symbol and allegory which it effects by appropriating the metonymic ground.

The A Priori and the Marginal Text

The "Unity" or "Generality" in which Coleridge's symbols participate is described by Robert Barth as an overwhelming "oneness" aimed to counteract Cartesian duality and reconcile the chaos of modern fragmentation.[33] In aesthetic terms, Coleridge adapts the definition of Beauty as the reduction of many to one. This is in itself an act of the understanding.[34] In *Lay Sermons*, he states that it is Reason which is responsible for man's tendency toward unification: "We can neither rest in an infinite that is not at the same time a whole, nor in a whole that is not infinite" (*Lay Sermons*, 60). Reason, as the factor of unification, identifies the part and projects an immanent whole. The effect of this emphasis on reason rather than, say, imagination, is that figuration—and the symbol in particular—becomes a pattern of logic, a syllogism. Poetry and religion are legitimized because they are grounded in the same processes that control more empirical phenomena such as mathematics (a similarity worked to the extreme by Samuel Beckett).[35] Clearly, prose is the principal medium for expressing logical relations. Speaking of literature in Ancient Greece, Coleridge remarks:

> prose must have struck men with greater *admiration* than poetry. In the latter it was the language of passion and emotion; it is what they themselves spoke and heard in moments of exultation, indignation etc. But to have an evolving roll, or a succession of leaves, talk continuously the language of deliberate reason in a form of continued preconception, of a Z already possessed when A is being uttered—this must have appeared *god*-like.[36]

His description of prose as almost cyclical, a "continued preconception" generated by "deliberate reason," reveals an organicism in the process.

The agent of this unifying "oneness" is Kant's a priori reasoning, translated by Coleridge as the "all in Each" (*Lay Sermons*, 49), or God.[37] This is an interpretation of Kant's concept of the a priori that underlies all experience but that cannot be discovered through experience (as space and time). Kant's emphasis is on the operational nature of the mind in the act of perception but Coleridge deflects the source of universality from the physiological to the theological.

However, it is at this stage that Coleridge's scheme begins to falter. It has been shown that he repeatedly refers to spatial and temporal relationships as *consequences* of the transcendent. In doing so he reveals his misapprehension that the Kantian a priori, wherever its source, preexists phenomena.[38] One implication arising from this misunderstanding is that Coleridge's aesthetic remains tied to a Platonic model of originating ideal and subsequent (inferior) representation. The scheme is a causal one and Coleridge uses the assumption of the "necessary link" in causality to legitimize both Christian and poetic symbolism. It is not only his attachment to a two-world theory that ultimately prevents Coleridge from achieving the unity he so desires, but more importantly his belief that one world follows the other. As long as Time continues to be an active factor, synthesis is forever postponed.

Coleridge blames his inability to achieve unity on the nature of rhetoric, which, as he shows in his distinction between copy and imitation, rests on conditions imposed by a medium which itself differs from the object it seeks to reproduce.[39] If truth is ineffable, if it is beyond words, then its apperception is subjective and mute; linguistic representation must fail inevitably. By this token, the fragment (and, by implication, the prose poem) can exhibit the required mode of visionary experience—the creative process—but cannot accompany the reader into an imaginative synthesis with the Idea. At the same time, logic is ultimately incompatible with the a priori because the latter cannot support causality, occurring instead together with the moment of perception. If De Quincey is to be believed, Coleridge was unable to extract himself from a logic-based epistemology.[40] Yet, Coleridge's prose work is too imbued with the Kantian type to entirely misrepresent the a priori. In fact, his work acknowledges the copresence of this ubiquitous faculty of interpretation by recognizing the need for a textual encasement to his poetry. This contextual envelope takes the form of a marginal gloss or preface that is designed to coincide or interact with the work itself.

> The end of the preface, if such an end is possible, is the moment at which the order of exposition (*Darstellung*) and the sequential unfolding of the concept, in its self-movement, begin to overlap according to a sort of a priori synthesis: there would then be no more discrepancy between production and exposition, only a *presentation* of the concept by itself, in its own words, in its own voice, in its logos. . . . The analytic procedure and the synthetic procedure would mutually envelop each other.[41]

If the prose poem is comparable to the critical fragment, as I have argued, then it is to the fragment as a textual a priori. The prose piece is revealed through the text but, being metatextual, critical, self-conscious, must somehow precede that text, being at once prefatory to and coincident with it. The prose poem, like the fragment is therefore a substitution anticipating its own realization.

The Wanderings of Cain exists as several different fragments, evidence of a writer attempting to introduce a particular line of reasoning from varying angles. This conscious accommodation of the infinite in the finite suggests that the symbol, as Coleridge describes it, continues to support irony. As we have seen, irony unites the whole and the part in the form of the fragment and it is this very aspect which saves the symbol from the stasis of its hermetic metaphoric counterpart—allegory (because, of course, the fragment rejects closure). As Lee Rust Brown points out, Coleridge's projected unified system "is a fiction of textual wholeness which maintains itself through the fragmentation of the literal textual corpus; and as such it can no more be recovered by critical archaeology than the whole of 'Kubla Khan.'"[42]

The prose poem genre is similarly ironic: it is conducted in the medium of prose, which is by nature expansive, and yet the prose poem is characterized by extreme brevity. Although Coleridge did not venture far into this genre he shows sensitivity to the concealed areas in any given composition and he struggles with the problem of how to represent them. Following his advocacy of the a priori, he strives to represent the marginal as necessary to the creation of the object text and inherent to it—a task that leads him to engage in the prose / poetry debate. Yet, despite writing only one prose poem, *The Wanderings of Cain,* he accurately identifies one of the genre's defining characteristics: its dual nature of coordinated autonomy and (contextual) dependence.

III

"To have conceived strongly, does not always imply the power of successful execution."
—S. T. Coleridge, Preface to *Osorio*

In this section I will discuss *The Wanderings of Cain* and "The Blossoming of the Solitary Date Tree" as Romantic texts that incorporate self-critical prose as a preface but fail because the commentary can only occur together with the work that remains an object for anticipation. In this way, these works point to the initial obstacles to prose poetry: namely distinguishing the equally concise forms of metatext and prose poetic text, if, in fact, they differ in that genre.

Parts of *The Wanderings of Cain* together with "The Blossoming of the Solitary Date Tree" were composed around the time of Coleridge's stay in Malta. Both poems are characterized by a sense of extreme loneliness and the desire to share experience. In the "Date Tree," this sentiment is repeated through a series of metaphors in the preface and the poem itself. In *Cain*, Coleridge takes this problem a stage further. The protagonist, ejected from Eden and rejected by God, attempts to induce a response from an external source to alleviate the pain of his overwhelming subjectivity. Such emphasis on the search for dialogue and coupling inevitably results in thematic doubles and these works are no exception. What is notable about these pieces is the way in which their formal qualities participate by giving voice to the Other through prose pieces. The prose poem, however, as a literary form of the critical fragment, seeks a synthesis of proposition and response where the text and the dialectical return occur together in the prose piece rather than by an alternation between preface and text, prose and poetry. In the "Date Tree," the boundaries are dissolving, but *Cain* approaches the establishment of a prose poem genre by generating its own collection of texts, which in turn stand for the unrealized work.

"The Blossoming of the Solitary Date Tree. A Lament"

"The Blossoming of the Solitary Date Tree," composed in Malta in 1804/5, was first published in Coleridge's collection of 1828, the same year as *The Wanderings of Cain* and both poems appeared with similar prefatory notes.[43] The "Date Tree" appeared in the "Prose in Rhyme" section of which it was, in fact, the only piece to actually diverge from nonmetrical verse. The poem highlights Coleridge's play with (prose) prefaces and reveals the process of composition in the space of the poem itself. Wheeler discusses the same aspect in "Kubla Khan." She concludes that in its problematizing of the boundaries of preface and text, Coleridge is turning the epistemological claim "that one cannot decide the extent of the mind's contribution to the construction of objects of experience" into an aesthetic claim, "that one cannot determine what is description and what is interpretation."[44] The reader, says Wheeler, who believes he is perceiving the artifact objectively is as mistaken as the philosopher who claims to see "the thing in itself." As a result, Coleridge also engages in the current prose / poetry debate.

The preface to the "Date Tree" claims that the first page of the manuscript is missing and with it the opening two or three stanzas. In its place, the two prose paragraphs at the opening of the poem are offered as substitutes.[45] This contrasts with *Cain*, which provides *its* alternative (versified) version outside the text in the preface. Between these works and others ("Kubla Khan" for instance), the distinction between preface and text, rough draft and finished piece, is blurred. The verse for *Cain*, for example, as a form of rewriting, appears in a letter, an appendix and a preface but never as a piece in itself. Together with its protagonist, Cain, the verse is thus condemned to eternal exile and substitution. Brown has argued that where the poem is a fragment it will always blame an external source for its incompleteness and in so doing can never actually be a poem but only ever "'symbolize'" one. In effect, he concludes, what the fragment gives us is "reading *in lieu* of reading."[46] This is an eminently appropriate definition of prose poems that are themselves only ever prefaces and incomplete substitutes for a projected work. Indeed, by Samuel Beckett's late prose, "reading *in lieu* of reading" is almost all we can assert. Ultimately, the prose poem is literally a usurper of recognized textual and public space (see Chapter 7).

In terms of the prose/poetry issue, the significant part of the preface to "The Date Tree" is the final sentence: "It is not impossible, that some congenial spirit, whose years do not exceed those of the author, at the time the poem was written, may find a pleasure in restoring the Lament to its original integrity by a reduction of the thoughts to the requisite metre" (*PW*, 2: 93). The condition that the reader-poet must be the same age as the historical poet suggests that indeed "restoration" and not "co-creation" is intended. In contrast to "The Ancient Mariner" where prose doubled the verse, this preface proposes that here, the verse has been engulfed and disfigured by the prose and that prose may, through reduction, give birth to the poetry inside it.[47] This preface parallels and helps to explain the apology that follows the metered lines in the 1828 preface to *The Wanderings of Cain*. Repeating the image of poetry as born of prose, Coleridge represents, as far as possible, the whole process of creation: "I have here given the birth, parentage, and premature decease of the 'Wanderings of Cain, a poem',—intreating, however, my Readers, not to think so meanly of my judgment as to suppose that I either regard or offer it as any excuse for the publication of the following fragment . . . in its primitive crudity" (*PW* [1828], 2: 108).

In the light of the "Date Tree" preface, this reads not so much as an apology for the published text proper as an acknowledgment of the gap between the prose work and the verse rendition as if the latter were, in fact, the original objective.[48] If this is so, the verse fragment is a trace of the "absent work" but is relegated to the preface and "Canto II," its substitute, suffers the embarrassment of inversion and juxtaposition and for *this* reason requires an apology for the usurpation.

Where the author of the "Date Tree" preface appears to be unperturbed by whether the poem is in verse or prose, the subject of the poem provides a second and ironical judgment. The significance of the title is explained in the preface: a date tree while regularly in blossom never produced any fruit until a branch from another date tree had been brought to it from a distance. The preface precedes this with a rabbinical myth, but while the poem that follows illustrates, in Shelleyan manner, the importance of compatible pairings it does not actually mention the date tree itself or the rabbinical myth that stated the argument, thereby creating a bond between title and preface that excludes the poem or, at least, reveals the gap between them.[49] Further, considering the unusual typography of the poem, in which two prose paragraphs are followed by metered lines, there is a subtle parallel to be made between the verse/prose dialectic and the gender relations they describe. Yet, whereas this combination may be seen to advocate the copresence of both literary forms as corresponding to the natural attraction of sexual opposites, Coleridge, in the *Biographia Literaria*, actually rejects any work that mixes the two. The difference between verse and prose is, for him, so wide that he perceives something "unpleasant" in having to alternate between such dissimilar states of feeling.

From the statements he formulates on the subject in *Biographia Literaria*, Coleridge clearly concerns himself with a poetry that may be identified as verse. Such poetry, he concludes, is the coexistence of passionate spontaneity for an appropriate subject with artificiality (meter).[50] In other words, the technical restraint of verse poetry is inherent in its heightened mode of expression. Therefore, Coleridge's opening paragraphs of the "Blossoming of the Solitary Date Tree," which he refers to in the preface as simply a "rude draught" must be identified as pieces of formless writing as opposed to either prose or prose poetry. In the same way, the theme of male / female coupling, which is expounded in the preface, is somewhat confused by the analogy of a mother and child in the poem itself. The child represents the reduced echo of its mother's song returning to the idea of the prose text "giving birth" to the poem.

If Coleridge associates subjects with a style of expression proper to verse or prose, the introduction of an intergenre, a prose poem, would require a separate category of sentiment entirely. That third category is never articulated, if identified, by Coleridge except by the interplay between the text and its prefatory elements.

In all three poems: *The Wanderings of Cain,* "The Ancient Mariner," and "The Blossoming of the Solitary Date Tree," the marginal prose (preface and gloss) is arguably the most assertive element. This prose threatens the protected code of poetry as existing in a rarefied plane by constantly drawing attention to context, the degree to which the project is successfully realized or still anticipated and by inciting a collapse of Coleridge's own distinct categories: prose / verse; formless writing / poetry, toward an imaginative synthesis of the two in a developing prose poetry. The "Date Tree" preface reveals that Coleridge himself cannot achieve prose poetry because he believes that the essentially formless character of prose forbids its own reduction to a new type of wrought-*prose* composition. However, he is significant in the study of prose poetry because in these works he has shown his continued attraction to the dialectics that characterize the genre: prose/poetry; text/context; marginal text/text proper; published fragment/absent whole. These attributes, considered as organic and inseparable, are also central to the play of the prose poem's form.

As a prose poem, *Cain* anticipates many problems that lie at the root of the inherently paradoxical genre. These difficulties include isolating the metatext from both its object-text and its own potential expansion into context. The concision and embryonic nature of the metatext is imitated but is repeatedly defeated by the copious character of the prose medium. Consequently the multiplication of object-texts that occurred with the *Cain* project is revealed as inevitable within a system of Romantic prose fragmentation. In the next chapter, I will take a closer look at these obstacles to the prose poem genre. Before that, below, I will attempt to establish a chronology for the texts that comprise *Cain* in order to establish them as part of the work. Having collected the fragments I shall spend the last pages of this chapter considering their relation to one another (aided by the dating) and offering an interpretation of their separate elements in order to glimpse the Absent Work at their core.

The Wanderings of Cain

The Wanderings of Cain denotes any one of four prose and one verse fragments written between 1797 and 1828. (for a hypertext edition, see http://pages.britishlibrary.net/nsantilli). The only published fragment, subtitled "Canto II," purports to chronicle the experiences of Cain in his exile after having murdered his brother Abel. Coleridge's tale is clearly a moral one because, rather than founding cities as the ancient myth relates, this Cain is met by a spirit who claims to be his dead brother. "Abel" persuades Cain that there is a separate and more powerful God of the dead whom he should worship. The text breaks off at the point where Cain, his son, and the spirit set off to find this deity.

In the apologetic preface appended in 1828, Coleridge describes how the work was projected as a collaboration with Wordsworth. They were to compose one canto each and the quickest to do so was to write the third so that the work could be finished in a single night. He goes on to describe a pathetic scenario in which he found Wordsworth apparently unable to write anything. Upon seeing this, Coleridge denounced his own project as "ridiculous" and abandoned it. When the fragment apparently drew approval from friends such as Sir George Beaumont some years later it was finally published independently of its overshadowing "coauthor" as a fragment in the first edition of the *Bijou* literary annual and also, with slight variations, in the first edition of Coleridge's own collected *Poetical Works* in 1828.[51] By 1834, Coleridge had excised the apology that claims the work is far from realizing his personal objective and the prose piece finally stood alone.

The ostensible objective of *The Wanderings of Cain*, according to its preface, was to imitate *The Death of Abel* by Gessner, which had proved so popular when it appeared in translation in 1761, and the influence is clear. Coleridge's projected tale begins where Gessner's closes—Cain in self-imposed exile—and it may be suggested that Coleridge was not just setting himself (and Wordsworth) a task of imitation but actively involving them in the previous work and, by implication, the original narrative, by providing a contiguous work in the form of a sequel.

In terms of source material for *Cain*, Werner W. Beyer has made several objections to the claims which Coleridge makes in his introductory preface. Beyer's principal argument is to show that "Canto II" and the fragments owe more to Wieland's *Oberon*, which Coleridge said he was translating in November 1797, than to Gessner's *The Death of Abel*.[52] In fact, through his own paraphrase, Beyer gives the impression that Coleridge almost lifted plot sequences and landscape settings from two of Wieland's cantos. On the other hand, if Beyer is right and many elements from *Cain* are taken from Wieland's *Oberon*, then it seems increasingly unlikely that the published Canto is the same manuscript that was "despatched . . . at full fingerspeed" in anticipation of Wordsworth's contribution.[53] The speed of enthusiasm or inspiration would be incompatible with such detailed selection, paraphrase and cross-referencing. We may therefore speculate that the original draft may have been destroyed in the face of Wordsworth "struggling with the sense of the exceeding ridiculousness of the whole scheme" ("Prefatory Note," *PW*, 99). In other words, "Canto II" and the original text may have been separate pieces, even if the published version was developed from the original jottings. Coleridge did return to Wieland. In 1811 he spoke of him as Germany's best poet and criticized Sotheby's translation.[54]

During the Romantic period, literature was taking steps away from accepted narrative norms. The fragment form, such as those in the *Athenaeum*, directly controverted the extended narrative that the new novel genre was establishing. In view of this, a text like *The Wanderings of Cain* appears ideally Romantic.[55] The status of the work as a sequel (to both Gessner and to a portion of the Bible itself) and of coauthorship is in line with Schlegel's own statement that all works should participate in a single, eternally developing book that will reveal the gospel of humanity (Schlegel, *Ideas*, 95).

However, in accordance also with Coleridge's concept of imitation, where similarity of objective moves toward an appreciation of differences within that similarity, *The Wanderings of Cain* acknowledges its predecessors but then departs from both the German and standard biblical versions of the story and its other poetical sources.[56] Ironically, Coleridge actively attempted to purge himself of any tendencies to poetical prose, which was proving a corollary to his own metaphysical meditation. His notebook for February–May 1799 shows him attempting to versify, in German, two lyrics from Gessner's prose idyll, *Daphnis*.[57] In 1802, he writes to W. Sotheby of his work in progress: another translation of Gessner into blank verse.

Coleridge's convoluted excuses in this letter for returning to translating Gessner include the need to "force myself out of metaphysical trains of Thought" that were being thrown up in poetical prose ("a metaphysical Bustard"), when he was actually trying to write poetry.[58]

In fact, "Canto II" tends to be considered chiefly as a preparatory exercise for Coleridge's subsequent work. In his celebrated book, *The Road to Xanadu*, Lowes unquestioningly accepts Coleridge's dismissive preface, which describes the poem's failure as indicative of "the exceeding ridiculousness of the whole scheme—which broke up in a laugh: and the Ancient Mariner was written instead" (*PW*, 2: 99–100). It is true that the poem was abandoned and failed not only to be realized as a completed (three canto) work, but was also unsuccessful in its own ageneric right. However, the failure referred to by Coleridge was that of Wordsworth whose "look of humourous despondency" suggests that his defeat was rooted in a simple unwillingness to write another man's plan or to stray from the quotidian subjects on which his thoughts were engaged at that time. Lowes's argument draws thematic similarities between *Cain* and the "Ancient Mariner" to prove that the collection of ideas with which Coleridge was juggling for a time (evidenced in the notebooks) rested fitfully in *Cain* but were actually resolved in the verse poem. Such an argument relies on accurately dating *Cain* as antecedent to the "Ancient Mariner." In the preface to the prose work, Coleridge sets the date of composition at 1798. If he is correct (and we must remember that the preface was written thirty years later), then it is impossible that its failure produced the "Ancient Mariner" because the initial date of that poem has been firmly fixed at November 1797.[59] Either the date (1798) is wrong or the author was mistaken as to which poem was produced instead.

The complexities involved in tracing the compositions and publication history of *Cain* is, ironically, an accurate reflection of the ambiguous regard in which Coleridge held this work. On one hand, he is content to minimize the importance of the prose piece by an apologetic preface in which he records that its failure at least precipitated the composition of the "Ancient Mariner." On the other hand, only a year earlier he lists *Cain* among "the flowers of my whole poetic life."[60] Moreover, these contradictions are being voiced thirty years after his initial attempt at the work. Coleridge's failure to specify which version of *The Wanderings of Cain* he means is symptomatic of its status as a plural text in which all relevant material is needed to explain the (absent) proposed work. A brief summary of the history of *Cain* should illustrate these points. Namely, that Coleridge worked on *Cain* mostly after the "Ancient Mariner" of 1797, indicating a significance not normally attributed to it. Also, that the changes that the work underwent produced a text that is not *The Wanderings of Cain*: Canto II, but is best understood as several fragmented states, like a collection of critical fragments or, subsequently, prose poems. *Cain* is a plural text, being, finally, not the single published fragment but different imperfect representations. Extant texts for the Work take their place beside "Canto II," eschewing marginal boundaries to participate in the creative process. Each text represents a fresh attempt to write *The Wanderings of Cain*. Therefore, all the fragments anticipate a projected authorized version that, in the nature of the Absent Work, is at once in concordance with the extant pieces and ultimately beyond them.

Fragments for the Cain Text

Coleridge includes a verse fragment at the end of his preface in which he claims that the verse is the product of his second and last attempt to write *Cain*.[61] However, besides the published "Canto II" fragment, two separate plans for the work have been uncovered. One appears in a notebook, the other on a loose folio sheet (see plates 1 and 2 and transcripts). The extended prose (Egerton, 2800, fol. 1–1v), is used by E. H. Coleridge to date *Cain* (more specifically, "Canto II").[62] He identifies William Bartram's *Travels in Florida and Carolina* [sic], which Coleridge was reading in 1798, as the source for the alligators and vast meadow in that unpublished version.[63] It is true that *Cain* was in Coleridge's mind when Hazlitt first visited him in spring 1798. They visited the Valley of Rocks and Coleridge identified it as the location for the published "Canto II."[64]

Of this extended prose piece, it has been suggested that it actually comprises two separate fragments that, moreover, are not necessarily in order.[65] It certainly appears sensible to assume that it was drafted in at least two sittings. The three paragraphs do not follow each other sequentially nor do they follow logically from "Canto II." The manuscript itself supports the theory of two separate compositions. A title that is possibly "Book 3rd" appears at the top of the page before the text beginning, "He falls down in a trance." A line is drawn across the page after "dancing from rock to rock in his former shape down those interminable precipices." Then, another title "*Cain*" appears to have been squeezed in some time after the first line of the second section had been written.[66] It is possible, then, that this brief section, which corresponds in its content to the verses, was intended to precede "Book 3rd." What is clear is that the second (and longest) section of MS *F*, which begins on the verso, "Midnight on the Euphrates" is a much more sophisticated account both thematically and in narrative technique to "Book 3rd." In fact, as the main narrative (concerning the near-sacrifice of Enoch) is related by Cain himself, any conclusion to this version must return to Cain's wife and children, who have found him and are listening to the tale-within-a-tale.

While E. H. Coleridge may be correct in identifying Bartram's *Travels* as a source for the alligators in this section, there appears to be a closer connection with a notebook entry that can be dated at precisely November 1804: "Earthquake this autumn at Almeria, destroying all but the Church ded. to the Tributary Source with an unfathomable Gulph around it, *full of alligators.*"[67] This is echoed quite clearly in the manuscript: "He is going to offer sacrifices to this being, and persuades Cain to follow him [?]to [?]come to an immense Gulph filled with water, whither they descend followed by alligators etc." (MS *Fv*). However, the italics in the notebook give pause for thought. It is possible that they denote a retrospective acknowledgment of Bartram's, and his own, similar descriptions.

The first paragraph of the MS *F* section, subtitled "Cain," is the briefest of the folio sections and forms, with "Canto II," the prose correspondant of the verse fragment.[68] In his letter to Byron, Coleridge alludes to a lost poem of which the verse is the only surviving part. The same fragment reappears ten years later in the conclusion to *Aids to Reflection*.[69] Therefore, although he speaks of the verse as having been written "years" after "Canto II," we cannot be more precise in our dating than to situate it between 1804 and October 1815. Nevertheless, *Cain* was first read by the public as a verse fragment and the idea of the work as a verse poem appears to have been preferable to Coleridge for at least eighteen years. In other words, the verse fragment may have been the last version of *Cain* to be composed and the first to appear in print despite the fact that it was superseded by the (possibly original) prose of "Canto II" in the *Bijou* and *Poetical Works*. Coleridge confirms the development by removing the verses from the preface to "Canto II" in 1834. Yet, again, this apparent preference for meter is difficult to assert with confidence. In 1826, two letters refer to a copy of *The Wanderings of Cain* that had been requested by the poet's nephew, Edward Coleridge. This is probably a request for a prose version, "Canto II" being yet unpublished but still, apparently, disseminated. A year later, Coleridge is preparing to give the manuscript of "Canto II" to Pickering for the latest *Poetical Works* and, unknowingly[?], the *Bijou* for 1828.

In his letter to Byron, Coleridge states his intention to publish *Cain* together with "Christabel." The coupling may be significant. If we accept that the first part of "Christabel" was composed some time between late 1797 and early 1798 and the second part in 1800, then there is clearly a link between the two works based around Coleridge's reading of Bartram. The description of the landscape in "Canto II" as a combination of desert sand and rocks (ll. 70–81) is clearly influenced by Bartram.[70] Much more compelling, however, is the image of the vulture caught by its wings in the coils of a snake, taken from the same page in Bartram, which appears in "Canto II" but also in Part II of "Christabel." Other thematic similarities with "Christabel" include a meeting between the protagonist and a supernatural being in a place outside the city; and the power of this being resting on its supposed knowledge of a deceased relative. Considering that both projects were begun at around the same time, we may suggest that when Coleridge continued with "Christabel" in 1800 (the year in which we know that he was reading from Bartram again) he also returned to work on *Cain*. This reasonable speculation allows us to propose a compositional date for "Canto II" of circa 1800.

The other draft fragment, more tenuously offered as a preparatory piece for *Cain*, is actually found in one of Coleridge's notebooks (no. 22):

> The Child is born, the Child must die / Among the desert Sands / And we too all must die of Thirst / for not a Drop remains. But whither do we retire / to Heaven or possibility of Heaven / But this to darkness, Cold, & tho' not positive Torment, yet positive Evil—Eternal Absence from Communion with the Creator. O how often have the [ ] Sands at night roar'd & whitened like a burst of waters / O that indeed they were! Then full of enthusiastic faith kneels & prays, & in holy frenzy covers the child with sand. In the name of the Father &c &c / —Twas done / the Infant died / the blessed Sand retired, each particle to itself, conglomerating, & shrinking from the profane sand / the Sands shrank away from it, & left a pit / still hardening & hardening, at length shot up a fountain large & mighty /
>
> How wide around its Spray, the rain-bow played upon the Stream & the Spray—but lo! another brighter, O far far more bright / it hangs over the head of a glorious Child like a floating veil (vide Raphael's God)—the Soul arises / they drink, & fill their Skins, & depart rejoic-

ing—O Blessed the day when that good man & all his Company came to Heaven Gate & the Child—then an angel—rushed out to receive them—[71]

Dating this piece is equally problematic and Kathleen Coburn, as editor of the notebooks, suggests a range of dates, setting the limits between 1804 and 1821, with her own specific proposal of 1815–16. Both Sultana and Coburn couple this notebook draft with the verse-*Cain*.[72] Indeed, the beginning of the notebook entry divides into a meter that resembles that of the verse fragment. The slashes which Coleridge uses to mark metered lines ("The Child is born, the Child must die / Among the desert Sands / ") appear throughout the first paragraph even where no meter is yet apparent. It may be that entry 2780, with its separate line indicators represents Coleridge's initial attempt to versify *Cain*. In the preface he introduces the verse fragment as: "the introductory stanza, which had been committed to writing for the purpose of procuring a friend's judgment on the metre" (*PW*, 2: 100). It is possible that the verse fragment, which contains a consistent meter, was made in preparation for the completion of MS *N*. At the same time, this entry seems to me to be thematically consistent with "Canto II" where the unredeemed (child and spirit Abel) are figured in the desert dying of thirst.[73]

Clearly, Coleridge's *Cain* project underwent several fundamental changes and in discussing *The Wanderings of Cain* we are obliged to understand the subject as a plural text. That is, we perceive the project as a work of several faces or identities that are nevertheless organically linked in the manner of Schlegel's garland of fragments. The several parts of *Cain* also participate in a similar unity to the Romantic critical fragments in the paradoxical nature of their interrelationship. The disparate fragments are connected yet distinct; sequential but not contiguous. There are plots but no synthesis. This dynamic between and within prose pieces (existing here almost by chance when the various fragments are collected together) is a characteristic that I will be identifying with the prose poem in its collection.

Returning MS N to the Cain Collection

In terms of imagery, there are two types of landscape in "Canto II" and its associated versions. These are the fertile wood and the barren desert. The bare and arid landscape is most appropriate to the Arabian setting but the forest provides a reference to the lost terrestrial paradise of Eden (Cain is the first to leave Eden entirely as Adam and Eve were expelled from the garden only). The notebook piece (MS *N*) returns the setting to the desert sands, which bizarrely turn into a fountain on the death of the Child from thirst (there is no mention of Cain or Abel here). The dead Child rises to drink from the fountain which heralds the arrival of another (?Christ-) child and thus becomes an angel.[74] The scene resembles the rescue of Enoch by the "real" Abel in MS *Fv*. In fact, this scenario helps to date the entry. On 16 July 1804, in Malta, Coleridge experienced a rare natural phenomenon: a series of small earthquakes was followed by a rainstorm.[75] In MS *N*, the Child is buried alive "in holy frenzy" by the desert sands that "roar'd & whitened like a burst of waters" and "at length shot up a fountain large & mighty."[76] If this entry was inspired by the phenomenon, it is improbable that it was written, as Coburn and Sultana claim, as a continuation of the verses. Coleridge had already employed a similar image in a letter of 1801 to describe the physiological effects of his ill health. "I seem to sink in upon myself in a ruin, like a Column of Sand informed and animated only by a Whirl-blast of the Desart" (*CL* 2: 663). In this case, the verse was created closer to the composition of the letter to Byron. If the reason for the letter actually was to submit a sample the meter, it would be reasonable that his material would be the opening of "Canto II," which also appears in the folio.

Water, which all Coleridge's characters seek, is the substance of "salvation." The fountain is a common image in Coleridge's writings but is here accompanied by a rainbow—God's postdiluvian covenant. The sun and the fountain are well-established separately as images of the ideal in Coleridge but figured together, as the sun reflected in the fountain as a rainbow, they represent the highest form of this idealism. In addition, we know that Coleridge was developing his own definition of "the ideal" during his sojourn in Rome in 1805–6 .[77]

Another notable element of this text is the phrase "roar'd & whitened." The same phrase (as "Roaring and whitening") appears in Wordsworth's (canceled) draft for Book V of the 1804 *Prelude,* which was abandoned some time around 10 March 1804, and Coleridge took with him to Malta a fair copy of the revised version (MS *M*). However, the appearance of the above phrase in MS *N* is compelling evidence for Coleridge having heard or read the canceled passages, possibly on his return from Italy in 1806.[78] This, in turn, may allow us more confidence in applying this date of 1806 to the composition of the notebook piece.

1 / THE PROSE POEM AND THE ROMANTIC FRAGMENT 57

The second 'paragraph' of MS *N*, which begins on a new page (*f88*), holds another clue to dating this piece: "How wide around its Spray, the rain-bow played upon the Stream & the Spray—but lo! another brighter, O far far more bright / it hangs over the head of a glorious Child like a floating veil (vide Raphael's God)." Clearly, identifying the reference to "Raphael's God" is crucial to elucidating the entry. Unfortunately, the image, the reference, and the nature of their association are all ambiguous and we are limited to reasonable speculation. Coleridge's return journey from Malta was via Naples, Rome, and Florence. He lingered in Rome from Christmas 1805 until May 1806. Throughout this period, he visited the Vatican as a tourist. Although we have no immediate notes that he may have made on the Raphael frescoes there, Coleridge was already an admirer and we may safely assume that he saw these works.[79] The painting that most strikingly resembles the images in MS *N* and is housed in the Vatican is the "Madonna di Foligno." Here we have the Madonna and Child seated on clouds against a halo of light like the sun itself. The shape of this golden orb is repeated below in a golden arc or rainbow that hovers over the head of a child-angel. Faces of numerous putti blend into the clouds surrounding the holy couple. It has been observed that a natural phenomenon (the arc of light, which substitutes the more traditional crescent moon at the Madonna's feet) is occurring. Also, that the red flash in the sky may further indicate that the painting had been occasioned by a meteor or similarly portentous event.[80] The notebook entry follows this by combining images of night and day in an apocalyptic scenario. As a myth devoted to change, here emphasized by the innocent child, *Cain* may be associated with Coleridge's interest in the millennial issue, which was being debated just prior to the origins of the poem, in 1796.[81]

If this is the painting that Coleridge is thinking of, then "God" is actually "Christ-child." Yet, it is unlikely that, struck by an image, he would later mistake one for the other: God the father for Madonna and Child. In addition, "Madonna di Foligno" was undergoing restoration in Paris at the time of Coleridge's visit.[82] Despite the uncanny resemblance between these two images, "Raphael's God" therefore, possibly refers to an additional source. The *Disputa* forms part of a large fresco by Raphael in the Vatican Palace. Appearing under the personification of Theology, this fresco illustrates the mystery of the holy sacrament. The sacrament exposed on the altar, leads the eye up to the Holy Spirit inside a gold disc (similar to the

Madonna and Child), followed by the enthroned Christ. Finally, God the Father forms the apex of the group. He floats within a golden ribbed vault which is filled by putti faces as in the "Madonna di Foligno." The fresco is very striking as the figures are almost life-size and fairly engulf the viewer who stands in the room. Both of these works, "Madonna di Foligno" and the *Disputa*, are among Raphael's earlier works and Coleridge's subsequent remarks suggest that this period was not to his taste, but, nevertheless, indicate an acquaintance with them. Thus, considering the concentration of Raphael-like images and, exceptionally, the reference to a canceled passage from the *Prelude* of 1804, we can propose that the text, MS *N*, dates from Coleridge's return to England in 1806 when he had Raphael's images in his mind and he may have read or heard Wordsworth's canceled passages.

A Revised History for The Wanderings of Cain

Regardless, then, of the compositional date of the 1828 version ("Canto II"), it is a fact that Coleridge returned to the project several times over eighteen years. It is possible that this was a reaction to the cooling down of the friendship between Wordsworth and himself and signaled a slightly defiant creative independence on his part. For whatever reason, Coleridge did not regard *Cain* in such a dismissive light as his later commentators, none of whom questioned the apology with which he ends his preface (1828), dissociating himself from the outcome.

Thus, in attempting to establish a sequence for *The Wanderings of Cain*, we can achieve only a rough table of supposition. The initial inspiration may be lost but three subsequent prose and verse pieces reveal an increasingly sophisticated sequence of events culminating in the surreal notebook entry. Finally, Coleridge publishes two versions of "Canto II," the most developed fragment, which is in prose, but he appends a preface. In this introduction, he incorporates the verse by claiming it is closer to his projected work: "assuring the friendly Reader, that the less he attributes its appearance to the Author's will, choice, or judgement, the nearer to the truth he will be" (*PW* [1828], 2: 108). In other words, the published fragment, "Canto II," which may have been composed at any time throughout the work's long history, is disclaimed just prior to its appearance as the least representative of the Absent Work, *The Wanderings of Cain*. As a prose poem, "Canto II" is finally deemed indistinguishable from

1 / THE PROSE POEM AND THE ROMANTIC FRAGMENT   59

the other fragments that group around the gap of the envisioned work: explaining but not presenting it. For Coleridge, who clearly regarded "Canto II" as incomplete in itself, the detached prose piece still required a verse composition to compensate for its shortcomings. On the other hand, Coleridge not only returned to the project at various intervals over an eighteen-year period, he also removed his disclaimer of "Canto II" in his own last collection of 1834, allowing the verse to end the preface and stand juxtaposed to "Canto II."

A clearer picture of the history of *Cain* might look like this:

1797–98	(?lost) original Canto & MS *F*
1800	"Canto II"
1800–4	MS *Fv*
1804–15	verses
1806	MS *N*
1825	verses published in *Aids to Reflection*
1826	Edward Coleridge requests a copy of *The Wanderings of Cain*
1827	*The Amulet* requests a copy of *The Wanderings of Cain*
1828	*The Bijou* publishes "Canto II" as *The Wanderings of Cain. A Fragment*; "Canto II" appears in *Poetical Works*.
1834	"Canto II" appears in *Poetical Works* without an apology after the verses in the Preface.

A conservative estimate of the initial period of composition, therefore, shows it extending from 1797 to 1806 followed by at least nine years of reconsideration (the switch from verse to prose and the removal of the preface). A key date for the compositions appears to be 1804, rather than 1797. This year saw Coleridge's departure for Malta. His physical and mental health was so bad that neither he nor his closest friends expected his return. He fed his depression as ever by examining the nature and origins of evil, guilt, and redemption, and continued to do so after his return to England. His recurrent interest in *Cain* may be therefore be attributed, in part at least, to his own sense of guilt and punishment at this time: the revulsion he felt for his wife and his love for Sara Hutchinson.[83]

Interpreting The Wanderings of Cain

Coleridge's feelings for Sara while he was so far away in Malta are clearly visible in "The Blossoming of the Solitary Date Tree." His desire for her response also has a bearing on *Cain*. Cain's wife and child look to him for answers, while Cain himself looks to Abel. The loss of a partner leads these characters to reflect on themselves and become aware of their own limits. Thus, Cain's torment possibly stems from an experience of the sublime: perceiving his own finite nature inside an infinite structure (the metaphysical desolation in the landscape of "Canto II"; his proximity to death in MSS *F/Fv*).

Placing the mortal inside images of transcendence (the ball of fire in "Book 3rd" [MS *F*], the two Abels in *Fv*, death and apocalypse in MS *N*) raises questions concerning the boundaries of mortality and the nature of the afterlife. The fact of life after death is never questioned in these texts, only its nature. Throughout the various textual versions, a basic dualism is established between the temporal and the supernatural. In part this corresponds to Cain physically crossing the boundary from Eden to primitive society, where he is met by visions and illusions.[84] The dualism also registers the transference of the Absent Work into the realm of representation. Correspondences between the subject and its search for response; life and afterlife are analogous to the relationships established between the prose pieces and between the individual texts and their marginal spaces. Coleridge represents the presences in these blank areas as supernatural to denote their disjunction.[85]

A central concern in these fragments is whether or not the afterlife is connected to one's present, conscious, existence. Put another way, how far the transcendent state reflects or depends on one's experiences. Coleridge firmly believed that the transcendent must be accessed through experience. Indeed, Cain, who is the first agent of death, finds himself in a living hell, reflected in the barren landscapes of "Canto II" and *Fv* and the "interminable precipices" of "Book 3rd" (MS *F*). When the "fiery shape" tries to persuade Cain to burn out his own eyes as penance for his crime, "Cain opposes this idea and says that God himself who had inflicted this punishment upon him had done it because he neglected to make a proper use of his senses &c." ("Book 3rd," MS *F*). He recognizes that his senses are the key to this post-Edenic world and his return to paradise.[86] However, this appears to be the antithesis of Abel's fate. The spirit "Abel" is, rather surprisingly, in great distress in MS *Fv* and here in "Canto II": "But Cain said, 'Didst thou not find favour in the sight of the Lord thy God?' The Shape answered, 'The Lord is God of the living only, the dead have another God.' Then the child Enos lifted up his eyes and prayed; but Cain rejoiced secretly in his heart (*PW*, 2: 106)."[87]

The image is surprising because Christianity would teach that Abel's innocence was rewarded in heaven. It follows that if there is a connection between one's deeds and one's eternal state after death, Cain's torment will be perpetual. If, on the other hand as these texts propose, there is *no* connection, and one's afterlife existence is in the hands of a separate "God of the dead," then the distress exhibited by the spirit Abel is a sad possibility. Good and evil would no longer be accountable in a realm whose values, if they exist, are unknown.

Despite feeling wretched in the face of God and physically tormented by him, Cain himself is easily convinced that Jehovah is not the sole god of the universe ("Canto II"; "Book 3rd," MS *F*; MS *Fv*). Indeed, Coleridge originally intended to pursue the identity of this alternative deity. When "Abel" offers sacrifice of his own blood, the manuscript reads: "A gleam of light illumines the meadow & a being of terrible majesty appears." Although the second part of this sentence is crossed out, the remaining elements of the gleam of light and the observation that "the countenance of Abel becomes more beautiful and his arms glistering" have overt parallels with the transfiguration of Christ.[88]

In the same way, it is only through the fragmented text that the Absent Work can be glimpsed. The attempt to verbalize a transcendental experience is inevitably doomed by the devices of expression. Here, the Absent Work, *The Wanderings of Cain* cannot be "restored," like the "Date Tree" stanzas, but only reflected in the fragments. However, the authors of the *Literary Absolute* show that the written fragment only serves to do more violence to the representation of the Absent Work: "the writing of the fragment, consequently serves to subtract this fragment from the Work, within the continually renewed ambiguity of the *small* work of art, thus serving, in sum, to fragment the fragment. Ultimately, therefore, it effectively dislocates the organic unity of the hedgehog and presents the fragmentation of the *Fragments* only as an ensemble of *membra disjecta*."[89]

Paradoxically, failure proves to be a fertile state because its achievement provides the possibility of innumerable further productions. As a collection, the fragments present particular aspects of the idea in *darstellung* like sides of a prism catching the light. Yet, more than this, subtracting the fragment from the Work creates a doubling: the concept as absent and the concept as partly represented (forever removed from its model by its own finity).

The folio texts offer reported rather than direct narrations: proposals and hypotheticals that resist analysis in a similar way to the Romantics' critical fragments. Coleridge's texts also anticipate genre, suggesting drama at the opening of MS *Fv* with the significant words, "Cain discovered . . ." and later, "soliloquy"; the entrance of Abel and Michael, *ex machina*, and so on. Line breaks and rhythmic phrases in MS *N* imply verse poetry and "Canto II" mimics a biblical prose. In fact, the pre-genre aspect of the *Cain* pieces support the identification with the Romantic "fragment-project" that "does not operate as a program or prospectus but as the *immediate* projection of what it nonetheless incompletes."[90] This subtle dynamic is visible in *Cain*, which indicates, in its textual trail, the complete *Wanderings of Cain*, but which continues to consist of the present, ambiguous and possibly partial set of fragments.

Cain's search, in his exile, for response, for outside acknowledgment of his existence, is only partly realized by the illusory appearance of his brother. The real Abel is the Absent Work that can never be adequately represented but that exposes the limits attached to any attempt to do so. In other words, the spirit Abel is a distortion of the real Abel who exists in eternity and is ultimately unsustainable like the fragment itself. On the other hand, by writing in the real Abel in *Fv* (floating down from heaven with St. Michael), Coleridge exposes the inevitable flaw. The real Abel cannot operate as a symbol because he already represents the Whole: the unknowable transcendence. Having been introduced into the text, Cain becomes obliged to choose between two representations of Abel and of God, confirming one and denying the other. What existed as the ideal, the Absent Work, is now a circumscribed element participating in a process of logic—questionably implying that the truth can be discovered through human reasoning. This appearance of Cain's actual brother dispels mystic ambiguity and affirms Christian dogma, counter-defining its fragmented double, the spirit "Abel," as illusory or worse, as evil.[91]

This conceptual doubling is repeated within the process of fragmentation. That is, whatever the fragment represents, the antithesis continues to be supported by the Idea as Whole. The fragment responds by incorporating irony and paradox (to indicate subsisting antitheses) in a further attempt to fulfil its substitutive role. For example, the fiery spirit claims both a severe and a merciful God who will reward the penance of blindness by "delicious sights and feelings" ("Book 3rd"). In addition, the temptation scenes of the supernatural beings anticipate future biblical passages: the ball of fire tempts Cain as the Devil tempts Christ and "Abel" is transfigured like Christ. Coleridge changes the fiery shape's suggestion of burning out his eyes (in "Book 3rd"), which echoes the Oedipus myth, to a request from the spirit "Abel" to sacrifice the blood from his son's arm in MS *Fv*. This latter scenario is immediately recognizable as a prefiguration of God's similar demand of Abraham in Genesis 22— an event that anticipates God's sacrifice of his own son in the New Testament.[92] Textual irony extends to the contrasting landscapes in the fragments of *Cain*, the barren desert and the fertile forest. In the early folio versions, the forest offers a place for the appearance of the Spirit. In fact, the word "desert" is crossed out in favor of "rocks woods, brooks forests &c." in MS *F*, "Book 3rd." This place may be an illusion, a false Eden, or it may mark the boundary between the sacred and the temporal. Although there is no firm evidence to prove that Coleridge read Dante's *Paradiso* before 1817, the fertile landscapes of *Cain* do contain similarities to the celestial forest that borders Eden in *The Divine Comedy*.[93] In "Canto II" and MS *N* however, the desert at night directly reflects the torment of unredeemed souls ("Eternal Absence from Communion with the Creator"). "Canto II," alone, employs anachronism to underline the purpose of the landscape as a vehicle for other contexts:

> Never morning lark had poised himself over this desert; but the huge serpent often hissed there beneath the talons of the vulture, and the vulture screamed, his wings imprisoned within the coils of the serpent. The pointed and shattered summits of the ridges of the rocks made a rude mimicry of human concerns, and seemed to prophesy mutely of things that then were not; steeples, and battlements, and ships with naked masts. (*PW*, 2: 104)

The imminent birth of civilization is represented here ironically by the fate of its future societies—the church and the military. Unwritten narratives are already present as traces, "fossilized" in the rock and in the panhistoricism depicted in Cain's countenance.

This process of contradiction as a sign of response from the Absent Work operates equally within the self. The protagonist of MS *Fv* is both an agent of death (to Abel and Enoch) and a victim. Similarly, Coleridge's manuscript reveals indecision on the point of whether Cain kills the tigers or submits himself to them.[94] Ultimately, Cain's free will is overtaken by the Christian symbolism that increases with the alternative versions. In *Fv* ("Midnight on the Euphrates"),

Abel and Michael appear theatrically *ex machina*, revealing Abel's salvation and celestial benevolence. MS *N* stands at the apex of the religious undertones that culminated in MS *Fv*. Correspondingly, internal paradoxes are heightened, implying a closer identification with the Absent Work. In "Canto II," Abel, who was killed "by the side of quiet rivers," is found to be apparently dying of thirst. This is also echoed in the notebook entry (MS *N*), "we too all must die of Thirst / for not a Drop remains." However, the thirsting "Abel" is in fact an evil spirit and the desert in MS *N* represents a godless place.[95] Also, in the notebook entry, the sand (by an unknown force) acquires water-like qualities and "drowns" the child before creating a fountain of immortality for which the child, Cain, and "Abel" had thirsted after their expulsion from Eden. Indeed, the Child, on drinking from the fountain together with the Christ-child (like the real Abel, another representation of the Absent Work), is transformed into an angel, a symbol of eternity.[96] There is no longer a sense of human control on the part of the protagonist, nor the narrator who acts as a witness rather than an interpreter. Ultimately the child is carried off (as in MS *Fv*) by its transcendent double and the two are united.

Despite the increasingly orthodox terms in the *Cain* texts, references to supernaturalism continue undiminished, from the fiery ball in the folio (MSS *F/Fv*) to the unnatural fountain in MS *N*. *The Wanderings of Cain* exposes our opposition of the biblical to the temporal by a kind of Gnostic dualism that is represented by the supernatural. The Spirit, for example, is neither sacred nor earthbound and yet participates in both of them—having empirical and divine attributes. The sand, too, in MS *N*, is part "blessed," part "profane."[97] Coleridge identifies the supernatural as a distortion of either the earthly or the divine. Yet, once in the world beyond Eden, no source can be confirmed—thus, with the exception of "Book 3rd" (MS *F*), all versions specify night—the time of secrecy dominated by the reflected light of the moon.[98] The horror of the supernatural is thus couched not in its distortion but in the unknown identity of its source. In addition, emphasizing the natural landscape sustains the ambiguity of these types of phenomena. Nature was currently considered to be both hieroglyphic of the lost language of God and a subject of scientific research.[99]

Cain desires the manifestation of a cosmic event as a rejoinder to his fears of solitude in subjectivity, a state that leads to visions and illusions when not tempered with a little empiricism.[100] In terms of composition, however, Coleridge regards the supernatural as the essence of poetry which is similarly a distortion and requires reductive interpretation: "but the Tale will be then most impressive for all when it is so constructed and particularized with such [traits?] and circumstances, that the Psychologist and thinking Naturalist shall be furnished with the Means of explaining it as a possible fact, by distinguishing and assigning the *Subjective* portion to its true owner."[101] This defense of marginal matter operating on a par with the text itself resembles his directions on restoring the "Date Tree." As with the "Date Tree," what Coleridge is proposing is a continuous project. We may, with some effort, reconstitute these texts, the "Date Tree," even *Cain*, but we are not restoring the Absent Work, only reading a collection of fragments in the peculiar way they demand to be read.

Although the Absent Work cannot be recovered from these pieces, Coleridge attempts, in *Cain*, to draw the unrepresentable a priori of imaginative perception into the discussion of the text (the prose paragraphs in the "Date Tree," the spirit Abel in *Cain*, for example). In 1805, a key time for the composition of the *Cain* fragments, Coleridge considered the well-known analogy between the body and the physical universe. He found the analogy incomplete: "it always seemed to me strange, and wilful and <almost> wicked to not to believe equally that what [?ever] cannot be seen, touched, or heard, bore an equal analogy to his soul."[102] This statement is clearly applicable to Coleridge's approach to his own texts here and their relation to the a priori. In *Cain* he tries to represent this copresence in both its subject matter (giving voice to the dead) and its form (the fragmented prose piece).

In conclusion, *The Wanderings of Cain* is a set of fragmented texts that can be partially reconstructed but which ultimately anticipate a projected definitive version. *Cain* as a collection of pieces (mostly prose texts approaching prose poems), eschews the solidity of fixed allegory to exist as part of an incomplete plurality. In this way, *Cain* corresponds to Schlegel's garland. The projected text is contained around the extant fragments as supernaturalism where the supernatural denotes, according to Coleridge's definition, an overproduction of possible circumstances. In Chapter 3, I will show how the space which Coleridge instinctively denotes as supernatural houses the mass of unselected contextual matter that enables the prose poem to sustain its strictly small dimensions. Crucially, Coleridge chose to publish "Canto II" in his *Poetical Works*. In contrast to the relative sophistication of MS *Fv*, the landscape of the Canto is noticeable for actually rejecting realism. Having emerged from the forest,

Cain and Enoch are drawn, by the moonlight, into a place that, unlike Eden, is unbounded. In other words, the plot moves from the particular to the universal: a semipastoral setting is transformed into an infinite expanse of white sand where the loss of an immediate context introduces the possibility of many others, as the anachronistic symbolism shows. While it may not be the most successful of the various texts of *Cain*, the ability of "Canto II" to tell one story and literally inscribe others is finally what recommends it to the prose poem genre.

It is true to say that "Canto II" and its satellites of marginal texts resemble the prose poem collection in their form and dynamics and as such, they contribute to our understanding of the genre's aesthetics. However, "Canto II" is probably too long to be a prose poem as it is longer than any recognized critical fragment—the genre it formally resembles most closely. In addition, the work was projected to be longer still, in three cantos, and we may take each version to be progress toward such an extension. Truncation in itself does not create a separate genre. Finally, *Cain* appears to be developing, latterly, into a verse poem in its notebook and metered versions. For all these reasons, while these fragmented texts anticipate the prose poem collection, they do not, finally, achieve it.

Egerton 2800:1r (MS *F*)

Book 3rd

He falls down in a trance. When he awakes he sees a luminous body coming before him. It stands before him an orb of fire. It goes on he moves not. It returns to him again, again retires as if wishing him to follow it. It then goes on & he follows. [*undecipherable, possibly crossed out*] they are led to [?]a desert near the bottom of the [?]rocks, woods, brooks, forests, &c &c. The [?]fire gradually shapes itself, retaining its luminous appearance, [?]on to the lineaments of a man: A dialogue between the fiery shape and Cain, in which the being presses upon him the enormity of his guilt, and that he must make some expiation to the true deity, who is a severe God, and persuades him to burn out his eyes. Cain opposes this idea and says that God himself who had inflicted this punishment upon him had done it because he neglected to make a proper use of his senses &c. The evil spirit answers him that God is indeed a God of mercy & that examples must be given to prevent & that [?]examples must be given

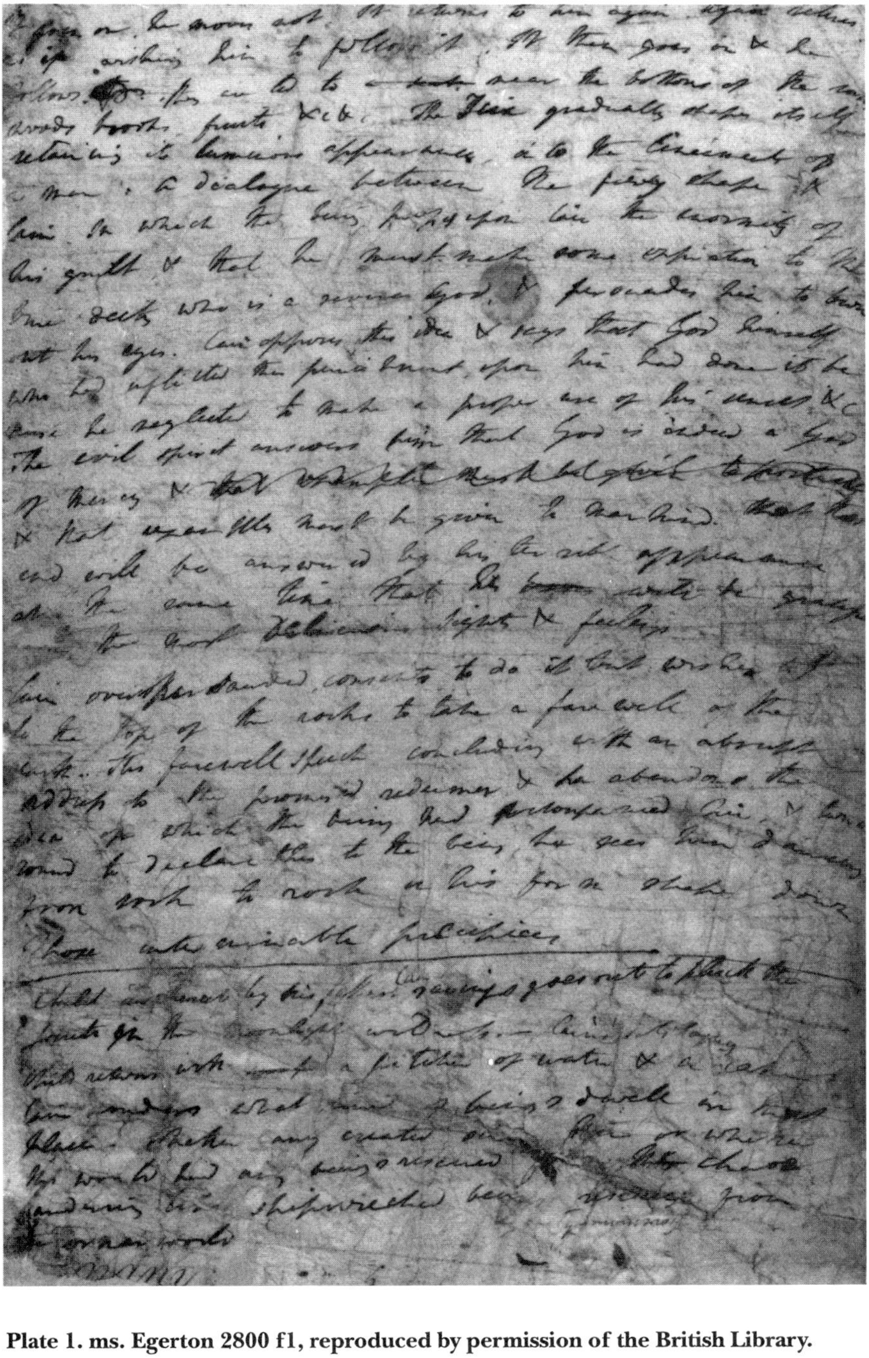

Plate 1. ms. Egerton 2800 f1, reproduced by permission of the British Library.

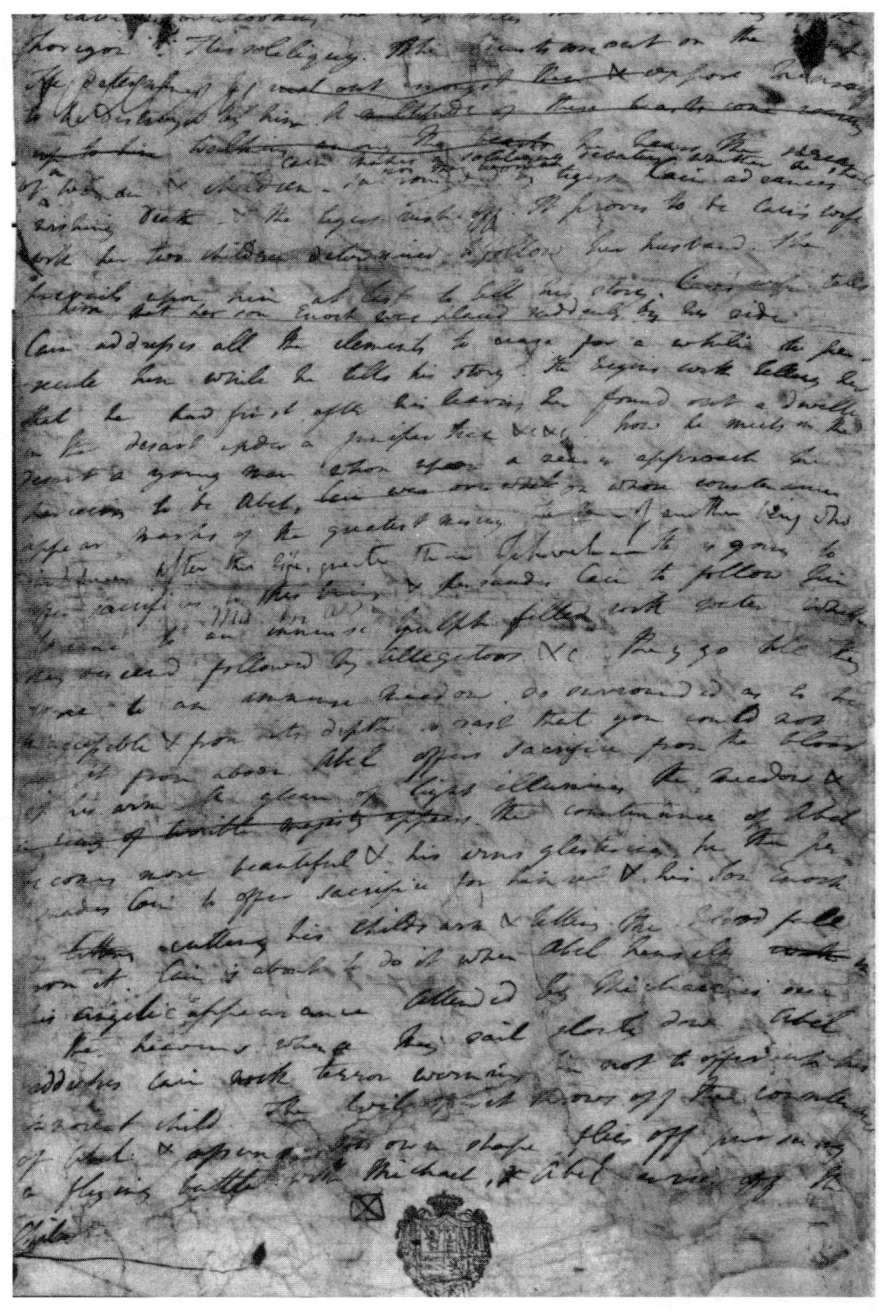

Plate 2. ms. Egerton 2800 f1v, reproduced by permission of the British Library.

to mankind. That this end will be answered by his terrible appearance at the same time that he [*crossed out*] will be gratified [?] with the most delicious sights and feelings.

Cain [?]over-persuaded, consents to do it but wishes to go to the top of the rocks to take a farewell of the earth. His farewell speech concluding with an abrupt address to the promised redeemer & he abandons the idea on which the being had [?]accompanied him, and turning round to declare this to the being he sees him dancing from rock to rock in his former shape down those interminable precipices.

Cain

Child [*illegible*]¹⁰³ by his father's ravings, goes out to pluck the fruits in the moonlight wildness—Cain's soliloquy—Child returns with a pitcher of water and a cake. Cain wonders what kind of beings dwell in that place—whether any created since man or whether this world had any beings rescued from the Chaos, wandering like ship-wrecked beings [?]rescued from [*illegible*, ?the other] world.

EG. 2800:1V (MS *Fv*).

Midnight on the Euphrates. Cedars, palms, pines. Cain discovered sitting on the upper part of the ragged rock, where is cavern overlooking the Euphrates, the moon rising on the horizon. His soliloquy. The beasts are out on the [?]ramp ~~He determines to rush out amongst them &~~ oppose [?]himself ~~to be destroyed by him.~~ A ~~multitude of these beasts come up to him. Walking among the beasts~~ he hears the screams of a woman & children—surrounded by tigers [*inserted* : Cain makes a soliloquy debating whether he shall save the woman] Cain advances wishing death—& the tigers rush off. It proves to be Cain's wife with her two children determined to follow her husband. She prevails upon him at last to tell his story. [*inserted*: Cain's wife tells him that her son Enoch was placed suddenly by her side.]

Cain addresses all the elements to cease for a while [?]to persecute him, while he tells his story. He begins with telling her that he had first after his leaving her found out a dwelling in the desart under a juniper tree &c, &c. how he meets in the desart a young man whom [?]upon a [?]nearer approach he perceives to be Abel. ~~Cain was overwhelmed~~ on whose countenance appear marks of the greatest misery. [?]He [?] of another being who had power after this life, greater than Jehovah [? —] He is going to offer sacrifices to this being and persuades Cain to follow him [?]to [?]come to an immense Gulph filled with water, whither they descend followed by alligators &c. They go till they come to an immense meadow so surrounded as to be inaccessible, and from its depth so vast that you could not see it from above. Abel offers sacrifice from the blood of his arm. A gleam of light illumines the meadow & ~~a being of terrible majesty appears~~. The countenance of Abel becomes more beautiful, and his arms glistering—he then persuades Cain to offer sacrifice, for himself and his son Enoch by ~~letting~~ cutting his child's arm & letting the blood fall from it. Cain is about to do it when Abel himself [?]~~walks~~ in his angelic appearance, attended by Michael, is seen in the heavens whence they sail slowly down. Abel addresses Cain with terror, warning him not to offer up his innocent child. The evil spirit throws off the countenance of Abel & assume[?s/ing] its own shape, flies off pursuing a flying battle with Michael. Abel [?]carries off the Child.

2
De Quincey and Baudelaire

DE QUINCEY'S NARRATIVES AND VISIONARY PROSE WRITINGS PROVIDE a natural step forward from the Romantic critical fragment. Having established that the fragment is essentially a prefatory genre, ultimately relegated to a parallel and marginal relation to some elected "text proper," De Quincey's texts offer a glimpse of that privileged spot. Consistent with the character of the writer, a man in constant flight from creditors, such promises are often urged but remain unrealized. His professed objective is to write a series of opium-induced dream visions—which, we may anticipate, would resemble prose poems in their dimensions and collective presentation. In fact, we read extended and embellished autobiographical accounts. However, his practice of juxtaposing two very different styles, journalistic and purple prose, symbolizes this desired move from prefatory announcement of intention (the critical fragment) to its presentation (the absent work). As a result, the work is always an image rather than a realization of its subject and similarly *prefigures* the prose poem rather than achieves it. De Quincey's idiosyncratic recycling of his own work, in the form of numerous revisions and reordering of material, means that in place of an autonomous text are a series of variables that, as a collective substitute, have come to be regarded as synonymous with his own image of a promised text. This "chaos" in itself has an influence on the presentation of prose poems in the form of reorderable collections. My aim, in the first part of this chapter, is to focus on those edges of the text that most closely approximate the gulf separating the fragmented text and the absent work, that is, the beginnings and endings. Section II looks more closely at how "The Oxford Visions" achieve their (reorderable) fragmentation. Section III examines the crucial, if overlooked, fact that Charles Baudelaire began writing prose poetry in the same year that he "rewrote" the *Confessions* and the *Suspiria de Profundis*. In 1860, a year after De Quincey's death, the first instalments of *Un mangeur d'opium*, Baudelaire's translation of the *Confessions* and the *Suspiria* appeared in France. His work on these narratives had begun in 1857 concurrently with his experiments on brief prose pieces that would come to be regarded as the first legitimate works in the prose poem genre.[1] This final section investigates the extent of De Quincey's influence on the emerging form.

Having studied De Quincey's narratives, which tended increasingly to distinct unit-based prose but never actually achieved full autonomy, Baudelaire was able to examine the nature of extended prose composition (and De Quincey's self conscious style in particular) while creating his own distinctly brief prose texts. However, as Baudelaire himself stated, beyond adapting the *Confessions*, his own translation was designed to make the works of the two authors indistinguishable.[2] Defining these new perimeters in his prose poems would therefore involve reconstructing the intertextual operation from which they sprang. As a result, the abridged passages of De Quincey's full-length works linger over the condensed new prose poetic form.

I

Beginnings

At the close of the original version of *Confessions of an English Opium-Eater* (1821), De Quincey pauses to contemplate the pain of birth: "Jeremy Taylor conjectures that it may be as painful to be born as to die: I think it probable: and, during the whole period of diminishing the opium, I had the torments of a man passing out of one mode of existence into another." (M.III.448).[3] This coupling of suffering and change introduces a leitmotiv to the *Autobiographical Sketches*, which opens the first volume of the authorized collected edition, *Selections Grave and Gay* (1853). The first of these, "The Affliction of Childhood" *begins,* conversely, with an emphasis on endings:

> About the close of my sixth year, suddenly the first chapter of my life came to a violent termination; that chapter which, even within the gates of recovered Paradise, might merit a remembrance. *"Life is finished!"* was the secret misgiving of my heart; . . . " *Life is finished! Finished it is!"* was the hidden meaning that, half unconsciously to myself, lurked within my sighs. (*Sel.* 1:1; M.I.28)

Somehow, the "first chapter" of his life, and therefore his narrative, is claimed as violently lost at its very outset. The beginning is presented in transition. This recurs in the revised version of the *Confessions* (1856) where the shadowy self of the narrator is "reborn" and the whole childhood experience reenacted. However, this narrative opens with a discussion not of himself but of opium and of Coleridge. De Quincey claims that, like Coleridge, he took opium as a medical treatment, in his own case, for ailments that were a consequence of his early life. In this way, the childhood incidents become the overshadowing object of narration, postponing and replacing the proposed text: a description of opium dreams now diminished to three brief examples at the end of the work: "For in these incidents of my early life is found the entire substratum, together with the secret and underlying motive of those pompous dreams and dream-sceneries which were in reality the true objects—first and last—contemplated in these Confessions" (*Sel.* 5:13; M.III.233).

In each case, birth and death are posited as gateways to another "mode of existence." They are therefore not subject to linear time (De Quincey is "reborn" at his recovery) but, like Wordsworth's 'spots of time,' can occur at any point.[4] In addition, these states are always associated with writing since the transformation signals a knowledge of the end through which the previous condition can be more accurately interpreted. In literary terms, De Quincey claims that the opium dreams represent the moment before the end, the climactic moment where the current condition is perfected. The ideal nature of this end is one of synthesis, collecting and presenting all elements in an experience of simultaneity.

Yet, it is the starting point (so eagerly pursued that it becomes, ironically, a final objective) that eludes De Quincey. More defensive than penitent, his priority lies in locating the source of his addiction, which will provide him with an immediate justification for the life he feels obliged to narrate. The subsequent narrative evolves by a movement of continual regression as he attempts to locate the crucial event through analytical retrospection. In other words, the texts are finally a substitute for a single starting point that, if ever found, would have engendered an entirely different work. This "Absent Work" is continually projected as the next piece. His preoccupation with sequence, thus revealed in the *Confessions*, derives, in part, from his reading of Kantian philosophy which he expounds in an article for *Tait's* magazine, June 1836, entitled "German Studies and Kant in Particular" on the problem of causality. If De Quincey can claim that his texts are produced in the pursuit of their own starting point—the source of authority that will, by necessity, generate the process of cause and effect coinciding with the proposed narrative—then he finds a fundamental flaw to this procedure in the theory that he propounds in the article. Kant's argument denies the existence of necessity as the catalyst in any procedure: the connection, in the event of succession, being contingent only. Kant opposes Locke's concept of knowledge rising out of experience and Hume's differentiation between perceived causation and necessary connection. Instead, Kant argues that causality is rooted in one function of the human understanding (the category of relation). Furthermore, this idea forms one of the a priori preconditions to any possibility of experience.

De Quincey is therefore left a problem for his defense, resting as it does on a claim of powerlessness within the indifferent machinery of events. Since necessity is denied him as the source of power, the starting point must disappear because there is nowhere and no point at which a system of authority can be introduced that will legitimize and predict the process. Yet, to remove the starting point would leave a series of impressions and associations of ideas where the role formerly assigned to necessity would be appropriated by the imagination. De Quincey approached this more modernist style in *The English Mail-Coach* (1849) but was later obliged to provide a note to the reader in order to supplement the resulting elliptical text.

In 1848, De Quincey published an article entitled, "System of the Heavens as Revealed by Lord Rosse's Telescopes" in *Tait's* magazine. The article is based on Kant's proposal that even if we knew the age of the earth, the information would not enable us to determine how much more time it had remaining since we are ignorant of the scale on which such a calculation would be based (for example, is one thousand years a long or short period of time for the earth?). De Quincey accuses Kant of dozing. Of course, the earth may be a phoenix: both old and young; bound to a series of fluctuating cycles as opposed to linear or human time—in the same way, we may add, as memory. In other words, with his characteristic scrupulousness, De Quincey refutes Kant's own proposed starting point (of assuming the objective reality of linear time for all things) as an inadequate hypothesis and goes on to deny the subsequent proposals which it logically, if erroneously, engenders.

De Quincey redresses the problem of sequence, however, by returning to Kant and the source of knowledge. If ideas are preconditions to the possibility of experience then a certain form of "nexus" is validated, but De Quincey's audience must be in possession of his ideas before they are able to participate in the experience of the proposed narrative, that is, the dreams. In other words, if apprehension is subjective, communication is rendered virtually impossible unless the reader is drawn into an ontological communion with the narrative self so that reading becomes a shared experience rather than an objective deciphering. An extreme example of this occurs in the revised *Confessions* when the young absconder is returned home.

> If in this world there is one misery having no relief, it is the pressure on the heart from the *Incommunicable*. . . . At this moment, sitting in the same room of the Priory with my mother, knowing how reasonable she was—how patient of explanations—how candid—how open to pity—not the less I sank away in a hopelessness that was immeasurable from all effort at explanation. She and I were contemplating the very same act; but she from one center, I from another. (*Sel.* 5:114–15; M.III.315)

Convinced that to make her understand even the briefest of his bad experiences at school will be enough to reconcile her to him, he grapples with the inadequacy of rhetoric by which he can effect only "the feeblest and most childish reflection" of what he has "suffered." Analogy to the writing process itself is quite clear here. The passage quoted above appears only in the revised version and reveals De Quincey's concern about the effectiveness of any form of revision (recounting being a form of repetition) when on one level it merely involves juggling with an essentially inadequate language system. His later recourse to "impassioned prose" registers this despair in real terms where the need to invent an idiom in order to write has serious implications for his neoclassical principles, which classify writing as an imitative art. Similarly, without a conscious attempt by his readers to adopt the author's mask, in an act of temporary self-alienation, De Quincey's text "dies away into a sigh" of unproductive self-pity that ultimately invalidates the legitimacy of its own ambiguous and fragile starting point.

This image of initiation as a retreating power source is repeated in the figures of authority: God, father, guardians, and the "immortal druggist" who mythically appears to sell the first tincture of opium to the narrator before vanishing completely.[5] In the face of such precarious origins, and by a Cartesian logic, De Quincey is led quite specifically into autobiography: "since no man surely, on a question of my own private experience, could have pretended to be better informed than myself" (*Sel.* 5:3; M.III.225). Even if his own self proves similarly elusive in this role, at least he is "not simply the best, but surely the sole authority" and more able to follow its course rather than wander around in the disorientating breeze of a sudden departure.[6] De Quincey, the schoolboy logician, constantly seeks to justify his textual point of origin in order to avoid Kant's own error of an argument generated from an unsound basis.

In the 1821 version of his *Confessions*, De Quincey identifies the end of the work with the exit by opium from the stage of the narrative: "Not the opium-eater, but the opium, is the true hero of the tale; and the legitimate centre on which the interest revolves. The object was to display the marvellous agency of opium, whether for pleasure or for pain: if that is done, the action of the piece has closed."[7] This passage again reveals De Quincey stepping aside from the crucial moment of initiation. In the 1856 version, a preface preempts the earlier problem by stating that what was intended as "a crowning grace . . . reserved for the final pages of this volume" that is, twenty to twenty-five dreams and visions, are lost.[8] In addition, both versions of the *Confessions* are concluded in diary form, which locates him decisively inside a time system where the past is portrayed as ever present yet simultaneously distinct from its current development. Yet, his very reluctance to hand over his work to the public, which manifested in missed deadlines and no definitive edition, bears witness to a continuing incomplete attempt to reconcile his fragmented self into a coherent whole. The partial alienation of the projected self means that De Quincey is able to "recognize" himself in past events but is not under pressure to "identify" with the character he has produced.[9] This is evident in the structure of his works, which, based on their silent source *The Prelude* (unpublished until 1850), are composed of "spots of time" that Lindop estimates De Quincey probably read in manuscript in 1810 or 1811.[10] The shadings in tone between pedestrian narrative and a "spot" or set piece reflects moments of recognition that occur during the otherwise objective perspective on his former self. In other words, an ambiguous and possibly substitutive starting point secures a split-self that, in turn, finds expression in a divided prose style.

De Quincey's double edged prose is crucial to a developing prose poetry that is rooted in dialectic and paradox (as its title suggests). As with Coleridge, De Quincey's aesthetic relies heavily on logic as an authority to support any form of artistic extension—here most obviously, narrative. However, it is clear that this system still gives De Quincey trouble with the edges of his texts: for example, no single starting point will, by necessity, generate his convoluted narrative. While De Quincey's texts seek to present detached moments, or visions, and thus move toward prose poetry, they are never finally released from his pressing need to authorize all forms of connection (between parts of a text and between a text and its audience).

Artistic Vision and Dreams

The principal antitheses of De Quincey's work are generally acknowledged (the split-self and the two prose styles: "literature of knowledge" and "literature of power") but the nature of the visions themselves requires analysis. Although the visions appear in the text more often as symbols of the anticipated work in its projected completion rather than as distinguishably individual narratives, they are not, themselves, homogenous. Two types of dream-visions can be distinguished. One is first experienced in youth and is crucial in that it serves to identify the child as an artist (I will continue to refer to this as the "artistic vision" in association with the Romantic aesthetic). The other is the result of artificial stimulation by opium and is therefore associated with adulthood.[11] Episodes that correspond to this second type I will hereafter refer to as "dreams" since they are, to a greater extent, purposefully induced by drugs and refer specifically to the dreamer's own life through which they may be interpreted. Wordsworth's epiphanies are of the visionary order while Coleridge's "Kubla Khan" and other fantasies may be considered as dreams. Despite this self-referentiality, the opium dreams are characterized by an expansion in space and time. Such forays into metaphysical forms emphasize the limits of prose language: "Time becomes infinitely elastic, stretching out to such immeasurable and vanishing termini, that it seems ridiculous to compute the sense of it on waking by expressions commensurate to human life." (*Blackwood's*, 57: 280; M.XIII.338–9)

Conversely, the artistic vision involves transcendence. It is often a sudden and unexpected experience in which the subject is made aware of the hitherto concealed structure of the moment. In the principal vision of the *Suspiria*, in which a shaft to God's throne opens up before the young author, De Quincey records that the experience: "exactly reversed the operation of opium. Instead of a short interval expanding into a vast one, upon this occasion a long one had contracted into a minute." (*Blackwood's* 57: 281). This minute comprises a vanishing focal point (God) and it is significant that the experience that signals De Quincey's birth as an artist should be anticipated by him to "rise again for me to illuminate the hour of death" (*Blackwood's* 57: 281; M.I.43). In this way, the artistic vision becomes one with the final moment, they being identical but prospective and retrospective, respectively. Such is the mirror-image relationship between De Quincey's artistic vision and the account of a drowning woman who saw every moment of her life at once, so that, "her consciousness became omnipresent at one moment to every feature in the infinite review" (*Blackwood's* 57: 742; M.XIII.348). Similarly, through the privileged vision of the artist, each moment is seen as if it has already passed. The prose poem, in these terms, would accord with the vision rather than the dream because it too holds an expansive content within a contracted space.

In "System of the Heavens as revealed by Lord Rosse's Telescopes," De Quincey denies that a revelation shows to men what they could discover for themselves but defines it instead as the manifestation of something that the "moral darkness of man" would otherwise prevent him from seeing. Similarly, he prioritizes his opium dreams in the *Suspiria de Profundis* over his own glimpse of God because opium introduces a randomness to each experience that cannot be predicted or, necessarily, understood. De Quincey surrenders to the permutations and is caught up in the infinitely expansive nature of the dreams. Ultimately, however, this very freedom prevents him from creating a coherent narrative. The point is best illustrated by the prose piece appended to "System of the Heavens" which was taken from a work by Richter.[12] In the narrative, "Dream-vision of the Infinite as it reveals itself in the Chambers of Space," a dreamer is taken up into heaven to be guided by an angel around that celestial house. On the journey, they pass "wildernesses of death," blazing suns and "eternities of twilight, that revealed, but were not revealed." Incredible architectural structures rise through the "self-repetitions," parallels and counterpositions of the constellations:

> Without measure were the architraves, past number were the archways, beyond memory the gates. Within were stairs that scaled the eternities above, that descended to the eternities below: above was below, below was above, to the man stripped of gravitating body: depth was swallowed up in height insurmountable, height was swallowed up in depth unfathomable. (*Sel.* 3:200; M.VIII.34)

This succession of identical structures complies with Burke's prescription for an architectural sublime and the repetitive clauses imitate the expansion by piling upon one another until reading them becomes a vertiginous experience. Finally the dreamer is defeated:

> Then the man sighed, stopped, shuddered, and wept. His overladen heart uttered itself in tears; and he said, "Angel, I will go no farther. For the spirit of man aches under this infinity. Insufferable is the glory of God's house. Let me lie down in the grave, that I may find rest from the persecutions of the Infinite; for end, I see, there is none." ...Then the angel threw up his glorious hands to the heaven of heavens, saying, "End is there none to the universe of God? Lo! also THERE IS NO BEGINNING." (*Sel.* 3:200–1; M.VIII.34)[13]

Similarly, De Quincey's "journalistic" narratives anticipate the dream-visions, but appear themselves to be infinite in their capacity for expansion (the nature of the dream, like the house of God, would be expansive too). The fact that De Quincey was prepared to write numerous dreams reminds us that they only symbolize the moment and are not the moment itself. At the other end of the scale, the artistic vision locates an end at every stage, often obscuring the beginning (for example, De Quincey's vision by his sister's deathbed replaces the chronological, the current time that is being transcended). Such a structure is reminiscent of the critical fragment that focuses on its crumbling edges: failing to realize its own coherence but fixed in anticipation of the beginning of a complete text—the Absent Work.

Suspiria de Profundis

In March 1845, the first instalment of *Suspiria de Profundis* appeared in *Blackwood's*. Judging it "a new *Opium Confessions*" and superior to the earlier work, De Quincey regarded "these final 'Confessions'" as "the *ne plus ultra*, as regards the feeling and the power to express it, which I can ever hope to attain."[14] Grevel Lindop records how the plans for the new work were thwarted partly by disagreements with Blackwood over its allocated space in the magazine. Of the proposed four parts only two appeared, of which the second was incomplete. Four years later this was followed by *The English Mail-Coach* (clearly an autonomous work but apparently included in De Quincey's plan for the *Suspiria*).[15] Lindop suggests that De Quincey's proposal to include the *Mail-Coach* and "The Daughter of Lebanon" show that he "had come to regard *Suspiria* as an undefined repository for all his more fantastic prose works."[16] In fact, according to his own comments on the genre, it is possible that De Quincey saw the *Suspiria* as a development of the novel form. In the article "On Novels," he identified what he believed to be the single redeeming feature of that genre—the power found in separate passages that have not been harmed in their abstraction from the whole. Alternatively, the *Suspiria* can now be partially reconstructed with the restoration of various manuscript prose pieces collected by Japp in the *Posthumous Works* although many were never rewritten, having been accidentally burned by the author.[17] Not only was the *Suspiria* incomplete in *Blackwood's* but De Quincey argues in his Preface to *Selections Grave & Gay* that he regards only those works which appear in collected editions as published (since magazines target a limited and specific audience). The *Suspiria* did not appear in the *Selections* as a unified work but as a project, only partially realized.

In his secondary role as reviser and editor, De Quincey acknowledges the displacement of the author by emphasizing an imperfect knowledge of the present excepting its imminent need for revision. At the opening of the *Suspiria*, he immediately mentions the *Confessions* (making an end of a beginning), states the fact that progress and the pace of life produce dissipation of thought and he introduces the present work as a reconcentration of the themes set out in the last. The *Confessions*, therefore, is a model for the *Suspiria*, which is reflected in the tighter construction of the latter.

On the whole, this concentration is effected by omission. Although the *Suspiria* offers the same theme of opium-induced dream visions reflecting the artist child, there is much less autobiographical narrative than was generated in the *Confessions*. The structure of the *Suspiria de Profundis* is more episodic marking the end of continuous narrative and the beginning of a unit-based form of composition, a disjunction that is only fully realized in the "Dream-Fugue" section of *The English Mail-Coach*. At the same time, the title of the *Suspiria* applies both to the whole work and to its individual sections. Thus, the individual episodes of which this work is composed do not relate to a larger context because that wider, final framework is never adequately established, confirmed or even seen to exist. Such a structure allows the incorporation of numerous prose pieces and an equal liberty to decant them (into "Autobiographic Sketches," etc.). Ironically, this freedom, offered by the form, conflicts with De Quincey's own dictatorial stance over his work. Protesting to Blackwood against the omission of "Levana and Our Ladies of Sorrow," he writes: "There are many passages which will lose all—not only effect—but even *meaning,* if torn away from the context."[18] Perhaps De Quincey was not himself aware of the license for decontextualization that he had legitimized. The conflict that exists between expansive tendencies of the compositional unit (especially in the dream sceneries) and De Quincey's insistence on authorial control becomes the final obstacle to the liberation of the independent prose piece.

If the form of the *Suspiria* is regarded as its weakest point, it is appropriately ironic that it is the single aspect retained by Baudelaire for his *Spleen de Paris.* Meanwhile, the episodic form of the *Suspiria* means that the separate units can continue to exist regardless of the particular frame they acquire. This works for De Quincey on several levels: he can use the same material in separate works, infinitely adding layers to an ever-incomplete text, so that secondly, and economically, he is able to maximize his income from minimum materials (it being a naïve reading that does not take into account the market value of each piece). Ideologically, it allows him to view his life as a pattern or musical theme that gains significance by continuing to exist under an unceasing series of variations. In this he preempts Pater's promotion of the music model to the apex of aesthetic form and the object of *Anders-streben,* of artistic borrowing, for all art.[19] A final advantage to De Quincey lies in the fact that the episodic composition allows him to conserve the fragmentary nature of the sections—and therefore his own ability to reevaluate them. In other words, only at the moment of the unforseen "end," his own death, can the set of possibilities be exhausted and a different analysis be precipitated—one that De Quincey feared because it occurs independently of the artist himself. His somewhat paranoid rewriting demonstrates that his fear centers on the loss of control over the position of interpretation and he engages in a power struggle with the Press, which he projects as the responsible agent of finality.[20] The relationship between De Quincey and the Press, however, is actually one of mutual necessity. As the *Confessions* showed, De Quincey needed to perceive an end in order to begin writing. His years of solitary study and meditation amounted only to procrastination, but once he became a regular contributor to the magazines, his output, however fragmentary at the level of individual articles, became profuse: "The magazines might not wait for De Quincey's truth; but *because* they would not wait, they got it."[21]

II

The Oxford Visions

In their mild disjunction, as set-pieces within a larger coherent narrative, criticism even now proves to be incapable of approaching these dreams without resorting to the clumsy deduction of whether these pieces are prose or poetry.[22] Virginia Woolf exhibits the archetypal confusion when faced with De Quincey's "prose-poetry." Having stated that "it is for his poetry that we read him and not for his prose," clearly advocating a distillation of the text, she then objects to the results this would produce: "A prose writer may dream dreams and see visions, but they cannot be allowed to lie scattered, single, solitary upon the page. So spaced out they die."[23] This type of criticism, which relies so heavily on the belief that all writing falls squarely within one of the two poles of prose or poetry, is too rigid to conceive of a genre that is "prose that, without ceasing to be prose, aims at producing the effects of poetry—at affecting the reader by means of rhythm and alliteration and by . . . subtler influences."[24] De Quincey spends too much time with images of inseparability (the rod and the flowers of the thyrsus; the bricks and the road in Cheapside) to be ignored on this point. His work is insistently organic. Thematically, opium is a necessary foundation for the dreams and cannot be separated from them. Similarly, this self-conscious practice of filling-in and purposefully including in his work the "ugly pole" of composition (i.e., the opium) shows that his aim is to provide a subdued background against which his impassioned prose can blaze with defined intensity.

In his perception of the organicism of his own works, journalistic and impassioned prose become interdependent. The former is not restricted to framing its counterpart in the role of "raw material" from which it is composed but is considered as inherent to it and the texts forcefully implement this. The context of "Levana and Our Ladies of Sorrow," "The Spectre in the Brocken," and "Savannah-La-Mar" is not restricted to the main portion of "The Affliction of Childhood" (as far as "The Palimpsest") and Part II of the *Suspiria*, creating a checkered structure of "mere" and "impassioned" prose.[25] Instead, the context breaks its traditional boundaries and permeates these short titled sections by way of footnotes and digressions that eventually undermine the intensity of vision and singularity of thought that would otherwise characterize them. It is precisely this problem of context (passages that connect these pieces to the larger narrative) that *prevents* the Oxford Visions from passing into prose poetry at all. The continuous nature of prose is not amenable to decisive shifts from one form to another but anxiously fills in any possible gaps, mainly, in De Quincey's prose, to sustain the single center of interpretation that he defended in the *Confessions*. This tendency to shrink from episodes lying "scattered, single, solitary on the page" means that he cannot fully render into prose the Romantic vision (by definition fragmentary) and thereby he initiates rather than achieves a model for the prose poem.[26]

Significantly, the first titled section (although not usually collected under the eponymous "prose-poems") is "The Palimpsest," a tablet on which several layers of writing are inscribed and overlaid. The image provides a model for the dreams proper, in which temporal events are absorbed into a synchronic pattern. There is a clear analogy to autobiography here where the dreams can be self-sufficient if they contain within themselves elements of their initial, several, contexts. This would go some way to explaining the paradox of the dreams being at once distinct from the surrounding tissue of "mere" prose and one with it in its accommodation of them.

"The Palimpsest" traces the movement effected by the individual dream episodes. That movement is one of accumulation and concentration followed by dispersion (in different contexts or simply in their rearrangement). Yet, again the conflict with De Quincey's demand for control restricts this final diffraction: "Insolent vaunt of Paracelsus, that he would restore the original rose or violet out of the ashes settling from its combustion" (*Blackwood's* 57: 741; M.XIII.345). Within a potentially independent prose piece, De Quincey here reveals his anxiety of resurrection, that is, decontextualization, when it is arranged by someone other than himself the author (Baudelaire makes much of the palimpsest image as if he is concerned to defend De Quincey's own preemption). The significance of the palimpsest is fully manifest when it is made analogous to the human mind, which stores "successive themes, having no natural connection." At the moment of death, fever, or opium stimulation, these past themes are reanimated. In the resurrection, their ghosts appear satisfyingly coexistential and their very repetition injects an intensity into the imperfect present that, without catalytically transforming its disparate elements, provides a model through which that present may be perceived under the unity of vision usually reserved for its future recall. In addition, the palimpsest offers a space for writing that authorizes the reordering of the occupying compositional units, hence: "the Grecian tragedy had seemed to be displaced, but was *not* displaced, by the monkish legend; and the monkish legend had seemed to be displaced, but was *not* displaced, by the knightly romance" (*Blackwood's* 57: 743; M.XIII.348).

This passage also legitimizes De Quincey's own rewriting practice and his repetition of those revisions. It is therefore with an ingenious sleight of hand that the end of a prose piece that denies a single origin in favor of an infinite succession of precedents should be diverted into a footnote. The first independent piece in a series of similarly defined prose pieces thus fails to determine its own radical boundaries which define it against traditional prose narrative. The mid-textual "end" peters out in marginal space. In fact De Quincey goes further to actively illustrate the point by removing (but by the same token *not* removing) "The Palimpsest" from the version of the *Suspiria* as it was incorporated into the *Autobiographic Sketches.*

"Levana and Our Ladies of Sorrow" is generally regarded as the first "prose-poem" proper in this sequence.[27] In just the same way as "The Palimpsest," this piece is almost totally given over to an explanation of its title; the actual dream being only narrated in the final paragraph. "Levana" also ends on a footnote. In this case the note attempts to place "Levana" in the larger scheme—or, rather, the larger context is contained in the circumscribed prose piece because the narrative whole is here claimed to correspond to the three Ladies. The note can only *attempt* to indicate the correspondence because that larger work was never completed. Again, the discriminative boundary collapses under the weight of context.

In "Levana" the Ladies are servants of God and the 'Madonna' is a defier who orders the dreamer to exist in a resurrected state of living death: "So shall he rise again *before* he dies. And so shall our commission be accomplished which from God we had—to plague his heart until we had unfolded the capacities of his spirit" (*Blackwood's*, 57: 747; M.XIII.369). This effectively raises the poet above ordinary mortal status and honors him with the (artistic) vision which is informed by an intuition of the end; a vision which De Quincey exhibits at the very opening of his *Confessions*. The artist can create patterns of being because to do so requires a level of completion inside the teleological framework that he—as an artist—possesses. Again, the distinction between "man" and "artist" is significant because it allows a comprehensive coexistence of the two states, making autobiography possible in that it permits the simultaneous and dual perspective of subject and author. In fact, as I have shown, it makes autobiography essential. The moment of self-recognition for the artist, when he perceives himself to be acting within these causal structures, has two contradictory consequences. On one hand it generates the creation of the art work as almost a *duty* implied with the bestowal of that "gift." On the other hand, that very vision of the end is described by De Quincey as a painful experience: "Either the human being must suffer and struggle as the price of a more searching vision, or his gaze must be shallow and without intellectual revelation" (*Blackwood's* 58: 44; M.XIII.351).[28]

In "Vision of Sudden Death" in *The English Mail-Coach*, De Quincey will actually refer to his authorial position as an "accursed gift." Despite the instinct to communicate, then, this vision of the end makes the artist recoil from the starting point since by initiating a beginning he is then responsible for the inevitability of the end that has just filled him with horror. The only alternative that will reconcile these antagonistic responses *and* reduce the risk of responsibility is in autobiography where the starting point is shared in the communication of the artistic experience itself.

By positing himself as victim of the three sisters, De Quincey opens up the field of possibilities that will link him, causally, to his present condition thereby tracing the pattern of his own individuality. He does this in the hope that recognizing his own design will fuse his split self into a comprehensible whole.[29] The experiencing protagonist/victim is set against the investigative narrator and intensifies the vision but it is a vision that is willed, being carefully manufactured, and cannot therefore provide a springboard to the desired transcendence of complete comprehension.[30] The section stops with the Madonna's "speech" and De Quincey is left unanswered and providing his own, inadequate response. All he can confidently assert is that his experiences of a living death and resurrection somehow places him in a unique position that only writing can now fully exploit. Yet, the beginning of writing is registered by the end of the text and the "capacities of his spirit" are dangerously bequeathed to the reader for a final analysis (despite the final attempt to contextualize them in the concluding footnote).

Following "Levana" in the *Suspiria* is "The Apparition of the Brocken."[31] This piece is more tightly constructed than the preceding ones as there is no preamble. However, the source of the relationship between the Spectre and himself is revealed prematurely and in a footnote. De Quincey exposes the nature of the Spectre as simply a reflection of its perceiving subject *before* he is able to narrate the experiment which will discover it.[32] What should proceed as an investigation culminating in empirical proof and metaphysical understanding is wholly undermined. By prematurely offering the reader a glimpse of the privileged vision afforded to the artist, De Quincey drains the subsequent narrative of its purpose. (In terms of technique, it reads like a performing magician unaware of his transparent sleeves.) "Make the sign of the cross, and observe whether he repeats it, (as, on Whitsunday,* he surely ought to do.) Look! he *does* repeat it" (*Blackwood's* 57: 748; M.I.53). Here the additional footnote (at "Whitsunday") takes the reading eye out of the text to inform one that Whitsunday often produces the right temperature and clouds to effect the phenomenon. After this, the exclamation and surprised response are difficult to support. De Quincey's "mistake" suggests a fear-induced attempt to draw his masked audience into a closer intimacy so that the alienated self can be united in a conceptual "we" in the face of its own fragmentation. The process is still incomplete until De Quincey, clinging to his didactic position, reveals the full extent of the image. "This trial is decisive. You are now satisfied that the apparition is but a reflex of yourself; and, in uttering your secret feelings to *him*, you make this phantom the dark symbolic mirror for reflecting to the daylight what else must be hidden for ever" (*Blackwood's* 57: 749).

The phantom is finally revealed as not merely an image of the self and its internal divorce involved in the production of the text but also a figure of silent sublimity in the same way as the Sorrowful Sisters. The Spectre ultimately represents De Quincey's projection of the "ineffable" sufferings of childhood, which, while not representable in linguistic expression, embody the title "Sighs from the Depths" and provide the vehicle for the dreams. The Dark Interpreter, which shadows the texts like a Greek chorus (and to whom the Spectre is analogous), is De Quincey's perception of the end: his artistic persona, which enables him to occupy the marginal position of combined subject and commentator.[33]

"Savannah-La-Mar" is the last in the prose-poetic sequence. The piece absorbs the preceding themes of the Interpreter, tragedy, injustice, and so on, including the death of Elizabeth. It is arguably the most successful of the Oxford Visions because its theme of immeasurable time is contained in a well-defined space ("Savannah-La-Mar" does not contain a preamble, digressions, or footnotes). In addition, in the image of the drowned city of Savannah-La-Mar, enshrined forever in the crystal dome of the ocean, De Quincey produces a subtle contrast between the proportions of its eternal fate in earthly terms and as a single element in the greater scheme of God's time and purposes. The connection is made by the Dark Interpreter:

> The time which *is*, contracts into a mathematic point; and even that point perishes a thousand times before we can utter its birth. All is finite in the present; and even that finite is infinite in its velocity of flight towards death. But in God there is nothing finite; but in God there is nothing transitory; but in God there *can* be nothing that tends to death. Therefore, it follows—that for God there can be no present. (*Blackwood's* 57: 751; M.XIII.361)

Hence, the dream-visions proper, the Absent Work, never appear because in their transcending synthesis, where all things exist in their complete state, presence is replaced by the past. De Quincey can only represent the visions faithfully, then, by positing them always as a project, hovering in the future and as always about to be made manifest. The prose poem form, adequately developed, would have been most appropriate to provide the alternative area needed for the promised visions. But De Quincey drains the new form of its potential power by using it prematurely in an initial attempt to communicate the artist's intuition of the end by which he is able to experience those dreams that are now displaced. The "Oxford Visions" are therefore not fully realized prose poems because they preempt the form best suited to a prose of vision (a prose that is both a beginning and an end) and as they stand they are compromised by an incomplete dissociation from narrative detail by context, footnotes, and so on.[34] De Quincey went some way to correcting his method especially in the "Dream-Fugue" from the more tightly constructed *English Mail-Coach* (see Chapter 3, section III).

III

Un mangeur d'opium

The *Confessions* first appeared in anonymously translated fragments in France in *La Pandore* on 29 and 30 September 1827. These went largely unnoticed until an adaptation, *L'Anglais mangeur d'opium*, by Alfred de Musset appeared in 1828 becoming an immediate popular success.[35] De Musset's editors suggest that Baudelaire was aware of this translation but that his dislike for de Musset's work prevented him from ever mentioning it.[36] Epistolary evidence shows that Baudelaire considered producing his own translation at the beginning of 1857. In that year, he sent Eugène de Broise a list of those whom he wished to receive a copy of *Les Fleurs du mal*. The list included three English writers: Browning, Tennyson, and De Quincey.[37] Of significance is a letter written to his mother that July:

> But I have jobs to do which cannot be done in a place without libraries, prints or galleries. First of all I must clear up the question of
> the *Aesthetic Curiosities,*
> the *Nocturnal Poems,*
> and the *Confessions of an English Opium-Eater.*
> The *Nocturnal Poems* are for the *Revue des Deux Mondes* ; the *Opium-Eater* is a new translation of a magnificent author who is unknown in Paris. It's for the *Moniteur.*[38]

"Poèmes nocturnes" was one of the working titles for Baudelaire's *Le Spleen de Paris* the first six of which were published in 1857 and which he continued to publish until his death ten years later. *Un mangeur d'opium* appeared in *Revue contemporaine* on 15 and 31 January 1860 before being collated with articles on wine and hashish to produce the single work, *Les Paradis artificiels opium et haschisch* in spring of that year. Therefore, Baudelaire was developing his prose poems concurrently with his work on *The Confessions*.[39] De Quincey's influence on Baudelaire is usually referred to only in passing with regards to the thyrsus image which the latter used for his famous prose poem on the subject (one that is itself often taken as the model of the genre as a whole).[40] However, this is the most tenuous link. I contend that the connection goes further. It was precisely his treatment of what he termed De Quincey's "bizarre" texts that guided Baudelaire into achieving the goal to which De Quincey's autobiographical work increasingly tended. In turn, he developed these extracted prose pieces into the first legitimate collection of prose poetry.

Charles Baudelaire was a man in very similar circumstances to De Quincey. Threatened continually by creditors and an overbearing mother, both men still tended to procrastination, which in turn led to missed deadlines and angry exchanges with their publishers. In the light of these similarities, Baudelaire's rewriting of the *Confessions* and the *Suspiria* also ran along comparable lines to the original compositions. Baudelaire's initial plan to produce a translation of the complete *Confessions* was thwarted mainly by his publisher's restrictions on the space he would allow for the work in the *Revue contemporaine*.[41] This problem was soon compounded when Baudelaire became aware of the existence of the *Suspiria de Profundis* and decided to include it in his translation. Finally, he resigned himself to a version of the *Confessions* (including the *Suspiria*) that was part translation, part paraphrase and summary and, increasingly, an abridgment. The rendering of foreign works into translated fragments was, at that time, a favored method in France. Indeed, original French works appeared purporting to be *un traduction* and the title became a concession to any work in the new and unfamiliar concise-prose format.[42] Through his similar reworking of the *Confessions*, Baudelaire took this practice one step further by subsequently producing not fake fragments but original prose pieces. However, he claimed in his preface that the prose poems were failed attempts to imitate Aloysius Bertrand's prose fragments, *Gaspard de la Nuit*, 1842, themselves "translations" of paintings by Rembrandt and Callot.

It is immediately evident that Baudelaire retains most of the *Confessions*, sacrificing more of the *Suspiria*, probably because his aim appears to be a "tidying up" of the original.[43] His utilization of the form of the *Suspiria* in the prose poem collection suggests that he regarded the original work as being overstretched in its accommodation of the contextual narrative that frames the visions. The reedited *Confessions* was to form part of his own *Paradis artificiels*, an investigation into the whole subject of drug-taking, so digressions and footnotes are edited out in order to produce a discussion on the power and effects of opium: the work that De Quincey "intended" to write but ostensibly failed to realize. The result, inevitably, is a tighter construction where discrete biographical context is actually juxtaposed with the dreams. However, such editing also dangerously presupposes a volume of extraneous material and is in itself a statement on the status of De Quincey's texts as reducible and, moreover, requiring reduction. Baudelaire's treatment of the *Confessions* to create the text that it was "meant to be" assumes an inherent flaw in the original text and offers a problematic response in its correction.[44]

Ironically, Baudelaire himself is still led, like De Quincey, into numerous apologies and statements of intention concerning the work as projected and what has been realized on the page. Indeed, the thyrsus image, which is generally the only accredited influence of De Quincey on Baudelaire's prose poems, may have been included at a later date and then only as a gibe against his publisher and an apology to his readers for having to omit the arguably organic and indelible digressions.⁴⁵ Elsewhere, Baudelaire describes De Quincey as "a dreadfully conversationist and digressionist author" almost turning his meanders into a profession.⁴⁶ In fact, he found these aspects of De Quincey's idiosyncratic prose difficult to edit as severely as he was required. The thyrsus thus becomes a symbol of the crucial factor of abridgment that he finally achieved and it was subsequently shifted away from De Quincey's extensive poetic prose to serve instead as a model for the relatively intensified prose poem.

Baudelaire's Translation

In a letter of 1858, Baudelaire describes the effect of the editing he is forced to make in his translation of the *Confessions*. The result of his part-translation, paraphrase, and commentary is an uneven foreshortening of the characteristically purple prose and produces a new narrative tone, "freer (in appearance) and more jerky."⁴⁷ That is, he identifies the difference in his own prose by its capacity to be both relaxed and jerky. This description clearly has a bearing on his often-quoted dedication to *Le Spleen de Paris* where he attributes the innovation of the genre to the suppleness of its prose: "Which of us has never imagined, in his more ambitious moments, the miracle of a poetic prose, musical though rhythmless and rhymeless, flexible yet strong enough to identify with the lyrical impulses of the soul, the ebbs and flows of revery, the pangs of conscience?"⁴⁸ Thus, the new language is produced in part by his attempts to distill De Quincey's struggling narrative.

However, another factor of the new prose is Baudelaire's role of commentator besides that of translator. Despite several statements concerning his intention to conflate the two texts (narrative and translation), Baudelaire's rejection of De Quincey's narrative "I" makes this goal untenable. Baudelaire's shift from autobiography to biography replaces the split self with a simple third-person narrative. Alan Astro reasonably states that Baudelaire's use of "he" for "I" has two opposing effects: it distances him from De Quincey's rhetorical excesses but also allows him to appropriate the language of an author with whom he identifies so closely.⁴⁹

The unification of this original dualism is also reflected in Baudelaire's single, consistently clear prose style, which in turn replaces De Quincey's alternation between journalistic and impassioned prose. For example, the famous description of the oriental opium dreams at the end of "Pains of Opium," where image is heaped upon image with the agitation they produce, is rendered more calmly in French:

> Je tombais soudainement chez Isis et Osiris; j'avais fait quelque chose, disait-on, j'avais commis un crime qui faisait frémir l'ibis et le crocodile. (*Mangeur*, 194; *Oeuvres*, 485)

> [I came suddenly upon Isis and Osiris: I had done a deed, they said, which the ibis and the crocodile trembled at] (*Sel.* 5:268; M.III.442)

Baudelaire translates the "deed" as a "crime," which particularizes the ambiguity and relaxes the pace of the sentence. Language considerations mean that certain effects such as alliteration cannot be imitated: "J'étais baisé par des crocodiles aux baisers cancéreux" for "I was kissed, with cancerous kisses, by crocodiles" (*Sel.* 5: 268; M.III.443). An additional element in Baudelaire's text is the announcement of De Quincey's death: a shadow that haunted the original work and necessitated a succession of fictional ends. It is ironic that another man's revision, something De Quincey feared more than death, should finally realize it.

De Quincey's Influence on "Le Spleen de Paris"

Baudelaire's acute observation of the potentials in circumscribing De Quincey's text is revealed from the start, in the opening to *Un mangeur d'opium*. Baudelaire eschews the "Notice to the Reader" in favor of a passage taken from the end of the section preceding "The Pleasures of Opium." The passage, now titled "Précautions Oratoires," is almost a single sentence of an extended apostrophe to the drug and is defined as a unit by the final echo of its opening phrase: "O just, subtle and mighty opium!" (*Sel.* 5: 213; M.III.396)[50] By decontextualizing the piece and placing it at the head of the translation, Baudelaire's first comment on De Quincey's work is an illustration of the autonomous tendencies of his prose. (In the *Confessions*, this passage does not even exist as a separate paragraph.) It is significant therefore that the detached passage is taken from an impassioned moment inside the general narrative as opposed to any of the dreams that De Quincey himself had composed as separate entities. Baudelaire borrows freely from both works in his collation and therefore could easily have opened with one of the more composed set pieces from the *Suspiria*. Ironically, Baudelaire also managed to place this "first" prose poem *before* the preface, obscuring the starting point with a rhetorical flourish.[51] In effect, De Quincey's apostrophe, set apart in this way, provides a model, in terms of extension and closure, for Baudelaire's new prose compositions: *Le Spleen de Paris* often appear to have been themselves lifted from a larger narrative and, in similar prayer-like apostrophes, employ some form of repetition as a framing device. It is noticeable that Stäuble-Lipman Wulf, as a scholar of French literature, instantly identifies De Quincey's now displaced text as a "poème en prose." By contrast, it is somewhat surprising that the famous thyrsus image, incorporated throughout the *Confessions*, never appears in direct translation, only by reference and allusion.

In general, attempts to identify points of influence between the two writers can never be conclusive owing to Baudelaire's interests preceding his reading of De Quincey and his subtle use of anything which he *does* take from the *Confessions*. Stäuble-Lipman Wulf claims on one hand that, having completed the translation, Baudelaire could no longer distinguish his own feelings from De Quincey's, but she nevertheless rejects the notion that the influence can be traced in the prose poems. And yet, several themes and phrases from these texts by De Quincey do find echoes in *Le Spleen de Paris*. For example, the episode in which the school porter drops the absconding pupil's suitcase down the stairs (and which Baudelaire translates in full), clearly contributes to the scenario, anticipation and "sense of the ludicrous" in "The Useless Glazier" where the narrator lures a glazier up to his flat in order to make him negotiate the stairs with his fragile merchandise before actually throwing the panes out of his window. Again from the *Confessions* comes De Quincey's narration of his first experiences of opium. The feelings it induces lead him to wander the London streets aimlessly, mixing with the crowd and losing himself in obscure alleys. Later, when the "honeymoon period" is over and his past returns in the shape of nightmares, De Quincey describes being tormented by "the tyranny of the human face."[52] Baudelaire, who generally presents himself in the prose poems as a *flâneur*, wandering through the streets of Paris, mixing with the crowd, includes an alternative piece in his collection called "One O'Clock in the Morning." In this prose poem the narrator celebrates being alone at last in his room: "At last the tyranny of the human face has gone, and I'll suffer no more except from my own self" (*Poems in Prose*, 53). Baudelaire resented the artistic power of opium (describing it as "an inexhaustible stock of caresses and betrayals" in "The Twofold Room"),[53] which accounts for his using De Quincey's hallucinated imagery in more "pedestrian" circumstances.

2 / DE QUINCEY AND BAUDELAIRE

Baudelaire's "Evening Twilight" provides the most telling example of De Quincey's influence on the prose poem. The piece was first written in 1855, that is, before work began on the *Confessions*. In this original version, the narrator contrasts the deranging effect of twilight on his friends with the happiness he discovers, at the same time of day, in himself. The poem was published with substantial changes in August 1857, after work on the *Confessions* had begun. The original piece is retained, with minor variations, but it is surrounded by new paragraphs before it at the beginning and after it at the end. It is the final three paragraphs that reveal a debt to De Quincey. The various images are reminiscent of the opening apostrophe to "juste, subtil et puissant opium!" and other passages in *Un mangeur d'opium*: the rise of labyrinthine cities from the darkness of solitude; the power generated by opposing forces; the sun and the night; fascination with the Orient.

The following and final paragraph does not refer back to the anecdotes that make up the body of the poem, to create closure, but rather continues expansively the image of light and dark:

> Or it suggests one of those ballerina's exotic costumes, whose dim transparent gauze hints at the splendours of a brightly coloured skirt, just as the delicious past shows through the darkness of the present; and the shimmering gold and silver stars which spangle it are the will-o'-the-wisps of Fancy, which only start to shine in the deep mourning of the night. ("Evening Twilight," *Poems in Prose*, 99)

The concept of a past that shines out like a star through the obscuring gauze of the present is clearly influenced by his reading of De Quincey. In fact, the passage follows his paraphrase of the English author:

> de même que les étoiles voilées par la lumière du jour reparaissent avec la nuit, de même aussi toutes les inscriptions gravées sur la mémoire inconsciente reparurent comme par l'effet d'une encre sympathique. (*Mangeur*, 184; *Oeuvres*, 481)

> [just as the stars veiled by the light of day reappear with the night, so too all the inscriptions engraved on the unconscious memory will reappear as if by the effect of invisible ink.]

Appropriately, the original context of the passage above is a developing formulation of the "Palimpsest," which states that no record can be erased by future emendations:

Of this, at least, I feel assured, that there is no such thing as ultimate *forgetting*; traces once impressed upon the memory are indestructible; a thousand accidents may and will interpose a veil between our present consciousness and the secret inscriptions on the mind. Accidents of the same sort will also rend away this veil. But alike, whether veiled or unveiled, the inscription remains for ever; just as the stars seem to withdraw before the common light of day, whereas, in fact, we all know that it is the light which is drawn over them as a veil; and that they are waiting to be revealed, whenever the obscuring daylight shall have withdrawn. (*Sel.* 5: 261; M.III.437)

Typically, this passage appears near the end in "The Pains of Opium." However, the same concept works vice versa, that is, looking from the present into the future, an idea that De Quincey expounds in similar terms just before "The Pleasures of Opium," in its preface, as it were: "And yet, if a veil interposes between the dim-sightedness of man and his future calamities, the same veil hides from him their alleviations; and a grief which had not been feared, is met by consolations which had not been hoped" (*Sel.* 5: 190; M.III.377). De Quincey's imagery shows the act of writing to be itself a dance with veils as it obscures and reveals the past in the present.[54] So too, the defamiliarizing form of Baudelaire's prose poems did not transform the elements he found in De Quincey but constituted a new perspective in which to present them: a perspective that, in its disjunction, had its roots in the source material itself.

The Prose Poem Collection and the Palimpsest

The general starting point for discussing the prose poem (Baudelaire's *Le Spleen de Paris*), then, contains the qualification that working on De Quincey's *Confessions* had a direct bearing on the construction of the first legitimate prose poems. This is borne out in the fact that little work was needed on the *Suspiria*. Partly due to the consideration of magazine space, but principally for aesthetic reasons, Baudelaire simply cut out most of the narrative before the Oxford Visions and translated "this melancholic gallery of paintings," the visions, as they stood (although he removed all footnotes). The sole exception is his rendition of "The Palimpsest." The original piece is an explanation of this ancient form of writing tablet, which received several impressions in succession, each one superseding the last. Ironically, the use of the palimpsest as a literary image is predated by Coleridge seventeen years previously in his Prefatory Note to *The Wanderings of Cain*.[55]

In place of, or *overlaying*, De Quincey's exemplum, which conflates Coleridge's image with another from Shelley, Baudelaire substitutes a section in which most of the discursive introduction is cut and another illustration is inserted.⁵⁶ In Baudelaire's prose piece:

> Un homme de génie, mélancolique, misanthrope, et voulant se venger de l'injustice de son siècle, jette un jour au feu toutes ses oeuvres encore manuscrites. Et comme on lui reprochait cet effroyable holocauste fait à la haine, qui, d'ailleurs, était le sacrifice de toutes ces propres espérances, il répondit: «Qu'importe? ce qui était important, c'était que ces choses fussent *créés*; elles ont été créés, donc, elles *sont*.» (*Mangeur*, 242; *Oeuvres*, 506)
>
> [A man of genius, melancholic, misanthropic and wanting to take revenge on the injustice of his age, one day casts into the fire all his works still in manuscript. And to those who were reproaching him for this horrific holocaust made in hatred, and which was, moreover, the sacrifice of all his own hopes, he replied, "What does it matter? What was important was that these things were *created*; they were created, therefore they *are*."]

The narrator goes on to apply this indestructibility to thoughts and actions past and future. That is, while this concept of permanence in the palimpsest may allow us a complacency in our retrospections, it makes the prospect fearful as future actions loom indissolubly before us. In addition, the narrator cites the dream visions as illustrations of the truth that nothing is entirely erased by the human mind. Yet, in terms of a collection of prose poems, the palimpsest, as De Quincey describes it, proves to be a pivotal image because it belies the concept of representational succession in favor of experienced simultaneity. De Quincey's insistence that the monkish legend is not displaced by the knightly romance contains direct implications for the following sequence of dream visions. Following the principle of the palimpsest, Baudelaire soon concerned himself with the possibility of a moveable order for his prose poems in *Spleen*.⁵⁷

Curiously, the scene that Baudelaire creates for the palimpsest episode (above) is reminiscent of the fate of the original *Suspiria*, which was lost to the flames of a small (accidental) fire (De Quincey narrates the episode in the preface to the *Confessions* of 1856). Baudelaire's scenario offers recognizable elements of his later prose poems: principally the character of the splenetic author/narrator protagonist and the soliloquy that provides the resolution. In addition, we witness the beginning of a style that uses anecdote and discussion without creating a specific plot. The final sentence of the inserted passage, "The palimpsest of the memory is indestructible" exemplifies this, being more provocative than conclusive.

There is another aspect of the palimpsest image that Baudelaire employs in his prose poems. After referring specifically to various "romances" in his literary illustration of the palimpsest, De Quincey's narrator introduces the Oxford Visions, which are revivified at the moment of delirium. Displacement of the visions (and the textual romances), by subsequent experiences is belied by the truth of the palimpsest. Analogous to either mind or text, the palimpsest counters linearity with copresence and nonchronological spontaneity. De Quincey employs the palimpsest image to disrupt the sequence of visions that follow, emphasizing the point by describing the visions as choruses concluding the overture of Part One. Similarly, Baudelaire's *Spleen* is a collection of often transient moments experienced in a city. Yet, the significance of recording these episodes appears to belong, rather, to the play of their interrelations. I will discuss the aspect of ordering and reordering in collections of prose poetry in the final chapter but it does appear to be associated with the Romantic image of the palimpsest passed here from De Quincey to Baudelaire.

As I have mentioned, the end of the *Un mangeur d'opium* was provided with an ironic point of departure. Baudelaire ends his translation with De Quincey's seminal idea: "Death we can face: but knowing, as some of us do, what is human life, which of us is it that without shuddering could (if consciously we were summoned) face the hour of birth?" (*Blackwood's* 58: 55; M.XIII.359). If death is sublimation into a desired synthesis, life, with its tenuous causality and proliferating misinterpretations, proves infinitely more fearsome. The prospect of the palimpsest is dizzying in its possibilities. Baudelaire ends his work with a notice on De Quincey's project for the *Suspiria*, which was in fact set in a footnote to "Levana." According to the note, the *Suspiria*, in its pared form, could be projected into a larger (absent) whole. De Quincey's death, announced by Baudelaire at the end of his translation of the *Confessions*, meant that the plan was fixed in this prospective form, outlined in a footnote. The irony of the processes involved is not lost on his French translator, who closes his text musing on the end that De Quincey continuously invoked but inevitably failed to realize in his work. The end of writing, in this case, corresponds literally to the death of the author:[58]

> Mais la Mort, que nous ne consultons pas sur nos projets et à qui nous ne pouvons pas demander son acquiescement, la Mort, qui nous laisse rêver de bonheur et de renommée et qui ne dit ni oui ni non, sort brusquement de son embuscade, et balaye d'un coup d'aile nos plans, nos rêves et les architectures idéales où nous abritions en pensée la gloire de nos derniers jours!   (*Mangeur*, 268; *Oeuvres*, 517)
>
> [But Death, whom we do not consult about our projects and whose consent we cannot ask, Death, who lets us dream of happiness and fame without saying yes or no, comes flying out of his ambush and, with a sweep of his wing, brushes aside our plans, our dreams and the ideal halls where we harbored thoughts of glory for our last days!]

Baudelaire posits De Quincey's death as the cause of his work's abruptness, suggesting that had he lived long enough, he could have investigated every avenue that writing opened up before him. By stating this, the end of De Quincey's text (as text proper or as the death of the author) marks the beginning of Baudelaire's interpretation of the *Confessions* as essentially a series of distinguishable prose pieces. Baudelaire's translation is piecemeal because causality is not pursued so fully. The outcome is also a moment of transition into a new "mode of existence" for both De Quincey and his work—now redefined as seeds to the concept of a prose poetic genre.

3
Contexts I: *The English Mail-Coach*

THE VISUAL DIMENSION OF THE PROSE POEM IS CHARACTERIZED BY its brevity. This formal severity instantly distinguishes the form from poetic prose, which, by contrast, is naturally expansive in its complex weaving of syntactical rhythm, as De Quincey's texts clearly show.[1] In fact, what emerges from an analysis of De Quincey's work in relation to the prose poem is the presence in the new genre of an undefined agent that forcibly separates prose pieces and sustains their isolation against our natural tendency, when reading prose poems in quick succession, to fuse them into a single narrative. However, if brevity is regarded unanimously as an essential property of the prose poem, the theories that supply the reason for this concision vary widely.[2]

Lyricism and a strong sense of closure provide the most common explanation of brevity in the prose poem. Michel Beaujour rejects these theories, comparing instead the prose poem to a picture, and he cites Bertrand's *Gaspard de la Nuit* (subtitled "fantasies in the style of Rembrandt and Callot"), Rimbaud's *Illuminations*, and Butor's *Illustrations* as evidence of the pictorial association. Historically, the French prose poem has been closely identified with the art book in which concise texts accompany and often imitate visual images. Beaujour claims that the art album provided a frame that supported a reading of the prose text as poetic. Tellingly, he is obliged to qualify this: "Paradoxically, these texts seldom get read very attentively in the luxurious context which is, so to speak, their artistic-poetical collateral. In order to become 'poems' in their own right, rather than skippable pages of stylish typography, they have to be published separately, in non-illustrated volumes."[3] While the size and content of the individual prose poem and its collective presentation continues to be affected by its association with the art book (Samuel Beckett/ Jasper Johns, *Foirades/Fizzles* participate in this tradition as, more subtly, do the pictures described in Charles Tomlinson's and Roy Fisher's prose poems), the comparison between the text and its "host" does not fully justify the shape of the genre.

The prose poem is recognized by its appearance of black boxed text on a white page. In this chapter, I seek to explain the significance of the white page within the aesthetics of the prose poem genre. The space is not accounted for within the simple and extremely ambiguous regulation that states the prose poem must be brief. Indeed, although the areas of blank page may designate the brevity of its host, the text, we have no explanation of its role, if any, in that text or its interpretation.

I take "brevity" to mean that the prose piece can be instantly identified as a discrete unit like a critical fragment. At the same time, however, I regard the genre's identifying brevity to be an illusion: the concision required is too severe to support plot or character development and hints instead at a previous act of reduction that has minimized the text without loss to the sense or the representation of its object. The blank space must play a role just like the walls of a locked-room mystery. In this chapter, my aim is to draw out any traces of suppressed narrative that may be lingering in these silent dividers. In other words, I will show that the brevity of the prose poem is, in fact, a deception. We know that some kind of narrative technique is in operation to achieve this degree of brevity because prose is predominantly referential in its construction and cannot simply stand in autonomous lines as can versified language. Instead, prose relies on an ever-present context to achieve the representation of its object. Thus, the brevity of the prose poem is "a trick of the eye" effected by a process that eliminates its context in an attempt to isolate the object "poetically," that is, purely, untrammelled. The catalyst of this process, the implied context, is the subject of this chapter and the next.

I

Context

The plurality of elements involved in context or circumstance are usually represented by contingent relations from metonymy to verisimilitude. In context-driven writing we are taken step by step on a thought process, and we mark those steps by accepting their reasonable juxtaposition. Both plot and narrative detail, for example, operate by assuring us of the possibility of their occurrence. However, the writer who embarks on an investigation into these assembled circumstances themselves risks the unchecked growth of the narrative as Sterne mines to advantage.

Like his novelist contemporaries, De Quincey expressly rejects brevity, and he states this clearly at the outset of the *Suspiria* and in answer to the traveler who asks for the shortest road to Keswick: "might it not be as well to ask after the most beautiful road rather than the shortest? Because, if abstract shortness, if τὸ brevity is your object, then the shortest of all possible tours would seem, with submission—never to have left London" (*Blackwood's*, 57: 273). In other words, De Quincey aims at the experience of the arabesque, the context, the flowers of the caduceus. Brevity, however, *is* forced on him by Baudelaire in his translation. Originally employed by De Quincey to defend his excessive material, the thyrsus image is simultaneously evoked and rejected in the paraphrase that Baudelaire substitutes: "No doubt I will abridge a lot; De Quincey is essentially digressive; the term *humourist* can be applied more appropriately to him than to anyone else; at one point he compares his thought to a thyrsus, a simple stick which takes all its charm and appearance from the foliage which envelops it."[4] The image is also displaced from the *Suspiria* to the beginning of the *Confessions* in Baudelaire's translation. De Quincey gets caught up in the luxuriance of the *caduceus* tendrils and not only turns context into digression but also into the main narrative. Baudelaire, in his paraphrase, brings the opposing concepts of abridgment and digression together under the image of the caduceus, confirming a relationship between brevity and the treatment of context. In addition, Baudelaire's subsequent prose poem, "The Thyrsus," which uses De Quincey's image to illustrate its own fundamental dualities, becomes a model for the prose poem genre.

While context can persuade the reader to accept a single interpretation, the process of *creating* narrative connections can prove expansive. In De Quincey's essay "Style," the orator attempts to limit contextual digression by systematically enumerating only the pertinent points of his speech. Yet even he is ultimately forced to quit in confusion when faced with the still manifold difficulties of passing from one point to the next. The episode is, unsurprisingly, narrated in a digression. Yet, the problem is not simply that the reader is tyrannically restricted to following a single path through the text while the writer indulges in the authorial freedom of interpretation (the very selection of circumstance). In the case of the prose poem, a clear lack of context on the page (indicated by the fragmentary form) denies passivity to the reader obliging him instead to participate in the lawlessly expansive creation-process in order to arrive at a point of interpretation. The reader, faced with prose but no context, instinctively provides the missing material. The prose medium sends him in search of circumstance and he will attempt to complete the text per se before finding an interpretation. In fact, the completion of the text may be taken to be consonant with the moment at which interpretation can take place. What has happened is a shift in roles: the writer writes the work but the reader writes the text by taking control of context.

II

Brevity

In 1857, at the start of his work on De Quincey and in the middle of his translations of Edgar Allan Poe's work (a project which spanned roughly twenty years), Baudelaire wrote an essay entitled "Notes Nouvelles sur Edgar Poe" in which he supports many of Poe's artistic theories. One of the principles of composition which Baudelaire reiterates in this essay is Poe's insistence on brevity whether in prose or verse.

> Among the literary domains . . . there is one of which Poe is especially fond; it is the *Short Story*. It has the immense advantage over the novel of vast proportions that its brevity adds to the intensity of effect. This type of reading, which can be accomplished in one sitting, leaves in the mind a more powerful impression than a broken reading, often interrupted by the worries of business and the cares of social life. The unity of impression, the *totality* of effect is an immense advantage which can give to this type of composition a very special superiority, to such an extent that an extremely short story (which is doubtless a fault) is even better than an extremely long story.[5]

It was a short step from translating Poe's tales to producing the "faulty" and extremely short stories for the *Poems in Prose* (*Le Spleen de Paris*).[6]

Poe himself emphasizes that his insistence on brevity in literature is an effect of the more important qualities: unity and totality. His understanding of art is that it presents itself as a single impression—the reader, he says, will become dissatisfied and lose his excitement (his "elevation of soul"), when he moves from one tone to another. In any two juxtaposed passages, one takes precedence over the other. Yet, taken separately, merits appear in the very piece one had previously considered to be the inferior. Accordingly, the text can only be truly appreciated when it is not attached to anything that may endanger the unity and induce a noticeable change of tone.[7] Poe's ideal text, it may be said, is achieved in the fragmentary form of the prose poem. But the success is effected at the expense of context.

Yet the writer's context is not simply expendable. Joris-Karl Huysmans, in the guise of his most celebrated protagonist, Des Esseintes, holds up the prose poem as his favorite genre and, in reference to its brevity, "the essential oil of art." For him, the circumscribed form of the genre evolves from the absolute precision involved in the creation of its sentences:

> The words chosen for a work of this sort would be so unalterable that they would take the place of all the others; every adjective would be sited with such ingenuity and finality that it could never be legally evicted, and would open up such wide vistas that the reader could muse on its meaning, at once precise and multiple, for weeks on end, and also ascertain the present, reconstruct the past, and divine the future of the characters in the light of this one epithet.[8]

In other words, the prose poem represents, for Des Esseintes, a telescoping of the novel genre, and its brevity is the consequence of eliminating circumstantial details now considered to be superfluous.[9] Compared to the novel, which may be defined by its foundation in the individual story with its concomitant details, the prose poem is not subversive but expurgatory. Huysmans's image implies that the prose poem is the kernel of a larger and rather more amorphous literature from which the prose poem is reduced but to which it may also return. In fact, Huysmans's metaphor of the essential oil is more useful to us than a simple call to concision as some abstract yet recognizable quality. An essence is extracted by distillation or reduction but can be reconstituted through a reversal of the initial process.[10] The space marks the reduction and anticipates reexpansion. There is clearly a parallel here between Huysmans's reversible metaphor and the reader/writer dialectic that operates around narrative context in the prose poem. I would like to look at this comparison a little more closely.

3 / CONTEXTS I: *The English Mail-Coach*   103

The Thyrsus and the Palimpsest

Roland Barthes announced the end of consumerist reading in which there is a gulf fixed between the producer of the text (the writer) and its user (the reader). Instead, he has referred us to the "readerly" text and the "writerly" text (*lisible* and *scriptible*, respectively).[11] The readerly requires only a passive reader who acknowledges the norms of the "classic" text and is led across the narrative paths that have already been selected. The "writerly" text, on the other hand, demands activity from the reader to participate in the creative process and coproduce the text.[12] Where the reader is offered a preconcluded text (the readerly), context is a given and I will refer to it as "expressed context." However, where, as in the prose poem, the text is fragmentary and the context required for its interpretation is missing (the visual effect being textual brevity, even fragmentation), the work may be said to contain an "implied context." The white space device begins to reveal itself. The circumstances and connections needed to make sense of the prose is recast as implied context and inhabits the area of blank space around the text in anticipation of reader-response. In the following pages, I will trace this process in De Quincey's writing: from the copiousness of expressed context, which is clearly unavailable to the prose poem, through his battle to bring it under control, to the point at which he is mostly successful, in *The English Mail-Coach*. Notably, this work is seen to be destabilized in its genre type and requires an explanatory preface. Finally, I will demonstrate the dynamic of the implied context as it exists in the established prose poem genre.

Expressed context is usually regressive:

> Supposing a reader acquainted with the true object of the Confessions as here stated, viz. the revelation of dreaming, to have put this question:
> "But how came you to dream more splendidly than others?"
> The answer would have been: "Because (*praemisses praemittendis*) I took excessive quantities of opium."
> Secondly, suppose him to say, "But how came you to take opium in this excess?"
> The answer to *that* would be, "Because some early events in my life had left a weakness in one organ which required (or seemed to require) that stimulant."
> Then, because the opium dreams could not always have been understood without a knowledge of these events, it became necessary to

relate them. Now, these two questions and answers exhibit the *law* of the work, *i.e.* the principle which determined its form, but precisely in the inverse or regressive order. The work itself opened with the narration of my early adventures. These, in the natural order of succession, led to the opium as a resource for healing their consequences; and the opium as naturally led to the dreams. But in the synthetic order of presenting the facts, what stood last in the succession of development, stood first in the order of my purposes. (*Blackwood's*, 57: 270; M.XIII.336)

In De Quincey's case, expressed context is used to legitimize the artistic vision, to reveal the concordance between the beginning and the end—an objective that is subverted by his own belief in the infinite complexity of causal structures. As a result, the Oxford Visions are overrun by marginal discourse of contextual detail to "prove" their visionary status. Ultimately, the parenthetical method proves unproductive and precludes the possibility of the visions appearing on the page in ideal isolation. De Quincey flounders. Moreover, the self-generative nature of context, in which digression acts on regression, prevents him from emerging from its now labyrinthine possibilities. He habitually gets lost in the contextual intermedium on which he has embarked and which is marked by its own peculiar sublimity.[13]

J. Hillis Miller interprets De Quincey's apparent disorientation inside his contextual maze as the search for God and likens the regressive structure of the narrative to the proliferation of motifs in Baroque art. Significantly for our discussion of reader-reaction, the Baroque period has been identified as a watershed in the history of the labyrinth. What had previously been a religious exercise in perseverance as the would-be pilgrim made his way across a path on the cathedral floor (which symbolized God as the mysterious designer), became, in the Baroque period, a battle of wits. The traveler was now expected to apply his own logic in order to solve the design now hidden amongst other similar, but possibly misleading, paths.[14] Wendy Faris neatly corresponds this double perspective of the original "unicursal" and modern "multicursal" designs to the diachronic and synchronic experiences of the literary text. On one hand, someone inside the labyrinth wanders around attempting to construct a pattern at each step (diachronically). On the other hand, synchronic vision perceives the whole and its inlaid design from above, as it were.[15]

The two approaches to a labyrinthine text return us to the reversible metaphor (Huysmans's prose poems as essential oil). Barthes's dialectical terms of reader-response have already been applied to two of De Quincey's key images: the thyrsus and the palimpsest. In that discussion, Michel Charles applies the terms "digressive" and "synchronic" to the thyrsus (by virtue of its wandering and spontaneous arabesque); "regressive" and "diachronic" to the layered tablet of the palimpsest as described by De Quincey.[16] However, Charles rejects the perhaps obvious conclusion that De Quincey employs two types of prose correlating to the two images, one branching outward in reaction against its present incompletion and the other retracing its steps to locate its own starting point. Instead, Charles regards the thyrsus as a model of writing and the palimpsest as a model of reading. He argues that De Quincey writes digressively in his attempt to provide a full and comprehensive text while the reader, faced with pages of these intertwining threads sets about retracing their paths to a starting point. This is, in effect, the same way that Baxter reads De Quincey, constantly aware of the continual play between the "text-as-written" and "text-as-read."[17] Without wishing to confuse matters, I need to point out that Charles's models take the opposite names of those in Barthes's statement. In Barthes's terms, the thyrsus becomes the readerly (because the reader takes up his traditional passive position) and the palimpsest, the writerly, as the reader is forced to put on the mantle of the writer in order to attain a level of completion which will submit to interpretation.

It is not a surprising coincidence that the image of the caduceus is intimately linked to the prose poem genre. This image, which Baudelaire appropriated for his prose poem, was subsequently elected as emblematic of the genre as a whole (Mallarmé being an early example).[18] However, the relationship between image and genre is instructive in terms of our developing aesthetics of the genre.

Baudelaire takes the thyrsus image (and not the more obvious writerly palimpsest) for his prose poem. Despite representing the guided reader who obediently follows its arabesque, the thyrsus is also held up as a model of omission—it is removed from Baudelaire's translation of De Quincey's *Suspiria* only to reappear as a decontextualized prose piece within a collection of similarly truncated fragments in *Le Spleen de Paris*. The thyrsus is thus "forgotten" only to reemerge as one image among many within a palimpsest structure of continual appearance and forgetting in the prose poem collection. The expressed context in the *Suspiria* (expounding the relation between narrative and opium) thus becomes implied in *Le Spleen de*

Paris.[19] For "The Thyrsus," Baudelaire adapts De Quincey's image to refer generally to the concept of inseparability. Considering Baudelaire's rejection of De Quincey (by dedicating the piece to Liszt and addressing himself directly to that musician), it is only the play of the palimpsest, aided by the implied context, that revives De Quincey's presence. The space is the container for the implied context, which sustains the paradoxical inseparability between brief text and context, which is unique to the palimpsest form and also that of the prose poem collection. The attribute of unity in the genre and in the image is paradoxical because the sign of connection is represented by an empty space between its distinct elements.[20]

In the transformation of the thyrsus image, Huysmans's metaphor has been successfully reversed: the thyrsus and the palimpsest prove to be opposite sides of the prose poem coin. The readerly connotation in De Quincey's *Suspiria* has become the writerly fragment in *Spleen* (the thyrsus couched in the palimpsest) and the amorphous nature of expressed context has been reduced in anticipation of a future expansion (the activation of the implied context when reading the prose poem). De Quincey finds it difficult to support the reversal of single but dialectical texts preferring to project the play between synchronic and diachronic in theory, as an ideal. Significantly, "The Palimpsest," the symbol of the double-headed text, heads the Oxford Visions, which aspire to greater concision than they achieve. Proof that De Quincey could theorize more successfully than he could realize the prose poetic structure.[21]

III

The English Mail-Coach

The English Mail-Coach offers us a work on the very brink of this ideal of the reversible text. The greater part of the work, which describes a near accident in which the narrator is involved, apparently leads us gently along a path of familiar modes of narration. However, the final part, the "Dream-Fugue" (in which the event is replayed several times in nightmare scenarios), not only eschews careful development for snatched variations on a theme of sudden death but also reveals links to other parts of the earlier narrative that can be induced by an imaginative (that is, an actively responsive) rereading. The narrative therefore reuses the same context (the circumstances leading up to the incident) in order to slowly extricate an independent textual unit, the dreams, from the larger work by turning expressed matter into implied context.

Although the work as a whole is divided into separate sections, we may assume that they cohere as a single unit in the same way that the Oxford Visions were the logical consequence of the first part of the *Suspiria*. However, at the close of the first section, "The Glory of Motion," De Quincey questions the idea of causality:

> perhaps I am wrong in ascribing any value as a *causative* agency to this particular case on the Bath road—possibly it furnished merely an *occasion* that accidentally introduced a mode of horrors certain, at any rate, to have grown up, with or without the Bath road, from more advanced stages of the nervous derangement. (*Blackwood's*, 66: 495)[22]

Together with his doubts concerning the "causative" agency of the Bath road, the narrator here denies his own starting point, revealing the tension between the palimpsest and the thyrsus, the writerly and the readerly. This passage contradicts his appended introduction in which he attempts to indicate the logical process of the work for those readers who had complained that they could not make any connections between the individual sections. In that introduction, De Quincey cites the near-fatal accident contained in the third section, "Vision of Sudden Death," as the center "from which the whole of this paper radiates." In other words, by introducing a causal logic, he apparently tempers the more avant garde aspect of his composition in order to respect the traditional mode of contextual prose. This climb-down is only ostensible, however, because by using the term "radiate," De Quincey does not confirm a causal connection so much as an associative one—an action that firmly indicates a move away from the tyranny of contextual narrative as exhibited in the *Confessions* and to a lesser extent in the *Suspiria*.[23] The extended and discursive nature of the first three sections suggests that they are an example of the "caprices, the gay arabesques, and the lovely floral luxuriations of dreams, [which] betray a shocking tendency to pass into finer maniacal splendours" (*Blackwood's*, 66: 495; M.XIII.291n). This is a clear reference to the caduceus image of the *Suspiria*, itself an image of narrative context. By contrast, the *English Mail-Coach* is cleverly constructed to vindicate digression by rendering it inherent in the detail of the Dream. Some elements are imported as they are, for example, the frantic movements of the female traveler in distress. Others tend to implication as in the avenue of trees at the site of the accident, which is transformed into an extended cathedral aisle in the Dream. Although the thyrsus is being promoted at this stage, the repetitive rhythm of brief subsections in the focal part four, "Dream-Fugue" concludes the work quite differently on a prose poetic structure that I have identified with that of the palimpsest.

The fugal form, which had emerged in the late seventeenth century, had by De Quincey's time lost its popularity but continued to be discussed in compositional theory.[24] The fugue marked the end of the Baroque extravagance of "unity in diversity" (which I have equated in principle with the expressed context as main narrative) and introduced the new era of organicism. Ian Bent observes the paradoxical way in which the fugue embraces organic form. An abandoned theme is used to initiate new sections. Extension is generated through repetition. In other words, the point of origin masks its own privilege by setting itself in a context that counteracts causality and even association because it is a reflection.[25] The fugal structure allows De Quincey to indulge in "maniacal" arabesques while developing more tightly structured prose pieces. Bent's account of nineteenth-century discussions of the fugal form bears a striking resemblance to De Quincey's own dilemma of double perspective: "composition and analysis in melodic and fugal materials were inextricably intertwined: as the composer of a fugue worked his materials, he was performing an implicit analysis of his subject."[26] With his characteristic refusal to surrender authorial control, De Quincey may have found in the repetitious fugue structure the perfect way to advocate a new treatment of context: the controlled freedom of reading as reordering. While the expressed context of the first three sections provides the logical background to the dream imagery, the multiple presentations of that context in the "Dream" create a formal interdependence that is later imitated by the prose poetic collection.[27]

"Dream-Fugue" resembles but does not achieve prose poetry because of its continuing (if partial) dependence on causality and expressed context. In the "Dream-Fugue" De Quincey comes closest to achieving what he had set out to do since the *Confessions*. This aim, to present a collection of opium dreams, shares ideals with that of the prose poem collection. Much of this common ground involves the problem of suppressing context, which in turn affects the causal structure of the work. The fugal form allows him to indulge in the spontaneity of the arabesque without simultaneously expanding the text uncontrollably.

3 / CONTEXTS I: *The English Mail-Coach*   109

The *English Mail-Coach* is a text in reduction and, in "Dream-Fugue," briefly participates in the delusive play of the prose poem collection. In the following section, I will turn to texts that have been published *as* prose poems. We may assume that these texts, by exhibiting the necessary extreme concision, claim to have been successfully reduced by the device that I have termed the implied context. These pieces, by Wilde, Dowson, and Roy Fisher, represent the achievement of De Quincey's attempts to produce self-contained prose pieces and have been realized by a strict control of context.

IV

The Implied Context and the Prose Poems of Wilde, Dowson, and Fisher

As I have argued in this chapter, the implied context is peculiar to the prose poem where it is used to create the illusion of autonomy. This type of context is differentiated from the expressed simply by not being physically present on the page. The implied context is "marked" by a blank space by which I mean that the space is an active element. Any information that would elucidate the minimum data given in the text is withheld, rendering an interpretation of the work dependent on the reader's supplying the correspondence—the missing signified. There are two obvious effects. Implication is never guaranteed so the text may be crafted to invoke a particular expectation that it can subsequently defeat. Wilde's prose poem "The Disciple" employs this device by using the pool in which Narcissus gazed at his reflection as a "character," thus establishing a well-known myth as the implied context. Wilde's "twist" is made possible by reinterpreting the myth: as Narcissus gazed into the pool, the water found its own reflection in his eyes. The pool does not mourn for the youth in Wilde's poem, but for its own loss. Wilde's solution is not to reinvent the story but to give expression to one of its myriad but distant possibilities. Another mode of displacement occurs in the "open work" where the text is designed to support a variety of contextual possibilities. Ideally, the interpretation is varied at each reading to produce a different experience each time.[28]

In contrast to the implied context as an ending "device" in Wilde's poem, Ernest Dowson's prose poem, "The Fortunate Islands" is generated at each step by the implied context. This poem quickly establishes the fairly conventional scenario where the narrator speaks to a group of sailors in order to record their tales: "'We have adventured,' they said."[29] The narrator, as if conscious of his own literary device, suggests topics that will provoke an anecdote from the men. He asks of the mariners' travels, of the "high perils" they must have undergone, of the fortunate islands they must have seen. His questions create an expectation for an expressed context that will introduce the framed passage of the mariners' tale (a heightened account of these episodes) but all is immediately subverted by their response, "We have found nothing." A second prompting, which is more general and contained in literary cliché ("I have looked for the woman I might have loved, and the friend we hear of, and the country where I am not"), still inspires a negative reaction: "We are old, withered mariners, and long and far have we wandered in the seas of no discovery. We have been to the end of the last ocean, but there was nothing, not even the things of which you speak." In effect, the suggestions offered by the narrator for a subsequent discourse are turned back upon themselves to become a reference not internally for the framed passage but for an external—and therefore implied—context. In addition, the speech of the mariner subverts expectations of a framed, heightened passage and substitutes instead an "adventure" without content. The terms he uses—"the last ocean," "the port of our nativity"—imply that the scene is also a symbolic one. In this case, "no discovery" cannot mean simply a lifetime's journey over clear blue seas, but it does not specify the nature of the symbol. Unlike Wilde's tale, we have no rubric before the set-piece begins except that the Fortunate Isles were reputed to be home to the heroes. Does the mariner mean that hero-worship is misguided optimism, that age and travel do not guarantee wisdom; or that our experiences are not, ultimately, of any importance in the larger scheme of things (symbolized by the collected writings of the narrator)? The "tale" that occupies the space of the expected tale is therefore only comprehensible if it is given a context at the moment of reading (and Baudelaire's "The Port" begs comparison with this piece). An implied context is marked in the prose poetic collection by the blank spaces that surround each piece. In Dowson's prose poem, the blank space is emphasized by the fact that the piece opens with the mariners "looking listlessly at nothing with their travelled eyes" and ends "And they fell into their old silence" thus directing responsibility for the context to the reader.

The similarity between the implied context of the prose poem and Romantic aesthetics (especially the Absent Work) is quite clear. In addition, the correlation between the ethos of the prose poem and the Romantic critical fragment also accounts for their visual similarity as successive brief texts. By situating itself at the edge of a work that is always invoked—anticipated but never realized—the prose poem, as a fragment, is able to offer itself in the place of any singly elected narrative by evoking, instead, a multiplicity of *possible* narratives. Consequently, we, as critical readers, can restore the vanished context or situation out of which the individual prose poem has arisen (and it may appear to us to be the only logical scenario). However, in relation to our reconstruction, we cannot assume either that we, as separate readers, have intuited the *same* context or that one interpretation is advocated over any other in the given text. Indeed, my own analyses below are restricted more than any other by these correlatives: I cannot embrace all readings and the interpretations I offer may appear to be only partial. The silent narratives, which are created by the reader through this active engagement with the given text, I have collectively termed the "implied context" because the prose poem itself must provide the implication that a larger work exists: it must identify itself as a part.

Roy Fisher's prose poems in his collection *Stopped Frames and Set Pieces* express a consciousness of their fragmented status by operating within a minimal time factor.[30] The episodes often occur in a matter of seconds:

> Furious, the boxer dog leapt in pursuit and was brought up short by its lead while in the air, only one foot touching the ground. The strength of its impetus, the whole weight of the body yanking on the strap, distorted it: the head seemed as if it was being twisted off, and the creature for all its heaviness and force had no more stability of shape than a slug hurled at a paving slab.
>
> In the second the dog's form was destroyed and before it reconstituted itself a fallen scrambling dog, it had an alternative form of paroxysm, a sudden precipitate out of energy, a bigger payout than was budgeted; dog-sized, big enough to remember, bursting out from the subsiding animal, twisting on into the world, detaching itself, a single plasm, weightless and self-determining.
> (*Poems*, 33)

What is notable about this piece is that while the opening sentence presents the event as a dog reacting angrily to something, the prose poem itself dwells not on the cause or effect of that situation, not even on the dog, but on the amorphousness of the reaction. The dog strikes a typical pose but the energy of the movement is stronger. Amusingly, the animal is overwhelmed, having "no more stability of shape than a slug hurled at a paving slab." Similarly, the second paragraph describes the split second preceding the animal's fall to the ground. The dog is finally redefined as but one concretion of the "precipitate out of energy." The description, then, of this larger energy, "bursting out from the subsiding animal, twisting on into the world, detaching itself" appears to take precedence over the animal itself, which will inevitably fall into a defining shape. In the same way, the contentless device of the blank space of implied context expands the work when it is generated and shapes the text into a solid block when it is not.

Stopped Frames and Set Pieces play on the distortion of the reduced text, which is a consequence of the omissions generated by the implied context. One piece, also untitled, is a description, in four paragraphs, of a broken Indian statue of a female dancer (*Poems*, 34). All that remains of the figurine is the torso: the head, neck, arms and lower legs are missing, one breast has been smashed. The statue represents the simultaneous distortion of a truncated object and the shift in its elements of signification. On one hand, the figure is reduced to a violently treated female torso, which is emphasized by the description of its imprisoning body ornamentation of a triple rope collar, a "constricting belt" that passes through the legs and "pendants of beaten metal stretching down toward the vanished knees." On the other hand, the navel, generally a redundant feature of the human body, becomes the dominating part of this statue, substituting itself for those that are missing: "It is eye, or mouth, or anus, or ear: all the body's orifices." Fisher is careful to minimize references to gender possibly to sustain an idea of "everyman" in the mistreated figurine. The navel shifts from incidental "scar crater" to the center of this new statue through amputation. He also emphasizes the navel as "an insignia of coming into life" that, beyond its substitutive role, represents the moment of independence, the mark of separation. There is clearly an analogy between the Indian statue and the prose piece as fragment that represents it. The missing limbs that "will have shown what it was intended to mean," are the context in which the existence of the statue and the explanation for its condition are couched. Fisher acknowledges the importance of the implied context in the prose poem when he refuses to allow it here: "There's no temptation to guess at the positions of the vanished head and limbs." This statement shows the narrator forcefully denying even a probability-based context. Fisher commonly attempts to eradicate, avoid, or ignore centers in his work in a postmodern attempt to prevent a false unity being projected onto given parts.[31] By denying a center of interpretation to the description of the statue, here represented by the amputated limbs, Fisher forces a reading based on a center (the navel/ the prose poem) that is self-evidently a substitute.

Attempts have been made to secure the prose poem within a larger framework but the latter has always been intertextual. For example, Michael Riffaterre regards any significance in the prose poem as being generated from a perceived interplay of intertextuality.[32] Jonathan Monroe and Margueritte Murphy are among others who claim the prose poem is dialogical, a view that draws in other literatures or discourses. Murphy's own theory of the prose poem as a subversion of any genre it appropriates makes the presence of other texts a necessary condition for the prose poem to come into being at all. These approaches paradoxically negate the surrounding blank space, which identifies the prose poem, by writing over it and making it accommodate quite separate works preconditionally. Such descriptions of the implied context require that it preexist the prose poetic text itself rather than enter into a palimpsest-like play. In these cases, the relation between the given text and that which is offered as "implied context" is associative rather than metonymic. In "The Fortunate Islands," intertextuality is not a principal concern although it does act as one form of implied context. Ultimately, it is not necessary to rely on "legitimate" genres in order to account for the prose poem.[33]

Closest to my reading is that of Michel Delville, who senses, in the work of Michael Benedikt, the existence of "an absent or undefined context."[34] However, Delville does not pursue this lost content, but explains its disappearance as the effect of the poetic axis. I will examine the role of the poetic and referential axes in Chapter 5, but in this chapter, I have sought to actually track the content and account specifically for the displacement of context. Although it does not appear on the page, context is nevertheless evoked in the reading process and continues to exert an influence over the text.

Suppressing external context arises from the objective of the prose poem, which is, ostensibly, to occasion the *darstellung* of the ideal work but is actually to substitute itself for that absence. Either way, the site of the prose poem claims an exclusive and privileged status that distinguishes it from the novel or other extended narratives such as De Quincey's works. This occurs because of the different narrative directions created by the different types of context: whereas the expressed context, in seeking a single course, functioned regressively, implied contexts are circumfluent around the text that they aim to elucidate.

V

The Space of Disjunction

Textual brevity introduces space as a conspicuous element in prose poem collections. In this final section, I would like to look at the nature of the space that defines the brevity we have been discussing as a characteristic of the prose poem genre. The innovatory aspects of the *Mail-Coach* that visually distinguish it from the *Confessions* are the gaps that a lack of causality introduce into the text, namely in the creation of the four main constituent parts and in the smaller subdivisions of the "Dream-Fugue." Space on the page can be understood as part of a textual rhythm. Thus the recurring internal hiatus in "Dream-Fugue" (which is the space of separation, interpretation, and location of the implied contexts), lends the work a rhythmic quality and enhances the final fugal structure. The Royal Mail hesitates before outdistancing its rival, the *Tallyho*, and the main narrative augments the ninety seconds in which the near-accident occurs. In "Dream-Fugue," the representation of this moment of crisis is averted by a gap: a period of stasis created by the trumpet blast from an animated bas-relief that fixes the association of rhythmic breakdown with structural hiatus.

A rhythmical breakdown, like Romantic fragmentation, indicates an impasse in the pursuit of representation. However, unlike the Romantic phenomenon, a rhythmical collapse does not necessarily signal the end of the work. In fact, what occurs is a disjunction; a temporary separation of form from content. The signal for a disjunction is the gap or silence effected at the severing break of an interruption. De Quincey exhibits a sensitivity to this literary form in his essay, *On the Knocking at the Gate in Macbeth*. This piece of criticism centers on the juxtaposition of the scene of Duncan's murder to its discovery. De Quincey observes the mechanics of the play which isolate ordinary, human activities from the murder and its perpetrators,

3 / CONTEXTS I: *The English Mail-Coach* 115

who exist in "a world of devils," by suspending the world of men through the temporary abolition of time. The completion of the murder coincides with the end of the scene:

> then the world of darkness passes away like a pageantry in the clouds: the knocking at the gate is heard; and it makes known audibly that the reaction has commenced: the human has made its reflux upon the fiendish: the pulses of life are beginning to beat again: and the re-establishment of the goings-on of the world in which we live, first makes us profoundly sensible of the awful parenthesis that had suspended them. (M.X.393)[35]

De Quincey advocates a spiralling design where each state of being is perfected at the moment of self-consciousness—registered by a pause and redirection in form (context to vision, for example). This system confirms the importance of literary boundaries and the environment of the text because to begin or end a piece of writing is posited as the current fulfillment, by default, of the desired state in the writer. The text is always prefatory and alternative because its parenthetical nature represents a move away from the state from which it arose. However, this plan proposed by De Quincey, illustrated by the scene in *Macbeth*, is actually more subtle in its movement between the text and parenthesis. The knocking on the gate begins in fact at 2.2.58 during the tense exchange between Macbeth and his wife and continues into the following scene in the porter's soliloquy, which prefaces the arrival of Lennox and Macduff. The sound interrupts the dialogue in scene two and is instrumental in bringing it to an end. In other words, the knocking, which signals the return to ordinary human life, is not suddenly heard, as De Quincey proposes, after the voluntary withdrawal of the murderers but is copresent with that other "world of devils," puncturing and finally overwhelming it (in the same way that its insistence must also overwhelm the porter's parody of hell). The interaction between text and subtext is, likewise, not in alternation but in concurrency. The previously suppressed variations in prose narrative are given a voice and a parenthetically placed platform from which to expose the disjunction.

The authorial footnote is one such disjunctive device in undramatized prose. The note breaks into and augments a logical discourse by stating or implying its relation to a larger whole and thereby qualifies the authority of the main text. De Quincey's footnotes are particularly obtrusive. They add to the tendency to disorientation in the discourse and provide a vehicle for admitting context into otherwise autonomous prose poems in the *Suspiria*, preventing their establishment as independent pieces. De Quincey also uses footnotes to emphasize the layering of time and personas involved in composition (that is, first as author, then editor, then author of the revised text, then editor and so on). This stratification thickens the density of the text just as its regression draws out the length. The work shapes itself by the unchecked development of its internal devices and therefore operates quite differently from the prose poem form. Hugh Kenner's incisive comments on the footnote describe the device as language forsaking oral communication in favor of "technological space." However, he regards technology not as a different mode of communication but simply as offering a different effect to the ear: "Parentheses, like commas, tell the voice what to do: an asterisk tells the voice that it can do nothing."[36]

Kenner, and Ricks in his counterargument, does not account for the fact that the footnote is physically divorced from its referent in the main text on the page and is distanced more than any other parenthetical forms such as the subordinate clause or the bracketed sentence. Existing in its own "technological space," the footnote is semi-independent, physically redirecting the argument away from the claims of the main text to some external source (which is either another text or, more simply, a possible redirection of the contextual narrative). Yet, claims to any extratextual material are based on the immediate context: the footnote's very existence being dependent on the narrative from which it springs. De Quincey draws attention to this in his article, "Sir William Hamilton": "'*Civilation!** And what may *that* be?' Look below, reader, into the footnote, which will explain it. Whilst you are studying that, I'll be moving slowly on overhead; and, when you come up from that mine to the upper air, you'll easily overtake me."[37] Once again, here, the textual rhythm of continuous narrative is punctured by an isolated prose fragment that both expands the contextual horizon by implication and redirects the focus back to the now pregnant text. Like the knocking in *Macbeth*, the footnote runs silently alongside the text, an invisible commentary that is occasionally vocal and coincident to the main text in the manner of musical counterpoint.

In this discussion, my aim is not to equate the footnote with the prose poem, indeed, I have already argued that it is precisely De Quincey's footnotes in the Oxford Visions that prevent them from becoming prose poems. Instead, I wish to indicate that both forms are semi-independent of the single direction of contextual narrative;

their similar functions of opening up the text by implying what it is not; and their role of breaking into the single line of contextual logic. Expressed context, in seeking to provide the *darstellung* of an artistically perceived truth, involves itself in the discourse of logic. Caught within the labyrinthine or unformulated structure of such explanation, this type of context causes the permanent postponement of the true text or its closest approximation, the preface (represented here by the prose poem). De Quincey's solution is to resort to "technological space" in an attempt to portray the polyphony of his incommunicable vision. Due to the expansive nature of the expressed context that he cannot relinquish, he is never wholly able to control the structure of his material—although the ideal for which he strives, the independent prose piece, is also that of the prose poem as genre exemplified by the pieces by Wilde, Dowson, and Fisher.

Moving away from De Quincey now and toward more established prose poems, the next chapter continues this discussion of the implied context by a demonstration of it operating within a specific collection, Geoffrey Hill's *Mercian Hymns*. The prose poetic structure of this work is created by the simultaneous disjunction and interrelation of its fragmented parts, resulting in a structure and rhythm that develop those first attempted in the Oxford Visions and the "Dream Fugue."

4
Contexts II: *Mercian Hymns*

GEOFFREY HILL'S IDEAS ON CONTEXT ARE BASED ON THOSE OF HOBBES for whom context represents contiguity, structure, and composition as well as custom, opinion, and circumstance: "there is scarce any word that is not made *equivocal* by divers contextures of speech, or by diversity of pronunciation and gesture.... It is therefore a great ability in a man, out of the words, contexture, and other circumstances of Language, to deliver himself from *Equivocation,* and to finde out the true meaning of what is said."[1] Hobbes is aware of the paradoxical nature of these proposals (that ambiguity is inherent to words and yet we must try to elicit "true meaning" from them). Yet he does not attempt to reconcile them. He continues to claim that truth exists even if every word is compromised as it is uttered. The process of extracting this "true meaning" from expression centers on the formal properties of language, which limit clarity while offering it flexibility—the ability to contradict itself, for example. Hill explains:

> Hobbes's "meaning," therefore, comprises an argument, a thesis which is unequivocal ... and a counter-argument, realized within the texture of his writing, which grasps that the equivocal and the ambiguous are intrinsic to human nature and civic history. One is so impeded by custom, opinion, circumstance, and all other forms of "tyrannizing"... that "the *contrary* must needs appear a great Paradox."[2]

Hill follows Hobbes (and, he adds, Bacon) by advocating the release of intentional meaning from these "circumstances of language." *Mercian Hymns* is one such attempt to tease out a "meaning" (which would necessarily include its own antithesis) from the historical tyranny of the ancient British ruler, Offa. Meaning is represented by the semiautobiographical figure of the young boy who plays the leader while retaining an essence of childhood.

Hill develops this dilemma of context by arguing that if language is the source of its own problem, it also provides the antidote in the form of style, namely disjunction and brevity. By momentarily separating structure and style disjunctively the poet creates an internal resistance to habit and custom.[3] In this chapter, I aim to show how Hill finds his own solution to Hobbes's paradox of eliciting meaning from context. In his collection of prose poems, *Mercian Hymns*, he does this by composing a deliberately equivocal text in order to manipulate custom (I use Hobbes's term "custom," as I understand it, to denote the received language of narrative, the readerly), turning the space of ambiguity into the implied context. Three sites in particular that he indicates as spaces of ambiguity are: etymology in the text proper, the appended endnotes, and the status of the titles against the individual hymns. This chapter divides into three corresponding sections where I shall look in detail at these spaces and their contribution to the text via the implied context. The first section precedes this analysis with a continuation of my discussion on the principle of disjunction. Hill's use of the three sites named above all produce a particular form of disjunction, a self-contradiction, which reflects the play on duality and paradox that the work sustains while affirming Hobbes's demand for a unified argument and counterargument.

In his critical writings, Hill has written that despite the completion of any poem, a part of it always remains inside "the 'imprisoning marble' of a quotidian shapelessness."[4] In the case of *Mercian Hymns*, the distinguishing form of fragmentary prose together with its archaeological theme suggests a resemblance to Coleridge's "The Blossoming of the Solitary Date Tree." In Coleridge's poem, the prose acts as the "imprisoning marble" in which is couched an unrealized verse poem to be restored by the reader. Seamus Heaney also subscribed to this subordinated status of prose in the "poem in prose" by turning his own sequence of prose poems, *Stations*, into the verse collection, *Station Island*.[5] Hill, on the other hand, has always considered technical form to be a highly significant element in any composition and "the only true way of releasing the simple, sensuous and passionate."[6] Like his protagonist Offa, Hill, as poet, is also a "tyrannical creator of order and beauty" in his imposition of strict poetic form as a means of evoking a work of harmonious beauty.[7] His concern for formal structure suggests that the prose of *Mercian Hymns* is essentially different from that of the "Date Tree," for example by its determined composition.

I

Hill's Theory of Disjunction: "The Antiphonal Voice of the Heckler"

Mercian Hymns comprises thirty hymns each of one to four versets of "rhythmical prose."[8] The sequence is suited to the prose medium because it literally traces the ancient and "poetic" spirit of Offa in the diurnal, the prosaism of the narrator's own childhood, while heightening the tension between them both formally and thematically. The young child (a reminiscence of the narrator) poses as the king and, conversely, the historical king plays out his role in a largely anachronistic setting. If the prose of *Mercian Hymns* is not simply formless, one would expect Hill, as an academic critic, to be able to articulate the reasons for his unusual choice of medium and structure. Unfortunately, he has been somewhat evasive on this point as this excerpt from his interview with John Haffenden demonstrates. Asked why he chose to write *Mercian Hymns* as a sequence of prose poems, Hill replies: "They're versets of rhythmical prose. The rhythm and cadence are far more of a pitched and tuned chant than I think one normally associates with the prose poem. I designed the appearance on the page in the form of versets . . . I did immediately see it as an extended sequence."[9]

Hill does not actually define or illustrate what he means by a "prose poem" here. In "Poetry as 'Menace' and 'Atonement'" (12), Hill describes the prose gloss to "The Ancient Mariner" as "(virtually a marginal prose poem)" but his phrasing and parenthesis indicate that he too has only a vague impression of the technical nature of this genre. I would argue that these "versets of rhythmical prose," if not indeed prose poems themselves, exhibit a successful treatment of context that confidently sustains a collection of minimalist prose pieces. As I shall continue to argue, the control of contextual matter by individual highly organized pieces that then participate in the dynamic of their own collection are central characteristics and concerns of the prose poem.

The prose poetry of *Mercian Hymns,* like the unstructured prose-poetry of the *Suspiria de Profundis* turns on the tyranny of duality. A sense of artistic vision (hymns V and XXIX) leads to autobiography, a split self and a corresponding split style.[10] The narrator, "I who was taken to be a king of some kind," is both poet and scholar, participating in the text and paratext, respectively: the hymns and the appended endnotes. On the other hand, the protagonist is both Offa and child, each one a distinct persona yet sharing characteristics of Hill himself.

Stylistically, Hill has defined writing as working in relative proportion with "hefting" and "tuning" words. These terms appear to refer to basic words used to make oneself understood (hefting) and others used judiciously with artistic precision. In Jakobsonian terms, "hefting" privileges the horizontal axis of combination while "tuning" operates on the vertical axis of considered selection. By restricting the terms to individual words, Hill avoids the prose/poetry debate.[11] Significantly, he sustains the antithetical nature of the contextual argument, as defined by Hobbes, by observing that a writer may "tune in" or "tune out"; that counterpoint may be harmonic or discordant. I take this alternative faculty of "tuning out" to refer to the subversive countertext represented by, for example, the footnote or any form of disjunction. We may infer that "at-one-ment," Hill's term for the reconciliation of aesthetic and technical form, occurs with the equilibration of tuning and hefting.

Hill's description of *Mercian Hymns* as a "pitched and tuned chant" reveals a concern with musicality, a dimension that is generally missed, perhaps because the colloquialisms lend many of the hymns a speech, rather than chant, rhythm.[12] In referring to his work as "pitched" and "tuned" with the additional possibility of tuning in or out, Hill emphasizes the rhythmic quality of orality rather than musicality per se and the influence of Gerard Manley Hopkins is quite clear here.[13] Hill quotes Hopkins's defense of sprung rhythm as closest to prose (and therefore speech) rhythm in his essay "Redeeming the Time." This essay centers, in part, on the success of the "stress-pitch-disjuncture" effected by Wordsworth in his "Ode: Intimations of Immortality."[14] Here, a weighty iambic pentameter ending the eighth stanza is followed by a "fresh time-signature," causing a dramatic rhythmic change at the beginning of the ninth. It is this idea of disjuncture as the mimetic medium of recognition that Hill employs in the prose of *Mercian Hymns*. The disjuncture signals an imminence that collapses at the moment of self-consciousness. At the same time, this breakdown of communication ushers in the implied context, the pregnant space, to complete the fragment. In "Redeeming the Time," Hill shows himself to be as sensitive as De Quincey to the musical qualities of language made manifest in the polyphony of textuality. In this article, he objects to George Eliot's pamphlet, *Address to Working Men by Felix Holt* because she "excluded the antiphonal voice of the heckler," which "has denied us the cross-rhythms and counterpointings which ought . . . to be part of the structure of such writing."[15] This statement is also a clear reference to the function of the implied context in prose writing that Hill perceives (or, rather, hears) as a voice of dissent, external to the text, which joins and embellishes it. In other words, the implied context must be activated to produce the antidote to tyrannical custom that imposes itself as meaning on what is, in fact, more representative as equivocal language.

Disjuncture itself can occur in style and subject as well as rhythm and Hill employs all of these in what is essentially a poeticizing of prose: an elimination of expressed context. Hill's use of recognition disjuncture shows clearly the influence of Hopkins's poetry, differing only in its technique of presenting experiential and transcendent reality. *Mercian Hymns* is not divided into a surface appearance and a faith-induced recognition as in Hopkins's work; there is no structural pause that needs a faith or the simulation of a faith to be crossed, but instead, a coexistence of experience and transcendence. Disjunction supersedes the footnote in indicating a greater whole but also operates in a more sophisticated way, making less of "technological space" and more of textual counterpoint.[16] Where De Quincey exploited technological space in an attempt to gain control, Hill displays his use of paginal space to exhibit his actual control over the material.[17] We are reminded of the fact that this is not "ticker-tape prose" but was deliberately designed on the page, perhaps with more sympathy toward Apollinaire than Baudelaire.[18] For example, the Old English style which Knottenbelt observes in the elliptical syntax and the caesura-like use of colons in *Mercian Hymns* is repeatedly, though not consistently, at odds with its contemporary subject matter.[19] Words are joined together by hyphens to create an effect of antiquity but this actually further complicates the reading by making single words rather than sentences the basic sense-making units. Together with the caesura, the hyphen draws attention to the antagonism of its elements as well as to their complementary interrelation and, reflecting this, leitmotivs of severance and connection run heavily through the work. Frequently oxymoronic, these compounds create minor disjunctions in their very descriptions: "the riven sandstone" (I); "They ransacked epiphanies," "They are scattered to your collations" (XII); "broken utterance" (XVII); "splinters of habitation" (XIX), where "sandstone," "epiphany," "collation," "utterances," and "habitation" are all types of fragmented units. However, it is the rhythmical aspect that ultimately redeems this work from the potential inertia of a plotless narrative. Enhancing the aural quality becomes integral to a syntactically resistant work where meaning is in danger of becoming only "an accidental byproduct."[20]

Hill allows the twin time spheres and their relative elements to coexist not alternately but in continuous referral between the "tuned" and the "tuned out."[21] Any recognition that provides an interrelation between the child and king does not occur in opposing structural units connected by a single rhythmic disjuncture but is consistently reenacted in the continuously staccatoed rhythm of cohabiting forces (ancient and modern; archaic words and contemporary idioms). For example, in hymn II, someone is playing with the name "Offa," twisting and contorting it in various ways. Knottenbelt takes this to be the child-poet experimenting with the sound: "he discovers that he can make it sound like a 'laugh,' then a 'cough.'"[22] In fact, it is more subtle than this. The hymn *itself* must be read aloud rather than just the name "Offa" enunciated in the manner of a laugh and then a cough, because the king's name actually rises out from the utterance of the text in a manner that evokes his spirit:

II

A pet-name, a common name. Best-selling brand, curt
   graffito. A laugh; a cough. A syndicate. A specious
   gift. Scoffed-at horned phonograph.

The starting-cry of a race. A name to conjure with.[23]

This gives us:

      gr*affi*t*o* (affo/offa)
      a l*augh*; a c*ough*. A (offa offa)
      sc*off*ed-*at* (offa) h*o*rned *ph*onogr*a*ph (offa).

The final phrase, "a name to conjure with" shows "conjure" to signify not only the child's juggling with the word but also the actual raising of the spirit of Offa (by the reader's breath) as an essence manifesting itself inside the modern world.[24] Appearing as it does at the beginning of the collection, this hymn demonstrates the coexistence of past and present brought together through the disjunctive rhythm of poetic utterance. The "reentry of transcendence into this sublunary world" (XXIII) recurs at each reading. In purely structural terms, context is absorbed by the text proper in *Mercian Hymns* and the challenge to single linear logic, previously sounded by parenthetical interruptions, is here produced by the frustration of regular reading rhythms in internal disjunction. The stylistic effect of disjunction, as in hymn I, is the kind of telegraphic style that Jakobson equates with metaphoric discourse, thus proving the relation between implied context in brief prose works and poetic discourse.[25] Significantly, the image of the arabesque, which is closely associated with prose poetry and context, abounds in *Mercian Hymns*. However, here De Quincey's organic expansion comes under the artist's control and is now an image rather than a process. The arabesque is represented by a pictorial image carved in stone rather than in its natural form (as roots and tendrils), that is, it too appears in a form of disjunction.[26]

Etymology

Prose poetry turns on paradox, as its title illustrates, and context is defeated in *Mercian Hymns* by the continuous movement generated by its active dualisms. The constant referral from one axis to another (eighth to twentieth-century time spheres, prose to poetic form and so on) causes the internal struggle, registered by disjunction, which generates the sequence. Hill labors to make the binary form sufficient material for contextual matter. If the self is split, then the two personalities may inform one another rather than rely on creative reading. In this way, Hill echoes De Quincey's insistence on authorial control.

In interview with John Haffenden, Hill has explained that he uses Offa's brutality to characterize his own childhood with its tyrannical streak.[27] By establishing this double perspective to his sequence, Hill is able to restrict the context: child informs king, king informs child. It is this interaction that allows for the context and, therefore, the perspective, to be reversed so that the other protagonist, Offa, can simultaneously recognize the child/artist in himself. Ironically, it is tyranny that induces form and therefore makes the artwork possible. The context (which is implied) consistently supports a two-directional reading:

>   ... Dreamy, smug-faced,
> sick on outings—I who was taken to be a king of
> some kind, a prodigy, a maimed one.
>
>   (V)

> "God's honour—our bikes touched; he skidded and came
> off." "Liar." A timid father's protective bellow.
> Disfigurement of a village-king. "Just look at
> the bugger..."
>
> (XVII)

> "Not strangeness, but strange likeness. Obstinate,
> outclassed forefathers, I too concede, I am your
> staggeringly-gifted child."
>
> (XXIX)

In hymn V, the raised spirit of Offa is incarnated in the child who is set apart from his peers. Thus, the mention of a king and a prodigy (attributed to Offa) are embedded in the oxymoronic portrait of a sick and dreamy "maimed" child. In XVII, the verset quoted above is sandwiched like a memory inside a narrative of a man driving. His recollection of the bicycle accident leads him to react by defiantly accelerating his "maroon GT." It is possible to read this either as a humorous device in which Offa appears anachronistically as a young boy and/or as the narrator of the hymn in a moment of self-recognition, his acceleration a reaction to a spontaneous déjà vu. Finally, the distinction made in the first verset of hymn XXIX, "Not strangeness, but strange likeness" also allows for the dual perspective in that poem by emphasizing the difference between the obscure and that which is unexpectedly illuminated, through recognition, in the apparently obscure. Hymn XXIX may be interpreted in two ways: Offa's ghost begins to withdraw while the boy plays ludo and, in his retreat, "enters" or plays a role in the boy's last dream; or, the poet as a child mutters the monologue before mentally withdrawing himself into a daydream about Offa.[28]

Mercian Hymns centers on a skilful performance of word-play. Discussing narrative masks and devices and whether or not they are compatible with the concept of a "sincere" work, Hill has quoted Simone Weil: "Simultaneous composition on several planes at once is the law of artistic creation, and wherein, in fact, lies its difficulty."[29] In other words, like Hobbes's context, artistic creation is defined by its plurality but that very pluralism is the cause of ambiguity. Although *Mercian Hymns* requires a cooperative reading, to decipher its stratified form, it is a strictly controlled experience. Technological space is replaced by rhythmic and syntactic disjuncture. The self-destructive quality of the internal rupture is echoed in the self-contradictory nature of the text (as both language and the subversion of language).

Hill manipulates his prose to alternate between the syntagmatic and paradigmatic planes. He employs very specific words whose individual histories cast shadows of implication over the immediate verset and beyond in the operational method of the work as a whole. The most common form of critical analysis therefore records the critic's procedure of lifting out and intensely scrutinizing the individual word.[30] Each one is academically observed in all its etymological, phonetic, and associative environments—in their paradigmatic plane in other words—before being replaced in the context, the syntagmatic axis, of Hill's poem.[31] However, if criticism unravels all the meanings of Hill's words and phrases (where "all" can never be "complete"), then it is being "set up" by the poem because the narrative is lost amid the excessive amount of information in a parody of the expressed context it has clearly eschewed. This element of absurdity arises because the critical analysis foregrounds elements that should only exist as faint echoes as in hymn II.

John Needham's analysis is symptomatic of the problem of a double reading. Needham carries out his investigation to prove that the etymological list of the words that make up *Mercian Hymns* collectively form an explanation of the work by reconciling the two time spheres that share the space of the word. However, he does not take account of the syntagmatic axis and this leads to fundamental problems in his interpretation. He is at a loss what to do with the products of his excavations: "There is obviously no way in which one can *show* that this is so; but one can at least note that the verbal texture is dense to the point of solidity."[32]

This is clearly not enough. The "proof" of this method is in the very exercise of excavation itself. For example, Needham lifts the word "livid" from the third verset of hymn XXVII and observes that it denotes a color but also, colloquially, anger, "which makes Thor an angry bloke as well as a Norse deity."[33] Needham is left holding "livid" in the sense of a leaden blue color with only a tenuous thread to link it to "butcher of strawberries." In fact, "livid" as a color suggests a corpse (Earth is his "ghost-bride"). Standing, as it does, at the head of the last four hymns all entitled "The Death of Offa," the implication is that Thor is being equated with this ancient king. However, it is Thor as a dead myth, resurrected through the modern (colloquial) image of "an angry bloke," which is also the destiny of the character of Offa, here reflected in the ruinous landscape of the third verset in its quasireligious scene of preresurrection chaos.[34] The single word, "livid" through *both* of its significations is therefore

4 / CONTEXTS II: *Mercian Hymns* 127

instrumental in holding together the sustained oppositions in the hymn: "'Now when King Offa was alive and dead'" in the first verset and "He was defunct. They were perfunctory" in the second.

Presenting the narrative of a historical process by a series of isolated words, rather than a succession of sentences, has a direct bearing on the nature of the work and threatens its accessibility. Needham instinctively registers this as stylistic effect: "dense to the point of solidity." Each word can be mined, indeed, almost *requires* to be investigated, familiar patterns of reading are thwarted and the result is a stilted and labored reading process. In fact, what is being thwarted is the tendency to admit, in prose, only the immediate semantic logic of the word in order to elicit a single meaning in terms of linear narrative. On the other hand, taken as radical poetry, the paradigmatic interpretation requires a narrative context in order to acquire any significance as an interpretation: the syntagmatic and paradigmatic directives constantly defer to each other.

Mercian Hymns sustains an ambiguous, prefatory, and incomplete nature (in other words, a symbolic nature, in Romantic terms) by the fact that it indicates the vast region for potentiality and possibility of an implied context. In fact, if De Quincey's incessant digressions and footnotes show his defeat by expressed context, Hill's resistant hymns illustrate a similar problem with context even after he has restricted and suppressed it. Both writers emphasize the process of progression by digression.

Such complex wordplay threatens to reduce Hill's poetry to the "cerebral conundrums" that he finds and dislikes in the work of his peers.[35] In addition, the prose pieces are in danger of appearing only as a collection of individual words whose sentence is imminent but never achieved because it is forever delayed by pun, paradox and irony through etymology. On the other hand, *Mercian Hymns* is the most explicitly autobiographical work of a writer who methodically attempts to eliminate the personality of the author from his work. Hill's method of representing the historical process, from Offa to his own childhood, etymologically reduces the personal aspect of pure lyricism.[36] By insisting on the centrality of the word, the prose objectifies the poetic—making it the subject of the work.[37] Yet, in redirecting the subject to Offa, Hill's implied context halts narrative flow in actual reading and fictional time. Once again, the narrative is postponed due to the regressive nature of its context. The act of critical analysis therefore participates in the paradox of context. Elucidation is necessary to render an interpretation for the poem but it gives expression to associations that are only implicitly present and never actually approved by the text (such as Annwn's commentary for hymn II—see note 24 above—where "Overseas Food Corporation" is not found anywhere in the text). We assume that meanings are lost and allowed, by Hill, to be lost because, as the etymology shows, meaning, like an implied context, can always be recovered. In terms of the prose poem, *Mercian Hymns* and its commentators, consciously or otherwise, demonstrate the most serious problem concerning the implied context, which is its resistance to expression. Once the implied context is expressed it loses the potentiality and pluralism that defined it together with the rhythmic disjunction, the quality of the blank space, in which it resided.

II

Endnotes

A second source of revealed context (beyond the etymology of the individual word) appears in the endnotes that follow *Mercian Hymns*, the majority of which provide sources for particular words and ideas. The notes have been described as "both indispensable and mischievous"[38] and are notable for their academic precision rather than their extensiveness or usefulness. Hill's expressed admiration for the work of T. S. Eliot makes a comparison with *The Waste Land*, as an annotated poem, a logical step in interpreting Hill's work: "The poem presents its broken or disfigured quotations like the salvaged fragments of some archaeological dig." This description could refer to either work but is, in fact, a response to Eliot's poem.[39] Here, in Drain's reading, the poem enters into a dialogue with other literatures in order to avoid isolation, in which case only the intellectual reader is granted any comfort, but the indirect nature of the correspondence between the endnotes and text suggest that there is little comfort to be had. We know that most of the notes return fragments of the poem to their original contexts—yet only partially: the sources themselves can only be cited, decontextualized again within the extension of Eliot's poem. In addition, as the "last section" of the poem to be read (there are no indicators within the text to instruct their parenthetical insertion), the endnotes give the impression that Eliot has been quoting rather than composing. *The Waste Land*, in its final telling, positions itself inside a larger literary canon and makes a part of itself. Hugh Kenner, characteristically, regards the notes to *The Waste Land* as simply "a consequence of the technological fact that books are printed in multiples of thirty two pages."[40] Eliot's notes famously frustrate rather than elucidate. For Kenner, the obtuse relationship between the various passages and their "sources" is proof of the speed with which they were added in order to fill up the spare pages and licenses a reading that ignores them.

Hill's notes may also have been born of technological circumstances and they certainly complement his reputation as a scholar-poet.[41] The first note, which refers to the original source of the work, is most rewarding in reading the poem. The reader is immediately directed to six latin prose hymns in *Sweet's Anglo Saxon Reader* that contain an interlinear translation in an Old English, Mercian dialect. Collectively they are titled *Mercian Hymns* thus also invoking intertextuality simultaneously with the main title of Hill's poem (the subtitles mimic this by enacting an interplay between themselves through repetition). Contained in this single source is the biblical aspect; the double axis reading based on concurrent texts (here the reference to interlinear translation); and the concept of recovered history. Further on, however, the notes are only vaguely helpful. Perusing the given references to *Larousse Encyclopedia of Mythology* as instructed, for example, one gains the idea of various representations of the horned god, Cernunnos, who appears in hymn XV, but little information relevant to that hymn. Hill attempts to combat the Eliot comparison by emphasizing his own "honesty." He begins by retracting his main title describing it instead as only "a suggestion" taken from the original *Mercian Hymns*, thus not actually appropriating it. At another point he acknowledges having picked up a word from a television quiz show (*Call My Bluff*, appropriately). Hill cites the date, episode, and the celebrity who correctly identified it. Whereas Eliot sank his poem in a bed of past literatures, Hill's endnotes defictionalize his work, exposing his compositional process from "fact" to poem and, with it, his "errors."[42] In other words, while Eliot's notes situate *The Waste Land* as heir to an inaccessible literary tradition, Hill's notes provide a critique of *Mercian Hymns*.[43] While in some ways the latter are as obscure and unhelpful as Eliot's, they are part of the autobiographical process that had regularly impelled De Quincey to step out from behind his own narrative mask in parenthetical asides. This process involves the appearance of a self-consciousness and thus a split-self in which the critic (who is also the author) curbs the poet's expression by representing tyrannical authority, academic precision, and technical form. Eliot reaffirms his own place in a long succession of "literary works." Hill, on the other hand, acknowledges "factual" rather than intertextual debts. His endnotes reveal a different type of prose: that of nonfiction which does not frame the work so much as challenge it. The voice of Hill's endnotes is the "antiphonal voice of the heckler," his "acknowledgements" the suppressed context that was that of the counterpointing footnote. Marginal spaces and voices are incorporated in the text itself: Ceolred is flayed *down* in the quarries (VII); a threatening, disembodied voice of a midnight caller and an invisible writer of venomous letters are thwarted in their "devices" (VIII).[44] Also, ironically, the only parenthetical sentence expresses anticipation of the resurrection of the dead.[45]

More recently, Alan Halsey's prose poem sequence, *The Text of Shelley's Death*, demonstrates another form of this internal broadening. The work, a collection, in different voices, of separate contemporary accounts of the poet's death, is presented as a scholarly variorum. This conceit admits direct contradictions to be juxtaposed and actually build up a picture of the scene:

> *var.* Shelley and Williams rapidly explored a large portion of the coast of Italy, his papers on board. I write a little
> *var.* much of the *Triumph of Life* was written as he sailed
> *var.* as he lay in his boat
> *var.* sat with his back against the mainmast [*var.* chestnut], reading *Faust* and Calderon, writing on loose scraps of paper nonsensical rhapsodies.[46]

Separate memories result in the *Triumph of Life* being mistaken for "nonsensical rhapsodies," or vice versa. But the effect is of a scene that cannot settle. The text is never established and remains open, modular, in a similar way to *Mercian Hymns*, by defining the text as inherently plural.[47]

Although Hill exercises a strict control over his poetical material, he betrays a disorientation over his objective in his use of the endnotes. This is partly due to the reverential tone and also to the wideranging degrees of association between the poem and its references. In other words, despite taking up the role of critic in order to direct and control the extent of context that is revealed (in a similar way to Eliot), Hill is actually defeated by the endnotes because his demystification results in an obfuscation of the contextual hierarchy. Providing the missing context confronts him with the problem of what exactly *is* contextual matter or what needs to be identified as such: where is the point at which an integral element of the poem must be disclaimed as belonging elsewhere. For example, Hill's note to hymn XXV illustrates the absurd but logical result of this practice of "honesty": "'quick forge': see W. Shakespeare, *Henry* V:v, Chorus, 23. The phrase requires acknowledgment but the source has no bearing on the poem." In other words, the danger of internalized context is that everything becomes implicated equally rather than in concentric and hierarchical rings of relation to the text proper.

There is clearly an analogy between De Quincey's use of footnotes and digressions in his battle against expressed context in the *Suspiria* and Hill's endnotes found in conjunction with implied contexts.[48] However, although both works strive toward independent prose pieces one cannot generalize for all prose poetry as De Quincey and Hill are unique in using this prose device. Consequently, this may mean that *Mercian Hymns* must also be excluded from the right to be titled a prose poem (as Hill wished, but for different reasons). In *New and Collected Poems 1952–1992* the endnotes do not appear—perhaps it has become a prose poem.[49]

III

Titles

In the spirit of historical stratification, each hymn has two titles: a traditionally descriptive title and a roman numeral. In the original Andre Deutsch edition the poems are presented beneath the corresponding roman numeral. This form derives from the Latin prose-hymns cited by Hill in the endnotes and is also suggestive of the labeling of excavated material from an archaeological dig.[50] In this edition, the descriptive titles are listed after the hymns, before the endnotes. However, they are omitted in both the Penguin edition of the collected poems and again in *New and Collected Poems, 1952–1992*. Therefore, the descriptive titles have never appeared in their traditional place above the hymn to which they refer.[51] In a recording of himself reading *Mercian Hymns*, Hill says each title once. Where two or three hymns follow in succession with the same title, he passes from one to the other without giving either the description or the number until the descriptive title changes.[52]

Excepting only hymns XXIII–XXV, "Opus Anglicanum," all of the descriptive titles state a relation to Offa whose name appears in each one: "The Childhood of Offa," "Offa's Coins," and so on. With Offa as the genitive, this form of titling turns everything into something in his possession from material objects ("Offa's Coins") to processes ("Offa's Laws"), to the logical, but ironic, "The Death of Offa"—which suggests that his mortality is somehow also under his control.[53] The descriptive titles play various roles. Together with the roman numerals they classify retrieved ruins (the fragmented prose). In addition, they establish the expectation of a narrative since, despite their repetitions, the descriptive titles seem to adhere to a loose form of chronology beginning with the naming and ending with the death of Offa. Finally these titles draw attention to the discrepancy between the object in the noun phrase (coin, law, sword, kingdom) and the corresponding poem as literary form. "Faced with such an initial incompatibility, the reader is forced to participate more actively in the text—to recognize and to interpret this cross-over between the enunciation of one code (plastic arts) and the exploitation of another (literature)."[54]

Reviewing states and abstractions as objects lends them a solidity that implies a closer relation, an analogy perhaps, between Offa's coins, laws, etc. and the individual prose hymn. The effect of introducing these themes as nouns is that it stills the progress of (numerical) succession by creating a material actuality of the image and text—emphasized by the solid block of prose, especially in hymns I and XIII. The titles therefore are involved in the double axis on which all elements of *Mercian Hymns* are based by implying a narrative on one hand and on the other eschewing process for an image-centered independent unit. By existing outside the text proper and yet suggesting ways in which the work should be read, the descriptive titles form a layer of context in the same way as the endnotes.

As well as this playful relation between the descriptive titles and their hymns there is also a parody of titles themselves in the discrepancies between the descriptions and the numerals.[55] The roman numerals appear in a successive series from I to XXX, indicating a fixed, possibly causal, narrative sequence.[56] The introductory tone of hymn I, which mimics the formal presentation of an important personage, and Offa's retreat in the last supports a directed narrative reading. Hill himself has stated that he saw the work immediately as an extended sequence.[57] He may have meant by this that he conceived of *Mercian Hymns* as continuing beyond the thirty hymns presented as the work: something that would be made possible by a repetition or a reordering. Although this could not occur with the sequential numerals, the descriptive headings are mostly repetitions. In fact, for the thirty hymns there are only fourteen titles, repeated up to four times mostly in groups but also at intervals. The change of implication here is quite forceful with a move from a single linear sequence to, if not a potentially reorderable collection, at least a selection of states that rotate in unison and syncopation to that implied linearity: the narrative is always a duality.

There is clearly a tension, then, between the sequence and the "state." For example, the death of Offa, which one would take to be a continual process in narrative terms and here indicated by the numerical sequence XXVII–XXX, is presented also as a tautologous state of possibly eternal repetition by the repeated descriptive title (it is also true that Offa's burial occurs in hymn IX, although the curate mistakenly reads the marriage service). On the other hand, for hymns III–V, "The Crowning of Offa," prepares us for a serial narrative. However, as numbered sections, such a reading is thwarted because although hymn III fulfills expectations (despite its anachronisms), "On the morning of the crowning we chorused our remission from school," hymn IV is not at all contiguous with the festive barbecue just described. The light, narrative tone is replaced by a mysterious soliloquy in an unknown voice and key words such as "mother-earth," "solidus," "Roman flues," and "tribe" suggest a shift backward rather than forward in time. The "I" of hymns III and IV mutates again in hymn V, but although the mention of elves, barbarians ("barbaric ivy") and scrollwork imply a further retreat, the subject claims to be a child and a king. Any continuous sequence in these episodes is seemingly indiscernable at a narrative level. As tautological utterances, where the three hymns claim to be the crowning of Offa, the discrepancies take a cryptic but decipherable twist. An effect similar to hymns I and II takes place where the spirit of the ancient king inhabits disparate objects and processes and is repeatedly evoked with their manifestations. Here, however, the reiteration of a single title for three hymns indicates an augmentation of the previously compressed time-scale. Each hymn is distinct in time and speaker but the spirit of Offa is diffused throughout suggesting an interrelation between the independent pieces. The child speaker of hymn III (whom we may take to be the young poet) is present also in the subterraneous "child's play" of accumulating time (IV) and again in the "desolate childhood" (V) of the king's journey of resurrection to "the presiding genius of the West Midlands."[58] In the same way, hymn III describes the barbecue chef as "a king," which invokes a regionally generic man stemming from Offa to the modern local, but also parodies the crowning, "a king in his new-risen hat." The crown theme is continued in hymn IV through the imagery of "the clogged wheel, his gold solidus." The versets of this hymn form an enjambment so the text enacts the physicality of the crown, which encircles a space in anticipation of the king himself. In hymn V, the two personas of child and king react with each other. The reemergence of Offa as presiding genius is paralleled with the growing self-consciousness of the child destined to be a poet and to invoke Offa in a (future) artistic work. This final verset of the subseries can be read alternately as referring to both characters in turn. The concurrence of both forms of titles works to resist a direct correspondence between linear narrative and the existence of a decontextualized state in "eternal return."

Such games with recurrence and evocation have a direct bearing on textual perimeters: beginnings and endings. No one has made a case for *Mercian Hymns* as a cyclical poem. The numerical sequence weighs against this form of reading and there are no outstanding repetitions in the first and last versets. In fact, the only cyclical movement is the potentially continuous reiteration of hymn I, created by its second verset: "'I liked that,' said Offa, 'sing it again.'" However, the death of Offa, the longest sequence in the poem, is a gradual process taking up four hymns. The fact that the king's death outweighs, in textual space, his lifetime achievements suggests that hymns I–XXVI are contextual ballast to explain the nature of his death: that he remains "alive and dead" in the Mercian collective unconscious. However, this interpretation cannot hold if we advocate a reading of reordering—something that is encouraged by the burial described before his death, in hymn IX. In fact, all of the individual hymns could be justified under the title "The Death of Offa" because he is characterized as reincarnated in each.[59] In this way, it is possible to regard the whole of *Mercian Hymns* as grouped in disorder around the end—but where or what is the end? Hill's poetic work immediately preceding *Mercian Hymns*, *King Log* (1968) contains the poem "September Song," an epitaph to a child who died (or was killed) during the Second World War, in September 1942. The poet recognizes the aspect of self-consolation involved in composing the poem.

He attempts a description of the ever-returning September. The poem ends: "This is plenty. This is more than enough."

Christopher Ricks, in his discussion of this poem, suggests that this final recoil is due to the poet's surprise that his English reserve has lapsed to allow this sentimentality.[60] However, together with *Mercian Hymns*, "September Song" seeks to invoke a dead personage into the present, a notion which collapses chronological time into kairoi.[61] The claim to "plenty" suggests that the container (be it an allusion to the harvest season, poetic form, or the structure of the moment) is full and it is this, rather than the achievement of a specific distance in a logical sequence, which denotes the end. Furthermore, although the statement "this is more than enough" is a second sigh against the unspeakable horrors of war, which he has dared to verbalize, it is also an acknowledgment that the end is, or should be, elsewhere: that the end of the printed page does not correspond to the poetical end. The final hymn on the death of Offa registers a similar retreat:

XXX

And it seemed, while we waited, he began to walk to-
    wards us   he vanished

he left behind coins, for his lodging, and traces of
    red mud.

In contrast to the previous hymns, which imitate the marble sculpture and excavated potsherd—especially hymns IV, XIII and XVII—by visibly emerging from the blank page, hymn XXX *remerges* with the consuming white space (between "towards us" and "he vanished" and the fractional last line) that, like De Quincey's context, breaks into the text. This is not a despairing fragment since the blank spaces have clearly been designed, as text, on the page. Hill retains full control. Instead, the blank spaces indicate a moment of transition at the end of a vision or dream.[62] The dream is overwhelmed by the unsupportable pressure of context and the language fades because, for Hill, language *is* context. Alternatively, the blank space represents the silences of both text and context in anticipation of something else: the true text that they have been circling (unfragmented). There are three possible outcomes: the appearance of a supertext (the absent work, which would be impossible by definition), recourse to contextual narrative as a substitute, or silence. If

Mercian Hymns is not cyclical, then silence may be said to prevail. However, after the final hymn come the alternative, descriptive, titles (a form of repeating the poem, perhaps) and the endnotes, which certainly are context.[63]

Despite their minimal form, the hymns, as prose poems, still draw the attention to the edge of composition and the problem that one can never quite eliminate context. The nature of the end remains ambiguously inconclusive but it seems to prefer noise to silence: a sense of the poet urging that there is more to excavate even if it is only to enrich the fragmentary material that has already been made available.[64]

5
Parallelism: Blake, Wilde, Beckett

At this stage of our inquiry, I would like to return to the Romantic neo-Platonist scheme of the Idea and its representation and apply it at sentence level to the style of the prose poem. In Chapter 1, I distinguished the Idea as the Whole from the Idea as the Absent Work, which is represented in part by the fragmented text. The fragment, as a literary genre, repeats its fraction of the Idea metonymically—that is, it centers on a quality or attribute and uses it to imply the whole that it is unable to encompass. This Absent Work, it can be seen, is open to interpretation through the implied contexts of the fragment-text.

The relationship that the fragment bears to the Idea from which it is torn (McFarland's "diasparact") is one of repetition with difference. In describing this relationship more fully in this chapter, I use the term "source" to denote the original state of the Idea, which is unrepresentable and can be understood intuitively. This is the Romantic Absent Work that I have substituted by its literary equivalent, the "implied context" in order to show the active relationship that it holds to the text both in its composition and in its reception (when it is read). In literary production, this intuited Idea is schematized as a concept by applying such qualities as to create a *model*: a particular structure, style, or other reproducible characteristic. Finally, attempts to realize the model produces *copies*, which are comparable to the literary fragment, the prose poem, as incomplete imitations. Table 5.1 sets out the correspondences among the various terms I have used so far. The contents of the two right-hand columns will be the subjects of this chapter. These terms are not fully synonymous. For example, the implied context is an actively operational Absent Work but both occupy the inclusive yet unordered stage prior to schematization.

TABLE 5.1

Platonic	*Romantic*	***Prose Poetry***	***Example***
Idea	*Absent Work*	*Implied Context*	*Bible*
Model	*Concept*	*Model*	*Parallelism*
Copy	*Fragment*	*Prose Poem*	*"The Artist"*

In this chapter, I will look closely at the prose of a substantial group of British prose poems that imitate the style of the King James Bible. In discussing the evolution of a biblical style I will use the terms "source," "model," and "copy" as I have defined them, above. The Bible, as a lost origin of its translations, stands as the *source*. Parallelism, the name given to the identifiable style of the King James becomes the *model*, and the various prose poems (by Blake, Coleridge, Wilde, Beckett) represent the *copies*, the realization of the model inside a literary framework. While I trace the development of the style, I shall be attempting to answer this question: What makes a biblical style valuable in writing prose poetry? Arguably, this style, by which I have identified a group of texts, is the closest we have to a general characteristic for the genre and a mark to distinguish its English form from its more successful European counterparts.

I

Biblical Style

In a statement reminiscent of Coleridge's response to Wordsworth's refutation of a prose/ poetry distinction, T. S. Eliot writes:

> There are doubtless many empirical generalisations which one may draw from a study of existing poetry and prose, but after much reflection I conclude that the only absolute distinction to be drawn is that poetry is written in verse, and prose is written in prose; or, in other words, that there is prose rhythm and verse rhythm. And any other essential difference is still to seek.[1]

Eliot's article is a direct reaction to what he perceived to be "a recrudescence" of the prose poem genre at that time in France, England, America, and Japan. The conviction that he displays in this article is remarkable, considering Eliot's own work in *vers libre* and

5 / PARALLELISM: BLAKE, WILDE, BECKETT

the prose poem—after all, his prose poem, "Hysteria" had been composed only two years earlier.[2] Eliot compares English (that is, Richard Aldington's) prose poems with their French counterparts. However, within the corpus of English texts that may be described as prose poetic, a significant number (pre- and post-Eliot) employ a style that does not exist in French but is exclusive to the English form of the genre.[3] The style is clearly reminiscent of the biblical books and creates, within the limited British corpus, a group of prose poems that evolved relatively independent of the parallel development of the genre in France. Blake's "The Couch of Death" echoes Psalm 139, Coleridge's *The Wanderings of Cain* is set between verses 16 and 17 of Genesis 4; De Quincey's *The Daughter of Lebanon* and Wilde's several prose poems are presented as imitation or even "fake" Gospels. On the other hand, although it is a common factor, this biblically styled prose poetry appears to be spontaneously generated; in each case I have found no evidence to suggest a line of influence or tradition between these specific works and yet, for example, the style of Samuel Beckett's late prose work also belongs to this group. Therefore, we may assume that this style lends itself to prose poetic form, that is, to brief prose texts. In this chapter, therefore, I aim to elucidate the specific nature of this style and its advantages for the prose poem.

Oscar Wilde's prose poem, "The Artist," provides a typical example of this biblical style.

> One evening there came into his soul the desire to fashion an image of *The Pleasure that abideth for a Moment*. And he went forth into the world to look for bronze. For he could only think in bronze.
>
> But all the bronze of the whole world had disappeared, nor anywhere in the whole world was there any bronze to be found, save only the bronze of the image of *The Sorrow that endureth for Ever*.
>
> Now this image he had himself, and with his own hands, fashioned, and had set it on the tomb of the one thing he had loved in life. On the tomb of the dead thing he had most loved had he set this image of his own fashioning, that it might serve as a sign of the love of man that dieth not, and a symbol of the sorrow of man that endureth for ever. And in the whole world there was no other bronze save the bronze of this image.
>
> And he took the image he had fashioned, and set it in a great furnace, and gave it to the fire.
>
> And out of the bronze of the image of *The Sorrow that endureth for Ever* he fashioned an image of *The Pleasure that abideth for a Moment*.[4]

While the subject of the prose poem is not religious, the oratorical tone is clearly imitative of Old Testament literature. Phrases such as "One evening there came into his soul"; "And he went forth"; key words such as "dieth," "endureth," and "abideth" are recognizably from the Authorized Version or in imitation of it.[5] Repetition of plain and direct sentences is also an identifiable characteristic of the Old Testament in translation and Wilde's prose poem clearly incorporates this device.

A source for this overtly "biblical style" lies over a century earlier in Bishop Lowth's identification and characterization of Old Testament texts. In the mid-eighteenth century, Bishop Robert Lowth, who occupied the Chair of Poetry at Oxford, gave a series of lectures promoting his belief that the Books of the Old Testament were originally received as metered poetry, but that the verse form had been lost over the centuries. In order to prove this hypothesis, Lowth had to find traces of a meter that he could restore, thereby recovering the "original" condition of the text. Although he could not detect a meter as such, he did discover what he described as a notable conformation in the sentences: "When a Proposition is delivered, and a second is subjoined to it, or drawn under it, equivalent or contrasted with it, in Sense; or similar to it in the form of Grammatical Construction; these I call Parallel Lines; and the words or phrases, answering to one another in the corresponding Lines, Parallel Terms."[6] That is, two or more clauses form internal semantic correspondences, consistently. This schema, which substituted for meter, Lowth was later to term "Parallelismus Membrorum" or, simply, "parallelism." For example: "Mercy and Truth are met together; Righteousness and Peace have kissed each other."[7] The mid-sentence semicolon acts as the clausal divider, much like the Old English caesura. In this case the two elements in A-clause [Mercy and Truth] and [met together], are answered in B by the parallel conformation of a pair of personifications [Righteousness and Peace] followed by the act of their literal and metaphorical embrace [kissed each other]. While the nature of the correspondence varied, the revealed pattern was enough for Lowth to confirm a biblical meter in which: "a complete sense is almost equally infused into every component part and . . . every member constitutes an entire verse. So that as the poems divide themselves in a manner spontaneously into periods, for the most part equal; so the periods themselves are divided into verses, most commonly couplets, though frequently of greater length."[8] He goes on to emphasize the fact that Hebrew poetry translates well into the prose of any other language.

Roger Pooley has estimated that a recognizable biblical style in prose first began to appear around 1650. However, he associates this early biblical idiom with the uneducated and the dissenting community who found in the translated Bible, "a flexible, readily learnable and impressive language which had nothing to do with Renaissance Latinity."[9] This forerunner of biblical style, in which phrases are lifted from the Old Testament and recontextualized in secular works, began to emerge at a time when the religious meditation was under threat by a burgeoning secular literature. Interest in the Bible *as text* did not wane but a separation between its expression and its message had patently occurred.[10] Similarly, K. G. Hamilton has written of the direction in which poetry and prose had been moving in the early seventeenth century: "rather than the tendency being towards a sharper distinction of the two forms, it is towards a greater clarity in the acceptance of prose as a norm of style, from which poetry may be allowed to depart, but always at its peril."[11] Of course, by the eighteenth century, poetry was beginning to take that very risk of separating from the prose norm. Lowth's lectures on the *Authorized Version* reverse this tendency by reasserting standard prose as the ideal idiom for modern poetry thereby causing a movement back toward the prose norm, leaving a minimal distinction between the two media.

Murray Roston shows how, until Lowth's time, the *Authorized Version* was regarded simply as a prose translation that could have no pertinence for poetical style.[12] In fact, the King James was often versified. However, the uniformity favored by neoclassicism meant that poetical versions of the Psalms, for example, were indistinguishable from those of Homer because both were rewritten to accord with contemporary principles of style, diction, and so on, resulting in a homogeneous mass. In addition, the poems were unrecognizable from the initial translation. Roston gives an example of Augustan paraphrase that reproduces this verse from Psalm CXXXIX, "If I ascend up into heaven, thou art there; if I make my bed in hell, behold thou art there." as:

> If thro' the Sky I urge my rapid Flight
> To regions blazing with immortal Light,
> 'Tis there the Seraph owns thy scepter's Sway
> Thy Glory beams intolerable Day.

> Or if to Hell I bend my downward course,
> Thy Justice there exerts its dreadful Force.
> Thy terrors howl around the dismal Cave,
> And frighted Devils tremble and believe.[13]

The comparative qualities of the original parallelism are inadequately represented by rhyming couplets in the verse. Indeed, Drummond's verse displays the artificiality commonly associated with much eighteenth-century poetry. In his Preface to the *Lyrical Ballads*, which is clearly (if indirectly) influenced by Lowth's primitivism, Wordsworth quotes a similarly styled sonnet by Gray to illustrate the type of poetic diction that his own "plain style" was attempting to counteract. On the other hand, Wordsworth feels obliged to defend his form of plain style from parodies such as Dr. Johnson's stanza, "I put my hat upon my head / And walk'd into the Strand / And there I met another man / Whose hat was in his hand" in which the "sense-units" are more *non*sense units.

Despite distinguishing also between the "languages" of prose and verse, Lowth claimed that the Hebrew poems divided into periods, that is, into rhetorical sentences, which could be regarded as verse units or couplets.[14] As a result of his lectures, he is generally considered to be responsible for releasing poetry from the constraints of verse, thus extending the sphere of poetry to reencompass that of prose. Smart's versions of the Psalms treat the parallelisms sympathetically and differ entirely from Drummond's.[15] We may compare the same passage from Psalm 139. This is Smart's versification:

> Should I to highest heav'n ascend,
> And with superior beings blend,
> There art thou in thy reign;
> Or should I in the depths immerge
> Of death and hell's contiguous verge,
> And thou art there again.[16]

The difference is striking. In conserving the parallelistic structure, Smart's diction is plain and his phrasing comes very close to natural speech. Lowth's description of the Old Testament poems dividing themselves "spontaneously" into periods highlights this principle of parallelism where the sense is coextensive with the period, as in prose, rather than the metered line, as in traditional verse.[17] In other words, while he is innovative in "proving" that part of the Old Testament is poetry, he encourages its rendition in prose—the effect of which would produce something like Wilde's prose poem.

The Biblical Style in Prose

The ease with which English prose is able to accommodate Lowth's biblical style is due to syntactic and stylistic sympathies between the two models. Syntactically, English, that is Old English, shares with Hebrew a tendency to paratactic structure.[18] Opposed to this form is the hypotactic nature of the Latin Period, which was subsequently incorporated to a degree into English rhetoric, but never wholly naturalized.[19] When Brian Vickers discusses Gorgian/Ciceronian "symmetry" in Bacon's prose, he emphasizes that the different syntactical (as well as social and religious) structures of the two languages (and cultures) mean that some aspects of the original are actually impossible to imitate in the English Renaissance.[20] Hebrew poetry, however, proves to be "remarkably translatable" as Ruth apRoberts claims, due, in part, to its parallelistic form. As she describes it, parallelism creates a self-exegesis, confirming and paraphrasing itself. The characteristic repetition clarifies and illustrates each statement, preserving the text before it is subjected to foreign translation.[21]

Secondly, Lowth's biblical style became popular, aesthetically, bcause the last major development in prose that occurred in the seventeenth century marked a return to the same Anglo-Saxon directness that had been marginalized by this neoclassical rhetoric. Although the reasons for the change continue to be debated, the outcome remains that prose emerged in its "modern form" by the end of the century.[22] Roughly speaking, a plain style came to predominate, overshadowing the Ciceronian period, which had hitherto held sway. That is, the long, composed, hierarchical construction of latinate phrasing and rhetorical matter was joined by a chopped, spontaneous style where plain diction was valued: "to reject all the amplifications, digressions, and swellings of style: to return back to the primitive purity, and shortness, when men deliver'd so many *things*, almost in an equal number of *words*."[23] Grammatical precision began to hold sway over the rhetorical devices of emotive persuasion.[24]

The stylistic debate itself lies beyond our field of inquiry but the shift has been variously attributed to "anti-Ciceronianism"; the influence of science and the Royal Society; current perspectives on epistemology and Puritanism.[25] The closest point of agreement amid all these conflicting opinions appears to be between Morris Croll and Stanley Fish who, for different reasons, both regard the new sentence as a reflection of the mental state of the writer.[26] The problem is further complicated by the fact that the nature of the plain style itself is a debatable issue. As one argument goes, the scientific style advocated by Thomas Sprat in his *History of the Royal Society* is not the plain style championed by the essayists.[27] However, a style in which each thought is represented in its order of succession often results in a series of snatched phrases related to each other by synonymy, antithesis, contrast, and so on.[28] This characteristic of the curt period is clearly similar to Lowth's later formulation of biblical style. Indeed, the late seventeenth century attic and the biblical style (as schematized by Lowth) share interests in brevity, basic syntax, and plain diction.[29] Pooley's estimate that a biblical style first appeared around 1650 would place its emergence contemporaneously with the deliberate shift to the attic style in Jones's scenario. In fact, considering their approximation, it is unsurprising that, for example, Sir Thomas Browne's sententiousness has been attributed at different times to both the fashion for the *style coupée* and to Hebraic influence.[30]

The quasi-biblical style of religious meditations such as Browne's was only gradually transferred to essays on more secular themes and then to the fictions of epistolary and autobiographical novels of the eighteenth century.[31] The influence of the plain style on literary prose fiction was therefore delayed and Lowth's support for such a style in poetry was, in some ways, rather radical. Basically, he historicized the Old Testament as a collection of ancient Hebrew poetry that could be revived, divorced from its sacred source, inside contemporary literature.[32] By the end of the eighteenth century, rather than simply *aspiring* to the presence inherent in the Logos by circling and incorporating sacred texts, writers were able to employ a repeatable model (the parallel form) in secular literature in a new way to approximate the ideal text.[33] However, Lowth's particular emphasis on the beauty of the Hebrews' plain vocabulary and basic expression did not always lead to an equally puritan and scientifically plain biblical style when it subsequently emerged in English literature.

Lowth often applauds the "dignity" of Hebrew poetry; the "plainness and inelegance" that forms the essence of its sublimity.[34] Yet his formulated style, which strives not to imitate but to achieve for itself a similar naïvety and originality, was almost immediately recognized as a repeatable model of primitive expression—a term that actually denotes the *in*imitable.[35] The popular success and confused authenticity of Macpherson's largely invented Ossian ballads, for example, can be attributed in part to its Lowthian influence. The Ossianic primitive fragment marks another link between England and France and their otherwise separate but contemporaneous steps toward a prose poetic genre. Lowth's treatise did not appear in France until 1812 but the success of the translated excerpts from Ossian did much to introduce the fashion for the primitive in Europe already in the late eighteenth century.[36] More importantly, Macpherson's parallelistic prose was published as abridged passages providing French readers with the coupling of parallelism and fragmented prose pieces. However, the objections raised fairly swiftly in France to the question of Ossian's authenticity led away from the possible transference of his biblical style. Instead, the focus of debate, which had begun with the appearance of Fénelon's *Télèmaque* in 1699, was redirected to a current debate on the legitimacy of the prose poem and poetic prose.

Lowth's parallelism, then, occupies a pivotal place in the development of a literary prose style, drawing together as it does the similarities involved in both Hebrew and Anglo-Saxon prose. On one hand, this newly discovered style continues the earlier neoclassical revival of ancient styles (Greek and Roman). On the other hand, parallelism stands at the head of a subsequent line of influence engendering the pre-Romantic nineteenth-century fashion for primitive orientalism and for Anglicized Hebraism in prose fragments.[37]

II

Biblical Style and the Poetic Function

In the second half of the nineteenth century, Gerard Manley Hopkins returns to the problem of parallelism and the verse/prose dialectic. He concludes, in an early essay, that all art "reduces itself to the principle of parallelism."[38] He defines parallelism as the relationship between noncontinuous (diatonic) units, either similar or contrasting and cites the New Testament to illustrate how the parallel works:

> Foxes (A) have (B) holes (C) and birds of the air (A') have (B—not B' here) nests (C') . . . the subjects of the clauses being changed the one does no more than say yes, the other no. Hebrew poetry is said to be of this nature. This is *figure of grammar* instead of *figure of spoken sound*, which in the narrower sense is verse.[39]

The overall impression is one of repetition, but crucially, verse parallelisms are the figure (or "repetition of") "sounds independent of meaning" while Hebrew poetry is the figure of meaning. Although Hopkins returns to parallelism on several occasions and his descriptions, as here, are helpful, he uses the style ultimately in attempt to distance poetry and verse from prose. His conviction regarding the difference between these forms derives from a Coleridgean sense that the writer's state of mind differs when writing poetry to when writing prose.[40] Despite the complexity of his argument, he fails to establish a convincing distinction between poetry and prose. He thus indirectly affirms the present claim that parallelism embraces both prose and poetry.

In the twentieth century, Roman Jakobson continues the investigation of parallelism and applies it to the study of poetics in general. At the opening of his paper, "Linguistics and Poetics," he makes clear his rejection of the hitherto common division between prose as "casual" and "designless" and poetry as "purposeful" and "noncasual." Instead, he states that all writing is goal-directed but variations in form (i.e., prose or poetry) are simply the result of a difference in their aims.[41] By using structural form as an effect rather than a cause of genre distinction, Jakobson is able to shift discussion away from a verse/prose dialectic to a more liberal concept of "poetry" that may inhabit verse and nonversified work alike: "focus on the message for its own sake, is the POETIC function of language."[42] The "poetic function" itself is defined as follows:

> *The poetic function projects the principle of equivalence from the axis of selection into the axis of combination.* Equivalence is promoted to the constitutive device of the sequence. In poetry one syllable is equalized with any other syllable of the same sequence; word stress is assumed to equal word stress, as unstress equals unstress; prosodic long is matched with long, and short with short.[43]

In other words, prosaic causal contiguity is replaced by a series of linguistic units whose sequence is directed and sustained by an internal correspondence. The initial process of selection occurs repeatedly, possibly at the expense of, say, narrative progression. I should add here that Jakobson describes "prosaic" works, conversely, as generated by a "referential function." In this case, the text acts primarily as a transparent surface always pointing beyond itself to some external reality. Significantly, Jakobson's functions are not exclusive. The poetic function does not exhaust the formal definition of poetry but remains its dominant determinant among others, for example, the referential function, which is more active in narrative texts, perhaps.[44]

Jakobson's "poetic function" provides us with a more specific vocabulary for discussing the parallelism of biblical style and its relationship to poetry and the prose poem. Indeed, parallelism itself is invaluable to the problem of the prose poem because it combats the difficulty of plot development and causal processes generally by making language, rather than content, responsible for their direction. In addition, prose may, without becoming *poetic prose,* employ the poetic function to reduce narrative in both its form and content while at the same time allowing the expansion of implied contexts, the narrative threads.[45]

To return to Wilde's "The Artist," we may now examine the framework of internal correspondences in the light of Jakobson's poetic function, which sees parallelisms operating at various levels. For example, the second image in bronze (*The Pleasure that abideth for a Moment*) requires the preexistence of the first (*The Sorrow that endureth for Ever*) and its title reflects this replacement. "The Artist" uses the reflection motif to place into question the whole notion of hierarchy that we have assumed is the basis of this parallelistic system of a model and its copies. The challenge is made by the fact that no value judgments are offered: ultimately, the image of pleasure may, in fact, be more beautiful than the first, which it destroys and yet incorporates.[46] While the image of pleasure supersedes that of sorrow, the act is represented as an artistic whim whose transience is literally inscribed into it. Not only does the title of the second reject the eternity claimed by the first, but the representation of "momentariness" coincides with the end of the prose poem itself. Indeed, the equations of the physically momentary with the literally brief and of "The Artist" with a biblical dialectic makes the prose poem analogous to the new image in bronze. In this, it is reminiscent of De Quincey's prose piece, "The Palimpsest" and Baudelaire's "Le Thyrse" ["The Wand"], which use their space for self-definition and regulate the extent of that space by actually enacting their own limitations (the palimpsest-like inability to sustain a self-contained text, for example).

III

Parallelisms in the Prose Poems of Blake and Wilde

William Blake wrote three prose poems, "The Couch of Death," "Contemplation," and "Samson," all of which appear in the *Poetical*

Sketches.⁴⁷ The prose form adopted for these pieces may have been influenced by the Ossian poems—but they in turn had incorporated Lowth's ideas on primitive poetry.⁴⁸ "The Couch of Death" concerns the last moments of a youth on his deathbed surrounded by his mother and sister. At the heart of the poem is an echo of Psalm 139 (the source for Drummond's and Smart's verses, above) in which the youth expresses his fears concerning God's judgment on him (the psalmic voice suggests the characteristically vengeful God of the Old Testament). Although he did not approach Hebrew until late in life and even then at a very basic level, Blake was steeped in the language of the *Authorized Version* and the style advocated by Lowth.⁴⁹ Other sentences combine the chopped spontaneity of attic structure with a more specifically Ossianic exclamatory tone:

> Parting is hard, and death is terrible; I seem to walk through a deep valley, far from the light of day, alone and comfortless! The damps of death fall thick upon me! Horrors stare me in the face! I look behind, there is no returning; Death follows after me; I walk in regions of Death, where no tree is; without a lantern to direct my steps, without a staff to support me.⁵⁰

However, "The Couch of Death" contains a number of less complicated parallelisms, notably where it comes closest to biblical imitation: "My hand is feeble, how should I stretch it out? My ways are sinful, how should I raise mine eyes? My voice hath used deceit, how should I call on Him who is Truth? My breath is loathsome, how should he not be offended? If I lay my face in the dust, the grave opens its mouth for me; if I lift up my head, sin covers me as a cloak!" (*Poetical Sketches*, 61). Here, the parallelisms are clearly marked, first by the successive confessions and questions: "My hand is feeble / how should I . . . "; "My ways are sinful / how should I . . . "; "My breath is loathsome / how should he . . . " These statements are answered by a second series of two-part repetitions (propositions and consequences): "If I lay my face / the grave opens . . . "; "If I lift up my head / sin covers me . . . . "

Blake extends the parallelism further by creating an antiphonal response by the mother: "O Voice, that dwellest in my breast, can I not cry, and lift my eyes to Heaven? Thinking of this, my spirit is turned within me into confusion! O my child, my child! is thy breath infected? So is mine" (*Poetical Sketches*, 62). He overlays this dialogue with another type of parallel, reminiscent of Smart's *Jubilate Agno*

(1758–63), that is constructed as a sequence of "Let..." and "For..." corresponding verses.[51] At the heart of Blake's poem, and forming the transition from one half of the parallel, the youth, to the other, the mother, there are two "As... Like" constructions:

> *As* the voice of an omen heard in the silent valley, when the few inhabitants cling trembling together; *as* the voice of the Angel of Death, when the thin beams of the moon give a faint light, such was this young man's voice to his friends! *Like* the bubbling waters of the brook in the dead of night, the aged woman raised her cry, and said, "O Voice, that dwellest in my breast, can I not cry, and lift my eyes to Heaven? Thinking of this, my spirit is turned within me into confusion! O my child, my child! is thy breath infected? So is mine. *As* the deer, wounded by the brooks of water, so the arrows of sin stick in my flesh; the poison hath entered my marrow." —*Like* rolling waves, upon a desert shore, sighs succeeded sighs; they covered their faces, and wept! (*Poetical Sketches,* 61–62, emphasis added.)

Overall, "The Couch of Death" contains several types of parallel: first at sentence level giving the Old Testament imitation; second, as larger, structural correspondences that indicate agreement between these parallels, that we now recognize as Jakobson's poetic function.

While Lowth advocated prose as the medium for translations from Hebrew, he chose to publish his own prose translation of Isaiah with sentences set out on separate lines. His chosen format was designed to highlight the poetical nature of the Hebrew while maintaining a prose translation.[52] This form, which is shaped by and serves the sense-units, was taken up by both Smart and Blake (who used it for his own "bible" comprising such as the *Book of Thel, Book of Los,* and so on). The return to lineation reveals that the influence of parallelism leads separately to prose poetry and free verse. *Vers libre* follows the psalmic structure in which the textual line is retained but is determined by meaning rather than meter.

If parallelism is to be identified with the poetic function, the ability to discern poetic correspondence from biblical resonances in "The Couch of Death" and other similar texts becomes problematic. As I have just shown, Blake's prose poem functions principally through the poetic function by emphasizing the self-reflection of the parallel. Both the poetic function and the metaphor establish comparative pairs (Hopkins's A and A'). Therefore the parallel, which provides the structure for the poetic function, also promotes metaphor and can be characterized as such. Indeed, the formal symmetry of parallelism participates in thematic concerns. The mirror-like structure of paired phrasal units, for example, readily gives rise to metaphor in which similarity and dissimilarity between two items develop our understanding of one or both of them. In Blake's piece, the mother, whose voice is described above as like the brook's bubbling waters, is first introduced as a reed "bending over a lake." The echo is tidy and unifying: the mourners are at once gazing into a lake and participating in its properties. However, as a result, these parallels produce a carefully poised equilibrium from which there is little incentive to construct a larger whole—a provocation that is an obligatory dynamic in the genre, as I define it, by virtue of the implied context. I shall address this problem fully in section IV when I discuss how the prose poem does move beyond metaphor. For the moment, I wish to illustrate the close, almost confused, relationship between the imitated biblical style and poetic or metaphoric structure.

Lowth assisted in reintroducing metaphor, which had petered out with Renaissance doublets in prose (the worldview itself had shifted away from an analogical frame of reference: the microcosm reflecting macrocosmic activities).[53] When he emphasized the "immoderate" use of metaphor in the Old Testament, metaphoric equivalence was foregrounded again, now with the parallel, as an artistic rather than scientific function, from metaphor and simile to allegory and parable. In other words, the ambiguity of the biblical/poetic in Blake's prose poem is due to the fact that the metaphoric equivalence of the Hebraic parallel is promoted almost to the point of dominance by the larger participating correspondences of the poetic function. The neatness of the work's self-referentiality eclipses any incompleteness of fragmentation.

While parallelism is therefore invaluable to the minimalist prose poem as a way to sustain intensity and effect closure, it is also clearly responsible for often limiting the piece to metaphor and allegory (at sentence level and as a whole respectively). This in turn may lead to failure for this genre (and many prose poems are simply not successful; no extra dimension being added by the prose to what might have easily passed for a minor poem). Occasionally, the stasis of equilibrium in the parallel serves a motif, for example, in Baudelaire's "The Looking-Glass." In this prose poem, the narrator asks a very ugly man who is looking at himself in the mirror why he should want to give himself such displeasure by doing so. The man replies that, following the Revolution, he has equal rights. Stamos Metzidakis shows how this prose poem collapses into a series of mirror-images that are ultimately invalidated: the last sentence, in which the narrator accepts the theoretical validity of the man's statement, remains inconclusive because one person is right but the other not wrong. In other words, there is no difference. In addition, repetition of the verb "se regarder" to refer to the man looking at himself and also to the question being posed, suggests that the narrator is in fact the mirror image of the man, who is speaking to himself.[54] "The Looking-Glass" clearly exhibits a strong poetic function—emphasized by the scenario of a man looking at his reflection—at the syntactic level of repetition and phrasal correspondence. Wilde's prose poem, "The Disciple" also functions on similar lines. The pool mourns after Narcissus's death but it is not for the loss of the boy or his beauty:

> "But was Narcissus beautiful?" said the pool.
> "Who should know that better than you?" answered the Oreads. "Us did he ever pass by, but you he sought for, and would lie on your banks and look down at you, and in the mirror of your waters he would mirror his own beauty."
> And the pool answered, "But I loved Narcissus because, as he lay on my banks and looked down at me, in the mirror of his eyes I saw ever my own beauty mirrored." (*Fortnightly Review*, 23–24)

Essentially, the scene enacted is the same as that in "The Looking-Glass": someone who appears to be witnessing another person looking at their own reflection is actually observing themselves in that very act. In Wilde's prose poem, this process is doubled by the fact that the pool is revealed as having imitated Narcissus (or vice versa—the poem actually challenges static perspectives). In fact, Wilde's reflective process satirizes conventional love lyrics where looking into each other's eyes is symptomatic of losing oneself in adoration of the other.[55] Thus, Wilde's pool looks through the transient beauty of the mortal Narcissus in order to contemplate a more stable ideal, which is the pool itself.

To return these images to the aesthetics of the prose poem, we may describe the genre as narcissistically seeking its source, which it partially reflects, aspiring to full presence like the Logos itself. Yet the source remains outside the text; leaving the prose poem as an anxious genre that falls away continually from true presence. The overtly metaphorical nature (or near-dominance of the poetic function) in "The Couch of Death," as we have seen, means that the succession of images and analogies limit the prose piece to allegory. The two prose poems by Baudelaire and Wilde are more successful because they use the parallel device to collapse into a series of statements that are at the same time opposites and identical.

Although the poetic function is strikingly similar to Lowth's parallelism and arguably finds its natural literary state in *vers libre*, we are reminded of the fact that Lowth himself encouraged parallelism to be translated as an English *prose* style. My own argument for the prose poem as essentially a prose genre makes it necessary here to investigate the distinction, if any, between the poetic function and biblical parallelism, which favors a prose medium. In Jakobsonian terms, this would mean that, in order to sustain the prose poem as prose, the poetic function (which at this point is identified by parallelism) may be promoted to a high frequency within the text, but cannot reach the status of the Dominant. In Chapter 1, section II, I set out the Romantic distinction between "allegory" and "symbol" and I discussed them with reference to the prose poem. I concluded that, if allegory can best be described as metaphoric and the symbol as synecdochic, the prose poem would take its place at the intersection of symbol and allegory, which it effects by appropriating the metonymic ground. This continues to hold true within a parallelistic structure. Indeed, as I will show in the next section, the nature of the metonym, to consistently refer to a projected larger whole, is essential in distinguishing the prose poem's biblical style from the poetic function.

IV

Furtherance

The nature of Lowth's parallelism is a continuing source of debate among biblical scholars. James Kugel claims that parallelism was invented by Lowth in order to confirm his own idea that the Hebrew texts are poetic (Kugel also rejects any prose/poetry distinction, claiming the dialectic would have been alien to these writers).[56] He allows that Hebrew texts are parallelistic but only in tendency not in principle. Although, in effect, Kugel is questioning the model in relation to its source rather than as model per se (that is, as literary model), his changes are valid in terms of formulating a model that is not identified with poetry or restricted to the poetic function. The most that Kugel will assert for biblical style is sequence. In fact, central to his argument is the characteristic tendency of Hebraic parallel to enforce "furtherance." In place of Lowth's three types of parallelism (synonymous, antithetic, and synthetic), he offers the observation that the B clause has a dual function being both retrospective and prospective. According to Kugel, the B clause reaffirms A and goes beyond it, emphasizing and developing it:

> Some differentiation is implicit in the very idea of parallelism: "the same thing in different words" means shunning actual repetition. . . . Instead, what differentiation seems to be about is the "afterwardness" of B. B follows A, and its containing differentiated verbal themes or other morphological and syntactic differentiations seems designed to draw attention to this circumstance, "*A is so, and what's more, B.*"[57]

In other words, the B clause, whatever its relation to A, always comes after A and this is more significant than the nature of their relation. His point is that, if the type of correspondence is, for example, synonymous, even then the equivalent elements are still contiguous: B will always follow A.[58] Thus, where, in the poetic function, the paradigmatic overwhelms the syntagmatic, Kugel's theory ensures that the act of furtherance occurs on the syntagmatic axis. In fact, furtherance is most conspicuous when it follows a parallelism, the repetition of A. The presence of the parallel prevents the prose from becoming wholly referential by restricting its expansion and aiding closure (thus Kugel identifies Hebraic parallelism as a medium in between modern prose and poetry categories).

Kugel's modification of Lowth's parallelism affects the literary model in two ways. Firstly, the new formula—A, A+B—provides the crucial extension to the essentially parallel or comparative base—the repetition of A.[59] In fact, it is this dimension of "incremental repetition" or "forward thrust" of the biblical model, which is its identifying mark, adapted to the point of exaggeration in its copies. Coleridge uses the technique for those passages in *The Wanderings of Cain* that are the most overtly "biblical": "he pursueth my soul like the wind, like the sand-blast he passeth through me"; "Yea, I would lie down, I would not rise, neither would I stir my limbs till I became as the rock in the den of the lion" (*PW*, 2: 102).[60] The sententiousness characteristic of curt attic prose is evident here. In addition, the prose device of "trailing" is present in which the last element, rather than the main subject, generates the next sentence.[61] Clearly related to Kugel's "furtherance," "trailing" continues the accommodation of the biblical model in plain prose style.

Secondly, Kugel's insistence on contiguity as the only significant relationship between parallel clauses requires a reading that is primarily metonymic. Kugel's B clause may contain an element of A but it is principally prospective, not coextensive as Jakobsonian critics have claimed.[62] Furtherance offers opportunities for a form of narrative plot because as a device it uses its space to establish consistent contiguity. To return to Wilde's prose poem, "The Artist," the technique of furthering is used to generate narrative progression, for example: "But all the bronze of the whole world had disappeared, *nor anywhere in the whole world* was there any bronze to be found, save only the bronze of the image of *The Sorrow that endureth for Ever.*"[63] Wilde uses furtherance as a way of conjoining successive elements that would otherwise appear in separate sentences associated only by their juxtaposition. By this manner of inching forward, furtherance gives the impression that the larger absent work can eventually be attained. The fractional advance suggests that the ground is being comprehensively covered. Indeed, the optical illusion of a brief prose piece, which we identified in Chapter 3 as the product of an implied context, is here assisted by the furtherance device.

Berlin, who continues to identify parallelism with a concept of the poetic function is left with a fragmented reading: "The lines, by virtue of their contiguity, are perceived as connected, while the exact relationship between them is left unspecified."[64] Clearly, the biblical style of parallelism can only become a literary model when it is distinguishable from the poetic function by incorporating the dimension of furtherance. This extra dimension incites recovery of the implied context by establishing a rhythm of delayed completion.

The "Waw"/ "And" Parataxis

In literary texts, it is the gaps between prose sentences or poetic lines that distinguish two units in a parallelism and in which is couched the significance of the device. Wordsworth had made the observation that meter consisted of the perception of "similitude in dissimilitude" and unlikeness with similarity.[65] Hopkins offered a similar description in his discussion of Hebraic meter, or parallelism, as having the dualism of "comparison for likeness' sake, to which belong metaphor, simile, and things of that kind, and comparison for unlikeness' sake, to which belong antithesis, contrast, and so on."[66] In prose composition, separate units are connected by conjunctions that indicate the nature of the relationship between its comprising parts. In other words, in adopting the biblical style, the prose poem relies on conjunctions to carry the weight of a sustained prose form while accommodating the metaphoric nature of internal correspondence. The progression from one clause to its related other is often indicated in Hebrew by the conjunction *waw*, which connects two units without submitting either to subordination. This word is generally rendered into English by the conjunction "and." The imported Hebrew style becomes, in English translation, syndetic parataxis, which was already being used in Old English texts.[67] Janel Mueller has shown that "and" is the most ambiguous of all forms of conjunction.[68] Hence, another characteristic of the "biblical style" model can be illustrated by another of Wilde's prose poems, "The Doer of Good":

> It was night-time and He was alone.
> And He saw afar-off the walls of a round city and went towards the city.
> And when He came near he heard within the city the tread of the feet of joy, and the laughter of the mouth of gladness and the loud noise of many lutes. And He knocked at the gate and certain of the gate-keepers opened to him. (*Fortnightly Review*, 22)

Every paragraph (except the first, above) in this poem in prose begins with "And." "And" may imply an association of similarity or simply a contiguous action. Therefore, not only do the conjunctions connect phrases within a sentence but they are used to generate the narrative process across sentences and paragraphs yet always under the guise of sense parallelism. At the same time, "and" offers only an addition rather than an unraveling of integral information. Anything which proceeds from the "and" is appended, an extra, it extends a situation that is already complete. It is noticeable that Wilde begins almost all his prose poetic narrative sentences with this conjunction, in direct imitation of the King James Bible. The prose poem uses the "and" conjunction to bridge these regular intervals while exploiting its closural properties to maintain a highly concise form.[69]

Wilde's prose poem, "The Master," illustrates one type of "and"–driven construction. This prose piece concerns a weeping man whom Joseph of Arimathea meets on his way home (having just buried Jesus). The prose poem ends with the man giving his reason for crying:

> I have walked upon the waters, and from the dwellers in the tombs I have cast out devils. I have fed the hungry in the desert where there was no food, and I have raised the dead from their narrow houses, and at my bidding, and before a great multitude of people, a barren fig-tree withered away. All things that this man has done I have done also. And yet they have not crucified me. (*Fortnightly Review*, 24)

The significant conjunction is that of the last sentence. In the final paragraph "and" has been employed to construct a list of miracles that appear to constitute this young man's identity as equivalent to the (unnamed) Christ. In other words, "and" connects not only the individual acts (turning water into wine, healing, and so on), but also connects the weeping man with Christ. At this point, then, "and" assists the metaphoric dimension of the piece. It is only in the final sentence that these analogies are "furthered" by a paradox. "And yet they have not crucified me" negates all elements in the catalogue of miracles by marking out the difference between the two men: a difference that the younger man does not desire but over which he has no control.[70]

"The Master" becomes an ironic comment on the whole concept of model and copy. While the young man aspires to embody the "naked repetition" of Christ, Wilde's style ironically undercuts his understanding of imitation by casting it as an act of seconding.[71] Wilde's protagonist attempts to eliminate all lines of difference in himself. However, his tragedy lies in not realizing that imitation does not preclude originality. In fact, imitators challenge the very assumption that an "original" product is always superior simply for the reason that it is the first to appear. At the same time, the imitator is protected by the preceding work, which acts as a shield in publication: the act of seconding reaffirms the status of the first and thereby exacts a share in the approbation.[72] Stylistically, repetition of the "and" conjunction is the key to this sameness and difference where the ultimate discovery of difference is couched in the repetition of similar structures. "And" indicates continuance, while the crucifixion motif sustains an obvious source for the implied context. However, it is at this point, where the prose piece achieves independence by the creation of a separate persona, that the text breaks off. The man is weeping because he cannot bear the extension of outliving his model.[73]

V

Samuel Beckett's Biblical Style

Samuel Beckett read much of the Old Testament from his King James Bible, which he has described as "riddled with mistranslations but extremely beautiful."[74] However, of the late prose, only a couple of sentences in "Lessness" have been recognized as imitative of the biblical style.[75] To return to our examination of the biblical model as refined by Kugel, all furtherance must involve repetition (A, A +B) through the metaphoric and emphatic character of the trope. The reverse is also true and all repetition, as Wilde's prose poem shows, must include an element of furtherance or extension. Samuel Beckett's late prose pieces capitalize on this aspect of repetition in the parallelistic model in order to release the narrative from a De Quinceyan labyrinth of overwhelming causalities.[76]

Texts for Nothing are generally taken to indicate the end of Beckett's creative period in prose (1945–50) and the beginning of truncated, intertextual pieces and fragments.[77] Porter-Abbott remarks that *Texts for Nothing* simply mark the end of Beckett's subscription to the common narrative curve of the linear trajectory: the oeuvre is *perceived* as interrupted because of the actual disruption of received narrative form. In addition, each of Beckett's subsequent prose works becomes an attempt to prevent the closure of the last. The assertion that Beckett seeks a stable continuum after the trilogy, beyond narrative plot, suggests that the *Texts for Nothing* and late prose pieces enter a universality that is both confirmed and denied by repetition. If universality is defined as a constant, Beckett can only conceive it as forever lost from the first moment of enquiry since the state of subjective existence is automatically one of change and flux.[78] Were the constancy of the subject to be guaranteed, that of the object could never be asserted. Regression appears to be the only logical direction if stasis is not possible.[79] Furtherance can only be halted by the coincidence of the same where repetition means the same thing on its latest replay:

> those were the days, I didn't know where I was, nor in what semblance, nor since when, nor till when, whereas now, there's the difference, now I know, it's not true, but I say it just the same, there's the difference, I'm saying it now, I'll say it soon, I'll say it in the end, then end, I'll be free to end . . . it's not necessary now, it's not possible now, that's how the reasoning runs. (*Text* XI, *CSP,* 109)

As long as the condition of the self continues to be comparable but not equivalent at different moments of consciousness, the narrator is obliged to "go on." Language can only be silenced when the self is entirely unified and self-conscious so that difference (and therefore language) denotes only that which is external to the self. This time would be indicated by the fact that "I" would have killed "he" in Beckett's split-self narrations, which are condensed in the fizzles, "Afar a Bird" and "I Gave Up Before Birth." The little body in "Lessness" is further than ever from ending as it decays into the landscape "little body same grey as the earth sky ruins only upright" (*CSP*, 153). Correspondingly, the syntax in "Lessness" comes closest to the most radical form of furtherance where the extension is barely distinguishable from its comparative base—that is, repetition.[80] While language offers the possibility for repeated words to be interpreted as furtherance through a perceived difference, the whole, or source, remains only partially recovered. In other words, Beckett's prose reveals his concern that extension and metonymy are the only tools that the writer has left with which to recover the lost purity of the repetitive continuum of equivalence. This attempt to achieve metaphoric figuration through metonymically oriented prose is one cause of Beckett's art of inevitable failure. Although metaphor would be misleading in its apparently complete correspondence, the expansive nature of prose offers a more striking glimpse of the larger whole but also of its own inability to encompass it.

Beckett's late prose piece "Still," for example, contains several corresponding sentences that, scattered across the text, give the impression of a nonprogressive state of "poetic closure" (that is, the self-referentiality of the poetic function). Juxtaposed, however, these correspondences only initiate reiteration but then introduce new elements that are available through the combination of repetition and the curt prose style:

> Sitting quite still at valley window normally turn head now and see it the sun low in the southwest sinking.
>
> Normally turn head now ninety degrees to watch sun which if already gone then fading afterglow.
>
> Normally watch night fall however long from this narrow chair or standing by western window quite still either case. (*CSP*, 183, 184)

Although the model of furtherance has been "diluted" or "chromatized" here over several sentences rather than generating its successor, the principle remains the same.[81] In the lines above, the habitual actions, which are confirmed at each stage by the repetition of "normally (turn head now)," are subsequently *un*confirmed in the same sentence. Moving the head while sitting is defined as a ninety-degree turn but later the position is possibly staring straight ahead while standing. There is little significance in the position itself but the alternatives confirm that another key phrase "quite still" is equally temporary, becoming "not still at all but trembling all over."[82] Beckett condenses this presentation of simultaneous alternatives into key phrases that are themselves repeated: "Quite still . . . not still at all" or "If not quite a single movement almost." Thus, furtherance works for the prose piece because it forces figuration beyond metaphor, indicating a larger, absent, if not inaccessible, whole that the current prose can only capture partially and successively.[83]

Incremental repetition lends itself to closure in the same way as the "and" clauses in Wilde's prose poems. Each repetition is both accumulative and indicative of closure.[84] Beckett plays on this aspect of his prose style in *Text* IX. Here, the narration inches forward only through the reassertion and extension of the initial statement, whose subject is itself a search for the end:[85] "If I said, There's a way out there, there's a way out somewhere, the rest would come. What am I waiting for then, to say it? To believe it? And what does that mean, the rest? . . . all dies so fast, no sooner born" (*Text* IX. *CSP*, 100).[86] Clearly, "the rest" is not synonymous with the "way out" and this inequality is precisely what generates the prose piece and delays the end. From this perspective, everything does die quickly because, as De Quincey discovered with causal narrative, one begins at the end and is obliged to regress to the starting point. The end itself is quickly over.

Furtherance is extension in any direction. Indeed, repetition is, on one hand, simply extension of the same. As the passage above shows, furtherance, when it involves reiteration by negation, as in "Still," may have the effect of stasis. Having proposed the notion of a way out, the narrator may subsequently deny the actual possibility of, or his own belief in, the idea. However, the initial thought, that the notion may logically exist, shadows the denial itself. Beckett's narrator cannot "go on as though I had asked nothing" because this second proposal only makes sense in relation to the first. He only has to say that he has *not* asked anything to prove that he has; the affirmative is couched in the very terms of its "unsaying."

One implication is that the "way out" offers a place of nonbeing, of no change and its concomitant suffering.[87] There is a kind of refrain-like closure about the last sentence in this *Text*: "There's a way out there, there's a way out somewhere, the rest would come, the other words, sooner or later, and the power to get there, and the way to get there, and pass out, and see the beauties of the skies, and see the stars again" (*Text* IX. *CSP*, 103). Ironically, this description of the way out is an allusion to Dante's repeated emergence from the successive circles of hell.[88] In other words, the necessity to begin (or end) again is seen as inevitable and not a single act of personal salvation. The furtherance to this "refrain" is indicated by the pun "pass out," which, as either a noble release from the flesh or a weak faint, forms a connection and a disjunction between Beckett's narrator, who is about to kick the bucket, and Dante's pilgrim, who travels with dignity to the very core of death.

In the final exit, language would be unambiguous, it too would end.[89] Until that time, the contiguous nature of language means that as soon as expression begins it fragments the whole that it represents by the exclusivity involved in naming and ordering, of repetition with furtherance. Beckett's narrators are obliged to go on, although to do so distances them further from the end, from the whole, with every new word uttered.

6
Beckett's Late Prose

FOR BECKETT'S CHARACTERS, WHO ARE OFTEN WAITING FOR DEATH, the question "what next?" is a pressing one. Even the anticipated moment, the only apparent certainty of death itself, is an unknown matter. In the last chapter we concluded that furtherance—in the form of stylistic expression—is an inherent aspect of the Beckettian model. Here, I will look a little more closely at the structural mechanism of this organic continuance as it develops in the prose poetic texts of Beckett's "late" work. If furtherance is central to the novels, then ensuring the next step is not only a narrative dilemma but also a contributing factor to their consistent contraction into fragment-like pieces.

Beckett's prose fiction can be characterized as having visible and persistent foreshortening. The early novels give way to short stories and, latterly, brief prose pieces. This textual reduction is generally taken to be symptomatic of Beckett's conviction in the inevitable, indeed, hoped-for, failure of the artwork: a set of variations on the theme of an impasse, first struck with *L'Innomable* in 1952.[1] At the same time, it has been noted that Beckett's latter concern is "with situations, not with the problems and resolutions that constitute plot. As a result his fictions have come to resemble prose poems, and his plays approach *tableaux vivants*."[2] This is a little misleading. The prose poetic pieces such as *Imagination Dead Imagine*, the *Fizzles* and the "Still" trilogy are not as static as their lack of plot may suggest. However, it is true to say that verbal economy is accompanied by the loss of successive "problems and resolutions that constitute plot." This is due to the fact that the first dimension that is lost to a narrative account when severe textual perimeters are erected is the causal process or fictional plot. Thus, the epic journeys of Mercier and Camier, Molloy and Moran are replaced by the pseudo-journey of repeated events in *How It Is* and finally by the protagonist in "Sounds" who barely makes it to the window. Beckett himself described his prose post–*How It Is* as residual of the earlier work.[3] This self-deprecation obscures the fact that, while these late works may carry the relationship of "part" to the "whole" of the novel, that part is not the superfluity of the narrative exercise but its heart.[4] If *L'Innomable* writes the Beckettian novel into an impasse, the late prose pieces provide the essence of any other fictional account like Huysmans's reversible metaphor (see Chapter 3). Works such as the *Fizzles* respond to the problem of individual plots by presenting instead the more abstract plane of narrative models. It is for this reason that I place Beckett's late works under the prose poetic genre, eliminating as they do the restrictions of choice in the contextual sphere that is represented by the single plot-line.[5] In other words, causality is the principal obstacle to decontextualization and the contracted forms of Beckett's late works provide us with the best example, after De Quincey, of that causal aesthetic in process.

"When the cause eludes me . . . I begin to feel uneasy"[6]

At the close of a bizarre essay on aesthetics, "The Two Needs," in which the artwork is represented (in a parody of rationalist logic) as the product of two incompatible needs, Beckett concludes: "For in the enthymemes of art, it is the conclusions that are missing and not the premises."[7] In other words, artists find it easier to continue the work than to find its logical end: "the path reflects better than the mirror."[8] In the same way, Romantic spontaneous expression does not offer a model for the completion of form or direction. The question concerning the nature of causality was inevitably one that was taken up again after Descartes's radical reformulation of epistemological premises. Aristotle's four causes (the material, the formal, the efficient, and the final) are replaced, in seventeenth-century metaphysics, by two main areas. First, the relationship between physical or mental events (ideas); secondly, the interaction of mind and body.[9] In Beckettian terms, this translates not only into immediate problems of the narrator's relationship to the narrated but also into questions of form and style—the movement from intuition through syntactical concretion to semantic representation as a coherent process. In fact, it may be enough to say that Beckett's oeuvre functions as a marginal gloss to the most audacious causal statement: Descartes's own *cogito ergo sum*. Not only does Beckett take advantage of the gap between the repetition of the single "I," but he reminds us that the *ergo* is made possible only by the self's conscious ability to doubt its own thoughts and experiences.[10] However, it seems possible that the influence extends beyond this. David Hume's *A Treatise of Human Nature* contains an extended discussion of causality and, considering his well-known interest in seventeenth-century philosophy (which Hume answers), it is likely that Beckett had read it.[11]

Hume separates causation from logic, an epistemology that the cultural dominance by science and mathematics had falsely secured.[12] Instead, he asserts that all reasoning is generated by comparisons. The mind, led by a propensity to habit and presented over a period of time with a number of similar occasions, eventually creates analogies between them. (Habit is the principle behind inference: prediction based on past experience and present, partial repetition.) Thus, in the case of causality, the mind abstracts the repetitions that characterize successive data to create a structure that will accommodate similar information in the future in chronological and contiguous sets. In other words, the mind has a tendency to establish systems, drawn from its remembrances, into which it decants the plethora of information that it receives. Cause and effect are identities created by the mind, they are not qualities inherent in the objects or situations themselves.[13] The narrator of *Watt* understands this concept: "Were there neither Galls nor piano then, but only an unintelligible succession of changes, from which Watt finally extracted the Galls and the piano, in self-defence?"[14]

Watt

Hume lists four principles involved in any occasion that might be recognized as a causal process. These are: chronological priority of cause; contiguity with the effect; constant conjunction of the two; and, most significantly, necessary connection. The last is important for being nonempirical.[15] Beckett was experimenting with the problem of causality even while he was writing the novels. Watt, for example, is occupied for quite some time by the problem of creating a necessary connection between Mr. Knott's slops and the hunger of the Lynch family's dog.[16]

Despite Hume's creation of two definitions of causation from synchronic and diachronic perspectives, Beckett retains the rationalists' use of geometric analogies for parodic purposes.[17] Following Descartes and the rationalists, he adopts the reasoning that mathematics confirms causation: a logical equation is true for every context and its result can be predicted. Accordingly, Beckett first applies the mathematical function of probability in order to openly determine the next action in a given (narrative) sequence.[18] Probability predicts the most likely effect of any particular cause but is in itself problematic beyond its tenuous premise, which postulates the reality of causal processes. Firstly, in order to calculate a factor of probability one needs to be in possession of all possible outcomes. In terms of narration, we see Beckett's characters studiously listing as many permutations as possible. *Watt* is full (if not overfull) of these lists, from the exchanged glances of the five judges to the combination of Watt's footwear on any particular day.[19] The device is only a little less absurd when it can be contained in a closed set of elements—such as Molloy's chances of sucking each of his sixteen stones as they circulate through his four pockets. The eventual outcome (an empirical not a mathematical reality) is therefore likely to repeat one of the possibilities already laid down. On the other hand, these potential outcomes are not guaranteed to occur: the reality may diverge widely from the calculation.[20] In other words, probability either affirms preknowledge of the result or is unable to detect it at all. Either way, the device cannot provide a system on which to base a narration. In the case of the judges exchanging looks: "And so on. Until of the five times eight or forty looks taken, not one has been reciprocated, and the committee, for all its twisting and turning, is no further advanced, in this matter of looking at itself, than at the now irrevocable moment of its setting out to do so" (*Watt*, 177). Here, a complete set of circumstantial possibilities becomes impossible to obtain, forever deferring the subsequent calculation. Similarly, although Molloy claims that sucking stones is habitual to him, the action is only described once because it would be impractical to represent each repetition of the same calculation and experiment. At the same time, although probability can be applied to any repeatable action, it is noncumulative. Predictions can only be made on a single scale of infinite repetition. However, the individual results of each repetition are independent of one another. The result of any one occasion cannot have a bearing on its subsequent repetitions. This lack of local interconnection breaks down even repeated events into quite separate occasions: there is no furtherance in probability, no incentive to "go on." Beckett solves this problem in the late prose. He minimizes activity to such an extent that he can record the slightest movement when it happens as an act of furtherance—the stylistics of which I described in the last chapter. Structurally, this solution places severe restrictions on plot.[21]

Not only is probability impractical as a way of advancing the narrative, it does not contribute to the discovery of a first or last cause, which Beckett's characters ultimately require. De Quincey, whose work is also directed by a need to find the starting point, is led into the trap of infinite regression by zenovian logic. By contrast, while Beckett's outlook is platonic in its adherence to an archetype it is also Humean in his insistence on an experiential element. This may owe more to the definitive shape that idealism lends a work rather than any actual conviction on Beckett's part.[22] Thus, Beckett is gradually able to impose the strictly brief prose poetic form on his prose, which De Quincey ultimately failed to achieve. However, Beckett and De Quincey appear to agree on the essence of structural form. This is Beckett's discussion of structure in Joyce's *Finnegans Wake:* "By structural I do not only mean a bold outward division, a bare skeleton for the housing of material. I mean the endless substantial variations on these three beats, and interior intertwining of these three themes [*sic. church, marriage & burial*] into a decoration of arabesques."[23]

Beckett's statement is reminiscent of De Quincey's numerous references to structural arabesques and musical analogies. In addition, Beckett commends Joyce's structure for its static and active duality generated, unusually, by harmonic movement. Beckett's own subsequent works may be seen, on the contrary, as an attempt to establish an impassive structure that achieves a mathematical stability. His anticipated failure to do so is based on the disparity between mathematical or geometric absolutes and circumstantial flux whose path cannot be anticipated. Thus, despite his studious pedantry, we are not given the outcome of most of Watt's observations. The narrator may follow up the farce of the judges' looks with an explanation of what would have been an effective system, but it is redundant at this stage. And, however efficient is Mr. Knott's clockwork regime, the narrator nevertheless records long lists of its individual movements as if he is not confident of the system's full automation because human spontaneity may occur at any time and disrupt it. Thus, what the novels contain are preparations for the calculation of the next probable step. The narrators lay out possibilities but they are abandoned because the answer is either included there already—or exists elsewhere entirely—and will not, on this small and finite scale, suggest itself through any recognizable pattern.

How It Is

Hume grounds his scepticism of causality in the factor of time that accompanies any event. Time separates objects that are perceived by us as successive and is not only the identifying factor in any causal sequence but also the instrument of its collapse. For something to be identified as a cause, one of its principles must be that it precedes the effect. However, Hume argues, if cause and effect are distinguishable entities (separated by their chronological difference) then they cannot be said to have a necessary link between them (where "necessary link," that is, consistent spontaneous connection, is another prerequisite of causality). Of course, in order to confirm constancy in the connection of two objects a ubiquitous witness is required; moreover, one who is not limited to his own experience and sense perception.[24]

Beckett's prose work from *How It Is* replaces the relatively arbitrary narrative plot with a narrative *system*. Here action is reduced almost to zero in an attempt to isolate the causal moment—if there is one: a point which will initiate process and predict its end.[25] Significantly, many of these pieces involve the shadow of a constant "unwitnessed witness of witnesses" (*Text XII*). In *How It Is*, the "plot" is meticulously defined and predicted throughout as "before Pim with Pim after Pim." A closed system is established and a witness is installed in order to create an account of necessitated movement. A finite number of men move to and from each other playing aggressor and victim alternately. The encounter with Pim is a model for what, it is claimed, occurs thousands of times concurrently. The narrator assumes a large population in order to verify his causal experiments. The witness is also a crucial element:

> all I hear is that a witness I'd need a witness
>
> he lives bent over me that's the life he has been given all my visible surface bathing in the light of his lamps when I go he follows me bent in two.[26]

In Part 2 of the work, the witness is given the name Kram, with his own ancestors and descendants, implying sustained observation. However, the situation in *How It Is* is ultimately retracted by its narrator: "all this business of sacks deposited yes at the end of a cord no doubt yes of an ear listening to me yes a care for me yes an ability to note yes all that all balls yes Krim and Kram yes all balls yes" (*How It*

Is, 159). Similarly in *Ping*, the reiterated phrase, "all known" also suggests that the account is narrated by Hume's ideal witness. Yet, the narration moves from the assertion of "all known" to the qualifications "only just almost never" and "perhaps." Finally to the admission that the infinite and even "elsewhere" are "known not." The piece ends on the less than certain statement "perhaps not alone" and an eye closing. Paradoxically, it is Beckett's commitment to reality, as opposed to allegory, which makes these abstract accounts, such as *Ping*, ultimately impossible: metaphysics is overtaken by reality just as we observed in narrations based on probability.[27]

Hume would regard this lack of witness in reality as the last obstacle to realizing causality. If causality does exist in actuality it is unavailable to us, because we are restricted in our perceptions by space and time. Instead, we rely on our (imperfect) senses and empirical observations to collect information that, after a period of observing similar instances, leads the mind to move immediately and independently from one object to another in a reaction we would now term "pavlovian."[28]

The investigation carried out in *How It Is* into causality is repeated in the torture that is inflicted on and suffered by the protagonists. Here, nails clawed into the armpit eventually, and consistently thereafter, produces singing until a thump on the head stops it, and so on.[29] In his later works, Beckett appears to compromise his attempt to realize the ubiquitous alien eye by shifting to the perspective of the fallible human witness of apparently successive events. He moves from seeking constant conjunction to necessary connection. *Imagination Dead Imagine* ends because the watcher has momentarily diverted his attention from the couple lying in the rotunda—whom he has been examining with absolute and geometrical precision. Suddenly the scene is irrevocable despite the detailed information previously gathered: the rotunda of bone-like substance, three feet in diameter, alternating between white heat and freezing blackness, housing two white bodies. Pieces of information remain—the color, environment, and the couple showing traces of life—but they have become fragments because the witness is unable to connect them in space and time. The speck is lost and the position of the people may have changed. The text can no longer support the scene as supposition. Even the precision of its geometrical properties cannot lend predictions because it has been applied to time and mobile objects.

Reduction in textual length is therefore strongly associated with the degree to which necessary links can or cannot be asserted. The prose poem genre begins to emerge at the point where narrative plot crumbles beneath an empirical gaze. Likewise, Beckett's works after *How It Is* can be described as prose poetic because, while they focus on the very nature of causal processes, they eschew plot. Or, rather, they circle the starting point of plot in an attempt to attain the origin of the axis where form and content meet. The aesthetic ideal behind most prose poems is to achieve this kind of organicism despite their effect of apparently disfiguring the prose text by their radical brevity and the corollaries which extreme reduction bring. However, as I noted in Chapter 3, the severe brevity of the prose poem makes a form/content synthesis impossible. The prose poetic structure is a trompe l'oeil in which meaning must participate.

II

Reducing Narrative Logic

In 1961 Beckett expressed the need for a form of writing that would accommodate the chaos of contemporary life but at the same time remain separate from it.[30] We may infer that if this form was nonchaotic, it must therefore be a specific literary genre. By his own proscription however, this form would not be created from a mixture of genres.[31] In this section, I will argue against the prevailing viewpoint of Beckett "tailing off" to suggest instead that his work follows a comprehensive line of inquiry into a "pro-chaotic" form and, further, that this form is prose poetic as I have described that genre in previous chapters.

Near the end of *Remembrance of Things Past* (a work of profound influence on Beckett), Proust's narrator discusses the proper subjects for novels. He advocates a universality grounded in, but transcending, realism, which is also free of theoretical discussions and moralizing: "And as to the choice of theme, a frivolous theme will serve as well as a serious one for a study of the laws of character . . . since the great moral laws, like the laws of the circulation of the blood or renal elimination, vary scarcely at all with the intellectual merit of individuals."[32] Beckett's frequent references in his fiction to bodily functions, more often anal than renal, supports this statement. He continues his assent through the late work, in his collection of prose poetic pieces that analyze "moments of life" ("Old Earth"), by titling them, *Foirades* and, in translation, *Fizzles*.[33]

If it is in these brief prose pieces that the ideal narrative form is to be found, situated beyond allegory and symbol, then their brevity is part of that aesthetic: "It is the thing alone. . . . The thing immobile in the void, there at last is the thing visible, the pure object. I don't see that there is any other."[34] The concept of the "pure object" being represented by its immobility emphasizes Beckett's belief that movement (as narrative plot) involves loss. Once the object interacts with its circumstances, which also introduces irreversible contingency, it is distorted and entropy increases. Hence the tendency in the late work to resemble memento mori : the skull as that pure object, "immobile in the void." This is a powerful image because it replaces the object prone to narration by the instrument of its contextualization. The mind recognizes itself as the protagonist but robbed of the reasoning faculty by which it projects its narration. The mind forced to contemplate the skull is possibly the nearest it can approach a "pure" subject: a mathematical zero. In addition, the dimensions of the skull are appropriate to the late prose and the prose poem, as I will show in the next chapter.

In 1934 Beckett reviewed Professor Feuillerat's book, *How Proust Composed His Novel*, which attempts to reconcile Proust's pre- and postwar manuscripts. Beckett opposes Feuillerat's attempts to reconstitute *Remembrance of Things Past* into a more uniform work, claiming that the professor is advocating the very realism that Proust detested. He accuses Feuillerat of distorting the work into a "narrational trajectory that is more like a respectable parabola and less like the chart of an ague."[35] By comparison, the almost violent brevity of the *Fizzles* prose pieces, which lurch from one style to another and one sequence to another (in its various published editions), are possibly influenced by this incisive observation of Proust's fitful narrative form.[36] Thus, Beckett opposes a narrative of realism because he finds no path of necessity in its causal sequences. However, relinquishing choice and hierarchy admits all chaos equally. He therefore reduces or omits plot from his work in favor of a series of attempts to rediscover necessity in any process; leading, ultimately, to the disjunction between form and content in the pursuit of "organised chaos."[37]

Temporality, which, according to Hume, creates the illusion of causality, is not confined to the object but infects the perceiving subject too. Beckett engages with this dimension as early as his essay on *Remembrance of Things Past* : "The aspirations of yesterday were valid for yesterday's ego, not for to-day's. We are disappointed at the nullity of what we are pleased to call attainment. But what is attainment?

The identification of the subject with the object of his desire."[38] In other words, with time, fragmentation of the self is deemed responsible for breaking up the linearity of process, which is plotted in advance by the individual under the term "desire." Desire is the wish to connect two objects, but, as one moves toward the other, the poles are already subject to division, it remains an ideal. Beckett's Cartesian narrators and protagonists are partly responsible for their own frustrated plots: "he'll go on, I'll be inside . . . he'll get up and go on, badly because of me, he can't stay still any more, because of me, he can't go on any more, because of me" ("I Gave Up Before Birth," *CSP*, 198).

At this point, communication between any subject and object appears to be impossible and we have a landscape in which independent centers of consciousness move about in mutual indifference. Many of Beckett's commentators pitch their tents at this point to highlight the sparseness of Beckett's universe in terms of physical bodies and occasions of their successful interaction.[39] Beckett concludes this particular section in the *Proust* essay by remarking that the identification of subject and object, which is the anticipated effect of desire, is ultimately unrealistic. Instead, the solution "consists not in the satisfaction but in the ablation of desire."[40] This is crucial for Beckett and initiates his battle against desire—the anticipation of an end—which is marked, ironically, by the beginning of his fiction writing and, as we have seen, a more subtle form of continuance.

A point of agreement between Proust and Hume is their assessment of general mental activity in the face of passing events. For Hume, knowledge could only arise from consistent comparisons and was limited to them. Proust believed that perceiving individual analogies released the universal essence of individual things.[41] Beckett's moody attachment to humanity (over systems) is probably influenced by this theory. However, if free will represents a maverick element in any equation, then this universality is in constant jeopardy; making an occasion of every event.[42] Proust went on to assert that perception is mostly generated habitually, that is, in accordance with preconceptions concretized from past repetitions. The result, as Beckett puts it, is "a compromise effected between the individual and his environment," which is Habit. Hume himself labels causality a habit of mind. This habit turns on the comparison of past and present events. In fact, habit, according to Hume, is the vehicle through which memories of past experiences are schematized and then projected into the future in the form of anticipation. The stages from experience to inference are these: habit deploys past repetitions of various principles (such as association) to generate belief. Once the mind holds certain beliefs the subject has been constituted and a foundation provided for the reason to work on.[43] We have already observed, in his use of parallelism, the effect on Beckett's syntax when he turned away from progressive causality in favor of a succession of comparisons. In the following section, I aim to show that habit (which is usually treated negatively in the Proust/Beckett dialectic) is actually the crucial force that, however slightly, propels the Beckettian text forward. The double-headed nature of habit links the "poetic" self-referentiality or repetition, by which it is initially defined, to the advancement of the prose narrative. Habit bridges the poetic and the referential because it anticipates future actions through past repetitions. By this act of furtherance, habit is essential to the structure and syntax of the Beckettian prose poem.

The Late Trilogies

The treatment of memory is a central point of influence between Beckett and Proust. But more importantly for our purposes, it is the articulation of these memories by habit, as prescribed by Hume, which is instrumental in transforming Proust's tome to Beckett's minimalist trios: "Still," "Sounds," "Still 3," and *Company, Ill Seen Ill Said, Worstward Ho,* and much of the late prose.

For Proust, Habit and Memory are two modes of existence. Beckett glosses these as "the boredom of living" and "the suffering of being" respectively in his essay, *Proust.* In fact, Proust's Marcel actually blesses habit, at the opening of the first volume, as the principle that gradually makes bearable the traumatic and incessant changes of life—such as moving home. Zurbrugg criticizes Beckett's term "suffering," but Beckett's concept of life is entropic and therefore "suffering" refers more to an inevitable material loss.[44] Beckett's use of the term "suffering" is also probably associated with the "pleasure-pain" principle that characterizes the stimulus of the Romantic artistic perception. In addition, this mode of recollection that one suffers is divided again, by Proust, into voluntary and involuntary memory, neither of which is negative. Voluntary memory is a process of logical reasoning and is formalized like habit in its search for constant conjunctions and necessary connections. Involuntary memory, on the other hand, can only occur accidentally because it restores a moment that had been lost until something in the present reignites it by being analogous to it. Crucially, involuntary memory is not a process because it bypasses both habit and voluntary regressive logic, spontaneously filling the container of the present with a revivified past. The restorative function of memory compensates for the divisions created by time.

The "Still" Trilogy

In isolation, Proust's involuntary memory clearly relates to De Quincey's artistic vision and operates in a similar way by eschewing the multiplicity of contexts that otherwise connect two moments. The so-called "'Still' trilogy" was not written sequentially or published together. "Sounds" and "Still 3" were written in May and June 1973 but not published while "Still" was written in 1974 and appeared in the same year in an edition with etchings by William Hayter and again in 1975 this time included in the *Fizzles* collection, *For to End Yet Again*.[45] The protagonist(s) in all three texts are waiting in anticipation of stillness, a sound, a memory, respectively. The present space of the text is used to contain a segment of the past, a remembered sensation of stillness, for example. Such a process relies on the thesis of conscious experience being an unconnected series of events. "Still" is another example of Beckett's increasing concentration on detail to the exclusion of the larger narrative that would ordinarily surround it. Inactivity opens up the scenario to exacting descriptions of minimal movement. Actual immobility in the protagonist is a resistance to process and narrative plot—although even this character will "get up certain moods and go stand by western window" or put his head in his hand.

Expansion is also resisted by the style of the narrative. The referential function is restricted by the high degree of (poetic) internal correspondence. For example: "sitting quite still at valley window," "go stand by western window"; "sun low," "afterglow"; "quite still" (repeated) and so on.[46] Adam Piette has recently written on Beckett's prose rhymes, which he interprets as "miniature acts of memory." For Piette, recognizing textual correspondences presents us with short-term sound effects that imitate larger structures of long-term memory.[47] Deleuze interprets Hume's perspective on repetition as follows: "Repetition by itself does not constitute progression, nor does it form anything. The repetition of similar cases does not move us forward, since the only difference between the second case and the first is that the second comes after the first, without displaying a new idea."[48] However, Piette's memory act highlights the successive nature of repetition within a creative structure. He identifies succession with accumulation and claims that repetition *is* progressive. In other words, he finds that the phonetic repetition serves to maintain the ever-forward propulsion of the subject that the associative principle imparts: the repetition is recognized *as* repetition because its recurrence has been both identified and anticipated.[49] However, Piette does not identify the agent of this propulsion beyond an initial assumption concerning the inherence of teleology within poetic prose.[50] I would contend that the missing element in this analysis is habit. If, as Piette asserts, "Beckett's prose rhymes act as faint, intricate reminders of persisting memory-traces within the forgetful textual voice," the reason for their presence, however minimal, is something beyond memory. The survival of repetition within the "forgetful voice" belongs to the generative quality of habit as defined by Hume.[51]

The present introduces a new context that prevents perfect identification and frustrates replication. Absolute stillness, for example, is impossible for any form of life. As the other *Fizzles* testify, breath itself prevents it:

> But casually in this failing light impression dead still even the hands clearly trembling and the breast faint rise and fall. ("Still," *CSP*, 183)

> Breath has not left him though soundless still and exhaling scarce ruffles the dust. ("For to End Yet Again," *CSP*, 181)

> No but now, now, simply stay still, standing before a window, one hand on the wall, the other clutching your shirt, and see the sky, a long gaze, but no, gasps and spasms, a childhood sea, other skies, another body. ("Old Earth," *CSP*, 201)

In other words, "still" is always a pun, signifying "continuing" rather than stasis. Furtherance, or habit—projection based on the closed system of the given—always finally overrides memory and repetition in these works.

In "Sounds," the protagonist uses the stillness to catch any noise he can and to discover its source, periodically going outside with a torch. However, failing in this too, he returns to "head in hand as shown . . . no such thing as a sound."[52] "Still 3" evades expansion by skirting any action at all. The piece opens with the protagonist returning from a journey that he cannot recall and about to resume his old position and listen for sounds: "Whence when back no knowing where no telling where been how long it was. Back in the chair at the window before the window head in hand as shown dead still listening again in vain" ("Still 3").[53] Immediately the narrator realizes that the two opening sentences are not successive and the rest of the work describes the gap between them. In playing with the causal principle as a structure, Beckett is thus able to reverse the process.[54] Language itself is a habit with the potential of re-creating (by repetition that grows into belief), a lost situation through the imagination. Thus, habit is crucial to any creative act because it is instrumental to the mind's recognition of logical forms that fictions then counterfeit. As Bruno Clément says, "not only is memory an invention but invention is also a memory."[55]

Night, which is the setting for "Sounds," and which the man in "Still" was trying to perceive as an event, has become indistinguishable from day because it is now always dark. In this marginal pause, he imagines a succession of male and female expressionless faces. These faces appear "one by one never more at a time" accompanied by the simultaneous alternation between blackness and whiteness, an image that resembles a slide show: "Size as seen in the life at say arm's length sudden white black" ("Still 3," 157). The slide show differs from the cine-camera, video, or film in the same way that the episodic narrative, or a collection of prose poems, differs from the single extension of the novel. The physical space between frames obliges the reason to supply continuous logical connections. Similarly, the loss of prepositions and punctuation marks serve to invite a reasoning rather than a reading of the text, despite the fact that the result may still be more "atomistic" than associative. The slide show is a modern palimpsest.[56]

"As the Story Was Told"

A few weeks after "Still" was composed, Beckett wrote "As the Story Was Told" for a commemorative volume in honor of the late German poet and playwright, Günter Eich.[57] This work is usually described as an "occasional piece," which suggests that it exists on the peripheries if not actually outside the oeuvre itself. "As the Story Was Told" is a sinister piece. The narrator lies in a hut hearing of a man being tortured nearby, apparently under his orders. The established system has been overturned: here, the judge relies entirely on accounts that are given to him, both written and spoken, a theme that is picked up in *Company*. Memory is being redefined as the recall of past language or speech as opposed to an image or event. No plot is needed. A person lying on their back in the dark is sufficient for both logical and textual economy. The piece ends with one of Beckett's beautifully cadenced sentences, which add poignancy to the figure of the narrator/judge who is quite literally kept in the dark: "No, was the answer, after some little hesitation no, I did not know what the poor man was required to say, in order to be pardoned, but would have recognized it at once, yes, at a glance, if I had seen it" (*CSP*, 212).

Here, ignorance provides the most provocative implication of the missing context. The narrator does not know what the prisoner should say but, *seeing it written, he would recognize it*—that is, he would know it as a repetition of something past. The partial projection of something past into the present returns us to the image of the Romantic fragment and the absent whole. Here too, the fragmentary text seeks to coincide with its lost ideal, which is both itself and the whole of which it remains a part. Mostly, in Beckett's work, the search substitutes for this absent text in the same way that De Quincey's Oxford Visions replaced the visions themselves.

The principal contribution of this prose piece, "As the Story Was Told," is in its relationship to the "Still" trilogy. The fizzles offer kernels of potentially extended narratives that, however, remain unsaid and in a state of ideal ambiguity or of multiple contexts.[58] "Still" is no exception. However, "As the Story Was Told" is a concretion of "Still": the first is not presented as the meaning of the latter but one interpretation that is valid only as far as its own narrative extends. The description of the torture room reminds the narrator of the summerhouse where, as a child, he would sit still for hours. Also, the image of a figure, a narrator, an author, attempting to attain mental stillness by clutching the ends of his seat's armrests is imaginatively reread as a victim's position of resistance to torture (a theme that is reminiscent of *How It Is*).[59] It is also possible that the narrative of the "occasional piece" is read as the projection of the "Still" protagonist's imagination (we know he is daydreaming because he stares at objects until they "go" and the eyes are described as "unseeing"). The victim is both Eich and the text's own writer, who can never produce the ideal text that he himself continues to desire or project.[60]

Several details also appear in Beckett's final trilogy, *Company, Ill Seen Ill Said,* and *Worstward Ho*. For example, the narrator in "As the

Story Was Told" and the protagonist in *Company* are lying on their backs in the dark listening to the sound of a voice. The summerhouse from childhood, first mentioned in "Still," reappears in "As the Story Was Told" and *Company*. In fact, the summerhouse episode in *Company* is recounted in one of two sections that were published separately as *Heard in the Dark* (*I* and *II*), suggesting not only another "concretion" but also, by its title, a connection to the earlier piece, "Sounds."[61]

Company, Ill Seen Ill Said, Worstward Ho

Company, Ill Seen Ill Said, and *Worstward Ho* are longer works than any of the "Still" texts. As extended narratives divided into sections, they are arguably prose poetic, based on the successful decontextualization of their residual prose poems, *Heard in the Dark I* and *II* (from *Company*) and *One Evening,* which appears to belong to *Ill Seen Ill Said*.[62]

Company retains the immobility of the protagonist, who deduces his position from experiencing effects consistent with lying supine in the dark. In an attempt to repudiate his isolation, he also infers that the voice that he hears is addressing him—although occasionally he doubts this and "reasons ill" in a series of suppositions designed to fill time and reaffirm his beliefs. In order to support the variety of possibilities that any one proposition may invoke, the narrator is forced to suppose parallel universes in order to contain them all within causal processes. The chore of exploiting as many implications as possible of any one proposition creates activity in passing time, invokes separate selves for company and requires only minimal mental effort: "The lower the order of mental activity the better the company. Up to a point" (*Company*, 15). This may account for the fact that the narrators of "As the Story Was Told," *Company*, and the old lady in *Ill Seen Ill Said* lie on their backs in the dark. Potential circumstances are severely reduced by this lack of light and activity.

Much of the contextual matter in *Ill Seen Ill Said* is suppressed. An old woman literally appears and disappears only to reemerge elsewhere and the shape of the text is dictated by her presences although she seems to be oblivious of the watchful eye of the narrator. Her absence is represented by a gap dividing the brief paragraphs that describe her so that the fragmentary state of the work imitates the "ill seen ill said" incompleteness of the vision and its representation. Warnings such as "careful," "on," "gently," reveal an account being expressed before the habit of composition can set in and shape the text but they also highlight the necessity and danger of continuing. The gaps in the text may indicate an unrecovered wholeness but the implication remains that, if revealed, those gaps contain chaos. In fact, the content of one such gap is shown in the companion prose poem, *One Evening*.

One Evening, was published a year earlier but was not then included or adapted in the longer work although thematically compatible with it. This piece describes an old woman who, looking for flowers to put on a grave, stumbles against a man lying face down on the ground. It is an account by someone practicing the skill of narrative contiguity cautioning himself occasionally, "Not too fast." The piece falls into two halves, repeating the initial account from a different perspective. The halves are separated by the comment, "That seems to hang together," which is repeated near the beginning and again near the end. The second section expands on the first by moving away from a narration focusing on the man, to a position close to the old woman. Where the first half reads: "He was found lying on the ground. No one had missed him. No one was looking for him. An old woman found him. To put it vaguely. It happened so long ago. She was straying in search of wild flowers" (*CSP*, 209), the second rewrites this as: "It happened so long ago. Cooped indoors all day she comes out with the sun. She makes haste to gain the fields. Surprised to have seen no one on the way she strays feverishly in search of the wild flowers" (*CSP*, 210).

Noticeably, whereas the opening offers an account from an omniscient perspective, the association of ideas is lacking. The information that no one had missed him does not *necessarily* follow from the fact that he is lying on the ground and so on. Immediately in the second half, however, we are given "she comes out with the sun," a subjective association in terms of the analogy itself and its perceived relevance to the account. The structure of the latter reminds us of the Humean concern for an empirical foundation that the ethereal, omniscient narrator inevitably lacks.

Indeed, the piece is carefully composed, if not to the extreme of *Lessness*, in order to minimize context. In addition to the geometrically arranged repetitions, the second section highlights potential gaps in the first (for example, between sentences six and seven) and fills them as above. The syntax of the second half of the piece is as sententious as the first suggesting that its function is not to elucidate. In the same way, *One Evening* situates itself in the gap behind a few sentences in *Ill Seen Ill Said* : "It is evening. It will always be evening. When not night. She emerges at the fringe of the pastures and sets forward across them. Slowly with fluttering step as if wanting mass. Suddenly still and as suddenly on her way again."[63]

The *Ill Seen Ill Said* passage occurs in the evening and *One Evening*, when the sun comes out. Encouraged by superficial correspondences, we come up against enough contradictions and paradoxes for the pieces to maintain their separateness despite their interplay. *One Evening*, like "As the Story Was Told," is occasional in the sense that it offers a single reconstruction of the multifaceted whole, represented by *Ill Seen Ill Said* and "Still" respectively. They can be read as the concretion of context; using the information already given in the associated larger work as a restriction against their own logical expansion.

Beckett's attempts to minimize if not eliminate altogether the copiousness of context can be seen immediately in the actual reduction of his works to the dimensions of the prose poem. Yet his insistent rationality prevents him from being satisfied with the simple suppression of circumstance. Instead, context (which includes the object's ability to move and speak) must be logically reduced to zero: its absence must be a necessary effect.[64]

Worstward Ho opens by stating the problem. Given the now habitual impulse to narrate, the writer requires a form that reveals the next step in any given sequence. "On. Say on. Be said on. Somehow on. Till nohow on. Said nohow on."[65] Expression itself cannot generate a process of necessary connection, however clearly the object of the work is defined. However, the *sound* of searching for that ideal expression can, at least, invoke the intertextuality in which, for Beckett, that ideal is couched. There is a marked musicality in this kind of prose (above) which began in *How It Is*. Barbara Trieloff has described the sound as most like medieval antiphonal chants. Echoes of Hopkins are therefore unsurprising.[66] Unlike the harmonious orchestration of poetic prose, the literary musicality that Beckett practices is more akin to Hopkins's staccatoed "sprung rhythm."[67] Marcel's repeated observation that music may often be mistaken for an attack of neuralgia is appropriate here too.[68] Beckett's is a music that fragments as well as unites and is painful to experience. In trying to abstract the image from its circumstance in his late work, he aspires to a musicality that he first identified in his early essay. There he describes music as "the Idea itself," which is nevertheless distorted by the listener who insists "on incarnating the Idea in what he conceives to be an appropriate paradigm." Beckett moves on to recommend the comedy of repetition in the form of vaudeville (over, say opera) and refers also to the musical instruction, da capo, as a "beautiful convention." Here too is explained the whole problem of the tendency of literature to particularize even as it abstracts; the counterattack of "exhaustive enumeration," which we observe in the novels, and the redemptive beauty of repetition in the "da capo" musical device.

Clearly, we could, ourselves, get lost in our own calculation of the intertextual permutations that are possible in these late prose pieces. However, permutation must be the key here. Many commentators have argued for Beckett's work to be viewed as a single sequence.[69] This seems reasonable up to a point—especially as I have myself presented the oeuvre as a systematic textual foreshortening (based on a developing narrative of causality). Indeed, I would agree that there appears to be a discernable logic that places *Watt* before "Lessness" although both revolve around closed systems. In the end, however, I would propose a two-tiered approach. While there appears to be a comprehensive line of development in the compositional output, there is also, especially in the late, "modular" prose pieces, a consistent intertextuality.[70] Such interconnections counteract the tendency to sequentiality by frustrating any sense of primacy, returning instead to permutation on a larger scale than Molloy's stones.[71] Intertextuality is a factor of equality in this respect for the same reason that I discussed in Chapter 5 with reference to Wilde's imitation of biblical sources. The first utterance (chronologically) requires a subsequent repetition to identify it as repeatable at all, just as the latter needs a precedent model on which to base its copy.[72] However, the ultimate failure to locate the necessary connection (which would guarantee a causal relation) between two bodies means that the late prose pieces respond to each other as independent or, if related, only contingently so, rather like probability and exactly as their residual status dictates.[73] Juxtaposed, one text may be interpreted as the particular of an expressed ideal but always with a separate symbol behind its own image. Problems arise because the nature of both logic and prose is one of continuity while human reason actually desires comparison. Hume's thesis of the mind's tendency to repeat memory through habit and project it in the imagination into truth-like fictions is very useful in our attempts to seek a methodology behind Beckett's increasingly prose poetic texts. In addition, Beckett sees

Proust's occasional involuntary memory as the closest phenomenon to his ideal of the pure subject and he attempts to distill this experience from the context of the novel itself but is led continually into furtherance, difference, and fragmentation.[74] Circumstance cannot be eliminated entirely but Beckett's overt identification of context with intertextuality goes some way toward making both a shape for the text and a stillness that defies the fragmentation of time, at least *look* like a possibility.

In terms of prose poetry, the "necessary link" that Beckett first set out to analyze is abandoned by the 1960s for brief, fitful narratives that function as synecdoches to their implied whole.[75] At the same time, the explicit intertextuality (emphasized by the increasing density of cross references) allows these pieces to participate in the comparative behavior of the mind that isolates events in memory recall. Indeed, the individual prose pieces in *Fizzles* were ordered differently in each of the four editions published in the same year (Editions de Minuit, John Calder, Grove Press, Petersburg). This decadent "sampling" of texts that reordering produces is characteristic of the prose poem.[76] By working in such a minimalist environment, Beckett attempts to identify either the essence of the object or the nature of the mind that represents it. Until then, "brief murmurs only just almost never all known": the late prose is nearly decontextualized, almost free.[77]

7
The Prose Poem and the City

> Now and then I would go to the window, part the curtains and look out. But then I hastened back to the depths of the room, where the bed was. I felt ill at ease with all this air about me, lost before the confusion of innumerable prospects.
> —Samuel Beckett, *The Expelled*

It is a critical commonplace that the prose poem was historically more likely to emerge in France than in England. English writing permitted a free style that blended the "poetic" with prose without scandal (as evidenced in Sir Thomas Browne's *Religio Medici* and Thomas Traherne's *Centuries of Meditation*). On the other hand, French literature up to the eighteenth century comprised, as Molière's Monsieur Jourdain discovered, prose and verse only and the verse carried strict rules and regular meters.[1]

If the prose poem in England is the product of a displaced Romanticism, then the emergence of the genre in mid-nineteenth-century France can be ascribed to the peculiar development of Romanticism in that country also. The enormous impact made on Europe by the German Romantic movement had had surprisingly little effect at the time in France. As Sabin puts it, "by English standards, romantic sublimity arrived in French poetry late and left early."[2] However, it was not purely the rebellion of poetry against verse in France that allowed for the new genre but the actual need for a new vocabulary to deal with changing cosmography that was emerging with the industrial age: the growth of the city.

I

Paris and London

The composition of Baudelaire's prose poems was contemporaneous with the systematic demolition and reconstruction of Paris by

General Hausmann under Napoleon III: "Even as Baudelaire worked in Paris, the work of its modernization was going on alongside him and over his head and under his feet. He saw himself not only as a spectator, but as a participant and a protagonist in this ongoing work."[3] This rebuilding had two major effects on the city. Firstly, the new wide boulevards, despite being designed to aid traffic flow and prevent the erection of barricades, spawned a new café society. These groups of people appropriated this created space to present themselves and their affairs to the rest of Paris.[4] Secondly, with Paris as an inviting public arena came the rise of the *flâneur*: a solitary man wandering in the crowds who often published *physiologies*, sketches of other passersby similar to the English sixteenth and seventeenth centuries' subgenre of the "Character." Immediately, then, French literature adapted itself to the city through its architecture and the redefined human relations organized *by* that architecture.

This side of the Channel had experienced a similar process at the turn of the nineteenth century, albeit at a slower pace and in response to social rather than political or military demands: "residential and economic segregation proceeded simultaneously with the redevelopment of central London. All over the city broad new streets were cut both to speed traffic into and out of the new middle class suburbs and to improve the character of the immediate area."[5] Although Blake, Lamb, and De Quincey all lived in the city (Blake and Lamb would not live anywhere other than London), English literature in general seems to have followed Wordsworth's lead and shunned the metropolis as a corruption of Nature's archetype. In his Preface to the *Lyrical Ballads,* Wordsworth goes so far as to denounce the literature spawned from "the encreasing accumulation of men in cities" as "evil" in a splenetic attack.[6] Until "The Waste Land" the realist city rarely features as a subject in English poetry.[7]

The seventh book of Wordsworth's *Prelude*, "Residence in London," despite forming the longest section of the work, portrays the capital in terms relative to the country. The grotesques, the sideshows of "dissolute men / And shameless women" are judged against a rural archetype that is the original model corrupted by the city. Indeed, the whole city is an aberration of the innately divine natural landscape and it requires language to decipher itself to itself, a Babel whose walls are texts.[8] In view of its biblical origins, the city, for Wordsworth, is symbolic of man's fall from grace and it participates in the mimicry that is symptomatic of its divorce from the rural idyll of Eden.[9]

Writing in the City

In his dedication to Arsène Houssaye, Baudelaire explains how cities provided the inspiration for the ideal prose style of his prose poems (see Chapter 2, section III). He concludes: "The notion of such an obsessive ideal has its origins above all in our experience of the life of great cities, the confluence and interactions of the countless relationships with them" (*Poems in Prose*, 25).[10] Baudelaire is making a very specific connection between the concept of the city as the setting for literature and the creation of a new (prose poetic) sentence.[11] As most of the prose poems in the *Spleen de Paris* collection are narrated by a solitary man strolling through the city, recording the scenes that are taking place around him, the roads are quite literally narratives. They represent, moreover, the myriad possibilities of narrative directions that are suppressed in the novel in the face of a single plot line and exist in the prose poem in what I have termed "implied context." The *Spleen de Paris* do not arise from the single fact of the relationship between road and text but emerge from the intersection of the solitary walker (subjective, lyric) and the objective mass of the city as "other" (dialogic, novelistic).[12] Baudelaire's technique is to present a tableau at a symbolic crossroads where the itinerant narrator intercepts a moment existing for the "other." Architecture in the prose poems comes into focus when a particular character is selected and treated in a separate space that is also the space of the prose poem. As a compact, static, collected structure (a collection of rooms and the city as a collection of buildings), the architectural construct provides a fertile analogy to the prose poem both in terms of its role in the city and as a manipulator of public space.

Baudelaire moved poetry into the sphere of narrative, replacing mountain crags and chasms with public buildings, streets and a whole new semiotic system based on professional, as opposed to supernatural, design.[13] Poetry set in the city made society and its individuals into legitimate objects for observation and contemplation.[14] The earlier Romantic emphasis on self-absorbed autobiography was augmented into a presentation of the new relation of the self to others in which Baudelaire exhibited the influence of De Quincey on his work by employing the same technique of examining the self by its relation to its immediate social surroundings. Baudelaire's prose poem "A Lost Halo" is based on this very act of relinquishing the inherited, privileged role of poet-priest in favor of active participation in the city. The narrator-poet is crossing the road when his halo falls from his head into the mud of the road. He does not have the courage to risk an accident in retrieving it: "I told myself that it's an ill wind and so on—now I can go around incognito, do all sorts of disgraceful things and mix with the scum of society, the way ordinary people do. So here I am, exactly the same as yourself, as you can see" ("A Lost Halo," *Poems in Prose*, 183). The colloquialism of "it's an ill wind that blows no one any good" marks the point in the narrative at which the poet surrenders his privilege for an equal and barely identifiable place within the city codes.[15] It is observable that Wordsworth's concept of the poet as a man speaking to men, which, I have suggested, could not occur within the traditional verse structure or in the landscape of the solitary country walker—which he refused to abandon—finally does emerge here at the same moment that poetry moves into the city and breaks out of its metrical norm.[16] In fact, T. S. Eliot registers his own debt to Baudelaire in his discovery of a new urban poetic. Baudelaire's work on the city provided

> a precedent for the poetical possibilities, never developed by any poet writing in my own language, of the more sordid aspects of the modern metropolis. . . . From him . . . I learned that . . . the source of new poetry might be found in what had been regarded hitherto as the impossible, the sterile, the intractably unpoetic. That, in fact, the business of the poet was to make poetry out of the unexplored resources of the unpoetical; that the poet, in fact, was committed by his profession to turn the unpoetical into poetry.[17]

Burton Pike identifies these "word-cities" as direct effects of Baudelaire's new literature in "modern urban rhythms of space and time—fragmented, short-range, immediate."[18] The analogy that can be made between architecture and the literary text centers on the organization of space and time respectively. In his article on the subject, "Texte et Architecture" Philippe Hamon sets out three points of similarity between the two forms: both can be described as "un *objet hermétique*,"[19] contrasting the inside and the outside; "un *objet discriminateur*," separating similar spaces by distinguishable differences; and "un *objet hiérarchisé*," organizing those spaces into a fixed order.[20] I shall take each of the above categories and apply it to the prose poem both as it initially appeared in Baudelaire's *Le Spleen de Paris* and in subsequent texts by English writers who, I propose, have been influenced by these values in Symbolist prose poetry. In this way I aim to refine the aspects that I have attributed to the development of the genre in Britain.

II

Hermeticism

According to Milan Kundera, the evolution of the novel is directed by a steady contraction of the horizon—where the horizon denotes the limits of knowledge and experience. Don Quixote's world seems boundless, but by the time of Balzac that horizon had been obscured by the metaphoric structures of social institutions: the police, the law, the state. In other words, history, in the shape of Time, has entered the novel.[21] Later, for Emma Bovary, the horizon of the diurnal bears down insufferably on the individual. Finally, history is internalized in the mind so that even dreaming is no longer possible: in Kafka's *The Trial* K's very thoughts are dominated by the Court.

The contraction of visible perimeters is enacted typologically and by narrative form with the prose poem. The foreshortening of beginning and end occurred, as I have suggested, in response to the Romantic tendency to fragmentation, but it was also, in part, due to the changing landscape of Europe whose movement from a strict neoclassical order through a neogothic sharpening of angles to the total reorganization of space in the industrial age was itself a movement of diminution. The gradual encroachment of the horizon becomes a seemingly severe hermeticism in the case of the prose poem, which presents its four edges to the single glance. This is to ironize the succession of framed passages that constitute the novel. Mary Ann Caws describes the framed passage in a literary text as a unified coherence set against the flux of narrative flow to which it remains "other."[22] As heightened moments that condense the larger narrative structurally or thematically and thereby provide its groundplan, these episodes inhabit a *privileged space*. Inside an extended narrative, privileged space is recognized either by an epiphany, which momentarily transcends the causality of plot, or as a set piece, which attempts a simultaneous representation of various narrative threads by a symbolic tableau.[23] Collections of prose poems represent a series of these privileged spaces without the context to connect them. Instead, the boundaries of the individual prose poem that distinguish the binary form of present text and absent context correspond to the frame of that privileged area. The exclusive status of the prose poem is used to affirm the significance of a context that it had initially silenced: unordered narrative is here paradoxically given voice through its apparent suppression.[24]

Within the city walls space is at a premium, due not just to economic concerns but also to the whole concept of a marked distinction between private and public; where the private, enclosed, interior space is privileged over the public exterior. Therefore the prose poem's manipulation of time, its simultaneous concentration and augmentation of directional or logical narrative is paralleled by its manipulation of space. Space is used to define more clearly the place of privilege and to emphasize the preconditions of that privilege. As a usurper of privileged space, which it inhabits to reveal its shortcomings (the very need to choose between the interior and exterior, the expressed and the suppressed and its criteria for doing so), the prose poem is mostly concerned with the borders of that privileged area, presumably because "to frame in is also to frame out." The frame is foregrounded because it is the area common to both sides of the dialectic.[25]

The Refrain

As early as 1801, Chateaubriand was using the repetitions and refrains of popular ballads to "poeticize" or seal his prose by endowing it with a cyclical as opposed to rectilinear quality.[26] By the mid-nineteenth century, a trend developed in France for retaining only abstracts from larger prose works and, in the case of foreign works, of publishing only abridged translations (Macpherson's *Ossian* and Young's *Night Thoughts* were particularly popular in this form). Suzanne Bernard describes how writers reapplied the poetic technique of repetition in order to define the new boundaries, reintroducing the refrain to bind these texts. The prose poetry that grew out of this experiment retained the device, to define its own area.

Liberation from verse and the alexandrine in French soon required containment and the refrain of the ballad lent itself to this need. The refrain, appearing predominantly at the beginning and the end of a prose poem, creates a boundary line that produces the inside/outside distinction: text is distinguished from the blank page, from context, from the previous poem and the succeeding one. The refrain also affects the text itself. Repetition suggests a return or ceremonial circling. In the context of (suppressed) narrative(s), the refrain-encased text lifts a moment out of the general flux of passing moments, nullifying the time scale because the prose poem now exists outside sequentiality, freezing continuity into a tableau.

Adrien Remacle's prose poem "The City," which appears in *Pastels in Prose,* makes traditional use of the refrain to order the individual sections and provide closure. In this prose piece, the narrator walks along a road but represents all the stages of man and refuses to mingle with the immediate crowd. There is no description of the city he is in, only of the City of Dreams, which he perceives "beyond the suns of the day, above the vapours of the evening." The refrain "*And he sings of that City as he walks*" is actually repeated only once before it is developed through furtherance: *"And he sings of that City as he walks by the waters,"* and so on, corresponding to the changing landscape as he approaches the city. The prose poem ends on a refrain which is quite different but clearly related to the opening: "*And he sings of the City, and he falls asleep in dreams."* Such high profile closure in some prose poems seems to belie the anarchy generally attributed to the genre.

> The *prose poem*, though it may have thrown off the shackles of a caducous tradition of rhyme and meter, is formally a profoundly conservative and traditional structure in its ceremonials of entrance and exit; that no matter how radical its content, how relentless its striving for apparent or real incoherence, the prose poem undergoes the secondary elaboration of syntactical coherence and its boundaries most often are clearly defined and marked.[27]

In France, the refrain is traditionally associated with musicality and constraint whereas in Britain, it tends to the visual, even the pictorial, and is not one of containment but release. Closures, in *Pastels in Prose* and other French collections isolate the text but in doing so also highlight it and announce its perimeters. On the contrary, closure in British prose poetry is generally suspect; textual perimeters tend not to be indicated, allowing freer movement in and around the text (with the context, etc.) Yet, this may also be seen as shyness of textual assertion and symptomatic of an inability to define a form as *indefinite* as the British prose poem. We can never be sure if prose pieces by British writers, except those that clearly imitate or otherwise respond to the French genre, are really prose poems or not.

Privileged Place

Hermeticism created by the refrain at either a syntactic or thematic level is translated in prose poetry as privileged space. The prose poem narrative imitates its own blatant manipulation of time—appearing as a decontextualized episode—by enacting the physicality of architectonic structure, which is analogous in its role of manipulating space. By appropriating the attributes of a three dimensional object, the prose poem draws attention to the public space of the page contrasted with its own concentrated mass of text. Manipulating causal narrative (as a necessary corollary of decontextualization) is therefore exhibited in plastic terms of spatial presentation.

The glazier in Baudelaire's "The Useless Glazier" is plucked off the streets of Paris in order to participate in a scene that the narrator directs. Fired by an *imp of the perverse,* the narrator draws the glazier into his room only to push him out again and physically abuse him, smashing all his panes of glass. This irrational behavior represents the sudden, swift action that interrupts long periods of contemplation and solitude and the prose poem, which, in a similar way, breaks sporadically into the blank page with its unconditioned "meter," provides an appropriate medium.[28]

Of all the possible narratives represented by the crowds of people in the streets of Paris, only one is selected, to be muted and "poeticized" then thrown back among the indistinguishable throng. By contrast, in "Miss Lancet," the narrator is himself drawn off the street into a private room by a girl who turns out to be mad and who reverses their identities as director and actor. She assumes control of the situation in which she is convinced that he is a doctor (despite his protestations to the contrary) and behaves accordingly. The narrator therefore only writes the scene by default: he has been cast, muted, and directed just as he treats the glazier. The city therefore proves to be an egalitarian construct in whose streets the poet is devoid of any Romantic, Wordsworthian, priest-like status but becomes instead interchangeable with its citizens as both writer and actor: participant and protagonist as well as spectator. Meanwhile, with its protracted perimeters, the *room* establishes itself as privileged space within the heterogeneity of the city and, between its walls, brings order to the confusion of narratives by momentarily decontextualizing them.

Baudelaire's "The Twofold Room" brings together the idea of personal space and the technique of the refrain. However, he does not contrast personal space with public space but with itself as a form of active suppression and he extends the idea of the refrain from semantic similarities into the reiteration of a whole scene. The poem is divided into two: a description of an ideal room and of the "real" room before the writer.

The ideal room is still but barely visible: the Idol is present but does not speak and the material objects, revert to nature. The first scene culminates in the poet's realization that this vision exists outside time. In a moment that bears a striking resemblance to De Quincey's reading of the knocking on the door in *Macbeth,* this timeless, "crepuscular" scene is interrupted and brought to an end by a loud knock at the door. As De Quincey had shown, knocking signals the return of time passing which Baudelaire too, claims to be incompatible with writing, so that the arrival of the newspaper's errand boy to collect the next instalment is seen as the first step on the descent into the "hell" of reality. The second half of the prose poem illustrates these infernal associations by corresponding to a blasphemy of the first. "Elongated" and "languorous" furniture is reinscribed as "dusty and chipped"; the cascades of muslin that fell over the windows become the network of lines traced by the rain in the dust and the Idol, the "Queen of Dreams," is now identified as the phial of laudanum.

The appearance of the opium forms the climax also to the second scene and leads into a reassessment of time. On entering the scene, time introduces narrative by referring to feelings both anticipatory and reminiscent. In other words, the contemplation of time, as a kind of refrain, distinguishes the two rooms from each other and from what is outside the text. Ironically it also reveals that there are not two rooms at all but just one. The distortion of time creates a similar effect in designated space. At the moment when time is reintroduced and the actual room is concretized, a single contextual situation emerges—the narrator taking opium in his room as a form of escapism. In a similar way, Ernest Dowson's prose poem, "The Visit" describes the arrival of Death personified at the narrator's bed. Death enters at the opening of the prose poem, that is, coincidentally with the reader engaging with the text. It becomes apparent that the narrator, looking at his own body on the bed, has become death itself. Thus, in the confined space of the prose poem, the narrator embraces the agent of closure (Death, who is personified on entering his room/text) and equates this synthesis with the reader's own passing through the room of the prose poem.

Samuel Beckett includes a prose piece appropriately entitled "Closed Space" in his collection, *Fizzles*. His use of the refrain suggests a continuing French influence: "Closed place. All needed to be known for say is known. There is nothing but what is said. Beyond what is said there is nothing. What goes on in the arena is not said. Did it need to be known it would be. No interest. Not for imagining. Place consisting of an arena and a ditch. Between the two skirting the latter a track. Closed place" (*CSP*, 199).

Even here, where Beckett's prose poetry is at its most ostensibly self-referential, the irony forces us to glance beyond the textual perimeters drawn by the refrain. An engagement with "Closed Space" clearly requires us to reject the assurance of a "closed place," of isolated expression, but instead to complete the landscape in order to interpret the symbolic significance of the subject (the arena) itself. In other words, the blank space that "marks" the place of the implied context works more subtly to defeat any semblance of a privileged space in the black area of text that it surrounds.

Dowson had included five prose poems in his collection, *Decorations* (1899). They show a discernable French influence in the use of anecdote, tableau, and high profile closure. One of these, "The Princess of Dreams," is a parody of the gothic genre in which both the city and its enclosures (rooms, cloisters, caves) play a large part. The tale recounts a journey undertaken to rescue the "legendary" princess by a clumsy and misguided liberator who, "thought that she awaited him." The fairy tale inevitably breaks down. After killing evil magicians as well as his own friends, the liberator arrives but does not free the princess, thus losing his identity. Even his adventures become questionable when his sword is broken by the porter who is described as "slow of wit." The figure of the princess undergoes the harshest transformation: "But there are some who say that she had no wish to be freed . . . Some say, moreover, that her tower is not of ivory and that she is not even virtuous nor a princess" (Dowson, *Poetical Works*, 134).

Sandra Gilbert and Susan Gubar assert, in their survey of the female figure in gothic fiction, *The Madwoman in the Attic*, that anxiety of space is a characteristic of the "female gothic."[29] In addition, secrecy is linked to confinement and escape from patriarchal institutions and these elements are to be found in Dowson's poem, where the mysterious princess is confined both by the presumptions of the liberator and the physicality of the porter.[30] Dowson's poem is a deconstruction of privileged space as impenetrable and finally, perhaps, illusory.[31] The interpreter, or liberator, of any text is not only responsible for defining that text and its boundaries but is ultimately excluded from its original site by virtue of his attempts. If the writer himself is excluded from his composition then the text, here the prose poem, can only preface the work proper.

It may be said that in abandoning traditional prose and poetic spheres, the prose poem also relinquishes the right to privilege any one value over another. In appropriating a single narrative strand from the field of its possibilities, the prose poem must also somehow acknowledge those unrealized avenues in which one assumes that the elected scene had originally been imbedded. I have attempted an explanation of this in the treatment of context that, I suggested, is referred to in the more successful texts so that it is present by implication in the reading process. I will now develop this inside/outside distinction to which the prose poem characteristically tends but which it is unable to defend.

Windows

Together with the private room, the *window* is a frequent feature of the urban landscape. Like the open door, windows prevent the complete detachment of an enclosed space.[32] A transparent wall, the window paradoxically divides and conjoins two spaces: excludes and includes; separates and continues. The interior claims equality with that which it excludes. In other words, the binary system that the urban setting appears to establish is actually a trompe l'oeil. The privileged text of the prose poem concurs with its architectural analogue by registering a similar obfuscation of the room and street dialectic. When Baudelaire's, Kafka's, Tomlinson's, and Beckett's narrators find themselves in a room, they are often looking out of the window.[33] The device of the window provides a clear reference to the implied context of unselected narratives that continue to inform the contents of the poem. Consequently, the play between private and public spaces, facilitated by the motif, breaks down the apparently rigid polarization of what is internal or external to the text—a distinction arising from a strong sense of closure that the prose poem exhibits but resists.

Baudelaire participates in the play of the window in his prose poem, "Windows."[34] The narrator does not gaze out onto the streets of Paris, involving himself in the activities outside while remaining physically indoors, as we may expect. Instead, he looks from the street through a window into a private room.

> Across the heaving waves of roof-tops I can see a woman who looks middle-aged: her face is already wrinkled and furrowed; she is poor; she is always bending over something; she never leaves her home. With her face and dress and movements, with almost no clues at all I have reconstituted that woman's history, or rather her legend, and sometimes I tell it over to myself in tears.
> Had it been a poor old man I could just as easily have worked out the story of his life. (*Poems in Prose*, 155)

The general thrust of the prose poem appears to condone impressionism as opposed to realism as the more evocative and therefore the more artistic form of expression. In the same way, the piece itself never moves further than suggestion. The window is normally presented as a space on the vertical plane (in the wall) eschewing the inside/outside dictum of horizontal space (in which a person moves) thus enabling the occupant to participate in activity outside while remaining, himself, indoors. Yet here, the window is being promoted as an instrument of concealment rather than access. The window hides more than it reveals (for example, the person / thing to which the woman is in constant attendance); the location of the room in question is not described and even the gender of the protagonist in the observed scenario is not decided. The middle-aged woman that the narrator makes out in the shadows could equally be a poor old man. In fact, the poem seems to unwrite itself in its vagueness. "Windows" describes itself as a tableau while never actually achieving one (we can be sure of nothing the narrator describes in the poem since he openly admits that it is an example of personal fantasy).[35] If he can create a story for the old woman, we never read it and the prose poem remains as a prefatory text to that yet absent work.[36] The single narrative occasion is defeated by the feasibility of several contingent accounts that are offered by the strolling narrator who is himself couched in the plurality of the streets. From his unique perspective, the prose poem straddles and therefore eschews the interior/exterior distinction.

More recently, John Ash has engaged with Baudelaire's Parisian crowds. Although his work is strongly informed by Baudelaire's work and also that of other French Symbolists and Decadents, Ash offers a revised critique of the crowd dynamic. In his prose poem, "The Lecture," his narrator refuses to select an individual from the crowd, preferring to view the mass in its hydra-like contortions. What develops is a hallucinogenic representation of the interweaving lines of pedestrian trails. In holding on to the abstract, amorphous nature of the crowd, the narrator's mind appears equally undisciplined. In such a brief space, he manages to abort two separate lines of thought and include both the Romantics and the Decadents in his speech, for example. It is also notable that he prefers a rooftop to a window view.[37]

The window plays a significant role in Kafka's work and this has been documented in an article by John Grandin.[38] Grandin links the leitmotif with Kafka's own flirtation with falling from a window in suicide. Paradoxically, although defenestration inevitably leads to death in Kafka's stories, the window itself is a symbol of life outside the claustrophobic, private room (of self and privileged text). In the prose poem, "The Street Window," for example, the protagonist is drawn to the window as a means of escape from his own privileged position of isolation (decontextualization), toward the chaos of un-ordered narratives in the streets and critically, self-annihilation. The prose poem must be seen to react to the pressure of the implied context (the move toward the window) but cannot internalize it. To accommodate the implied context would result in the prose poem's collapse.

Skullshapes

Charles Tomlinson's interest in, and practice of, visual art, accounts for his precise descriptions of physical objects. In fact, most of the eight prose poems in *The Way of a World* (1969) read as if the poet were engaged on a still-life painting.[39] This emphasis on visual art engages with the French prose poetic tradition of illustration but does so in a manner that eliminates the duality of both visual and linguistic art in favor of a single work, which illustrates its own premises concerning their relation.[40] The scene that the poem "paints" exhibits the traits with which the language is concerned and, vice versa, the insistence on the poem as a description of a painting presents language as a necessary product of sight and of the particular vision of the artist.

"Tout Entouré de Mon Regard," which is apparently an artist's apologia, does provide an explicit statement concerning where Tomlinson's personal horizon lies. The prose poem describes the act of seeing and proposes that the only boundaries whose existence we can assert are the limits of one's own vision. This implies that all places are coextensive with the area accessed by the eye. Yet this visual sweep is only a half-circle with the subject at the center of its diameter. The remainder of the circle, "which balances in darkness behind you," is a separate room that one cannot access but that acts as a receptacle for the elements excluded in the artistic glance; collected *out of sight* in a suppressed mass of opposition.[41] The even balance is reflected in the form of the poem by the beginning of each paragraph (the numbers below refer to the paragraphs of the piece): where paragraphs 1 to 3 describe the view that one sees and 4 to 6 describe that which is behind and invisible.

1. "surrounded by your glance"
2. "To [the question]"
3. "It is [like a phalanx]"

4. "surrounded by your glance"
5. "To [see]"
6. "It is [infinity]"

("Tout Entouré de Mon Regard," 190)

The clear symmetry of the piece indicates a relationship between the two spaces which is less a binary opposition than a doubling—as in Baudelaire's two rooms.[42]

Like Baudelaire's "Le Thyrse," although "Tout Entouré" is not the first prose poem in the sequence, it establishes the terms on which the others base their logic. If the enclosed space of the poem's location—thematically and structurally—is bounded by the single glance and its double, then the eye becomes its converging point and, to follow the logic of "Tout Entouré," it is the skull itself, a "helmeted cavity"[43] that comes to symbolize that closed space, being the dividing line between the inside of the mind (where the image appears) and the sense sockets (eyes, but also ears, nose and mouth) as "windows" to the outside world.[44] Baudelaire's Parisian rooms have become skulls as the containers of artistic vision and hold a similar relationship to the chaotic context of the unmediated outside world: "If the skull is a memento mori, it is also a room, whose contained space is wordlessly resonant with the steps that might cross it, to command the vista out of its empty eyes" ("Oppositions," 189).

In Beckett's prose poem, "La Falaise," written for a Bram van Velde exhibition, the middle stretch of a cliff is observed through a window. The watching eye looks for human life but, failing this, imaginatively produces human remains from a shadow on the rock. Out of these remains, the eye glimpses one particular skull to contemplate before the text ends. Ocular vision is ultimately denied superiority over that of the "mind's eye," which replaces the window motif.[45] "For to End Yet Again" retraces the last moments of a body before it literally falls into ruin. In this prose piece, the skull is the "remains of the days" and "last place of all black void within without," it is almost a fossil, a ruin rendered impotent as it is no longer capable of separating inside from out. Here, the skull forms the final resistance to boundlessness, the last room from which we emerge into the anonymity of universality.

The horizon has clearly shrunk. It cannot be internalized but its room has become the dead animal's head where interior and exterior are reconciled, where "'over there' and 'in here' compound a truce neither signed" (Tomlinson, "Poem," 192), where the skull is "at once manifest surface and labyrinth of recesses," "lines of containment, lines of extension" ("Skullshapes," 191). According to Wesling, Tomlinson prefers lines of containment.[46] However, it is noticeable that Tomlinson takes more care with beginnings (of poems and of individual paragraphs) than endings. The control exercised on the prose is not imposed by any traditional method of closure, such as the refrain. He offers his own explanation in the very structured poem, "A Process," which is also the last in the group of prose poems: "The beginnings have to be invented . . . And the ends? The ends are windows" ("A Process," 193).

In other words, the ends must remerge Romantically with the outside world, which, beyond artistic mediation, is unknown, or at least not ordered into a comprehensible whole. Whatever happens, or would happen, is simply beyond the immediate glance which turns out to be itself just "a play of universals" ("Skullshapes"). The prose poetry of Charles Tomlinson, then, becomes a *relative* text, appearing on the page in its own space: in relation to other prose poems and to its own implied context—represented by its blank frame.

To conclude this discussion of hermeticism in the prose poem, we can now confirm that the process of obstructing the horizon by the architecture of the industrial age undergoes a further contraction (as Kundera proposes) in the twentieth century. The horizon extends no further than the mind of his protagonist. At this point, topography becomes an illusion. In the end, "there is an end, but no way; what we call the way is shilly-shallying."[47] The labyrinthine tunnels in Beckett's "He Is Barehead" ridicule and finally negate each other. Murphy's movements are prescribed by the walls that, ultimately, can only occasion difference rather than progress. The prose poetic text therefore, rather than designate place, participates in the contradiction of the city: "an effort to define space and arrest motion, it also partakes inevitably of the ceaseless activity of differing inherent in all forms of sign making."[48]

III

The Prose Poem as a Discriminative Object

If we can assert that the ostensibly sealed form of the prose poem is belied by its relation to context whether that context is visible on the page or implied by the text, then we can add that closure is undermined by the discriminative forces at work in the composition; that the prose poem is in a constant state of self-comparison. In denying a hermeticism to these works, we are proposing instead a differential foundation. Not simply a "tradition of subversion" as Margueritte Murphy has termed the genre, but a form that requires visible boundaries around which to play. The prose poem acts as a mirror, reflecting what is other, thereby undermining its own presence while never actually achieving an alternative identity: furtherance and the metonym prevent it. In the end, while we may not be able to confidently identify the nature of its form (be it prose, poetry, dialogical, subversion, and so on) all we can be sure about are the lines around which it settles but by which it refuses to be contained (the rod of the thyrsus, the walls of the room, the refrain, the beginning and the end).[49]

British Cities

Wordsworth's mistrust and dislike of London, which he describes in Book 7 of *The Prelude* stems partly from his inability to adapt his vision to cityscape.

> O, blank confusion, and a type not false
> Of what the mighty City is itself
> To all, except a straggler here and there—
> To the whole swarm of its inhabitants—
> An undistinguishable world to men,
> The slaves unrespited of low pursuits,
> Living amid the same perpetual flow
> Of trivial objects, melted and reduced

> To one identity by differences
> That have no law, no meaning and no end—
> Oppression under which even highest minds
> Must labour, whence the strongest are not free.
> *(The Prelude* 1805, VII: 696–707)

Wordsworth is unable to distinguish an order in city life such as that which is yielded by the countryside or the Alps. Divorced from natural archetypes, the city appears as a chaos which the poet can only support if he believes that the soul of Nature is present beneath the mortal urban mask. Thus, London can only be poeticized when it "doth like a garment wear / The beauty of the morning" (Wordsworth, *Composed Upon Westminster Bridge*). However, despite the confusion of a concentrated population, the city offers a fundamental distinction that Wordsworth misses. The distinction is that provided by the building, which identifies and separates private and public space into indoors and outdoors. Wordsworth's narrative of London is notable for taking place almost entirely out of doors. Landmarks such as St. Paul's and Westminster are simply names in a rapid list. His single account of an interior is that of his experience in a theater or circus, but he exposes it as a mimicry and distortion of nature. From Wordsworth's perspective, the theater effaces itself in time and place in order to simulate other scenes, locations, and epochs. He also describes a religious sermon delivered in an oratorical tour de force in which popular literature is mixed indiscriminately with the biblical. In other words, buildings, where they do appear in "Residence in London," are not places of defined containment but are prostituted to the general disorder of the city.

Wordsworth is not the only English writer to reject interiors.[50] The idea of space as an architectural concept was only gaining popularity in the late nineteenth century.[51] It was Ruskin, whose influence on the British public in matters of art and taste together with his connections in the literary world made him well-positioned to introduce this concept of space to the forum for discussion in England. However, his writings on architecture show that he has an eye primarily for painting. In *The Stones of Venice* and *The Seven Lamps of Architecture* as well as his various lectures, Ruskin approaches each church and palace as if it were hanging on a gallery wall. He concerns himself almost exclusively with façades without mentioning the experience of the interior.[52] Like Wordsworth, he appears to accept the building, the concrete and metaphoric symbol of civilization, only if it exhibits imitations of the natural landscape, which it obscures by its presence. Thus, the leaf-like design of the Gothic window is morally as well as artistically more correct, for Ruskin, than the squared, neoclassical equivalent and, appropriately, Gothic tracery is designed to resist (en)closure.[53]

Roy Fisher's City

By the mid-twentieth century, the city becomes the embodiment of the postmodern dilemma of difference. In 1961, Roy Fisher published *City*, a collection of appropriately mixed verse and prose poems based on landscapes of real and imagined cities.[54] Like Wordsworth and Ruskin, Fisher the *flâneur* wanders through the city but rarely, if ever, goes inside. However, the mid-twentieth-century English town, like Baudelaire's Paris, is undergoing a process of transformation during which the inside and the outside are confused. For Baudelaire, this was through a building program that made outdoors a more public place with boulevards, street lighting, and shopping arcades. For Fisher, it is the war, poor public funds, and the erosion of time that destroy the city making wastelands that are streets without buildings or buildings without occupants. Fisher may set his collection in the city, but it is one with an "invisible heart," with purposeless and decaying "lost streets" that are not worth lighting; in other words, it belies its own definition as organized society.

While he does not consider the interior aspect of the city, Wordsworth does describe the effect of alienation on the individual caused by the anonymity imposed by vast communities.[55] In the last prose piece in *City*, the narrator explains that, despite his desire to find a unified world around him, his imagination fragments his view, it "sweeps across what I see and suggests what I do not" so that he can make no distinction between the real and the imagined. In a similar dilemma to Beckett's and Tomlinson's artistic perception ("La Falaise," "Tout Entouré"), Fisher believes he must absent himself, but without a perceiving subject, the landscape is unfinished and in decay like the statue that is discovered in a garden, "almost as if it had been abandoned as too heavy by those who were trying to move it—either in or out" (*City*, 28).[56] Baudelaire's attitude to the city is also ambiguous. While embracing a new status of anonymity and as actor rather than director, many of the prose poems in *Le Spleen de Paris* center on the paradox of solitude in the city and many do not specifically take place there at all. Meanwhile, those that *are* set in the city express the "regret of being in Paris, the desire to be elsewhere, the seeping melancholy of Parisian life."[57] Near the end of the collection, the soul of the poet cries out to be—"Anywhere!—Anywhere, so long as it's outside this world!" ("Anywhere Out of the World," *Poems in Prose*, 193). In other words, the city represents a fatal attraction to the poet making it analogous to femininity and desire perpetually postponing the promise of its streets: the fusion of subject and object, self and other, prose and poetry.[58]

Although of all British poets he comes nearest to Baudelaire's *flâneur* by allowing the randomness of innumerable streets to provide a collage-like content and in his splenetic tone, Fisher seems to have no interest in people. Where Baudelaire juxtaposed interiors and exteriors, the *flâneur* with the crowd, Fisher uses demolished buildings and abandoned tenements as traces of his own leveling treatment. His streets transform individuals into "a composite monster" and, like the buildings themselves, their presence is known only by the fact of their absence: if they are mentioned at all it is to say that they have just left: "I am not able to imagine the activity that must once have been here. I can see no ghosts of men and women, only the gigantic ghost of stone" (*City*, 21). People are generally identified as couples and families who inhabit the impenetrable interiors. On the other hand, these people are ignorant of "the manifold airs that blow through the streets" (*City*, 26). There is a tone of bitterness and jealousy in the *flâneur*'s response to the city's residents: "She goes off past the Masonic Temple with a young man. . . . Just for a moment, as it happens, there is no one else in the street at all. Their significance escapes rapidly like a scent" (*City*, 22). It is as if the couple have ruined his picture, encroaching, as narratives, on a tableau.[59] While much of the dynamics of these prose poems arise from this peculiar antagonism between interior and exterior, the discrepancy reveals a larger concern. Fisher has responded to the crisis in modern urban development (disrepair, loneliness, violence) but he continues to seek a Wordsworthian landscape of great stillness. He registers relief in the idea that extreme architectural ruin leads to rural rebirth: "There is not a whole brick, a foundation to stumble across, a drainpipe, a smashed fowlhouse; the entire place has been razed flat, dug over, and smoothed down again. The bald curve of the hillside shows quite clearly here" (*City*, 14).

We may conclude that however much the prose poem is marginalized (to the status of a preface, footnote, etc.) or deconstructed, it is always discriminated from its context by the framing device of its blank frame. However, the dichotomous structures involved, (inside/outside, prose/poetry, and so on) are subject to collapse, a fact which is illustrated by the potent images of the ruined city and fragmentary prose poem respectively. The images of the shifting city and the prose poem use the partly vanished border to evoke a restless content that is unable to settle within defined areas. In addition, the bordering space of the prose poem is itself an active element in this genre but its twin functions of containing suppressed narrative and of separating one poem from another actually frustrate a confident identification of a prose poetic text based on a perceived hermeticism and self-discrimination. The blank frame is therefore independent of the work and a part of it in the same way that the prose poem is related to the Absent Work that it prefaces in an infinitely tessellated system. The frame is a precondition to presentation but being itself a contradictory preface, it blurs the very edges it surrounds. Derrida shows that the line of the border that discriminates two areas is itself subject to division. As he puts it, the "internal edges of a passe-partout are often beveled."[60]

IV

The Prose Poem as a Hierarchical Object

A principal consequence of the consideration of space in the development of an aesthetic for the prose poem is that the genre adheres to a visual arrangement, which means that it can only be adequately examined as a collection. This cooperation of literal and metaphorical space is one of the most original aspects of the prose poem: it was a factor in its emergence in France in the nineteenth century and continues to inform modern compositions. Philippe Hamon writes that the architectural object can be considered primarily by literature as "a system of constraints defining enclosures, of organizations comprising principal and dependent bodies, of the text and pre-texts, of levels and landings."[61] Hamon refers in this passage specifically to a hierarchy of containment. However, hierarchy is broken down with the relocation of the poet (from his Romantic ruralism) to the heart of the city throng: "Multitude and solitude are equal and interchangeable terms for the active and productive poet" ("Crowds," *Poems in Prose*, 59). However, to be inside the building/text is also to be inside the city/ the collection that its narrator, Baudelaire and Fisher's *flâneur*, is often seen attempting or wishing to escape, as if the desired, privileged interior has become a cage or prison.[62] It is noticeable in Fisher's *City* that many of his prose descriptions of urban areas are situated at or evoke the edge of the town. At one point, the narrator does say "I cannot enter that countryside; nor can I escape it" (*City*, 29) as if he is unable to access that landscape but is constantly reminded of it in his exile.[63]

Manchester, for John Ash, acts as a model that he accesses remotely, through memory. Yet the model is not stable because the city is characterized as a set of images referring to other places and other narratives. In "Early views of Manchester and Paris: Third view" (from *The Goodbyes*, 1982), we are never sure which city we are seeing: perhaps both, possibly neither. These places, in turn, are "*like* film sets" (emphasis added). In other words they resemble, or are read in terms of, fictional re-creations. The film set is given prior authority for the source of these collective façades in Ash's phraseology. As part of this masking process, the architecture refers back to the past, real or imagined, and in other parts, divests itself for refashioning (that is, renovation) in the face of (the narrator's) principled opposition.

Such spontaneous opposition to any new building implies a perceived severence with the established set of semiotics that are culturally disseminated through media like the cinema. Yet, these superficial reflections playing off the solid stone and brick are affected by the condition of the memory that evokes it. Ash examines these motives of memory and its antagonism to change. "The Big House" (also from *The Goodbyes*) is a prose poem that describes a derelict house beside a felled tree. The piece speaks of loss (that of personal place and the past), through the decaying concretions of reality. In the second paragraph, this familiar feeling of fond memory or nostalgia is challenged: "The sentiment is questionable: regret for a vanished order which, if it still existed, we'd dream of destroying like any nation of the colonised."[64] This backward glance of regret and nostalgia is countered by subconscious motives and reference to the national psyche. The personal past with its lyrical associations is rejected here and revealed to be as much informed by shared culture as the places we have built under the illusion of distinct identity.

Alan Halsey's prose poem sequence, *The Art of Memory in Hay-on-Wye*, looks more at the effect of memory over time and finds that local anecdote moves into the collective memory, then into local history and eventually manifests in a published account (Halsey's text). Both Ash's and Halsey's places are captured in a state of flux, both visually and through time. The city, or its equivalent, is reconstructed before its ruin is reenacted: a destruction that is mediated through the questionable motives of memory. These poets have used the city (or town), the characteristic, if not almost "traditional" theme of the prose poem and used it, as a relic, to confront us with the complex psychology involved in reminiscence and alert us to the harsher truth concerning our nostalgia for the ruined places of our past.

The Prose Poem Collection

Having contained and distinguished various episodes, prose narratives traditionally order them into logical sequence and proportion (subplots to main plot, etc.). The prose poem, however, generally appears in the form of a collection either exclusively—*Le Spleen de Paris, Mercian Hymns, The Cut Pages*—or together with verse poems or illustrations, for example, Fisher's *City* and Beckett's *Fizzles*, respectively. Finally, the anthology provides another format for the genre: Stuart Merrill's *Pastels in Prose*, Michael Benedikt's *The Prose Poem: An International Anthology*, Dennis Keene's *The Modern Japanese Prose Poem*, G. H. Godbert's *Anywhere Out of the World*. More recently, Loydell and Miller, *A Curious Architecture*, and Friebert and Young, *Models of the Universe*. This characteristic form of presentation proves to be a correlative to thwarted narrative because redefined textual boundaries represent a challenge to inherited reading norms. Baudelaire immediately raises the issue of the prose poem collection in his dedication to Arsène Houssaye:

> I am sending you a modest work of mine, of which nobody can say without injustice that it has neither beginning nor end, as everything in it is both head and tail, one or the other or both at once, each way. I must ask you to appreciate the admirable convenience of such an arrangement for all concerned—for you and me and the reader. We may break off or skip wherever we wish—I, my revery, you, the manuscript, and the reader his perusal; for I have not strung the latter's wayward will to the endless thread of some unnecessary plot. Take out the vertebra and the two halves of my tortuous fantasy will join together again quite easily. Slice it into any number of chunks and you will find that each has its independent existence. (*Poems in Prose*, 25)[65]

The dedication serves to challenge the single order of the published edition, the nature of the relationship between the prose poems and the idea of the collection as a static unit. Barbara Johnson argues that if the work is decapitated (being alternatively head and tail) then hierarchy is replaced by *différence*. The dedication and preface lose their privileged positions in the collection (at its head) and become interchangeable with the prose poems themselves—made possible by their similar dimensions.[66] In fact, reordering the collection is actively encouraged by Baudelaire and his successors: Baudelaire urges us to chop it into numerous of fragments, that is, to break it up even before one has begun to read them as they stand; Beckett's prose pieces repeat details in companion pieces, sustaining both linear and modular readings; Geoffrey Hill uses recurring titles to reject any sense of a poem's fixed place; Roy Fisher abandons titles altogether so that the pieces float freely over the pages.

Baudelaire's emphasis is not so much on the "established order" being broken down as on the felicitous results of its regrouping. The main advantage of reordering the collection, then, centers on the effect produced by the newly evolved juxtapositions. The analogy, in his dedication, of the serpent (all head and tail) highlights this aspect where the prose poem itself does not undergo a change but the gaps between the poems alter their significance and reflect that change on the collection as a whole.[67]

Encouraging a randomly selected reading also prevents the collection being mistaken for a single piece with its concomitant line of development. The mistake is a tempting one to make. Michel Butor offers one such interpretation: "Baudelaire says . . . that he 'does not tie the recalcitrant will of his reader to the interminable thread of a superfluous plot.' This as much as states that there is a novel in his book, but one in which he has taken out anything that was not immediately poetic."[68] The implication here is that Baudelaire had written an entire novel and then removed any pedestrian narrative leaving him with what is in effect, a series of epiphanies. The narrative whole, it is claimed, is subsequently lost amid the emergence of previously suppressed possibilities now provided by the reader's personal interpretation of the blank spaces. For Butor, *Le Spleen de Paris* is "un roman inconnu," an unknown novel, of which the poems are extracts.[69] Yet an attempted reconstruction of this "lost novel" would be patently absurd.[70] One is immediately struck by the sheer heterogeneity of the fifty prose pieces and there is nothing to guarantee even the single identity of their narrators.[71]

The status of the poetic collection is generally an ambiguous one. Defined as a single work, it problematizes the role of the single piece within the larger one and the problem persists with the collection of poems in prose: Is *Mercian Hymns* a prose poem? If so, what does that make "The Naming of Offa?" On the other hand, if we regard the individual piece as the prose poem, and the sum of those pieces as a collection then we are implying that the relationship of the prose poems to one another is arbitrary, which may be true for *Le Spleen de Paris*, but is untrue for *Mercian Hymns*. We would also be reiterating the "mistake" of confining the fragment to the hedgehog analogy, which ignores the rhythmical dynamics of the steady pulse of short texts.[72]

Baudelaire's prose poems first began to appear as *feuilletons* in the Parisian press. The *feuilleton* (literally, a "series") was a short piece usually written by an outsider in a reflective tone that appeared next to the editorial and was therefore one of the first pieces in the newspaper to be read.[73] In other words, the prose poems originally participated in the collage aspect of the newspaper, representing a textual reflection of the heterogeneity of the city. The collage, more like an anthology than a collection, is a potentially infinite structure. The various texts of which it is comprised abandon their own immediate contextual possibilities in order to participate in a new whole. However, although an anthology comes into being and is defined by the collection of texts that, paradoxically, lack both interconnection and a coherence to a larger form, its collage is not defined by a new pattern that its disparate parts may create, but the components replace any anticipated teleological design. Having now recognized the prose poem as an exposé of the perimeters of public space, we may assume that constant movement within the prose poetic collection proves necessary for a genre that is dedicated to the demystification of its own privilege.

Meanwhile, mid-nineteenth-century England saw the rise of what has been termed the "structured collection." In this form of presentation, the titled work comprised a number of separate pieces whose relation to one another and to the whole, although tending to fall into specific groups (generic, thematic and so on), was unstated and left up to the reader.[74] Of the structured collection, John Woolford estimates that "it would not be too much to say that the 1850s saw it emerge into something like cultural predominance."[75] Yet even the availability of this appropriate and popular form together with the example of Merrill's *Pastels in Prose* (an anthology that contained some specially written sequences) did not translate into the emergence of a prose poetry collection in England at that time: Wilde reserved his prose poems for table-talk while Dowson's were collected together at the back of his book of verse, *Decorations*.

Clearly, insisting on permutation in the prose poetic genre affects the architectural analogy. The variable collection provides a new way to explore the manipulation of public space. Like the new shopping arcades in Paris, textual exteriors are falsified and contained beneath a single roof. Hamon manages to reconcile the "pure presence" of the building with the substitutive play around a lost origin that occurs in a sign-based system such as language. He points out that the building also has an amnesiac quality by which it allows itself to be used for functions other than those inscribed in its original plan. Even in the case of churches, the same building is often converted by a series of different denominations throughout its history.[76] In other words, the relationship among texts in a collection or anthology continued to be supported by the architectural analogy. The landmarks of the city participate in a similar fluctuation.

Twentieth-century British prose poems continue to be presented predominantly as a collection—although not always one exclusively of prose poetry. T. S. Eliot slipped "Hysteria" into the Prufrock collection; Roy Fisher's *City* is a mixture of verse and prose as is Charles Tomlinson's "The Near and the Far" in *The Flood* and his sequence of eight prose poems in the otherwise verse poems in *The Way of a World*. In fact, Jonathan Monroe has registered concern that this liberal inclusion of prose within the more familiar verse collections may prove fatal to the prose poetic genre itself, costing it "much of its autonomy and polemical force even as it enjoys a newfound respectability."[77]

To conclude, the ideal prose poem is not hermetic, despite its appearance, because it relies on the dialogue between itself and its context (the exiled reference). Devices such as the refrain do not necessarily implement closure but act as parallelistic furtherance. The prose poem is discriminative also because of the relationship to context. The genre attacks the idea of privileged as opposed to public space by focusing on and blurring its own boundaries, which appear to support such a system.[78] However, appearance is important in any trompe l'oeil and the prose poem is no exception. Individual pieces require well-defined borders in order to question the privilege that they confer on the text. On one hand, physical and textual boundaries are necessary in the creation of sense-making systems, but, on the other, they carry the risk of restricting the very linguistic and physical movements that they admit. The prose poem responds to the problem of its own place in the public arena by challenging the static connotations of "place." The genre highlights its restlessness, which is due to the dynamic nature of its context. Splitting its context between that proper to the content and that created by the sum of other pieces gathered under the same roof, the prose poem proves to be not hierarchical but collective. The genre ultimately finds its own significance in its sustained oscillation between the relationship of a fixed self to a relative other and of combined surface play within a reorderable collection.

Notes

Introduction

1. Jonathan Monroe, *A Poverty of Objects: The Prose Poem and the Politics of Genre* (Ithaca and London: Cornell University Press, 1987).

2. Margueritte Murphy, *A Tradition of Subversion: The Prose Poem in English from Wilde to Ashbery* (Amherst: University of Massachusetts Press, 1992).

3. Stamos Metzidakis, *Repetition and Semiotics: Interpreting Prose Poems* (Birmingham, Ala.: Summa Publications, 1986). Metzidakis records his debt to Riffaterre's description of the prose poem as a work generated by the reader's perception of an intertextual matrix that replaces the standard frame of verse. See Michael Riffaterre, *Semiotics of Poetry* (Bloomington and London: Indiana University Press, 1978), 117–24.

4. Terdiman supplements the notion of time and process to Saussure's basic model in order to give voice to the external, the "text's environment." *Discourse/Counter-Discourse: The Theory and Practice of Symbolic Resistance in Nineteenth-Century France* (Ithaca and London: Cornell University Press, 1985), 17–29.

5. Murphy, *Tradition of Subversion*, 6.

6. Stephen Fredman, *Poet's Prose: The Crisis of American Verse*, 2nd ed. (Cambridge: Cambridge University Press, 1990), 6.

7. Thomas O'Beebee, *The Ideology of Genre: A Comparative Study of Generic Instability* (Philadelphia: Pennsylvania State University Press, 1994), 125.

8. Ibid., 130.

9. Dennis Keene, ed. and trans., *The Modern Japanese Prose Poem* (Princeton: Princeton University Press, 1980), 18.

10. John Simon, *The Prose Poem as a Genre in Nineteenth-Century European Literature* (London and New York: Garland, 1987), 699. I use the term "prose poetic" advisedly. Hill and Beckett do not give their work the title of prose poems.

11. In 1893, Wilde used the term 'prose poem' to describe his "obscene" letter to Lord Alfred Douglas. Wilde first used the term in reply to his blackmailers and continued to defend the epithet during all three trials. However, his attempt to sonnetize the letter was decried as tantamount to sanitizing it. Throughout the course of these trials, the prose poem came to be equated, in the mind of the reading public, with at least immodesty and at most French decadence and sexual depravity. The view was articulated by the Solicitor-General in his closing speech at the third trial at which Wilde was convicted: "It has been attempted to show that this was a

prose poem, a sonnet, a lovely thing which I suppose we are too low to appreciate. Gentlemen, let us thank God, if it is so, that we do not appreciate things of this sort save at their proper value, and that is somewhat lower than the beasts." H. Montgomery Hyde, *The Trials of Oscar Wilde* (London: William Hodge, 1949), 326. The prose poem (which was, in fact, a fake—it was a letter), was thrust to center stage but again proved to be the site of political and artistic struggle and was censored from the English literary canon before it could be properly introduced.

12. MacLeod's brief prose pieces are heavily influenced by Macpherson's Ossian poems and Pierre Louÿs's *Chansons de Bilitis*; Geoffrey Hill in interview with John Haffenden, *Quarto* 15 (March 1981): 21. (Simon, in fact, names the 'verset' as the French term for the separate parts into which the prose poem was divisible. [Simon, *Prose Poem as a Genre*, iii]); Letter to Beckett's American publisher, quoted in Peter Gidal, *Understanding Beckett: A Study of Monologue and Gesture in the Works of Samuel Beckett* (London: Macmillan, 1986), 256–57.

13. Christopher North, "Winter Rhapsodies," *Blackwood's Magazine* 29, no. 177, February 1831 (II): 282.

14. George Barker, "The Jubjub Bird or Some Remarks on the Prose Poem," in *The Jubjub Bird or Some Remarks on the Prose Poem and a Little Honouring of Lionel Johnson* (Warwick: Greville Press, 1985), 1.

15. David Gascoyne, *Collected Poems, 1988* (Oxford: Oxford University Press, 1988), xvi.

16. In her Preface to *The Prose Poem in France: Theory and Practice*, eds. Mary Ann Caws and Hermine Riffaterre (New York: Columbia University Press, 1983), Caws presents this collection of essays as a response to the perceived impasse produced by Bernard's single work, "It may well be that the topic calls for multiple approaches" (vii). The concept of definition in the prose poem is itself problematic. For example, Monroe sets out to identify the genre's paradigmatic functions. Murphy also offers instead "a model for reading prose poems" (*Tradition of Subversion*, 2). Metzidakis does ultimately supply a formula that, while not mentioned by Murphy in her thesis of subversion, is clearly based on a similar concept of the genre: "I shall define it [the prose poem] as any short text which, by dint of transgressing the canons of accepted literary discourses, borders on a non-literary or 'para-literary' discourse" (Metzidakis, *Repetition and Semiotics*, 125).

17. The only British-based anthology currently available in the United Kingdom is *A Curious Architecture*, eds. Rupert Loydell and David Miller (Stride, 1996). However, in his introduction, Loydell states that the two editors had different ideas on the exact, identifiable nature of the prose poem and he presents the collection as personal selections (contributors are British and American). A more historically oriented anthology, *Freedom to Breathe: Modern Prose Poems from Baudelaire to Pinter,* edited by Geoffrey Godbert, is forthcoming from Stride in 2002.

18. See Yves Vadé, *Le poème en prose et ses territoires* (Paris: Éditions Belin, 1996), 9.

19. Almost immediately after De Quincey's work had been collected, publishers and critics alike have recognised a tendency in his writing to the independent prose piece. From 1866, excerpts from his work began to appear under titles such as 'Detached Gems' and *Lyrics in Prose*. In 1900 J. H. Fowler makes the connection specific in his introduction to *Essays from De Quincey* by claiming that the author's "impassioned prose" is synonymous with prose poetry.

20. Donald Wesling, *The New Poetries: Poetic Form Since Coleridge and Wordsworth* (Lewisburg: Bucknell University Press, 1985), 172.

21. Johnson's deconstruction of the prose poem relies ultimately on a reading in which the genre is founded on a principle of displacement and difference through its accidental origination. See Barbara Johnson, *Défigurations du langage poétique: la seconde révolution baudelairienne* (Paris and Montreal: Flammarion, 1979), 19.
22. Vadés, *Le poème en prose et ses territoires*, 11–16.
23. Tzvetan Todorov, *Genres in Discourse*, trans. Catherine Porter (Cambridge: Cambridge University Press, 1990), 60–61. Todorov's comments are directed at flaws in Bernard's argument but continue to apply to more recent works. Todorov himself regards brevity as poetic and the poetic element in a prose poem as thematic, that is, differing in each text.
24. Reviewer of *English Lyrics*, an anthology, in *Spectator* (January 1898).
25. Fredman, *Poet's prose*, 5. See also LeRoy C. Breunig, "Why France?" *The Prose Poem in France*, 12.
26. We may already have missed this debate altogether. Monroe muses on the possibility that the genre has reached its logical conclusion, aided by the efforts of its own practitioners and commentators: "the prose poem today is at a crossroads of its history, arrived at by what we may call a 'crisis of respectability'" (Monroe, *Poverty of Objects*, 332).
27. Kenneth Cox, "Roy Fisher," *Agenda* 19 (1991): 38.

Chapter 1. The Prose Poem and the Romantic Fragment

1. *Republic,* trans. Paul Shorey, in *The Collected Dialogues of Plato*, eds. Edith Hamilton and Huntington Cairns, Bollingen Series LXXI (Princeton: Princeton University Press, 1989), 10: 822–23.
2. Ibid., 823.
3. Plotinus, *The Enneads*, trans. Stephen MacKenna (London: Faber & Faber, 1962), 422.
4. See Blanchot on the effect of the literary manifesto during the French Revolution: "In short, literature announces that it is taking power." Maurice Blanchot, "The Athenaeum," trans. D. Esch and I. Balfour, *Studies in Romanticism* 22 (1983): 167.
5. Werner S. Pluhar, introduction to Immanuel Kant, *Critique of Judgment* (Indianapolis: Hackett, 1987), xxxiii n.10. Pluhar differentiates the two world theory of Leibniz and Wolff and that of Kant. For the former two philosophers, the phenomenal world is the world in itself as apprehended through the distortion of experience. According to Kant, this essential world remains blindly inaccessible and therefore unrelated to the sensory world.
6. Immanuel Kant, *Critique of Pure Reason*, trans. J. M. D. Meiklejohn from 2nd ed. 1787, ed. A. D. Lindsay (London: J. M. Dent, 1991). Hereafter, *CPR*.
7. Cf. Kathleen Wheeler, *German Aesthetic and Literary Criticism* (Cambridge: Cambridge University Press, 1984), 18: "The capacity for self-consciousness and self-criticism is connected with the ability to be so detached as to be able to enjoy a parody of oneself because of the limitations which have not yet been overcome."
8. Cf. P. B. Shelley, *A Defence of Poetry*. In the highest examples of poetry, expression "is probably a feeble shadow of the original conceptions of the poet." *Shelley's Prose*, ed. David Lee Clark (Albuquerque: University of New Mexico Press,

1954), 294. A century later, Benedetto Croce also makes the distinction between the art work as intuition and as material fact. The creation of a work of art is an intensely private, even religious, experience "when we have achieved the word within us . . . there is no need for anything else." Putting pen to paper is a practical as opposed to an aesthetic fact, "the work of art (the aesthetic work) is always *internal*; and what is called *external* is no longer a work of art." *Aesthetic,* trans., Douglas Ainslie, quoted in Raman Selden ed., *The Theory of Criticism* (London: Longman 1989), 255.

9. Rodolphe Gasché, foreword to Friedrich Schlegel, *Philosophical Fragments,* trans. P. Firchow (Minneapolis: University of Minnesota, 1991), xx.

10. Paul de Man, "The Rhetoric of Temporality," in *Blindness and Insight,* 2nd ed. rev (London: Methuen, 1983), 210–11.

11. Gasché, foreword to Schlegel, *Philosophical Fragments,* xiii.

12. Kant, *CPR,* 82: "Totality is nothing else but Plurality contemplated as Unity."

13. Schlegel, *Philosophical Fragments,* 31–32; ibid. 45.

14. Monroe, *Poverty of Objects,* 70.

15. Philippe Lacoue-Labarthe and Jean-Luc Nancy, *The Literary Absolute,* trans. Philip Barnard and Cheryl Lester (Albany: State University of New York Press, 1988), 44.

16. Blanchot, "The Athenaeum," 172.

17. In fact, German literature had already seen the prose poems of Gessner's *Idylls,* which appeared in 1756. They contained characters from ancient mythology, borrowed a simple and repetitious style from the Bible and were structured as brief prose pieces but were nevertheless rejected by the Romantics in a cultural backlash following a period of immense popularity for Gessner.

18. Schlegel, *Philosophical Fragments,* 21.

19. The irony, again, plays on the boundary of limits and includes the subject / object conundrum that describes the creation theory where the author is both transcendent and also immanent in the traces of himself which he leaves in his work.

20. Monroe, *Poverty of Objects,* 59–60. Monroe's list of attributes common to the German theoretical fragment and Baudelaire's prose poems contain many qualifications and is occasionally quite vague. For example, "a relative lack of formally distinctive features" is self-defeating in a comparative assessment and "the quality of sudden insight" could equally apply to several other genres.

21. Lacoue-Labarthe and Nancy, *Literary Absolute,* 57. The Romanticism of De Quincey and Samuel Beckett, for example, stems directly from a self-conscious difficulty in approaching the starting point.

22. Ibid., 47. "The empty place that a garland of fragments surrounds is a precise drawing of the contours of the Work." Cf. Schlegel, *Athenaeum,* 77. Schlegel uses the garland image to describe a dialogue, the Socratic being the ideal form of criticism for the Romantics.

23. Cf. Gasché, foreword to Schlegel, *Philosophical Fragments,* xxvii: "[fragments] are not leftover pieces of an integral whole, broken parts of a former or anticipated totality; they are that whole itself *in actualitas*—the only way in which the supersensible substrate occurs, or becomes present."

24. Karl Solger, *Erwin* quoted in Wheeler, *German Aesthetic,* 9: "The symbol would be a thing of the imagination which, as such, would be the presence of the idea itself in existence." The conditional terms of this statement suggest that, for Solger, the symbol is never practically realized.

25. S. T. Coleridge, "The Statesman's Manual," in *Lay Sermons*, ed. R. J. White, vol. 6 of *CW*, 30.
26. S. T. Coleridge, "Allegory," in *Coleridge's Miscellaneous Criticism*, ed. Thomas Middleton Raysor (London: Constable, 1936), 28.
27. Ibid., 30. Cf. Lee Rust Brown, "Coleridge and the Prospect of the Whole," *Studies in Romanticism* 30 (1991): 252–53. "Just as allegory involves the reference of a present sign to a prior text, symbol promises a transition from the present sign to a future text." From this, Brown concludes that "both allegory and symbol, as Coleridge defines them, hypothesize a temporality which is not given but constructed either backwards or forwards in a perpetually renewed moment of cognitive vision." John A. Hodgson challenges the ostensibly simple polarity advocated by Coleridge. Symbol and allegory, he reveals, actually intersect in Coleridge's hands. *Coleridge, Shelley, and Transcendental Inquiry* (Lincoln and London: University of Nebraska Press, 1989), 6–20.
28. S. T. Coleridge, "Allegoric Vision," *PW*, 2: 117.
29. Cf. *Biographia Literaria*, ed. James Engell and W. Jackson Bate, vol. 7 of *CW*, I: 304–305. Also, see Hodgson, *Coleridge, Shelley*, 21–23. Hodgson argues that Coleridge's "determined metaphor" (that is, one logically and causally connected to the image for which it substitutes) is a fallacy as the very notion of a metaphor implies an arbitrary correspondent.
30. Baudelaire's prose poems often refer, in the first instance, to verse poems in *Les Fleurs du Mal* and secondly to their symbolic subject. The parallelism of the prose to the verse means that they tend to the metaphoric as defined above.
31. David Lodge, *The Modes of Modern Writing: Metaphor, Metonymy and the Typology of Modern Literature* (London: Edward Arnold, 1977), 94.
32. I will discuss this in more detail in Chapter 5 where I equate the prose poem's larger metonymical design with the quasi-biblical style it tends to adopt at sentence level.
33. J. Robert Barth, S. J., *The Symbolic Imagination: Coleridge and the Romantic tradition* (Princeton: Princeton University Press, 1977), 20.
34. Coleridge, *Biographia Literaria* 2: 11. Coleridge attributes this definition of Beauty to Pythagoras, but Orsini doubts its authenticity. G. N. G. Orsini, *Coleridge and German Idealism* (Amsterdam and London: Feffer & Simons, 1969), 13; for Coleridge's concept of "understanding" see S. T. Coleridge, *Logic*, ed. J. R. de J. Jackson, vol. 13 of *CW*, 68: the act of the understanding is "no other than that by which a multiplicity of given presentations are comprehended in some one representation."
35. Cf. Thomas McFarland, "Aspects of Coleridge's Distinction Between Reason and Understanding," in *Coleridge's Visionary Languages*, ed. Tim Fulford and Morton D. Paley (Cambridge: D. S. Brewer, 1993), 169: "The continuing agenda of Coleridge's philosophical life was an attempt to defend Christianity against the rationalism of the French Enlightenment."
36. S. T. Coleridge, "Wonderfulness of Prose," in *Shorter Works and Fragments*, ed. H. J. Jackson and J. R. de J. Jackson, vol. 11 of *CW*, I: 441.
37. In Appendix C to "Statesman's Manual" (*Lay Sermons*, 59–60), Coleridge distinguishes Reason from Understanding. Reason is concerned with comprehending the single whole while the Understanding establishes logical relations between projected empirical parts.

38. Orsini, *Coleridge and German Idealism*, 78; also, Hodgson, *Coleridge, Shelley*, 11. Hodgson illustrates the temporalized a priori by posing Coleridge's problem of finding synecdoches to abstract concepts such as God: "We may determinedly allegorize the transcendent, which is a priori, by means of its consequences—and in no other way."

39. Coleridge, *Biographia Literaria* 2: 72 n4. Cf. Edmund Burke's anticipation of a structuralist logic, "nothing is an imitation further than as it resembles some other thing; and words undoubtedly have no sort of resemblance to the ideas for which they stand." *A Philosophical Enquiry into the Origin of our Ideas of the Sublime and Beautiful*, ed. J. Boulton (Notre Dame and London: University of Notre Dame Press, 1958), 5(v): 172.

40. See, Thomas De Quincey, "Samuel Taylor Coleridge," in *Sel.* 2: 159–60; M.II.153: "I can assert, upon my long and intimate knowledge of Coleridge's mind, that logic the most severe was as inalienable from his modes of thinking, as grammar from his language."

41. Jacques Derrida, *Dissemination*, trans. Barbara Johnson (London: The Athlone Press, 1981), 30–31.

42. Brown, "Prospect of the Whole," 244.

43. E. H. Coleridge is responsible for the dating of this poem. However, Sultana argues that correlations between the poem and a clutch of notebook entries (and Coleridge's lonely mood) suggest an earlier date of composition, circa April–July 1804. See David Sultana, *Samuel Taylor Coleridge in Malta and Italy* (Oxford: Basil Blackwell, 1969), 189. Coleridge recited a variant version of the last three stanzas of the "Date Tree" at the close of one of his lectures on literature (Lecture 2, 30 January 1818). This version appeared on the following day in the *New Times* under the heading "Imitation of one of the Minnesinger of the Thirteenth Century." See Coleridge, *Lectures 1808–1819 on Literature*, ed. R. A. Foakes, vol 5 of *CW*, II: 30. The text appears at II: 78. Marshall Suther points out that the similarity of the prefaces to *Cain* (1828) and "Kubla Khan" (1816) is rarely observed but he misses this additional parallel comparison with the "Date Tree." Suther, *Visions of Xanadu* (New York and London: Columbia University Press, 1965), 115.

44. Kathleen Wheeler, *The Creative Mind in Coleridge's Poetry* (London: Heinemann, 1981), 29.

45. Cf. Max F. Schulz, *The Poetic Voices of Coleridge: A Study of His Desire for Spontaneity And Passion*, 2nd ed. rev. (Detroit: Wayne State University Press, 1964), 159–60. Schulz suggests that Coleridge composed most of stanzas 3–6 in Malta and wrote the rest much later, possibly when he needed the fragment for *Poetical Works* of 1828.

46. Brown, "Prospect of the Whole," 239 and 241.

47. Cf. Wheeler, *Creative Mind in Coleridge's Poetry*, 54. Wheeler repeatedly uses terms of reduction to describe the prose gloss to "The Ancient Mariner." She associates this with the idea of abstraction, which is also decontextualization.

48. This is the impression he gives in his letter to Byron, Calne, 22 October 1815, where the verse fragment appears for the first time as the first stanza of a longer poem reproduced from memory—Coleridge claiming to have lost the only copy (*CL* 4: 601–602). Additional evidence that *Cain* was projected as a work of verse is that the fragment also appears in *Aids to Reflection* in 1825, that is, three years before its inclusion in the Prefatory note to the first publication of *The Wanderings of Cain* in prose.

49. Cf. Coleridge, *CN* II, 2140 (July 1804). Coleridge's observations on the flora of Malta include notes on the date tree leaf, "a complete circle." He adds "I should like to see Linnaeus on this Subject," although it is unclear whether Coleridge was currently reading Linnaeus or intending to refer to him.

50. *Biographia Literaria* 2: 64–65. Coleridge comments that certain verses by Wordsworth would have pleased him more in prose, being more suited to it by the simplicity of their subject. Also, Coleridge's response to Macpherson's *Ossian* (which he is known to have read between February and March 1796, that is, before he wrote *Cain*) was to render a couple of passages into rhyming verse poetry: "Imitated from Ossian" and "The Complaint of Ninathóma." For Wordsworth, meter is superimposed upon spontaneous expression as a form of presentation that is more pleasing than prose to reread.

51. Appearing in the second volume with "The Ancient Mariner," "Christabel," and the "Prose in Rhyme" poems. Coleridge had reluctantly given the manuscript of *Cain* and those of four other pieces in verse and prose to William Pickering, publisher of the *Poetical Works* and the *Bijou*. Pickering allegedly passed on the manuscripts to the editor, W. Fraser, without Coleridge's knowledge and they appeared in his new literary annual, the *Bijou*, earlier the same year (1828). "Canto II" is printed under the title, *The Wanderings of Cain. A Fragment.* Cf. Coleridge to Alaric A. Watts, 24 November 1827, *CL* 6: 710–12. Valerie Purton, in *A Coleridge Chronology* (London: Macmillan, 1993) 138, incorrectly assigns Leonard Horner as the addressee (*CL* 6: 709). The "Prefatory note" and the versified fragment of *Cain* are substituted in the *Bijou* by the editor's own general preface. Here, Coleridge is thanked for offering his poems to the editor. Fraser points to the merits of *Cain* in his call for the publication of all Coleridge's poetry. His support for *Cain* must be weighed against his possible mendacity on the question of authorization.

52. Werner W. Beyer, *The Enchanted Forest* (Oxford: Basil Blackwell, 1963), 55–65, and Appendix II (192–203); also, Rosemary Ashton, *The Life of Samuel Taylor Coleridge: A Critical Biography* (Oxford: Blackwell, 1996), 116.

53. One recovered fragment, (headed 'Book 3rd') does read like a first draft. There are only vague references to Wieland and it least resembles any other fragment (the landscape is not detailed, there is no son of Cain, and the spirit does not disguise itself as Abel). Clearly, if Canto II was not composed at the original sitting, then we are unable to date it at all. However, it may be that the verse fragment is connected to Canto II and this would explain Edward Coleridge's request for a copy of *The Wanderings of Cain* (the recently[?] composed Canto II) as late as 1826 but just two years before its first publication.

54. "Recollections of May 1811, recorded by Justice Coleridge," in *Specimens of the Table-Talk of the late Samuel Taylor Coleridge,* ed. H. N. Coleridge, quoted in Beyer, *Enchanted Forest,* 201.

55. Coleridge's frequent termination in the fragment form shows this sporadic process of writing to be a natural consequence of seeking an elusive wholeness. Typically, Coleridge's wholes are figured prospectively and retrospectively: in his letter to Byron he describes "Christabel" as "not yet a Whole" (Coleridge to Byron, 601); in the preface to "Kubla Khan" he writes that upon waking he retained "a distinct recollection of the whole" (*PW*, 1: 266).

56. *The Wanderings of Cain* positions itself in the gaps of its two source texts. It continues Gessner's story and it inhabits the interval between verses 16 and 17 of

Genesis 4. Unless otherwise stated, all references to the Bible will be to the King James *Authorized Version*.

57. Coleridge, *CN* I, 396, and Notes.
58. Coleridge to Sotheby, Keswick, 19 July 1802 (*CL* 2: 814).
59. See *The Letters of William and Dorothy Wordsworth I. The Early Years, 1787–1805*, ed. Ernest De Selincourt, 2nd ed. rev. by Chester Shaver (Oxford: Clarendon Press, 1967), 194.
60. Coleridge to Alaric Watts, August 1827 (*CL* 6: 699): "I am informed that they [the staff of *The Amulet*] had *rather have*—what? Why the 'Wanderings of Cain,' the Poem on 'Youth and Age,' and one or two others of which they had heard my acquaintance speak in rapture!"
61. "If, as the critics would have it, the prose poem repeats the 'same theme' as the verse poem, it is in order to question both the idea of *same* and the idea of *theme*. . . . For it is not prose that is here opposed to poetry, but poetry that, reworked by prose, has separated from itself." Barbara Johnson, *The Critical Difference* (Baltimore and London: The Johns Hopkins University Press, 1980), 43 and 44. Johnson is referring to Baudelaire's prose poems, *Le Spleen de Paris*, which followed, and occasionally paralleled, his verse poems, *Les Fleurs du Mal*. However, her comments are strikingly pertinent to *Cain*.
62. Reprinted by E. H. Coleridge, "Note on Coleridge," *The Wanderings of Cain* (an alternative version), in *Athenaeum*, 27 January 1894, 114. E. H. Coleridge also prints an edited text of the manuscripts in *Poetical Works*, reprinted (Oxford: Oxford University Press, 1969), 285–86 n.
63. Wordsworth mistakenly dates the composition of the "Ancient Mariner" as spring 1798. It is possible that he was thinking of *Cain*, which the poets also planned as a collaboration. Cf. W. J. B. Owen, introduction to *Lyrical Ballads 1798*, 2nd ed. (Oxford: Oxford University Press, 1987), vii. It would be a coincidence if the poem was discussed on two excursions both of which coincided with attempts (jointly or otherwise) at writing the *Cain* project. E. H. Coleridge suggests that a collaboration for *Cain* may have been attempted on more than one occasion (see *Athenaeum*, 114). More recently, Valerie Purton has dated one version of *Cain* as closely as "early November" 1797 (Purton, *Coleridge Chronology*, 30). However, her source for this may simply be Coleridge's preface, which is unreliable.
64. "Coleridge told me that he and Wordsworth were to have made this place the scene of a prose-tale, which was to have been in the manner of, but far superior to, *The Death of Abel*, but they had relinquished the design." *The Complete Works of William Hazlitt*, ed. P. P. Howe (London: J. M. Dent, 1931), 17: 120. As well as substituting Wieland's poem for Gessner's as an immediate source text for *Cain*, Beyer rejects Coleridge's claim (in the preface and to Hazlitt) that he used the Valley of Rocks as the poem's striking setting Beyer points out that the landscape of Canto II does not correspond to the terrain of the Valley and claims that Hazlitt's own description is also inaccurate. The combination of desert and rocky mountain-forest actually derives, according to Beyer, from Cantos VII and VIII of *Oberon* (Beyer, *Enchanted Forest*, 53–54). However, in October 1804, Coleridge visited the old Roman forum at Neapolis in Sicily. From there he climbed up to the village of Targea where he saw a mountainside of old tombs (Coleridge, *CN* II: 2202). In the same entry, Coleridge compares this rocky field to the Valley of Stones, which, he later claimed, was the original location for *Cain*.
65. John Beer, *Coleridge's Poetic Intelligence* (London: Macmillan, 1977), 297, n41.

66. Coleridge MS., Eg. 2800. There is also a fainter line drawn across the page after "Cain's wife tells him that her son Enoch was placed suddenly by her side." However, it appears that this sentence (in which the child's name first appears) was written after the line had been drawn.

I will identify these manuscript fragments as the folio texts, MS "*F*" (and "*Fv*" to denote the verso that begins, "Midnight on the Euphrates"). When necessary, I will distinguish parts of the folio by their "title," e.g. "Book 3rd." I will continue to use the italicized *Cain* to denote *The Wanderings of Cain* as a whole (that is, as a collective title for all fragments, published and unpublished).

67. Coleridge, *CN* II: 2257.

68. The content of the extant verse actually corresponds to just one sentence of the prose: "Child [?af'-feared] by his father's ravings, goes out to pluck the fruits in the moonlight wildness."

The published "Canto II" incorporates details from "Book 3rd" and "Cain" in MS *F*, but only from the second paragraph of *Fv* ("Cain addresses all the elements . . . Abel carries off the Child"). This may indicate that there are, in fact, *three* texts, the third beginning "Midnight on the Euphrates." Reapportioning the manuscript in this way does not affect subdivisions within the work or number of sittings, such as the second demarcation found in the middle of the last section.

69. Coleridge to Byron, 601; Coleridge, *Aids to Reflection*, ed. John Beer, vol. 9 of *CW*, 390.

70. See William Bartram, *Travels Through North and South Carolina, Georgia, East and West Florida, The Cheriokee Country* [. . . &c], 2nd ed. (London: J. Johnson, 1794), 216.

71. S. T. Coleridge, British Library, Add. MS. 47520. Hereafter, MS *N*. (Reprinted in Coleridge, *CN* II: 2780.)

72. Coleridge, *CN* II: 2780, Text and Notes. Coburn suggests that Coleridge may have attempted to complete *Cain,* as a companion piece to "Christabel" when he was preparing to publish the latter in 1815–16. However, this may also apply to the verse-*Cain* which was sent to Byron at that time. The close of the piece is partly written over a previous entry of 7–16 February, 1804 (see Coleridge, *CN* II: 1901, a memo to send Samuel Daniel's poems to Lady Beaumont). Another entry, datable 1821, appears above the piece, possibly inserted in a space. However, Coburn does not rule out MS *N* as a post-1821 composition. Coburn identifies textual similarities with the verses (the lonely boy in the night). Sultana, on the other hand, comes to his conclusion from the circumstances surrounding the notebook entry (Sultana, *Malta and Italy*, 90).

73. Cf. Simon, *Prose Poem as a Genre,* 625. Simon finds several poetic meters in "Canto II" including blank verse, a distich and a hexameter, all of which he finds "disturbing" in a piece of prose. Ironically, Simon also claims that in fact the notebook entries provide "prose poems in the best sense" (626) although his examples are of poetic prose—a flowing prose style rather than a fragmented genre, a distinction I will return to in the following chapters. By describing poetical prose as a wingless bird ("a metaphysical Bustard"), it is clear that Coleridge was attempting something quite different in his return to prose for "Canto II."

74. The Child as an active character in *Cain* is developed throughout MS *F,* the verses, MS *N* and "Canto II." However, the risen Christ-child image of the notebook draft indicates a step forward in Coleridge's poetics and the *Cain* project in particular. According to E. S. Shaffer, a principal obstacle to the original *Cain* was any

representation of the Divine. In the 1790s, rationalism avoided subjects such as the crucifixion and the Resurrection despite their centrality to the Christianity under discussion. See Shaffer, "Kubla Khan" *and The Fall of Jerusalem* (Cambridge: Cambridge University Press, 1975), 60.

75. Sultana, *Coleridge in Malta and Italy,* 180. Cf. *CN* II, 2146 and 2147. Notebook entry *CN* II, 2101, contains an interesting collection of observations when considered in relation to *Cain.* Two days after landing at Valletta, on 20 May 1804, Coleridge was introduced to General Villettes. There, in the Palace of the Governor he notes seeing a painting of Cain killing Abel (Coburn attributes the painting to Bartolommeo Passante). Of the following day, Coleridge records a storm and "hard rain." He also notes being told that his bad night was due to the sirocco wind. Extreme weather is implied in MS *Fv* ("Midnight on the Euphrates") when the protagonist addresses the elements "to cease for a while to persecute him while he tells his story." But, perhaps most significant is the specific mention in Canto II of a "sand-blast," which, if a siroccan wind, would be evidence for claiming it as a non-original, post-1804 composition.

76. Coleridge had experienced the sirocco wind in Malta and Sicily (Coleridge to Sir George and Lady Beaumont, Malta, 1 August 1804, *CL* 2: 1147 and *CN* II, 2101). According to Sultana, Coleridge immediately showed an interest in the sirocco, a hot wind from the Sahara, proposing to keep a journal of it and its effects on his health (Sultana, *Coleridge in Malta and Italy,* 136). At the same time, "he appears to have been inclined to dread the sirocco in Malta as much as rain in England" (136–37). In his letters home, however, Coleridge consistently makes light of the weather, describing the sirocco to the Beaumonts as "a mere Joke compared with our close *drizzly* weather, in England" and mentioning offhandedly that "we have had an Earthquake or two" (Coleridge to Sir George and Lady Beaumont, 2: 1147).

77. Coleridge, *CN* II: 2828. For other references to this image in Coleridge and Milton, see J. B. Beer, *Coleridge the Visionary* (London: Chatto and Windus, 1959), 240. On Maundy Thursday (3 April 1806), Coleridge observed the eternal qualities of change and permanence together in the fountains outside St. Peter's (Coleridge, *CN* II: 2832).

78. I am indebted to John Woolford for this acute observation. The passage, "Roaring and whitening" (from MS *W*) appears in W. Wordsworth, *The Prelude 1799, 1805, 1850,* eds. Jonathan Wordsworth, M. H. Abrams, and Stephen Gill (London and New York: W. W. Norton, 1979), 499. There is no other evidence at present to suggest that Coleridge had access to the canceled passages. Cf. Jonathan Wordsworth, "The Five-Book *Prelude* of Early Spring 1804," *Journal of English and Germanic Philology* 76 (1977): 23. Coincidentally, there is a lost manuscript of March 1804 that is described as a "companion-volume to [ms] *M*." In addition, the memo concerning Daniel's poems, which entry 2780 (MS *N*) partly obscures, was redundant from 8 March when the volumes were dispatched to Lady Beaumont (*CN* II: 1901 Notes).

79. In fact, Coleridge does make references to Raphael's frescoes in his lectures of 1808 (*Lectures* I: 208).

80. Roger Jones and Nicholas Penny, *Raphael* (New Haven and London: Yale University Press, 1983), 89.

81. See Ian Wylie, *Young Coleridge and the Philosophers of Nature* (Oxford: Clarendon Press, 1989), 62–64. According to Bishop Ussher's calculation, from 1796, the

world would have two hundred years to run, ending in 1996. Wylie finds references in the notebooks for this year to Thomas Burnet's *Telluris Theoria Sacra,* which claims that earthquakes and sea commotions are the principal signs of apocalypse. This is possibly a subtext in *Cain,* which surfaces in the apocalyptic phenomena of the notebook entry.

82. The painting was removed to Paris in 1797 and returned to the Vatican in 1815. See Luitpold Dussler, *Raphael: A Critical Catalogue of His Pictures, Wall Paintings and Tapestries,* trans. S. Cruft (London and New York: Phaidon, 1971), 31.

83. Coleridge to George Fricker, 4 October 1806 (*CL* 2: 1189 and 1192). Coleridge wrote to George Fricker in 1806 explaining his rejection of Unitarianism. His reasons center on "the incapability of man to heal himself" after the Fall. According to Tim Fulford, "Canto II" is "an intense dramatisation of the powerlessness into which guilt plunges the interpretative faculty" and articulates, through Cain's loss, Coleridge's own fears of a break with Wordsworth. Yet, Fulford claims that, without a conclusion, the piece is not a moral tale: "it might be called a work of disconfirmation, and for that reason one of the first English Romantic texts." *Coleridge's Figurative Language* (London: Macmillan, 1991), 67–68.

84. David Jasper notes in *Coleridge as Poet and Religious Thinker* (London: Macmillan, 1985), 9, that the interdependence of the spiritual and the physical, understood through irony, was a popular theme in European Romanticism, reaching its fullest expression in France in the work of Vicomte de Chateaubriand and, in particular, Pierre-Simon Ballanche's prose poem *Orpheus* (1827).

85. Marshall Suther reads "Canto II" as a human psychological drama projected by Cain himself. Although such a reading is inevitably problematic, it would explain the similarity of Abel's complaints to Cain's and its paradoxes (Suther, *Visions of Xanadu,* 119). Suther uses the folio texts (MSS *F/Fv*) to explain the published version but he ignores the fact that of the two Abels in MS *Fv* one is an evil spirit who tempts Cain into sacrificing his son. As it stands, we cannot tell whether the Abel of the published version is the true Abel or not. His hysterical shrieks, his account of a different Lord for the dead and the ominous landscape all suggest that the same plan of the supernatural in *Fv* is being followed. If this *is* the case, then Suther's reading of Abel as simply the redeemable aspect of the personality (as opposed to Cain the damnable side) is jeopardized.

86. This concept may have come from Coleridge's reading of David Hartley (*Observations on Man*) whose empiricist beliefs led him to the claim that those who studied the natural world had proportionally more developed moral senses (see Wylie, *Young Coleridge,* 75–76).

87. Cf. MS *Fv*: "how he meets in the desart a young man whom upon a nearer approach he perceives to be Abel . . . on whose countenance appear marks of the greatest misery."

88. Cf. Luke 9:29: "And as he prayed, the fashion of his countenance was altered, and his raiment *was* white *and* glistering." There are Gnostic overtones throughout these drafts, fueled mainly by their essential dualisms: the echo or reinterpretation of canonical texts and the distinction between the God of the living (the Demiurge?) and the dead (the androgynous God open to infinite interpretation, much like the Absent Work).

89. Lacoue-Labarthe and Nancy, *Literary Absolute,* 50. Thomas McFarland also deconstructs the 'ideal' image by showing how, etymologically, the word 'symbol' "implies a putting together of something torn apart . . . and though the emphasis

on putting together honors the idea of a whole, the inescapable fact is that the symbol as such is always jagged, is always a fragment incomplete in itself. . . . The symbol is a diasparact." *Romanticism and the Forms of Ruin* (Princeton: Princeton University Press, 1981), 27.

90. Lacoue-Labarthe and Nancy, *Literary Absolute*, 43.

91. "Canto II" minimizes its supernatural aspect by involving Enos as a co-witness to the appearance of "Abel." The ambiguity of the dead man's existence is turned into objective fact.

92. Cf. Paul Maguson, *Coleridge's Nightmare Poetry* (Charlottesville: University Press of Virginia, 1974), 64. Maguson regards this episode in Cain as a gloss on the similar occasion in "The Ancient Mariner" (III.160). Also, see Beer, *Coleridge's Poetic Intelligence*, 114. Beer claims that the end of MS *Fv* resembles the Apocryphal *Book of Tobit*, in which Coleridge had an interest. Tobit's son compares himself with Adam, and the angel Raphael pursues a released daemon thus foreshadowing Christ binding Satan.

93. See Dante, *Purgatory*, Canto 28. For example, the forest is impenetrable to sun or moon ("Canto II"); the various flowers are in flushed hues (Verses: "And fruits and flowers together grew / On many a shrub and many a tree: / And all put on a gentle hue"). Also, compare Milton, *Paradise Lost*, Canto 4: 148 with *CN* II, 2501, 2565, and 2787. These entries all refer to the sight of fruits and blossoms together on trees in Malta, the earliest is dated March 1805. The notebook editors suggest that the *Cain* verses were already written, which elsewhere they date at 1798 (see *CN* II 2799, Notes). Alastair Fowler notes that "the simultaneous concurrence of all stages of growth was a well-established feature of earthly paradises." Introduction to John Milton, *Paradise Lost* (London: Longman, 1991), 199 n. The absence of seasons is subverted by the desolate landscape of "Canto II." Coleridge possessed two copies of Dante's work in 1804 and transcripts begin to appear in the notebooks from 1805. S. T. Coleridge, *Marginalia*, ed. G. Whalley, vol. 12 of *CW*, II: 131.

94. "He determines to rush out amongst them . . . to be destroyed by him . . . Cain advances wishing death." The active / passive duality of the self is a recurrent theme in Coleridge's work, cf. "The Pains of Sleep" ll. 28–29: "all confused I could not know / Whether I suffered, or I did"; "To William Wordsworth" l. 112: "And when I rose, I found myself in prayer." Kessler identifies two metaphors that "reveal [Coleridge's] need to find a Being that is not defined, hence limited, by his senses and sensory language: a blind Arab in the desert listening for a voice; and a parent . . . seeking the answering voice of a child." Edward Kessler, *Coleridge's Metaphors of Being* (Princeton: Princeton University Press, 1979), 176.

95. Cf. "The Blossoming of the Solitary Date Tree," ll. 60–61. The speaker equates the silence of his loneliness with a blind Arab in a "lonesome tent" in contrast to the "fields, forests, ancient mountains" etc. that actually surround him.

96. In MS *Fv*, the water image is specified as the Euphrates (one of the four rivers running out of Eden) and is the place where Cain's wife and child are returned to him. Also, father and child are made to pass through a water-filled gulph before offering sacrifice to the god of the dead, in a parody of Christian baptism or purification from original sin. Finally, water actually substitutes landscape in "The Ancient Mariner" where it becomes the prevalent image of supernatural (possibly divine) forces.

97. In Blake's "Mock on, mock on, Voltaire, Rousseau," the sand, thrown against the wind, is both empirical and divine ("Blown back they blind the mocking

Eye / But still in Israels paths they shine"). For further discussion, see Thomas McFarland, "Patterns of Parataxis in Anglo-German Cultural Currents," in *English and German Romanticism*, ed. J. Pipkin (Heidelberg: Carl Winter, Universitätsverlag, 1985), 244–45.

98. See Notebook 43, quoted in Maguson, *Coleridge's Nightmare Poetry*, 51. Coleridge claims that the supernatural in poetry occurs "when the Poet of his free will and judgement does what the Believing Narrator of a Supernatural Incident, Apparition or Charm does from ignorance and weakness of mind,—i.e. mistake a *Subjective* product (A saw the Ghost of Z) for an objective fact—the Ghost of Z was there to be seen." Also, Arden Reed, *Romantic Weather* (Hanover and London: University Press of New England, 1983), 113. According to Reed, the absence of sunlight generally leads to spectral apparitions as substitutions in Coleridge's poetry. The moon is also an image of knowledge without religion and this too is appropriate to *Cain*, of which three drafts refer to the moonlit night ("Canto II," MSS *F/Fv* and the verses).

99. Cf. Wylie, *Young Coleridge*, 66–68; 81–91. Coleridge held these twin disciplines to be complementary. He perceived contemporary progress in scientific research (the discovery of electricity, oxygen, etc.) to serve the ultimate goal of deciphering nature in the Golden Age.

100. See Ronald C. Wendling, *Coleridge's Progress to Christianity* (Lewisburg, Pa.: Bucknell University Press, 1995), 124. "Coleridge moves toward a far less ecstatic transcendentalism and more practically minded Christianity—one that incorporates, in fact, as much as it can of the empirical tradition from Aristotle to Locke without ceasing to be itself."

101. From Coleridge's Notebook 43, reprinted in *Inquiring Spirit*, ed. Kathleen Coburn, rev. ed. (Toronto and London: University of Toronto Press, 1979), 191.

102. Coleridge, "The Soul and the Universe," in *Shorter Works and Fragments*, 154.

103. af'feared—E. H. Coleridge

CHAPTER 2. DE QUINCEY AND BAUDELAIRE

1. Baudelaire's prose poems began to appear in August 1857 although a couple had already been published two years previously. *Un mangeur d'opium* was first seen in serial form between 1858 and 1859. In 1860, it was produced as a book with a piece on hashish under the collective title, *Les paradis artificiels*.

2. Charles Baudelaire to Auguste Poulet-Malassis, Paris, 16 February 1860 (*Correspondance*, ed. Claude Pichois and Jean Ziegler [Paris: Éditions Gallimard, 1973], 1: 669): "It was no easy business to apply dramatic form to this summary and to introduce order into it. Moreover, it involved mixing my personal feelings with the opinions of the original author and producing a blend in which the two were indistinguishable. Have I succeeded?" Earlier, he had referred to his translation as a "delicate stew," presumably as an image of this amalgamation.

3. In the subsequent 1856 version for his own collected edition, *Selections Grave and Gay*, "Jeremy Taylor" is corrected to "Lord Bacon" (*Sel.* 5: 275).

4. Cf. D. D. Devlin, *De Quincey, Wordsworth and the Art of Prose* (London: Macmillan, 1983), 70: "For De Quincey the shape of *The Prelude* did not lie in a narrative curve, but in the repetition of those 'spots of time' which were the structural units

of the poem. These gave objectivity to subjective experience; and by cutting across time, by gathering past, present and future into one visionary object or involute, they made a structure based on the passing of calendar time unnecessary, impossible and, indeed, a lie."

5. *Sel.* 5:194; M.III.380. Cf. Edmund Baxter, *De Quincey's Art of Autobiography* (Edinburgh: Edinburgh University Press, 1990), 12–13. Baxter shows how De Quincey also reacts in a similar way when he escapes from school, inducing a shift in the "mode of existence," an act that forces him into writing.

6. J. Hillis Miller argues that the Memnonian wind of God's love is transformed by the death of De Quincey's sister into the Sarsar wind of death, which indicates that God is inaccessible if not absent. *The Disappearance of God* (Cambridge: Harvard University Press, 1963), 22.

7. Thomas De Quincey, *Confessions of an English Opium-Eater and other writings*, ed. Grevel Lindop (Oxford: Oxford University Press, 1985), 78.

8. *Sel.* 5:xiv; M.III.221.

9. In the opening of "Lord Rosse's Telescopes," De Quincey tries to be casually objective in referring to a previous article but cannot resist identifying himself as the author: "Several years ago, some person or other (in fact, I believe it was myself)." *Sel.* 3:169; M.VIII.7.

10. Grevel Lindop, *The Opium-Eater: A Life of Thomas De Quincey* (London: J. M. Dent, 1981), 187.

11. I should note here that I am not concerned with the medical implications. I treat opium as a narrative agent only. The division into opium dream and artistic vision is relevant only in its effect on the form of the text. In addition, night dreams are classified as "artistic vision" because "He whose talk is of oxen, will probably dream of oxen" (*Blackwood's* 57: 269; M.XIII.334).

12. De Quincey had previously translated this piece and had published it in the *London Magazine*, March 1824. Of the present version, De Quincey claims in the same article that " I may call it partly 'my own,'" since it is based on a single reading of twenty-five years previously. In fact, he recalls, Richter did not have enough "Grecian" severity, his style being too elaborate for "a dream considered as a work of art" (*Sel.* 3:198 and 199; M.VIII.33).

13. We are reminded of Piranesi's *Carceri* which De Quincey likens to the opium dreams in the *Confessions*. Richter's dream also prefigures Samuel Beckett's prose piece "He Is Barehead," where the protagonist is drawn through an infinite, labyrinthine journey toward his birth.

14. Recorded by A. H. Japp, quoted in *The Opium-Eater*, 355.

15. Cf. A. H. Japp ed., *The Posthumous Works* (New York and Hildesheim: Georg Olms Verlag, 1975), 1: 4. *The English Mail-Coach* is listed third between "The Affliction of Childhood: Dream Echoes" and "The Palimpsest."

16. Grevel Lindop, introduction to De Quincey, *Confessions of an English Opium-Eater and Other Writings*, xxiii.

17. Lindop recounts, in his biography, that the opium-eater's "trained imagination and 'photographic' memory" enabled him to reproduce various other pieces that had been lost in the post and so on (Lindop, *The Opium-Eater*, 223). It is therefore curious that, for a work that clearly held much importance to him, De Quincey did not attempt to rewrite these pieces.

18. Quoted in Lindop, *The Opium-Eater*, 358.

19. See, Walter Pater, *The Renaissance*, ed. Donald L. Hill (London and Los Angeles: University of California Press, 1980), 105–106.

20. Cf. Baxter, *De Quincey's Art of Autobiography*, 22: "[In the *Selections*] De Quincey destroys the historical actuality of the publication of his texts in journal form by repeatedly referring to other works as if they had still to be completed. . . . The destruction of a given historical actuality (that the work has been once and for all published in a specific form) articulates De Quincey's reaction to the Press: within his work he attempts to subvert the way the Press tends to render his writing permanent and finished."

21. Devlin, *De Quincey, Wordsworth*, 13.

22. V. A. De Luca's idea that De Quincey's texts are really poems swamped by journalistic detail has been vigorously attacked, particularly by Robert Maniquis and Edmund Baxter.

23. Virginia Woolf, "Impassioned Prose," *TLS*, 16 September 1926. Reprinted in V. Woolf, *Granite and Rainbow* (London: Hogarth Press, 1958), 32–35.

24. J. H. Fowler ed., introduction to *Essays from De Quincey* (London: Adam and Charles Black, 1900), xxv.

25. De Luca's description of the Oxford Visions as "semi-didactic, semi-visionary prose-poems" neatly illustrates the general confusion in critical responses with regard to both De Quincey's writings and the prose poem form per se. See, *Thomas De Quincey: The Prose of Vision* (Toronto and London: University of Toronto Press, 1980), 70.

26. Cf. Josephine McDonagh, *De Quincey's Disciplines* (Oxford: Clarendon Press, 1994), 23 and 32. McDonagh makes the distinction between De Quincey's political and aesthetic Romanticism. Political Romanticism stood for social fragmentation and the chaos of unpredictable effects caused by revolution (reflected in the *Mail-Coach*). In his literary reminiscences, De Quincey appears nostalgic for the lost era of a dehistoricized Romanticism.

27. As I do not regard the Oxford Visions to be prose poems in the generic sense, I shall use the hyphenated term as a sign of its approximation.

28. See also, "The Household Wreck" (M.XII.190), where Agnes has only just been charged with shoplifting: "In a moment, in the twinkling of an eye, and yet for ever and ever, I comprehended the total ruin of my situation." The narrator rejects all rational hope to which others could yet sensibly apply, "I felt as certain, as irredeemably, as hopelessly certain, of the final results as though I had seen the record in the books of heaven." Such an outburst appears to be an overreaction until the end of the narrative has been unraveled.

29. R. Maniquis introduces the element of bias into the split-self in "Lonely Empires: Personal and Public Visions of Thomas De Quincey," *Literary Monographs* 8 (1976): 58. "Innocence is wholeness: guilt is fragmentation. The 'real' self floats within a stream of discontinuous selves, and it is always this real self that is innocent. Discontinuous selves mark the presence of guilt, which is always alien, never *his*." Although it is a tidy theory that proposes that the style of the *Confessions*, rather than the confessions themselves, unify its disparate (and therefore guilty) contents, it is problematic since De Quincey himself denies any sense of guilt, at the opening of the work.

30. De Quincey reveals in a footnote that "Levana" "was in fact a legend recurring in sleep, most of which I had myself silently written or sculptured in my daylight reveries" (*Blackwood's* 57: 747; M.XIII.369n).

31. According to Japp's recovered plan for the *Suspiria*, "Levana" was to be followed by "The Solitude of Childhood" (which was an expression of a death-wish) and then "The Dark Interpreter." This second prose piece is not a dream sequence but a brief definition of the Interpreter followed by typical digressions. Japp represents this piece as a full explanation of the figure who is briefly compared to clouds in a gale in "The Apparition of the Brocken" and another shadowy figure in "Savannah-La-Mar."

32. This is possibly one of the "Freudian slips" *avant la lettre* that De Quincey's work often seems to invite. Maniquis reads this piece as a Freudian unveiling of the hidden that turns out to be self-identification. Maniquis makes other analogies with the Spectre (as the Dark Interpreter), for example with Bunyan's Interpreter in *The Pilgrim's Progress*. "The Dark Interpreter and the Palimpsest of Violence: De Quincey and the Unconscious," in *Thomas De Quincey Bicentenary Studies*, ed. Robert Lance Snyder (Norman and London: University of Oklahoma Press, 1985), 115–19.

33. De Luca claims that the Spectre "represents the dreamer's imagination at the outer verge of its individuality, at the point of transaction with large and autonomous powers which assert their presence in the sleeping mind" (*Prose of Vision*, 78). Yet, conversely, the dream visions are more likely to stem from a generation of highly individual energy that requires the man as artist, here embodied in the form of the Interpreter, to communicate in a manner accessible to those outside the contracted sphere of the self.

34. In Masson's idiosyncratic organization of the *Collected Works*, the "Oxford Visions" are dispersed. Those passages that did not appear in *Autobiographic Sketches* are reprinted in volume XIII, *Tales and Prose Phantasies*. Ironically, they are also reordered, ending with "Levana." Masson defends his action by referring his readers to the final footnote in "Levana" which offers a key to the larger Absent Work. In addition, he argues, "Levana" is "the finest thing that De Quincey ever wrote. It is certainly the most perfect specimen he has left us of his peculiar art of English prose-poetry" (M.XIII.362n).

35. De Quincey's name, which he did not use in the British magazines, signing himself only "X.Y.Z.," was not published in these translations. Michèle Stäuble-Lipman Wulf gives a comprehensive account of the history of the *Confessions* in France in *Mangeur*, esp. 33–38.

36. Alfred de Musset, *Oeuvres complètes en prose* ed. Maurice Allem and Paul-Courant (Paris: Gallimard, 1960), 1021. It is known that Baudelaire read a work on hallucinations that contained a long quotation from de Musset's translation, but there is no evidence to prove he was acquainted with the rest of de Musset's rendering.

37. Baudelaire to Eugène de Broise, Paris, 13 June 1857 (*Correspondance*, 1: 407).

38. Baudelaire to Madame Aupick, Paris, 9 July 1857 (ibid., 1: 411).

39. The date that Stäuble-Lipman Wulf proposes for Baudelaire's first reading of the *Confessions* is based on a deduction of the edition he used as a source text. She revises G. T. Clapton's early dating of 1839–1844, long before the publication of the *Suspiria*, suggesting something nearer to both the translation and the prose poems, that is, circa 1857, when Baudelaire first mentions the work in his letters (Stäuble-Lipman Wulf, *Mangeur*, 43–54).

40. Cf. Murphy, *A Tradition of Subversion*, 50. Also, Todorov, *Genres in Discourse*, 65–66. In his discussion of the fundamental dualism in Baudelaire's prose poems,

Todorov retains the thyrsus as symbolic model but he does not mention the link to De Quincey.

41. Deals with the *Moniteur* and *Revue Française* having broken down completely. See, Baudelaire to Alphonse de Calonne, Paris, 10 November 1858 (*Correspondance*, 1: 522): "I assure you that it was no easy thing to fit the description of a very complicated book into a SMALL space and without losing a single nuance."

42. See Bernard, *Le Poème en Prose*, 24–25 and 35. Translations of works such as Young's *Night Thoughts* into abridged prose were very popular but also instrumental in liberating poetry from the constraints of verse in the pre-Romantic era. In these translations, narrative and digression were eliminated to produce a heightened unity and intensity that was not available in the novel or the epic genres.

43. Clapton claims that the inclusion of details in *Un mangeur d'opium*, which had been corrected in *Selections Grave and Gay*, reveal that Baudelaire did not know of the 1856 revision or, possibly, preferred the shorter version. G. T. Clapton, *Baudelaire et De Quincey* (Paris: Les Belles Lettres, 1931), 13. An original source for the *Suspiria* seems to be virtually impossible to confirm. Stäuble-Lipman Wulf suggests that the American collection may have served for both of the texts but she adds that *Blackwood's* may also have been consulted for the *Suspiria* (*Mangeur*, 43–46).

44. Baxter distinguishes between failure and flaw in De Quincey's texts, a distinction that is helpful in separating the effect of the work (failure can be Romantic or comic) and criticism of its relation to what Baxter terms an implied "aesthetic absolute" (Baxter, *De Quincey's Art of Autobiography*, 9–11). Baudelaire's treatment does fall into the second category but criticism must be qualified by the fact that his preference for a full translation was thwarted through the directives on length issued by his publisher.

45. "The Thyrsus" from *Le Spleen de Paris* is dedicated to Franz Liszt but could equally apply to De Quincey. "The straight line and the arabesque; intention and expression; unyielding will-power and oblique Word; the one and only end and the multiplicity of means; the all-powerful amalgam of genius—what analyst will make so bold as to divide and separate you?" ("The Wand" [Le Thyrse], *Poems in Prose*, 145). Cf. *Mangeur*, 365. Stäuble-Lipman Wulf includes evidence put forward by M. Zimmermann and R. Kopp for other possible sources of this prose poem.

46. Baudelaire to Auguste Poulet-Malassis, Paris 16 February 1860 (*Correspondance*, 1: 669).

47. Baudelaire to Alphonse de Calonne, Paris 10 November 1858 (*Correspondance*, 1: 522). Baudelaire is comparing this narrative tone to that which he employs in *Haschisch*.

48. Baudelaire, *Poems in Prose*, 25.

49. Alan Astro, "Allegory of Translation in Baudelaire's *Un Mangeur d'opium*," *Nineteenth-Century French Studies* 18 (1989–90): 168–9.

50. The passage begins, "O just, subtle, and all-conquering opium!" (*Sel.* 5:212; M.III.395). As Lindop and others have pointed out, De Quincey's apostrophe is an echo of Raleigh's conclusion to his *History of the World*, "O eloquent, just and mighty Death!" Baudelaire had to battle with his publisher to use this piece as the opening. He broaches the argument by stating that an author of his renown would not normally participate in such pettinesses as he has had to endure. He goes on: "The same thing this morning! An opening was painfully sought for and prepared. At last I found the beginning which, in its solemnity, resembles the first bars of an orchestra. But '*voilà*'! you decide that, for an opening, it would be wiser to incorporate an

obituary notice." Baudelaire to Alphonse de Calonne, 5 January 1860 (*Correspondance*, 1: 651).

51. See Chapter 1 on the prefatory aspect of the prose poem.

52. *Sel.* 5: 266; M.III.441. See also, *Sel.* 5: 210; M.III.394.

53. *Poems in Prose*, 39.

54. See Baudelaire's own comments in *Un mangeur d'opium* (*Mangeur* 154; *Oeuvres*, 467–68) on the advantages of first, as opposed to habitual, perception (prefiguring Proust's aesthetic).

55. Thomas A. Reisner, "De Quincey's Palimpsest Reconsidered," *Modern Language Studies* 12 (1982): 93–94. Reisner cites the *Bijou*, 1828, as evidence of Coleridge's use of the term, however, the note did not appear in the *Bijou* but in the *Poetical Works* only, that year. Coleridge's reference is to a device used by the Ancients while De Quincey is thinking more of medieval parchment. Shelley's use of the image, also as an analogy to the human mind, occurs in *The Triumph of Life* (1822), ll. 405–12 as a succession of animal tracks on the beach.

56. Baudelaire's passage is inserted between the case of the drowning woman (after the paragraph ending "now this mystery is liable to no doubt; for it is repeated, and ten thousand times repeated by opium, for those who are its martyrs") and the literary palimpsest (paragraph beginning: "Yes, reader, countless are the mysterious handwritings of grief or joy which have inscribed themselves successively upon the palimpsest of your brain;"). *Blackwood's* 57: 743; M.XIII.348.

57. See his Dedication to Houssaye (*Poems in Prose*, 25/27). I will examine this aspect of the Collection in Chapter 7.

58. A final effect of Baudelaire's use of the third-person narrative, which is pointed out by Astro, is the fact that it distances the translator from the complicity required by all writers of Confessions, and De Quincey in particular, that one believes in the writer's innocence (Astro, "Allegory of Translation," 168). This clearly goes to the very heart of De Quincey's confessional writing, as I stated at the beginning of this chapter.

Chapter 3. Contexts I

1. Arthur Symons, clearly confusing poetic prose (style) and prose poetry (genre) in "A Word on De Quincey," defines prose poetry as "the *style* of Ruskin" (my emphasis). *Studies in Prose and Verse* (London: J. M. Dent, 1904), 51.

2. Murphy is the only critic to challenge this general consensus that the prose poem must be brief, by posing the reasonable question, "How long is brief. . . . ?" (*Tradition of Subversion*, 63). The challenge is not sustained, however, probably because the convention is a useful one.

3. Michel Beaujour, "Short Epiphanies: Two Contextual Approaches to the French Prose Poem," in *The Prose Poem in France*, 46–47.

4. Baudelaire, *Mangeur*, 104. Michel Charles points out that *"essentiellement digressif"* is an oxymoron. "Digression, régression (Arabesques)," *Poétique* 40 (1979): 397–400. He makes sense of the image by explaining that, despite the dialectic nature of the caduceus, De Quincey favors the arabesque (the route of the vagabond) whereas Baudelaire prefers not to make the choice and to suspend his aestheticism in a kind of hermaphrodite state.

5. Charles Baudelaire, "New Notes on Edgar Poe," trans. Lois and Francis Hyslop, in *Edgar Allan Poe: Critical Assessments*, ed. G. Clarke (Mountfield, E. Sussex: Helm Information, 1991), 2: 396.

6. Cf. T. S. Eliot, "From Poe to Valéry," in *To Criticize the Critic* (London: Faber & Faber, 1978), 31. Eliot claims that although Poe "dabbled in verse and in kinds of prose," he did not achieve success in any one genre but that this variety was appreciated by the French who mistakenly considered it to be a fragmented whole.

7. E. A. Poe, "The Poetic Principle," in *Selections from the Critical Writings of Edgar Allan Poe*, ed. F. C. Prescott (New York: Gordian Press, 1981), 228–256, esp. 228–29.

8. Joris-Karl Huysmans, *Against Nature*, trans. Robert Baldick (Harmondsworth: Penguin Books, 1959), 199. Huysmans's own collection of prose poems, *Le Drageoir à épices*, had been published ten years previously in 1874.

9. Baudelaire had expressed a very similar notion in his essay on Poe: "There must not creep into the entire composition a single word which is not intentional, which does not tend, directly or indirectly, to complete the premeditated design" ("New Notes on Edgar Poe," 396). Huysmans's theory is surely influenced by Mallarmé, whose best prose poems Des Esseintes claims as the masterpieces of the genre. Mallarmé (who also translated Poe) was influenced by Poe's commitment to *le mot juste*.

10. Cf. Coleridge, *Biographia Literaria*, 2: 62. "Essence, in its primary signification, means the principle of *individuation*, the inmost principle of the *possibility*, of any thing, *as* that particular thing. It is equivalent to the *idea* of a thing, whenever we use the word idea, with philosophic precision." Coleridge also speaks of reduction and restoration of a text in his preface to "The Blossoming of the Solitary Date Tree."

11. Roland Barthes, *S/Z*, trans. Richard Miller (London: Jonathan Cape, 1975), 4. Cf. Ron Silliman, *The New Sentence* (New York: Roof, 1987), esp. 10–15 and 63–94. Silliman advocates the "new sentence" as a response to the capitalist demand for a product of reading, which results in styles of (transparent) Realism. The new sentence erects barriers at sentence level to prevent this transparency and to redirect attention to the language itself. This also has an effect on context, the referent, or the product. Here, the sense of a meaning that is external or elsewhere (that is, at the level of interpretation), is hindered by the foregrounded grammatical constructs of the sentence. In other words, whereas I am suggesting that the ambiguity of the signified develops as a result of an overproduction of contexts, Silliman's new sentence impedes the very move to a contextual level.

12. Cf. Beaujour, "Short Epiphanies," 56. According to Beaujour, the prose poem exposes the "uninitiated" bourgeoisie who are unsettled by their thwarted attempts to read prose poetry in traditional ways. The initiated, by contrast, are the "modernist aristocracy of consciousness" who are presumably aware of the *scriptible*.

13. Cf. John Beer, "The Englishness of De Quincey's Ideas," in *English and German Romanticism*, 337. Beer has suggested that De Quincey believed a center of security and peace lay at the "heart" of any true labyrinth, the nightmare of being inside a labyrinth, therefore, always contained the immediate possibility of turning into an "experience of peace." Moreover, Beer adds, it was "as important to engage with the terms of the labyrinth as to enjoy the peace at its center." Beer's gloss on De Quincey's concept of the mental maze might explain his motive for persisting in these convoluted projects. Cf. McDonagh, *De Quincey's Disciplines*, 72–73. McDonagh

observes that De Quincey's discussions of the literatures of power and knowledge are raised in the context of the overproduction of books. However, in "The Poetry of Pope," this overproduction becomes a source of sublimity as "the capacity to overwhelm became an aspect of textuality."

14. Paolo Santarcangeli quoted in Wendy B. Faris, *Labyrinths of Language: Symbolic Landscape and Narrative Design in Modern Fiction* (Baltimore and London: Johns Hopkins University Press, 1988), 3. See also Miller, *Disappearance of God*, 7.

15. Faris, *Labyrinths*, 4 (originally formulated by Philip West).

16. Charles, "Digression, régression (Arabesques)," 400–401.

17. Baxter, *De Quincey's Art of Autobiography*, 20.

18. Mallarmé's concept of the prose poem was a text of precise words combined with infinite complexity—he uses the thyrsus image to illustrate this point in his essay "Music and Literature."

19. In fact, De Quincey's expressed context is also applicable to another of Baudelaire's prose poems, "The Twofold Room," which turns on the problems of perception under the influence of opium.

20. Josephine McDonagh explains that cleansing the palimpsest's surface "implies a present that is always new and has no history; each new inscription is thus devoid of context, being placed in a present that is always isolated from its past." "Writings on the Mind: Thomas De Quincey and the Importance of the Palimpsest in Nineteenth Century Thought," *Prose Studies* 10 (1987): 213.

21. De Quincey explains that he gave up his piano lessons because, as he played, he could not occupy the twin positions of performer and listener simultaneously: "Too soon I became aware that to the deep voluptuous enjoyment of music absolute *passiveness* in the hearer is indispensable." *Sel.* 5:59; M.III.270. Cf. Michel Delville, *The American Prose Poem: Poetic Form and the Boundaries of Genre* (Gainesville: University Press of Florida, 1998), 33–34. Delville examines the effect of Huysmans's concept on Joyce, a writer who works beyond the era defined by the Victorian novel. Joyce's *Epiphanies* are conceived as self-contained units that are linked together (in a rectilinear direction) to produce a full-length narrative, *Giacomo Joyce*, the supporting structure of which remains visible in its epiphanic moments into which it may again contract.

22. This passage does not appear in the 1854 edition (M.XIII.291n).

23. By symbolic reflection, the Mail-Coach itself as the "organ of publication" radiates news and patriotism through the country. The *Confessions* submits to contextual tyranny and is augmented in its revised edition; the *Suspiria*, on the other hand, manages to undergo an abridgment due to its unit-based system.

24. Ian Bent ed., *Musical Analysis in the Nineteenth Century* (Cambridge: Cambridge University Press, 1994), 1: 24.

25. Cf. Calvin S. Brown, Jr., "The Musical Structure of De Quincey's *Dream Fugue*," *Musical Quarterly* 24 (1938): 341–50. Brown carries out a detailed analysis. He argues that De Quincey was more precise than he is ever given credit for in his attempt to create a piece of word music. In his revision of the piece he eliminated a number of maverick elements which do not adhere to the laws of the fugue.

26. Bent, *Musical Analysis*, 23.

27. See Chapter 7, section IV. The contrast between expressed context and the new type of pared narrative finds an image in the two coaches in this work. The Royal Mail carried an insignia "displayed only on a single pannel, whispering, rather than proclaiming, our relations to the state; whilst the beast from Birming-

ham had as much writing and painting on its sprawling flanks as would have puzzled a decipherer from the tombs of Luxor" (*Blackwood's*, 66: 490; M.XIII.281–2).

28. See Umberto Eco, *The Open Work*, trans. Anna Cancogni (London: Hutchinson Radius, 1989), chapter 1. Eco replaces the traditional dualism of being and appearance by an infinity located at the core of the finite work—a Romantic/postmodernist Symbol. Gertrude Stein's *Tender Buttons* functions in this mode of contextual displacement.

29. *The Poetical Works of Ernest Dowson*, ed. Desmond Flower (London: Cassell, 1967), 129.

30. Roy Fisher, *Stopped Frames and Set Pieces*, in *The Cut Pages* (1971). Hereafter, references are to *Poems 1955–1980* (Oxford: Oxford University Press, 1980).

31. See A. Kingsley Weatherhead, *The British Dissonance* (Columbia and London: University of Missouri Press, 1983), 34–35.

32. Michael Riffaterre, *Semiotics of Poetry* (Bloomington and London: Indiana University Press, 1978), 124. The onus remains with the reader to perceive (although not necessarily articulate) the play between the prose poem and the literary texts from which it emerges. Riffaterre therefore also identifies implied contexts (which he terms "derivations") but they are not organically related to the prose poetic text or appear to hold a metonymic relation to it and consist of literatures rather than circumstances.

33. Cf. Max Jacob, "Preface of 1916," trans. Zack Rogow in *The Dice Cup: Selected Prose Poems*, ed. Michael Brownstein, various translators (New York: Sun, 1979), 5–8. Jacob insists on the prose poem being "situated," that is, on its being recognized as existing in its own artistic space. For him, the prose poem must be seen in isolation, as a jewel, rather than as a reference to other genres. One receives a little shock from the piece or from the margins surrounding it.

34. Delville, *The American Prose Poem*, 137.

35. De Quincey borrows this hiatus device for the trumpeter in section 4 of the "Dream-Fugue" and a similar phrasing is used to describe the revivification.

36. Hugh Kenner, *Flaubert, Joyce and Beckett* (London: W. H. Allen, 1964), 39–40. Cf. Christopher Ricks, *Geoffrey Hill and "The Tongue's Atrocities"* (Swansea: University College of Swansea, 1978), 12. Ricks agrees with Kenner's statement that the footnote is inaccessible to the ear but he rejects the distinction between the footnote and the parenthesis. For Ricks, parentheses may describe either the syntactical unit inserted into the larger text or the typographical indicators, which include square or round brackets, commas, dashes, and so on. His argument rests on the assertion that the voice does not make a distinction between any of these.

37. *Hogg's Instructor* 9: 273–4; facsimile in Baxter, *De Quincey's Art of Autobiography*, 85/6. Cf. M.V.321. Masson moves the footnote numerical indicator from "civilation" to "explain it." This frustrates the point of intersection between the two levels of discourse, disrupting the disruption.

Chapter 4. Contexts II

1. Thomas Hobbes, *Humane Nature* (1650) quoted in Geoffrey Hill, "The Tartar's Bow and the Bow of Ulysses," in *The Enemy's Country* (Oxford: Clarendon Press, 1991), 22 and 25.

2. Ibid., 24.

3. Geoffrey Hill, "Redeeming the Time," *Agenda* 10/11 (1972–73): 104. Revised and reprinted in Geoffrey Hill, *The Lords of Limit* (London: Andre Deutsch, 1984), 88.

4. Hill, "Poetry as 'Menace' and 'Atonement'," *Lords of Limit*, 2.

5. *Stations* (1975) are extremely similar to *Mercian Hymns* from their prose form to their subject of the growth of the young poet and his association with the landscape.

6. Geoffrey Hill, "Under Judgment," interview by Blake Morrison, *The New Statesman*, 8 February 1980, 212.

7. Geoffrey Hill, interview by John Haffenden, *Quarto* 15 (1981): 21.

8. Hill's own description in interview by Haffenden, 21.

9. Ibid.

10. Cf. Calvin Bedient, "On Geoffrey Hill," *Critical Quarterly* 23 (1981): 22. "The 'prose' I take to be earnest ballast drawing Hill down to actuality; the nonetheless paced, sonorous writing as his intention to celebrate it; and the wrought economy his refusal to be intoxicated by it (the more so as it is confused by dreams)."

11. Hill, *The Enemy's Country*, 33. Hill sees words in all writing falling under these two classifications. He even observes hefting and tuning in the work of Dryden where he senses a conflict between his celebrated plain style and the perceptible artistry which he ostensibly denounces: "it appears that Dryden bears in mind two kinds of '*labor*': the tenacity of the craftsman and the drudgery of the hack. It is a matter of angry pride with him to redeem the circumstances of the second by exercising the skill and judgement of the first" ("Unhappy Circumstances," ibid., 6).

12. When it first appeared, the tone of *Mercian Hymns* proved inaccessible. "The poem hoards its words frugally, with the sparseness of a primitive economy, thus forcing each phrase to flex its potential to the full. The loss entailed by this stringency is a drastic shrinking of tonal diversity—a kind of tight-lipped, poker-faced emotional anonymity which, one guesses, would weary if the book was not as brief as it is" review of *Mercian Hymns*, *Times Literary Supplement*, August 1971, 1024.

13. De Quincey's varied repetition in "Dream-Fugue" is another example, although here too we may make analogies to musical bass (pitch), melody (tune), and counterpoint (tune out). Cf. Eleanor McNees, *Fucharistic Poetry* (London and Lewisburg, Pa.: Bucknell University Press, 1992), 150. McNees shows that Hill borrows his term "pitch" from Hopkins' "freedom of pitch" and turns it into "an acknowledgment of the right rhythm, a poet's ability to maintain a stride and to step out of that stride."

14. Hill is adapting the Linguistics expression "stress-pitch-juncture."

15. Hill, "Redeeming the Time," 94; Hill, *Lords of Limit*, 90.

16. Cf. Hill, "Redeeming the Time," 95; Hill, *Lords of Limit*, 90. Hill quotes Coleridge's comment that his (Coleridge's) copious parentheses are "'the *drama* of Reason'" and adds, "his parentheses are antiphons of vital challenge" (99; 93), putting his own practice squarely within the same mould.

17. Cf. Peter Levi, S.J., "Geoffrey Hill," review of *Mercian Hymns*, *Agenda* 9/10 (1971–72): 100. "In romantic poetry the lines spill out into their surrounding silences, and make them resonant, but in these poems the context of language is used to the bone, very exactly, and this means that each stanza completely fills the surrounding silence."

18. Cf. Lodge, *Modes of Modern Writing*, 88: Lodge argues that, other than convenience, there is no reason why prose should not be printed on continuous paper like ticker tape. According to Lodge's reasoning, *Mercian Hymns* would have to be classified as verse since only in that medium is the arrangements of lines and spaces significant. In a prose text, on the other hand, the important spaces are those of punctuation that bear on the sense of the work.

19. E. M. Knottenbelt, *Passionate Intelligence*, Costerus New Series, 77 (Amsterdam: Rodopi, 1990), 154.

20. Grevel Lindop, "Myth and Blood: The Poetry of Geoffrey Hill," *Critical Quarterly* 26 (1984): 149.

21. Cf. Hill, *The Enemy's Country*, 34. "The extent to which any writer is, or is not, aware of 'overtones,' 'harmonics,' in the language, the degree to which it is possible, necessary, or desirable for a reader to 'hear' the harmonics, are matters of nice speculation." McNees (*Eucharistic Poetry*, 149) describes Hill as feeling obliged to "register his antiphonal voice against the common and often debased language of his age."

22. Knottenbelt, *Passionate Intelligence*, 161.

23. Geoffrey Hill, *Mercian Hymns* (London: André Deutsch, 1971). No page numbers.

24. David Annwn reads hymn II by interpreting the words rather than reading them at all. Thus, "'curt graffito' could be 'fuck' or 'piss off.' . . . A syndicate could be the O.F.C. (Overseas Food Corporation)" and so on in an attempt to achieve the *o* and *a* vowel sounds. David Annwn, *Inhabited Voices* (Frome: Bran's Head Books, 1984), 66. Annwn's personal catalogue seems to be an excessively derivative way to invoke the name "Offa."

25. The style of language in these two hymns in particular bear a striking resemblance to Jakobson's observations on contiguity disorder: "contexture-deficient aphasia . . . diminishes the extent and variety of sentences. The syntactical rules organizing words into higher units are lost; this loss, called a grammatism, causes the degeneration of the sentences into a mere 'word heap.'" Roman Jakobson, "Two Aspects of Language and Two Types of Aphasic Disturbances," in *Selected Writings* (The Hague: Mouton Publishers, 1971), 2: 251.

26. "the crypt of roots and endings" (IV); "scrollwork of fern" (V); "the silver veining, the gold leaf, voluted grape-vine, master-works of treacherous thread." (XXIII, of tapestry); "tendrils of the stony vine" (XXIV).

27. Haffenden interview, 21. Harold Bloom has called *Mercian Hymns* a "*Prelude-*in-little" in a reference to both the "growth of a poet's mind" and the spots of time of which it is composed. "The Survival of Strong Poetry," introduction to *Somewhere Is Such a Kingdom, Poems 1952–1971* by Geoffrey Hill (Boston: Houghton Mifflin, 1975), xxii. Cf. David Gervais's analysis of Wordsworth's influence on Hill. "An 'Exemplary Poet': Geoffrey Hill's Wordsworth," *Agenda* 34 (1996): 88–103, esp. 95.

28. In the first reading I take the speaker of the first verset to be Offa who is then transferred to the third person by the change of key effected by the phrase "So, murmurous, he withdrew from them" where the murmur is the preceding monologue and the two are held together by the conceit of "concede" and "withdrew." The word "dice" as plural of 'die' contains the associative meaning of a device to engrave coins (coinage being a significant element in Offa's reign), now comically reduced to a child's ludo accessory. The pronoun "his" ("his dice whirred in the ludo cup") therefore quite possibly refers to the child-king here.

29. Simone Weil, *The Need for Roots*, trans. A. F. Wills, quoted in Geoffrey Hill, "'The Conscious Mind's Intelligible Structure': A Debate," *Agenda* 9/10 (1971–72): 14.

30. Cf. Haffenden interview, 21: "In handling the English language the poet makes an act of recognition that etymology is history."

31. Cf. Alan Brownjohn, review of *Mercian Hymns*, *The New Statesman*, 6 August 1971, 183: "one is not asked, as reader, to live the poems so much as to pace about them, with benumbed fascination, as one might on some bafflingly fragmentary and impressive historical remains."

32. John Needham, "The Idiom of Geoffrey Hill's 'Mercian Hymns,'" *English* 28 (1979): 140.

33. Ibid., 147.

34. The scene of a "shadowy, thrashing midsummer hail-storm" (XVII) is at once biblical and Shakespearean (reminiscent of the heath in *King Lear*).

35. Haffenden interview, 19. Grevel Lindop writes of their "frigid patterning" ("Myth and Blood," 149).

36. Cf. W. S. Milne, "'Decreation' in Geoffrey Hill's *Lachrimae*," *Agenda* 17 (1979): 69. Milne argues that Hill's self-effacement has aesthetic/religious connotations. The poet's mortality is set against the transcendent quality of the artwork.

37. According to A. M. Roberts, "Reflexivity and Impersonality in the Poetry of Geoffrey Hill" (Ph.D. thesis, University of London, 1991): 228, *Mercian Hymns* gives shape to experience but as a poem is itself shaped by "the structures and pressures of language."

38. Cathrael Kazin, "'Across a Wilderness of Retrospection': A Reading of Geoffrey Hill's *Lachrimae*," *Agenda* 17 (1979): 56 n.3.

39. Richard Drain, "'*The Waste Land*': The Prison and the Key," in *The Waste Land in Different Voices*, ed. A. D. Moody (London: Edward Arnold, 1974), 29.

40. Hugh Kenner, "The Invisible Poet," in *T. S. Eliot, The Waste Land*, eds. C. B. Cox and Arnold P. Hinchliffe (London: Macmillan, 1968), 172. In its printed format the poem was longer than thirty-two pages but too short for sixty-four.

41. Seamus Heaney has described Hill as a "scholastic imagination." "Englands of the Mind," in *Preoccupations* (London: Faber & Faber, 1980), 151.

42. Hill is politely scrupulous in his notes. Hymn XXIII: "I have, with considerable impropriety, extended the term"; XXV: "'wire': I seem not to have been strictly accurate."; XXVII: "based on a ritual phrase used of various kings though not, as far as I am aware, of Offa himself."

43. The subtlety of this incorporation of extraliterary context into a work already in prose is not taken up by William Bedford in his essay, "True Sequences of Pain: 'Context' in the Critical Prose and Poetry of Geoffrey Hill," *Agenda* 30 (1992). Bedford states that in *Mercian Hymns*, past and present provide critiques of each other but he makes no distinction between context that is applied at the moment of reading (implied context) and that offered in Hill's notes.

44. Appropriately, "quarry" is both a site of excavation and an object of intended prey. Other subterranean images appear throughout: "I wormed my way heavenward" (V); "out of England's well" (XIII). Cf. Hill's antiphonal voices in "Ovid in the Third Reich": "I have learned one thing: not to look down / So much upon the damned. They, in their sphere, / Harmonize strangely with the divine / Love."

45. Hymn XXIV: "('Et exspecto resurrectionem mortuorum' dust in the / eyes, on clawing wings, and lips)." Cf. Baxter, *De Quincey's Art of Autobiography*, 89–90, on

the relation between death and parenthesis in "Sir William Hamilton." Baxter shows how the reading process of descending into the footnote and returning to the "upper air" of the main text is an artful dramatization of the essay's discussion of resurrection: the reader reincarnates De Quincey.

46. Alan Halsey, *The Text of Shelley's Death* (Herefordshire: Five Seasons Press, 1995), 24.

47. Cf. Alan Halsey, *The Art of Memory on Hay-on-Wye*, 4th ed. (Textual Instability, 1996). Although the pieces in this prose poem collection are distinguished by roman numerals, suggesting a rectilinear narrative, the reading process actually requires cross-referencing of the individual prose poems to connect the dispersed details of subnarratives. The weaving of the reader's eye around the text as a whole creates a narrative in itself that is consistent with the dimensions of personal memory. Indeed, Hay-on-Wye finally exists only in the memory, even for the narrator: "We could rebuild Hay-on-Wye somewhere in the west of Ireland: leave the present place of that name to the people who want it. Meaning Mr Morelli and the D.B.R.W." (XXXIX).

48. Cf. Hugh Haughton, "'How fit a title . . .' : Title and Authority in the Work of Geoffrey Hill," *Geoffrey Hill: Essays on His Word*, ed. Peter Robinson (Milton Keynes and Philadelphia: Open University Press, 1985), 146. "Under its studied mask of impeccable scholarship, [*Mercian Hymns*] remains an astonishing portrayal of the poet's quest for poetic authority—and meditation on the disturbing analogies between the language of poetry and the language of power." Significantly, De Quincey's use of the term "power" is being used in its literal sense and is now opposed to poetry. "Power" has, ironically, become identified with "knowledge," which is context.

49. Retrospectively, Alan Wall confidently identifies *Mercian Hymns* as "a sequence of prose poems" comparable to *Le Spleen de Paris*. "Geoffrey Hill's *Canaan*," *Agenda* 34 (1996): 38–39.

50. Cf. "'The Tongue's Atrocities,'" 19. Ricks points out that one cannot *say* roman numerals, that to call, for example, Larkin's poem, "MCMXIV," "nineteen fourteen" is to lose entirely the sense of epitaph and recorded history.

51. Geoffrey Hill, *Collected Poems* (Harmondsworth: Penguin, 1985); Geoffrey Hill, *New and Collected Poems, 1952–1992* (Boston and New York: Houghton Mifflin, 1994). A qualification is needed here. In saying that the descriptive titles are omitted from the work I refer to the text proper and the endnotes that follow in the Andre Deutsch edition. The titles do appear in both of the *Collected Poems*, beside the roman numerals in the list of contents.

52. *The Poetry and Voice of Geoffrey Hill*, sound cassette, in association with the Poetry Center (New York: Caedmon, 1979).

53. Offa is an active and controlling subject in these hymns despite their title: "when King Offa was alive and dead" (XXVII); "he withdrew from them" (XXIX); "he began to walk towards us" (XXX).

54. Nichola Anne Haxell, "The Name of the Prose: A Semiotic Study of titling in the Pre-Baudelairian Prose Poem," *French Studies* 44 (1990): 163. Hill is clearly aware of this game because in hymn XXIII he reverses it: the title is "Opus Anglicanum" and the poem produces a tapestry.

55. Haughton points out that almost all of Hill's titles (for his collections) are taken from previous literary sources and he associates this with the poet's persistent themes of authority and commemoration of the dead ("'How fit a title . . .',"

133–37). The sub-titles of *Mercian Hymns* create a microcosm by intertextualizing themselves as a parody of the title of the work and its interlinear source.

56. Cf. Martin Dodsworth, "*Mercian Hymns* : Offa, Charlemagne and Geoffrey Hill," in Robinson ed., *Geoffrey Hill: Essays on His Work*, 49: "[*Mercian Hymns*] is not a collection but a single sequence of thirty prose-poems"; also, Knottenbelt, *Passionate Intelligence*, 155: "As one might expect from a narrative sequence of prose poems—and again as in the Old English chronicle poems—[*Mercian Hymns*] has a logical conclusion."

57. Haffenden, interview, 21.

58. Hill, *Mercian Hymns*, Acknowledgments (unpaginated).

59. The hymns could also go under the title of "Opus Anglicanum," which acts as the needful contrast in Hill's aesthetic of the heckler.

60. Ricks, "'The Tongue's Atrocities,'" 16.

61. See Frank Kermode, *The Sense of an Ending* (New York: Oxford University Press, 1967), 88. The occurrence of a *kairos*, in the nature of the end "is not a universal end, merely an image of it."

62. "he entered into the last dream of Offa the King" (XXIX).

63. Cf. Halsey, *The Text of Shelley's Death*. The prose poem sequence is followed by two sections of end matter: "Reversions on the Text," where the scholar/editor interprets the motives of those who provide accounts of the doomed sailing trip. He also makes comments on the resulting text. For example, he notes that everyone and everything in the *Text of Shelley's Death* has two names, inciting us to attempt an interpretation of this fact. The second end section, "Towards an Index of Shelley's Death" reads like a concordance. It is an alphabetical list of phrases taken from Shelley's poetry. Like *The Art of Memory*, Halsey sets up echoes that provoke cross-referencing, not just within his text, but outside, to its sources.

64. Cf. Dodsworth, "Mercian Hymns," 61: "In the world of *Mercian Hymns* revelation is vouchsafed, but the natural world is reluctant to accommodate it."

Chapter 5. Parallelism

1. T. S. Eliot, "The Borderline of Prose," *The New Statesman*, 19 May 1917, 158.

2. Three other prose poems by Eliot have also been recovered (held in the Berg Collection at the New York Public Library). "Introspection," "The Engine" I and II, and "While you were absent in the lavatory" appear in Christopher Rick's collected edition of Eliot's previously unpublished papers, *Inventions of the March Hare: Poems 1909–1917* (London: Faber & Faber, 1996).

3. Henri Meschonnic is concerned with the task of producing a French translation of the Bible on a par with the King James. The Bible *is* mentioned in accounts that trace the development of the French prose poem but the influence is on the creation of a florid poetic prose (see Maurice Chapelan's introduction to *Anthologie du poème en prose* [Paris: René Julliard, 1946], viii–ix). Fénelon provided the model for this type of prose in *Télémaque*. It was later, with the appearance in France of Macpherson's *Ossian* poems, that brevity began to be imposed. Macpherson's work was imbued with the English biblical style, yet French prose poetry still tended to render this biblical influence in solely Psalmic lines, which produces a slightly different model, more like Whitman's style.

4. *The Fortnightly Review* 56 (1894): 22. "The Artist" first appeared, as did two other prose poems by Wilde, "The Disciple" and "The House of Judgment," in the Oxford undergraduate magazine, *The Spirit Lamp* between November 1892 and June 1893. These, with three more, were later published in the *Fortnightly Review*, 1894. All six finally appeared together in *Lord Arthur Savile's Crime and Other Prose Pieces* in 1908.

5. Cf. Charles Swann, "*The Picture of Dorian Gray*, The Bible, and the Unpardonable Sin," *Notes and Queries* 236 (1991): 327. Swann identifies the source for a sentence of the prose poem "The House of Judgment" (and a passage in *Dorian Gray*) as 2 Kings 24:4.

6. Robert Lowth, "Preliminary Dissertation" to *Isaiah* (London: J. Dodsley and T. Cadell, 1778), x–xi.

7. Psalms 85:10.

8. Robert Lowth, *Lectures on the Sacred Poetry of the Hebrews*, trans. G. Gregory (London: J. Johnson, 1787), 1 (III): 68.

9. Roger Pooley, *English Prose of the Seventeenth Century, 1590–1700* (London and New York: Longman, 1992), 100, 164. Pooley quotes Hester Biddle's 1662 address as an example of "biblical style": "Oh you high and lofty ones! who spendeth God's creation upon your lusts, and doth not feed the hungry, nor clothe the naked" (ibid., 100). The educated continued to use Hebrew, Greek, and possibly Latin texts at this time (101). See also, Harold Fisch, *Jerusalem and Albion: the Hebraic Factor in Seventeenth-Century Literature* (London: Routledge and Kegan Paul, 1964), 49–50: "there can be no doubt that a *literary* use was made of this Biblical model [the Psalms] after the manner of the current practice of literary 'Imitation' applied to the ancient orators and poets of Greece and Rome."

10. According to Thomas Preston, recent research in this field reveals, "an almost astonishing interest in religious works generally and biblical criticism specifically." Despite the increase in the number of printing presses in the next century, which resulted in the production of books per annum being quadrupled, the number of these religious publications continued to increase or at least remained stable. Thomas R. Preston, "Biblical Criticism, Literature and the Eighteenth-Century Reader," in *Books and Their Readers in Eighteenth-Century England*, ed. Isabel Rivers (Leicester: Leicester University Press and New York: St. Martin's Press, 1982), 98–99.

11. K. G. Hamilton, *The Two Harmonies: Poetry and Prose in the Seventeenth Century* (Oxford: Clarendon Press, 1963), 23–24.

12. Murray Roston, *Prophet and Poet: The Bible and the Growth of Romanticism* (London: Faber & Faber, 1965), 126.

13. T. Drummond, *Poems Sacred to Religion and Virtue* (London, 1756), quoted in Roston, *Prophet and Poet*, 131.

14. Lowth, *Sacred Poetry* I (XIV–XVI), esp. 308–13. Lowth distinguishes between prose as the language of reason and poetry as the language of the passions.

15. See Stephen Prickett, *Words and* The Word: *Language, Poetics and Biblical Interpretation* (Cambridge: Cambridge University Press, 1986), 114–15. Prickett traces two separate traditions that stem from Lowth's work: the theoretical Higher Criticism via Michaelis et al. in Germany and the formal influence on Romantic poetry in Britain. According to Prickett, the two areas were briefly reunited in Britain in the 1790s but the theoretical side was quickly suppressed as radical and unpatriotic after the French Revolution and did not reemerge until the 1820s.

16. *The Poetical Works of Christopher Smart*, ed. Marcus Walsh (Oxford: Clarendon Press, 1987), 3: 358.

17. Smart's version is ultimately verse and therefore the sense-period is made to coincide with the end of the line.

18. C. S. Lewis argues that the *Authorized Version* has had a much more limited influence on English literature than that with which it is generally credited. Quotations are used to embroider a work and, he claims, similarities in style between the two languages is not proof of influence but means only that a similar rhythm is unavoidable. For example, Lewis asks if the sentence "At the regatta Madge avoided the river and the crowd" reminds one of "In the beginning God created the heaven and the earth" and, if it did, whether that fact would be significant. C. S. Lewis, *The Literary Impact of the Authorised Version* (London: The Athlone Press, 1950), 16.

19. Ruth apRoberts, *The Biblical Web* (Ann Arbor: University of Michigan Press, 1994), 34.

20. Brian Vickers, *Francis Bacon and Renaissance Prose* (Cambridge: Cambridge University Press, 1968), 113.

21. apRoberts, *The Biblical Web*, 14 and 39.

22. "The plain style wins the day. The fact itself is not in dispute." Stanley E. Fish, *Self-Consuming Artifacts: The Experience of Seventeenth-Century Literature* (Berkeley and London: University of California Press, 1972), 379.

23. Thomas Sprat, *History of the Royal Society* (1667), ed. Jackson I. Cope and Harold Whitmore Jones (Missouri: Washington University Studies, 1958), 113.

24. The battle between grammar and rhetoric was of deep significance because prose stood as the standard for all vernacular writing in England. See Janel M. Mueller, *The Native Tongue and the Word: Developments in English Prose Style 1380–1580* (Chicago and London: The University of Chicago Press, 1984), 11–13. Mueller shows that standard English, which emerged in the fifteenth century, was rooted in a consciously literary style due to the fact that the use of the vernacular in documentation antedated the establishment of a standard spoken English.

25. Morris Croll and R. F. Jones have been the main protagonists to debate seventeenth-century prose styles. Croll takes the view that the change occurs at 1600 and reenacts the classical situation in stylistics which is being imitated. Croll's "anti-Ciceronianism" (manifesting in "loose" and "curt" attic) is a reaction against rhetoric. Jones, instead, argues for a "stylistic revolution" occurring around 1660 perpetrated by scientists and the Royal Society. Robert Adolph defines the shift as a move toward utilitarianism, which encompassed the arts and humanities as well as theology and science. Harold Fisch supports the Puritans as the main promoters of the plain style while others such as Joan Webber place the cause for change within the Puritan-Anglican debate. More recently, Stanley Fish has described the emerging plain style as "self-satisfying," that is, supported by a belief that the truth can be accessed by following the language of reason (Fish, *Self-Consuming Artifacts*, 380).

26. Croll describes the purpose of "Anti-Ciceronian" or "baroque" prose as "not a thought, but a mind thinking," where the experience of conceiving a thought is integral to the idea itself. "The Baroque Style in Prose," in *Seventeenth-Century Prose*, ed. Stanley E. Fish (New York and Oxford: Oxford University Press, 1971), 29. Stanley Fish, on the other hand, adds a new pair of dialectic couplings to describe the two prose styles. After "Anglican-Puritan, Painted-Plain, Ciceronian-Senecan, Scientific-Rhetorical, Utilitarian-Frivolous—I add a new pair, Self-Satisfying and Self-

Consuming." "Self-Satisfying" denotes a prose that leads the reader to a point of certainty and clarity while "Self-Consuming" describes a prose that moves away from clarity toward increasing complexity (Fish, *Self-Consuming Artifacts*, 378). In both theories, which are otherwise quite different, the prose acts as a window through which one observes the mental processes of the author.

27. John M. Steadman, *The Hill and the Labyrinth* (Berkeley and London: University of California Press, 1984), 92. According to Steadman, the scientific style strove to achieve the ideal language of one word for one thing while the essayists' plain style, although it was more direct than current rhetoric, was still another *style*.

28. Cf. Ian A. Gordon, *The Movement of English Prose* (London: Longmans, 1966), 109: "The new prose of short statements, to which fresh ideas could be immediately added by parataxis or simple coordination, allowed a writer like Donne or Burton to think in the act of writing." The Baroque era saw a similar exposition of logical thought in the new maze labyrinths that concealed the center and necessitated active reasoning by the pilgrim to discover it (cf. Chapter 3, section II).

29. Again, terms are never generalizations here. Adolph describes the brevity of Tacitus's writing as effecting ambiguity "to the point where his prose approaches poetry." In Bacon's hands, however, the same desire for brevity is to assist clarity and definition. Robert Adolph, *The Rise of Modern Prose Style* (Massachusetts and London: The MIT Press, 1968), 30–31. Fish points out that, in practice, the apparently straightforward structure of the plain style may on occasion be more difficult to understand than some Ciceronian rhetoric (Fish, *Self-Consuming Artifacts*, 379). However, this too makes the style comparable to the obscure statements of the prophetic passages in the Bible.

30. Morris Croll regards synonymy in Thomas Browne's work as evidence of the curt style—presumably as a development of earlier forms such as Elizabethan doublets (Croll, "The Baroque Style in Prose," 34–5). On the other hand, Whallon argues that the predominance of synonymy over antithesis in Browne's work suggests the influence of Hebrew poets rather than the more indigenous alliterative tradition or antithetical style of the curt attic. William Whallon, "Hebraic Synonymy in Sir Thomas Browne," *ELH* 28 (1961): 335–52.

31. Cf. James R. Sutherland, *English Literature of the Late Seventeenth Century*, The Oxford History of English Literature, eds. Bonamy Dobrée and Norman Davis (Oxford: Clarendon Press, 1969), 220–21: "So long as the potential essayist was isolated in a country rectory or meditating his past life in a rural retirement, he tended to write sententiously on moral and religious subjects, and with little real awareness of a reader to be addressed. But after the Restoration, with the rapid development of a well-organized literary community in London, the author-reader relationship was correspondingly transformed. . . . The breakthrough did not come until the early years of the next century, when the periodical essay paper, with a regular body of subscribers and therefore of constant readers, was firmly established."

32. It would seem that the dearth of quality prose-fiction in this period is due to the fact that the psychological insight afforded by the "anti-Ciceronian" prose was not coupled with the contemporary fashion for action and plot until much later (see also, Sutherland, *English Literature*, 218).

33. Cf. Thomas Traherne, *The Centuries*. Traherne prays repeatedly to be left with the imprint of God on him so that he may be inspired and his words (presumably as poetry) may be like the Psalms of David. He fuses his narrative "I" with that of Adam and later with a spectator to the crucifixion in an attempt to share their

experience. The prose style, however, a mixture of Ciceronian and attic, is not "biblical" in the Lowthian sense.

34. Lowth endorses Longinus's definition of sublimity in *Sacred Poetry*, see esp. 1(XIV): 307.

35. Sir William Jones, a contemporary leading Orientalist, confirms this view. Having defined "original and native poetry" as "the language of violent passions, expressed in exact measure, with strong accents and significant words," he goes on to say that "in defining what true poetry ought to be . . . we have described what it really is among the Hebrews, the Greeks and the Romans, the Arabs and Persians . . . but what did David or Solomon imitate in their divine poems? A man, who is really joyful or afflicted, cannot be said to imitate joy or affliction" (quoted in M. H. Abrams, *The Mirror and the Lamp: Romantic Theory and the Critical Tradition* [New York: W. W. Norton, 1958], 87–88). The same has been said of Bunyan's style, which "was not any convention of pastoral rusticity but the actual language as spoken on the roads and in the towns of East Anglia." According to N. H. Keeble, Bunyan's work became deeply unfashionable for over a century (despite his initial success) because he refused to refine his style for the second part of *The Pilgrim's Progress* and his reputation was only revived by the Romantics' interest in native diction (inspired by Lowth). N. H. Keeble, Introduction to John Bunyan, *The Pilgrim's Progress* (Oxford: Oxford University Press, 1984), xx.

36. Cf. Suzanne Bernard, *Le poème en prose de Baudelaire jusqu'à nos jours* (Paris: Librairie Nizet, 1959), 28. Bernard explains how translations of Macpherson's work eliminated his digressions to produce unified moments of heightened intensity.

37. More recently, Edward Said has identified Lowth as one of the pioneers (with Eichhorn et al.) in biblical studies, which instigated the influence of the Orient on the West. However, he qualifies this advocacy by arguing that prefabricated "Orientalism" has been "almost a European invention" and, from Lowth until World War II, a specifically Anglo-French "cultural enterprise." Edward Said, *Orientalism* (Harmondsworth: Penguin Books, 1985), 1, 4, and 17.

38. G. M. Hopkins, "Poetic Diction," in *The Note-Books and Papers of Gerard Manley Hopkins*, ed. Humphrey House (London and New York: Oxford University Press, 1937), 92.

39. G. M. Hopkins, "Rhythm and the Other Structural Parts of Rhetoric—Verse," in *The Journals and Papers of Gerard Manley Hopkins*, eds. Humphrey House and Graham Storey (London: Oxford University Press, 1959), 267. Cf. Silliman, *The New Sentence*. Silliman argues that, for Language poets, the sentence is distinct from the utterance by having structure and closure. The group claim for the sentence the same qualities of the line in verse. That is, it is regarded as a unit that is quantified by the paragraph, operating as the stanza. In other words, Hopkins's focus on clauses as the characteristic figure of prose, is expanded to encompass the more solid measure of the sentence.

40. See for example, G. M. Hopkins, "Poetic Diction" and "On the Origin of Beauty." Coleridge makes similar claims, in his response to Wordsworth's Preface, in *Biographia Literaria*, vol. 2: "A poem contains the same elements as a prose composition; the difference therefore must consist in a different combination of them, in consequence of a different object proposed" (11) and later, "the very *act* of poetic composition *itself* is, and is *allowed* to imply and to produce, an unusual state of excitement, which, of course justifies and demands a correspondent difference of language" (71).

41. Roman Jakobson, "Linguistics and Poetics," in *Selected Writings* III: 19. In "Poetic Diction" Hopkins describes poetry as the *consequence* of parallelism. The more marked the parallelistic structure, the stronger the parallelisms will be in its expression and diction (93). Moreover, the vividness that poetic diction represents is clearly regarded by Hopkins as terse and concise in contrast to the diffuse "chromatic" extension of prose parallelisms. W. H. Gardner, *Gerard Manley Hopkins (1844–1889): A Study of Poetic Idiosyncrasy in Relation to the Poetic Tradition* (London: Martin Secker and Warburg, 1944), 109.

42. Jakobson, "Linguistics and Poetics," 25. Hopkins had already defined poetry (in contradistinction to verse): "Poetry is in fact speech only employed to carry the inscape of speech for the inscape's sake—and therefore the inscape must be dwelt on" ("Poetry and Verse," in *Journals*, 289). Jakobson's formulation clearly echoes Hopkins in thought and expression.

43. Jakobson, "Linguistics and Poetics," 27.

44. See Roman Jakobson, "The Dominant," in *Selected Writings* III: 751–56. Jakobson describes the dominant as a sort of catalyst that "substantially changes the poem's structure with regard to sound texture, syntactic structure, and imagery; it alters the poem's metrical and strophical criteria and its composition" (752). It is the dominant that orders the various functions of language into a classifiable literary form.

45. Hopkins states that poetry requires repetition in order to "detach it to the mind." The mind then understands the poetic as an essence that may be copied and repeated (Hopkins, "Poetry and Verse," 289). The text is thus separated from contextual circumstance, from some larger whole, but free to develop organically from its own unity.

46. All of Wilde's prose poems contain this challenge: in "The Disciple," Narcissus's pool confesses to be mourning for the loss of its own reflection in the mirror of Narcissus's eyes; "The Doer of Good," who replicates the life of Christ, cries for not having been crucified too, and similarly with the rest.

47. Blake was reluctant to publish this collection of juvenilia and ignored the expectations of his patrons that he would publish or at least circulate his *Poetical Sketches*. G. E. Bentley, Jr. *Blake Records* (Oxford: Clarendon Press, 1969), 25–26. Cf. Michael Phillips, "The Reputation of Blake's *Poetical Sketches* 1783–1863," *Review of English Studies* 26 (1975): 19. According to Phillips, however, the assumption that the *Poetical Sketches* were unknown from their private printing in 1783 to the publication of Alexander Gilchrist's *Life* in 1863 has now been qualified. A number of copies are believed to have been circulated privately although only twenty-three are extant.

48. Cf. Roston, *Prophet and Poet*, 146, and David B. Morris, *The Religious Sublime: Christian Poetry and Critical Tradition in Eighteenth-Century England* (Lexington: University Press of Kentucky, 1972), 165. Macpherson was a divinity student in 1753, the year that Lowth's lectures were published. Hugh Blair had also reiterated the importance of parallelism in primitive and oriental studies in his own *Lectures on Rhetoric and Belles Lettres*, written circa 1759 and published in 1783 the same year that "The Couch of Death" was composed. John C. Villalobos offers a convincing argument that Blake responded directly to Lowth's work. In his introduction to his translation of *Isaiah*, Lowth claims that, in addition to its similarly fragmentary state, Aristotle's *Poetics* shares its depth of authority with that of the Old Testament. He describes the *Poetics* as "the great Code of Criticism." Blake's famous inscription on his

Laocoön engraving of 1820: "The Old and the New Testaments are the Great Code of Art," which is usually used as proof of Blake's interest in the Bible, can actually be read as a criticism of Lowth's classicism. Blake's misquotation or reinscription of Lowth places the Bible (as art) above the highest degree of rationality possible in the *Poetics*. John C. Villalobos, "A Possible Source for William Blake's 'The Great Code of Art'," *English Language Notes*, 26 (1988): 36–39. Finally, there is a similarity between the opening of "The Couch of Death" and Klopstock's crucifixion scene in *The Messiah* (*Messias*, 1748–1773), which, in 1763, was one of several popular German translations (see Morris, *The Religious Sublime*, 158).

49. Cf. Sheila A. Spector, "Blake as an Eighteenth-Century Hebraist," in *Blake and His Bibles*, ed. David V. Erdman (West Cornwall, Conn: Locust Hill Press, 1990), 213. Spector's investigation into Blake's actual knowledge of Hebrew shows that he knew the Hebraic alphabet and was capable of incorporating words and phrases, "but we have no evidence that he could do more than use a dictionary."

50. William Blake, *Poetical Sketches* (London, 1783), 60–61. The structure employed by Blake (and Macpherson) is Lowth's parallelisms. The passage quoted above echoes Psalm 23: "Yea, though I walk through the valley of the shadow of death, I will fear no evil; for thou *art* with me; thy rod and thy staff they comfort me." Meanwhile, in contrast to the Psalmist's dignified pace, Blake's breathless tone is clearly Ossianic: "I sit in my grief! I wait for morning in my tears! Rear the tomb, ye friends of the dead. Close it not till Colma come. My life flies away like a dream! why should I stay behind? Here shall I rest with my friends, by the stream of the sounding rock." "The Songs of Selma," in *The Poems of Ossian*, trans. James Macpherson, ed. William Sharp (Edinburgh: J. Grant, 1926), 411. Also, cf. Kathleen Raine, *Blake and Tradition* (Princeton: Princeton University Press, 1968), I: 124. Raine describes the difference between Blake and Macpherson as that between a symbolist and an imagist poet, respectively. She argues that Blake's imagery in the "Ossianic fragments" in *Poetical Sketches* (and here she quotes from "The Couch of Death") is "without a pronounced symbolic dimension." However she identifies the poetic prose as the source of this deficiency, which he mended by turning to verse.

51. Cf. Émile Hennequin's prose poem, "Minoration" in the prose poem anthology, *Pastels in Prose*, trans. and ed. Stuart Merrill (New York: Harper and Bros., 1890), 197. Hennequin's text is an anti-prayer beginning "Let all that is be no more" and continuing in a similar series of proposals, "Let . . . ," beginning on a new line, much like Smart's work. In "Minoration," these seven lines are answered by a paragraph dominated by "and": "And perhaps existence will lose some of its harshness; and perhaps in a tideless calm some souls will find repose . . . "

52. Lowth explains in his "Preliminary Dissertation" that he is following the structure of Jerome's translation of the same Book. Jerome himself follows universal opinion that the prophecies are in prose, but he sets them out in lines divided by cola. The form is that used for verse but Jerome specifically warns his reader not to mistake it for meter (Lowth, *Isaiah*, iii).

53. "The popularity of metaphors declined with the decline of the concept of the world as metaphor, to be replaced by less imaginative and more rational figures of speech, like the cautious and prosaic simile" (Steadman, *The Hill and the Labyrinth*, 19).

54. Metzidakis, *Repetition and Semiotics*, 74–75.

55. Cf. Gregory W. Bredbeck, "Narcissus in the Wilde: Textual Cathexis and the Historical Origins of Queer Camp," in *The Politics and Poetics of Camp*, ed. Moe

Meyer (London and New York: Routledge, 1994), 53–58 and 66–68. Bredbeck regards the abundance of self-referentiality in "The Disciple" as a form of autoeroticism associated with both Narcissus and sexual inversion. As a form of objectless sexuality, this "auto-textualism" (67) reacts against the "straight" (subject/object) referentiality, registered by the relationship Wilde/tradition, to create an unprejudicial and sustained dichotomy of difference. Neil Bartlett touches on the similar rhythms of male sexuality and religious texts. He concludes that by playing on the ambiguous distinction, Wilde aspires "to the true rigour of religious writing." Neil Bartlett, *The Uses of Monotony: Repetition in the Language of Oscar Wilde, Jean Genet, Edmund White, and Juan Goytisolo* (London: Birkbeck College, 1994), 16.

56. James L. Kugel, *The Idea of Biblical Poetry: Parallelism and Its History* (New Haven and London: Yale University Press, 1981), 69. Also, cf. Henri Meschonnic, "Translating Biblical Rhythm," in *Biblical Patterns in Modern Literature*, no. 77, eds. David H. Hirsch and N. Aschkenasy (Chico, Calif.: Scholars Press, 1984), 232. Meschonnic too rejects any prose/poetry distinction in the Bible. He argues that repetition, which is fundamental to parallelism, is universally emphatic and "in no way distinguishes poetry from prose." Instead, the Bible can only be described as consisting of verses and divided between the spoken and the sung.

57. Kugel, *Idea of Biblical Poetry*, 23, emphasis added.

58. Cf. William Whallon, *Formula, Character, and Context* (Washington: Center for Hellenic Studies, 1969), 148–51. Whallon argues that the root of parallelism is a national fund of word pairs that occur either in a series ("prose") or joining hemistiches ("poetry"). Kugel's formula still applies here because Whallon claims that the tradition for using set word pairs is purely stylistic. Pairing gives emphasis: "and drink not wine nor strong drink" (Judges 13:4); "I have drunk neither wine nor strong drink" (1 Sam.1:15); "they are drunken, but not with wine; they stagger, but not with strong drink" (Isa. 29:9). Compare Blake's fine detail in "Samson": "Now therefore drink no wine, and eat not any unclean thing" (*Poetical Sketches*, 69).

59. apRoberts objects to Kugel's application of his theories to literary criticism. She points out that, in some cases, B *is* a repetition of A but that synonyms are never merely repetitions. However, Kugel's definition of the B clause appears simply to suggest that its relationship to the A clause is not as significant as the fact that it comes afterward and closes that thought. apRoberts opposes Kugel's rejection of poetry and prose in the Bible as somehow demeaning to it (apRoberts, *Biblical Web*, 130). Whallon also proposes that the distinction between passages where word pairs are adjacent and where they are evenly distributed as prose and poetry respectively are modern classifications but that the original relationship was very close (Whallon, *Formula, Character and Context*, 148).

60. Coleridge borrowed the latin version of Lowth's lectures from the Bristol library in 1796, the same year in which he read Ossian (*CN* I, 161 Notes). Prickett sums up Lowth's influence on Coleridge's growing definition of poetry in terms of "antithetical parallelism" in *Biographia Literaria* (*Words and* The Word, 117–18; also, Fulford, *Coleridge's Figurative Language*, 83–86). Later, Coleridge describes the poetic parts of the Bible and Ossian as "slovenly Hexameters" (*CL* ii, 857).

61. Adolph, *Rise of Modern Prose Style*, 53. Adolph describes "trailing" as "characteristic 'Anti-Ciceronian' movement," arising from the lack of syntactic connection between members. Coleridge appears to have something similar in mind when he speaks of the correct motion of a reader, "at every step he pauses and half recedes,

and from the retrogressive movement collects the force which again carries him onward" (*Biographia Literaria*, 2:14).

62. Adele Berlin and Linda Waugh retain the prose/poetry distinction in order to emphasize that Hebrew poetry is capable of "*transcending the linearity* proper to any linguistic text." L. Waugh quoted in A. Berlin, *The Dynamics of Biblical Parallelism* (Bloomington: Indiana University Press, 1985), 13. Berlin and Waugh's approach tends to treat the "poem" spatially, like a picture. Parallelism in prose, on the other hand, is subordinated to the chronological process which it serves.

63. Emphasis added. Compare De Quincey's prose piece, *The Daughter of Lebanon, Sel.* 5:278: "of him that made Lebanon and the cedars of Lebanon." Lowth explains that the phrase "cedars of Lebanon" was commonly used to denote kings and princes of the gentiles, in parabolic terms (Lowth, *Sacred Poetry*, 1 (13): 295). De Quincey's parallelism, then, perfectly exemplifies furtherance in the biblical model.

64. Berlin, *Dynamics of Biblical Parallelism*, 6.

65. Wordsworth, *Lyrical Ballads*, 173.

66. Hopkins, *On the Origin of Beauty*, in *Journals*, 106.

67. See Berlin, *Dynamics of Biblical Parallelism*, 6; Bruce Mitchell and Fred C. Robinson, *A Guide to Old English*, 4th ed. rev. (Oxford: Basil Blackwell, 1986), 100: "*Hypotaxis* : When I came, I saw. When I saw, I conquered. *Asyndetic Parataxis* : I came. I saw. I conquered. *Syndetic Parataxis* : I came and I saw and I conquered."

68. In Mueller, *Native Tongue and the Word*, 19–23, conjunctions are described as devices of growth that condense intricate concepts of comparison by invoking similarities and differences between two elements simultaneously. Mueller goes on to illustrate the variety of types of "and" constructions with sentences that use a similar construction but infer different concepts (e.g.:"The scene of the movie and of the play was in Chicago." Here, "and" simply substitutes the repetition of "the scene of." However, in "Mary and Elizabeth left London," we cannot tell whether or not they left together). Similarly, "to and fro," or "Henry and Anne embraced" cannot be written in longhand, as it were. For Mueller, this linguistic ambiguity is often found at the center of theological paradoxes.

69. For example, "And he took away the treasures of the house of the Lord, and the treasures of the king's house; he even took away all: and he took away all the shields of gold which Solomon had made" (1 Kings 14:26). Cf. Mueller, *Native Tongue and the Word*, 35: "What becomes remarkable about Lowth's definitions . . . is that Hebraic sense parallelism makes creative capital of the very sameness-and-difference relations that inform the workings of sentential conjunction. Thus, as Lowth indeed recognized, synonymic and antithetic sense parallelisms comprise the paradigmatic types of composition in this mode; they subsist together in syntactic and semantic complementarity."

70. Murphy argues that Wilde's prose poems subvert the English Bible, in particular Jesus' parables, which they take as their model (*Tradition of Subversion*, 34). However, the parable form itself has been revealed as unstable in its own allegorical device: "The paradox of parable is that it is a likeness that rests on a manifest unlikeness between what is given and what cannot by any means be given directly. A parabolic 'likeness' is so 'unlike' that without interpretation or commentary the meaning may slip by the reader or listener altogether." J. Hillis Miller, *Tropes, Parables, Performatives* (New York and London: Harvester Wheatsheaf, 1990), 136. Wilde appears to be aware of a degree of paradox in the biblical parables when, in "The

Teacher of Wisdom" the prose poem consists of a hermit refusing to tell his knowledge of God, that is, refusing to give a parable. In addition, Jesus' parables do not rely on a final "twist-in-the-tail" as Wilde's do. The resemblance is clearly more stylistic than thematic.

71. The term "naked repetition" was coined by Gilles Deleuze in his *Différence et Répétition*. Steven Connor interprets Deleuze's concept as "repetition which is humbly obedient to its original, which merely and simply reproduces it without any addition or distortion." Steven Connor, *Samuel Beckett: Repetition, Theory, and Text* (Oxford: Basil Blackwell, 1988), 5–6.

72. Cf. *English Prose*, 100. Pooley argues that the *Authorized Version* had most impact on the uneducated who adopted the authoritative style when attacking authority itself.

73. Wilde's view of prose is a little ambiguous. On one hand he employs the devices of the abrupt antithetical epigram. On the other hand, he aspires to a more latinate construction, cf. W. B. Yeats, "My First Meeting with Oscar Wilde," in *Oscar Wilde: Interviews and Recollections*, ed. E. H. Mikhail (London: Macmillan, 1979), 1: 144. Also, Wilde's letter to Will Rothenstein, 24 August 1897, *The Letters of Oscar Wilde*, ed. Rupert Hart-Davis (London: Rupert Hart-Davis, 1962), 636: "When I said of W. E. H. that his prose was the prose of a poet, I paid him an undeserved compliment. His prose is jerky, spasmodic, and he is incapable of the beautiful architecture of a long sentence, which is the fine flower of prose-writing."

74. Charles Juliet, *Conversations with Samuel Beckett and Bram van Velde*, trans. Janey Tucker (Leiden: Academic Press Leiden, 1994), 167: "He reminds me that his family was Protestant and points out that the Protestants are very fond of the Old Testament."

75. Leslie Hill looks at allusions to the King James in the trilogy in *Beckett's Fiction in Different Words* (Cambridge: Cambridge University Press, 1990), 108–11. Alan Astro quotes Susan Brienza's examples of a biblical tone in the sentences: "It will be day and night again over him" (reminiscent of the refrain in the creation narrative, "and there was evening and there was morning"); "there will be stir in the sky" (similar to "let there be light"). Astro himself takes the postdiluvian landscape of ruin to approximate the fate of Sodom and Gomorrah. Alan Astro, *Understanding Samuel Beckett* (Columbia: University of South Carolina, 1990), 193.

76. Connor distinguishes between "open" and "closed" repetitions that correspond to metonymic and metaphoric figures respectively. "Closed" repetitions involve exhaustive possibilities. "Open" repetitions, on the other hand, offer a selection from an unlimited set of permutations (Connor, *Repetition, Theory, and Text*, 30–31). Unlike De Quincey's similar narratives, however, Beckett sustains the expansion of both forms of repetition, which are executed with careful calculation rather than awesome bewilderment.

77. H. Porter-Abbott, "Beginning Again: The Post-Narrative Art of *Texts for Nothing* and *How It Is*," in *The Cambridge Companion to Beckett*, ed. John Pilling (Cambridge: Cambridge University Press, 1994), 107 and 112.

78. Cf. E. M. Scarry, "Six Ways to Kill a Blackbird or Any Other Intentional Object: Samuel Beckett's Method of Meaning," *James Joyce Quarterly* 8 (1971): 278–89. Scarry investigates Beckett's underlying paradox that, while all intentional acts are bound to their object, the intention may be universal while the subject is by nature mutable. Beckett's struggle is characterized by an attempt to rid himself of the indelible object to achieve this universal condition.

79. Cf. Deirdre Bair, *Samuel Beckett* (London: Jonathan Cape, 1978), 221: "Beckett argued and then tried to demonstrate that once the [chess] pieces are set up on the board, any move from then on will only weaken one's position, that strength lies only in not moving at all. The ideal game for Beckett was one in which none of the pieces was moved, for from the very first move, failure and loss were inevitable." Beckett illustrates this point by the lunatic chess game in *Murphy* where the protagonist, forced to play white, loses to Mr. Endon's bizarre moves of nonengagement.

80. Cf. Martin Esslin, "Samuel Beckett—Infinity, Eternity," in *Beckett at 80/Beckett in Context*, ed. Enoch Brater (Oxford: Oxford University Press, 1986), 118. Beckett described to Martin Esslin the plan of "Lessness" as six "statement groups" of ten sentences each. These were picked out at random and the process repeated. "What *Lessness* represents in its form is an image of eternal return: the finite number of elements are here arranged in a manner which is both random and yet governed by a rigid formula" (119).

81. Gerard Manley Hopkins describes two types of parallelism in "Poetic Diction" and *On the Origin of Beauty*. The alternatives are abrupt or chromatic.

82. Cf. *Text* IV, *CSP*, 83–84 : "I stay here, sitting, if I'm sitting, often I feel sitting, sometimes standing, it's one or the other, or lying down, there's another possibility, often I feel lying down, it's one of the three, or kneeling. What counts is to be in the world, the posture is immaterial, so long as one is on earth." The last sentence, here, varies the furtherance model by inverting the second and third parts turning the model into A, +B, A.

83. Cf. Andrew Renton, "Disabled Figures: From the *Residua* to *Stirrings Still*" in Pilling, ed., *Cambridge Companion to Beckett*, 168. Renton argues that Beckett cannot express nothing because "expression occurs despite itself." Thus, even an art of antifiguration is itself a form of figuration, with Beckett's texts always standing in lieu of its projected subject. Renton interprets the command to "go on" in the post-trilogy prose as a rereading of the novels aimed at producing a new metaphor: intertextuality, or self-reflection is now the only analogy available. However, although Renton observes that "Still" is a substitute narrative and "What Is the Word" cannot achieve closure, he does not conclude that to "go on" is part of the figuration, which, surely, it is, and precisely what leads it beyond metaphor.

84. Cf. Leonard B. Meyer, *Emotion and Meaning in Music* (Chicago and London: University of Chicago Press, 1974), 129: "it would appear reasonable to consider the law of completion as a corollary of the law of continuation, since all incompleteness is, in some sense, a lack of good continuation and since that which is complete must have been well continued."

85. Cf. John Fletcher, "Ecrivain bilingue," in *Samuel Beckett* eds. Tom Bishop and Raymond Federman (Paris: Editions de l'Herne, 1976), 217. Fletcher describes Beckett's personal style of French, which was a style of rhythm rather than the idiosyncratic style of a foreigner. This rhythm was achieved in various ways including a supplement of three or four words to a phrase that both extended the meaning and created an echo. In other words, Fletcher is describing Kugel's "furtherance."

86. Cf. De Quincey, *Autobiographical Sketches* (quoted in Chapter 2, section I), which similarly opens with the realization: *"Life is finished !"*

87. Beckett speaks of "the suffering of being" in his essay on Proust.

88. Cf. John Pilling, "Fizzles" review of *For to End Yet Again and Other Fizzles*, in *Journal of Beckett Studies* 2 (1977): 97. Pilling points out that, whereas *Text* IX ended

with an echo of Dante in the *Inferno*, the fizzle "Old Earth" begins with his last words in the *Paradiso*.

89. "As we cannot eliminate language all at once, we should at least leave nothing undone that might contribute to its falling into disrepute. To bore one hole after another in it, until what lurks behind it—be it something or nothing—begins to seep through; I cannot imagine a higher goal for a writer today." Beckett to Axel Kaun, July 1937, trans. Martin Esslin, quoted in *Disjecta: Miscellaneous Writings and a Dramatic Fragment*, ed. Ruby Cohn (London: John Calder, 1983), 172.

Chapter 6. Beckett's Late Prose

1. I base my readings, in this chapter, on Beckett's English texts, whether written originally in English or not. Beckett's translations (of his own and other people's work) are always separate compositions. *The Unnamable*, however, appeared seven years after *L'Innomable*.
2. J. D. O'Hara, "Beckett Piece by Piece," *The Nation*, 19 February, 1977, 217.
3. Brian H. Finney, *since how it is: a study of Samuel Beckett's later fiction* (London: Covent Garden Press, 1972), 10, see note 73, below.
4. Cf. Connor, *Repetition, Theory, and Text*, 37: "the attempt at metaphorical substitution sustains an endless metonymic sequence."
5. Perloff does not see a need to debate her identification of the *Fizzles* as prose poems. See Marjorie Perloff, *The Poetics of Indeterminacy: Rimbaud to Cage* (Princeton: Princeton University Press, 1981), 201. However, in *Poetry On and Off the Page* (Illinois: Northwestern University Press, 1998), she analyzes "Still" as an example of "non-linear poetry" by lineating and marking the stresses of the sentences. This appears to translate the prose piece into verse, despite her appellation.
6. Samuel Beckett, *Mercier and Camier* (London: Calder and Boyars, 1974), 60.
7. "Les Deux Besoins," in *Disjecta*, 57. An enthymeme is a syllogism in which one of the premises is inferred or probable.
8. Ibid., 55.
9. W. von Leyden, *Seventeenth-Century Metaphysics: An Examination of Some Main Concepts and Theories* (London: Gerald Duckworth, 1968), 200, 202.
10. Descartes's "I" "is first treated as a quasi-objectified essence, and then the resultant 'me' is simply identified with the 'soul.' . . . Descartes has slipped across the threshold from the subjective 'I' to the objective 'soul' by going through the portal 'me'." Thomas Weiskel, quoted in Eyal Amiran, *Wandering and Home: Beckett's Metaphysical Narrative* (University Park, Pa: The Pennsylvania State University Press, 1993), 20.
11. Cf. John Pilling, *Samuel Beckett* (London: Routledge and Kegan Paul, 1976), 117. Our only firm evidence is that Beckett told Richard Ellmann of a witty exchange between himself and Joyce on the subject of Hume. However, as Pilling remarks, "of Hume's important sundering of cause and effect—which might be expected to appeal to the Beckett of *Proust*, irritated by the 'vulgarity of a plausible concatenation'—we hear nothing."
12. von Leyden, *Seventeenth-Century Metaphysics*, 204. Hume's doctrine is often a response to Malebranche and the Occasionalists whose influence on Beckett is well documented (220–21).

13. David Hume, *A Treatise of Human Nature*, ed. L. A. Selby-Bigge (Oxford: Clarendon Press, 1896), 103. Cf. S. T. Coleridge to Rev. John Prior Estlin, 13 February 1798: "Hume's system of Causation—or rather of non-causation. This is the pillar, & confessedly, the *sole* pillar, of modern Atheism" (*CL* 1:385–86). Coleridge's response to Hume is in Kant's a priori as he understands it (that is, involving chronological priority, see Chapter 1, section II).

14. Samuel Beckett, *Watt* (London: John Calder, 1976), 76.

15. See, Tom L. Beauchamp and Alexander Rosenberg, *Hume and the Problem of Causation* (New York and Oxford: Oxford University Press, 1981), 4.

16. Frederik N. Smith argues that Beckett is parodying Arnauld and not Descartes in these instances where logic is applied to everyday events. "Beckett and the Seventeenth-Century *Port-Royal* Logic," in *Critical Essays on Samuel Beckett*, ed. Lance St. John Butler (Aldershot, Hants, England: Scolar Press; Brookfield VT: Ashgate Pub, 1993), 218.

17. Cf. Beauchamp and Rosenburg, *Hume and the Problem of Causation*, 5. In the first definition, cause is described as prior and contiguous to another object. In the second definition, necessary connection is highlighted as an essential quality of any cause. I take the first emphasis on constant conjunction to represent a diachronic perspective because it describes a design revealed across time. In the case of necessary connection, subjectivity is required, implying a synchronic perspective.

18. Cf. Hugh Kenner, *Samuel Beckett: A Critical Study* (London: John Calder, 1962), 112: "Utter ablation of choice will confer utter freedom, which is by definition access to some plane on which all possibilities are equally available because all have been cleansed of identity and significance: and this is the world of number."

19. The combinations available to Watt apropos of his footwear comprise socks, stockings, boots, shoes and slippers that are not necessarily worn in pairs. See also, Beckett, *Mercier and Camier*, 82. Hume identifies two kinds of probability: that founded on chance, which, "properly speaking, is merely the negation of a cause" and that which arises from causes (Hume, *Treatise*, 124–25).

20. Molloy abandons the scheme because the best solution proves to unbalance him physically, demanding that one pocket be left empty. He registers an incompatibility between form (the distribution of stones) and content (the pleasure of sucking the stones) of the desired action: "when I abandoned the equal distribution, it was a bodily need. But to suck the stones in the way I have described, not haphazard, but with method, was also I think a bodily need. Here then were two incompatible bodily needs, at loggerheads. Such things happen." *Molloy*, trans. P. Bowles (Paris: The Olympia Press, 1955), 99–100. His expression echoes that in "The Two Needs," where Beckett compares "two needs" to the Pythagorean incommensurability of the hypotenuse and its side.

21. Kenner identifies this as the source of Beckett's inevitable failure and one that he takes from philosophical systems of thought: "That things and events are extracted in self-defense from an unintelligible continuum of changes is one of philosophy's self-cancelling propositions, assailing the very act of its own affirmation" (Kenner, *Samuel Beckett*, 99). That is, the method of isolating an object to give meaning to a continuum that is still proceeding, actually disables that object at the moment of its extraction.

22. Beckett told Harold Hobson, "I am interested in the shape of ideas, even if I do not believe in them." Quoted in Kenner, *Samuel Beckett*, 100.

23. Beckett, "Dante . . . Bruno. Vico . . Joyce," in *Disjecta*, 22.

24. Smith identifies the importance of a witness as one of the subjects covered in the *Port-Royal* book, which may have been Hume's source ("Beckett and the Seventeenth-Century *Port-Royal* Logic," 219).

25. Leo Bersani and Ulysse Dutoit, *Arts of Impoverishment* (London and Cambridge: Harvard University Press, 1993), 60. The repeated phrase of the narrator in *How It Is,* "I say it as I hear it," "initiates an infinite regression of sources." Cf. Amiran, *Wandering and Home,* 12. Amiran argues that change and reduction, such as that implied by a thesis of regression, actually affirms the existence of the object, "so long as it is littler it is there."

26. Samuel Beckett, *How It Is* (London: John Calder, 1964), 19.

27. David Lodge suggests that "ping" may successfully be substituted by "God" (following the Godot pun). This interpretation would also make sense of the "legs joined like sewn," the hanging hands, nails, scars, and torn flesh. However Lodge only suggests this reading as one allusion rather than as the significance of the textual symbol or allegory. David Lodge, "Some *Ping* Understood," *Encounter* 30 (1968), reprinted in Butler, ed., *Critical essays on Samuel Beckett,* 157.

28. Hume, *Treatise,* 165.

29. Unlike the other signals, which are arbitrary, the thump on the head has the practical effect of pushing the mouth into the mud. Cf. Beckett, *Molloy,* 22–23. Molloy has similarly taught his mother to understand one to five thumps to the head as indicative of "yes," "no," "I don't know," "money," and "goodbye." The system is comically flawed simply by the fact that his mother cannot count beyond two. Also Nicholas Zurbrugg, *Beckett and Proust,* (Gerrards Cross: Colin Smythe and Totowa, New Jersey: Barnes and Noble Books, 1988), 118. Zurbrugg clearly resents the fact that this episode in *Molloy* so clearly parallels and parodies Proust's narrator tapping on the wall, this "miraculous tapping communication which allows Marcel and his grandmother to transcend both spatial barriers and the discursive barrier of habitual conversation." For Zurbrugg, Beckett's allusions to Proust's work in his own are the pure parody of someone who has ceased to worship it and is embarrassed by the influence. This ignores what Beckett is saying about communication, especially in the torture sequence of *How It Is.*

30. Beckett, interview by Tom Driver, *Columbia University Forum* (summer 1961), reprinted in *Samuel Beckett: The Critical Heritage,* eds. Lawrence Graver and Raymond Federman (London: Routledge and Kegan Paul, 1979), 219: "The form and the chaos remain separate. The latter is not reduced to the former. That is why the form itself becomes a preoccupation, because it exists as a problem separate from the material it accommodates. To find a form that accommodates the mess, that is the task of the artist now."

31. See Beckett to his American publisher, 27 August, 1957: "If we can't keep our genres more or less distinct, or extricate them from the confusion that has them where they are, we might as well go home and lie down." Quoted in Gidal, *Understanding Beckett,* 256, n. 11.

32. Pl. 3: 882; P. 3: 916.

33. *Foirades* comes from the verb *foirer,* to suffer from diarrhea and, figuratively, to fail. See Rubin Rabinovitz "*Fizzles* and Samuel Beckett's Earlier Fiction," *Contemporary Literature,* 24 (1983): 320n.

34. Samuel Beckett, "La Peinture des Van Velde," trans. and quoted by Vivian Mercier in *Beckett/Beckett* (New York and Oxford: Oxford University Press, 1979), 101–02.

35. "Proust in Pieces," *The Spectator* (22 June 1934): 976, reprinted in Beckett, *Disjecta*, 64. Cf. George D. Painter, *Marcel Proust: a biography* (London: Penguin Books, 1990), 1: 12. If, as Painter suggests, Proust's commitment to sentences requiring unnaturally long breaths in a work of epic proportion can be traced to his own asthmatic condition, then each of Beckett's *Fizzles* offer a parody of the precious breath: "a fart fraught with meaning" (*How It Is*, 29). An obsolete meaning of "fizzle," is to break wind quietly (Rabinovitz, "*Fizzles*," 320n). Baudelaire interpreted Poe's guidelines for compositional unity as offering, metaphorically, a reading in a single breath (see Chapter 3, section II).

36. Proust repeatedly substitutes physical effects for their cause: the physical indication of Françoise's jealousy may be mistaken for "a slight stroke" (Pl.3: 360; P.3: 367); and the narrator entertains the possibility that his own renewal of grief may actually be the beginnings of heart disease (Pl.3: 533; P.3: 544). Proust's most consistent coupling of physical suffering is with musical pleasure, which I shall return to later on. Zurbrugg makes the highly questionable claim that Beckett contradicts Proust's view of music's healing properties by "characterizing music as a source of irritation rather than as a source of revelation" (Zurbrugg, *Beckett and Proust*, 126).

37. Cf. Judith E. Dearlove, "'Syntax Upended in Opposite Corners': Alterations in Beckett's Linguistic Theories," in *Samuel Beckett*, eds. Morris Beja, S. E. Gontarski, and Pierre Astier (Columbus: Ohio State University Press, 1983), 125. Dearlove describes the disjunction by the increasing artifice in the structures of the 1960s pieces that "points toward their underlying structural meaninglessness, whereas the arbitrariness beneath their order gestures toward a more fundamental absence of order."

38. Samuel Beckett, *Proust*, in *Proust and Three Dialogues* (London: Calder and Boyars, 1970), 13–14. Beckett's narrator in *The Expelled* echoes Marcel's contradictory state of mind:"Yes, I don't know why, but I have never been disappointed . . . without feeling at the same time, or a moment later, an undeniable relief" (*CSP*, 24). This is almost a paraphrase of Pl.3: 460; P.3: 469. There are many similar examples of relief at failure in Proust: daydreams of Venice and Florence (Pl.1: 386–94; P.1: 419–27) and the impossibility of happiness (Pl.1: 624–25; P.1: 672).

39. Cf. Judith E. Dearlove, *Accommodating the Chaos* (Durham, N.C.: Duke University Press, 1982), esp. 112: "The burden of selecting an interpretation from the implied possibilities rests on the reader because a deceptively analytic prose refuses to assume absolute meanings, because a highly articulated structure is made to imply a more fundamental absence of relationship." Jessica Prinz describes the characters in *Fizzles* as "irredeemably alone," confined physically and/or mentally. "Foirades/Fizzles/Beckett/Johns," *Contemporary Literature* 21 (1980): 483.

40. Beckett, *Proust*, 18. Beckett's remark is a gloss on Pl.3: 450; P.3: 458, "it is not the satisfaction, but the gradual reduction and eventual extinction of desire that one should seek." Cf. René Descartes, "My third maxim was to try always to conquer myself rather than fortune: to change my desires rather than the order of the world" (*The Discourse on the Method* in *Selected Philosophical Writings*, trans. J. Cottingham, R. Stoothoff, and D. Murdoch (Cambridge: Cambridge University Press, 1988), 32. Descartes speaks of past philosophers who regarded the limits of their own reason and thought as the extent of their desire. Beckett takes this a stage further by presenting thought and reason in the medium of fiction as themselves the articulation of the desire to shape an end to the narrative, that is, to engage in the storytelling process at all. Leopardi says much the same in *A se stesso*, which Beckett

quotes in both *Proust* and *Molloy*. The concept reappears in the third of the three dialogues with Georges Duthuit where Beckett describes the object of all art as "doomed to become occasion" (Beckett, *Proust*, 124).

41. As a skeptic, Hume cannot support the perception of universals, believing instead that one is limited to one's own separate experiences, which we are happy to relate to each other where no necessary connection exists.

42. Cf. Kenner, *Samuel Beckett*, 142. This random element is the surd that can be categorized as two types. One is chance and is oblivious to the subject while the other operates within the will as an arbitrary decision. Also, see John Pilling, "The Significance of Beckett's *Still*," *Essays in Criticism* 28 (1978): 146–47. Pilling remarks that after a second attempt to write an end to *The Lost Ones* in 1970, "it is difficult not to believe that he had seen how fraught with problems the ostensibly attractive device of permutation was."

43. Cf. Introduction to *CPR*, 35. A. D. Lindsay points out that Hume's theory does not explain the phenomenon inherent in mathematics, which Kant termed a priori synthetical propositions. The concept would be significant to Beckett considering his keen interest in mathematics. Cf. Gilles Deleuze, *Empiricism and Subjectivity: An Essay on Hume's Theory of Human Nature*, trans. Constantin V. Boundas (New York: Columbia University Press, 1991), 68: Experience and habit "stand alternatively for the presentation of cases of constant conjunction to the inspecting mind, and for the union of these cases inside the mind which observes them. Because of this, Hume always gives causality two related definitions: causality is the union of similar objects and also a mental inference from one object to another."

44. Zurbrugg, *Beckett and Proust*, 114. Zurbrugg takes "suffering" to be wholly negative without taking into account Proust's own idiosyncratic use of physical pain and Beckett's metaphysical use of the term.

45. French prose poetry of the nineteenth century was often published in illustrated volumes. Beckett has a similar practice, as here with the *Still* text and also with the Petersburg edition of *Foirades Fizzles*. Jasper Johns created thirty-three etchings that were published together with the collated English and French versions of the five original *Fizzles* ("I Gave Up Before Birth," "He Is Barehead," "Old Earth," "Closed Space," "Horn Came Always").

46. James Knowlson and John Pilling catalogue the "poeticisms" of "Still" in *Frescoes of the Skull: The Later Prose and Drama of Samuel Beckett* (London: John Calder, 1979), 177–78.

47. Adam Piette, *Remembering and the Sound of Words* (Oxford: Clarendon Press, 1996), 45, esp. 43–45 and 210–11. Curiously, however, the prose pieces that are most emphatically concerned with memory (such as "He Is Barehead" and "Horn Came Always") contain very few of these internal rhymes.

48. Deleuze, *Empiricism and Subjectivity*, 67.

49. However, Piette confuses prose poetry and poetic prose. His attempt to compare a passage from *David Copperfield* with Wilde's "The Disciple" ends in confusion because Wilde's assonances per se do not create the type of furtherance that Piette expects in a piece of prose (Piette, *Remembering and the Sound of Words*, 19).

50. Ibid., 4–5. Piette aligns himself with Shelley's "search for an ideal symphonic harmoniousness . . . [an] organic force of persuasion towards bodily and spiritual unity" through musical "sound-repetitions."

51. Cf. Dearlove, *Accommodating the Chaos*, 110. Dearlove offers a typical example of perceiving habit as a negative quality: "Habituation deadens our powers of

observation, turning 'such variations of rise and fall' into 'countless rhythms.'" I have tried to argue that Beckett relies, latterly, on these "countless rhythms" to symbolize (in Coleridge's sense of actively participating in) the myriad of variations that his prose is unable to encompass.

52. "Sounds," in *Essays in Criticism* 28 (1978): 155–56. Cf. Brian Finney, "*Still* to *Worstward Ho*: Beckett's Prose Fictions Since *The Lost Ones*," in *Beckett's Later Fiction and Drama*, eds. James Acheson and Kateryna Arthur (London: Macmillan, 1987), 67–68: Finney suggests that the trip outside represents a mimed reenactment of a past event.

53. "Still 3," *Essays in Criticism* 28 (1978): 156. De Quincey describes sitting motionless at an open window as a typical position when experiencing his opium dreams (*Sel.* 5.210).

54. Cf. Jonathan Culler, *The Pursuit of Signs: Semiotics, Literature, Deconstruction* (London: Routledge and Kegan Paul, 1981), 183–84. Culler argues that, while narrative is based on causality, Nietzsche shows us that causality may be a "rhetorical operation" where we work "backwards" from experiencing an effect to the search for a possible cause. Applied to narrative, this obliges us to acknowledge the difference between accounts in which either the event determines meaning or that event is itself determined by "discursive requirements" (186).

55. Bruno Clément, "VLADIMIR: La présence d'Ivan Tourgueniev dans l'oeuvre de Samuel Beckett," in *Beckett in the 1990s* eds. Marius Buning and Lois Oppenheim (Amsterdam and Atlanta: Editions Rodopi, 1993), 73. Clément's comment is based on his comparison between *Ill Seen Ill Said* and a prose poem by Turgenev, *Rencontre*. Cf. Deleuze, *Empiricism and Subjectivity*, 72: "In brief, habit has opposite effects upon the imagination and on the judgment: on one hand, extension, *and on the other*, the correction of this extension."

56. Marcel's magic lantern offers a similar effect (*Swann's Way*).

57. John Pilling, "Beckett after *Still*," *Romance Notes* 18 (1977): 280.

58. The texts that followed *How It Is* established this form of minimalist detachment: "All that goes before forget" (*Enough*); "Imagination dead imagine" (*All Strange Away*); "No trace anywhere of life" (*Imagination Dead Imagine*).

59. James Hansford suggests that the hearer of the story (who is also the narrator) is in fact the man in the tent (the tent and the hut now read as not separate places but "essentially the same, as speaker and hearer are the same" and distinguishable only after prolonged imaginative concentration. James Hansford, "Seeing and Saying in 'As the Story Was Told,'" *Journal of Beckett Studies* 8 (1982): 78 and 80.

60. For Pilling and Knowlson, the narrator seems to be unaware of the consequences attached to his rejection of the manuscripts. His refusal to accept responsibility for his action is, in contrast to Hansford's reading, taken as tantamount to rejecting any causal link between himself and the writer (Pilling and Knowlson, *Frescoes of the Skull*, 183).

61. Decontextualization was possibly first begun with the abstraction of an episode in *How It Is* published as "The Image" in the first issue of *X*, circa 1962, a review edited by Mary Hutchinson and Sonia Orwell. It is reprinted in *As the Story Was Told* (1990) in which John Calder sets the date of composition in the 1950s, predating the composition of *How It Is*, but not appearing separately until after the publication of the larger work. (A fragment from Beckett's unpublished novel, *Dream of Fair to Middling Women* had already appeared as "Text" in *New Review*, 1932).

62. The two *Heard in the Dark* pieces are actually juxtaposed memories in *Company* and so undergo an additional separation when abstracted.
63. Samuel Beckett, *Ill Seen Ill Said* (London: John Calder, 1982), 24.
64. Cf. Renton, "Disabled figures," 176: "*Company* offers the event without its consequence, and *Ill Seen Ill Said* presents the consequence without the event."
65. *Worstward Ho* (London: John Calder, 1983), 7. Cf. Finney, "*Still* to *Worstward Ho*," 77–78. Finney suggests that the title *Worstward Ho* is a parody of Charles Kingsley's *Westward Ho!* an adventure novel with an excessively intricate plot. Clearly Beckett's concern at this stage was also with the problems of expansion in narrative plot as well as metaphysical states of being by which his exhortations to "go on" are generally explained.
66. Barbara Trieloff, "'Babel of Silence': Beckett's Post-Trilogy Prose Articulated," in *Rethinking Beckett*, eds. L. St John Butler and R. J. Davis (London: Macmillan Press, 1990), 97. With regard to Hopkins, I am referring specifically to the sentences "Seat of all. Germ of all" (*Worstward Ho*, 10; 18; 30). The expression adapts Hopkins's phrase, "womb-of-all, home-of-all, hearse-of-all night" (*Spelt from Sibyl's Leaves*). Other similarities in these two pieces occur in their apocalypse through the fragmentation of imagery; juxtaposition of contrasts together with plays on words, notably "Disremembering, dísmémbering," which is exactly what Beckett's narrator attempts to do. Hopkins wrote of his poem, a sonnet in sprung rhythm, that it is "oratorical" and should be read aloud. *The Letters of Gerard Manley Hopkins to Robert Bridges*, ed. Claude Colleer Abbott, 2nd rev. imp. (London: Oxford University Press, 1955), I: 46.
67. Cf. Marjorie Perloff, "Between Verse and Prose: Beckett and the New Poetry," *Critical Inquiry* 9 (1982): 426. Perloff argues that Beckett's "free prose," which is grammatically correct but with "indeterminate referents," influences American prose poetry such as John Ashbery's *Three Poems*, which is not in the *Spleen de Paris* tradition of prose poetry. See also, Perloff, *The Poetics of Indeterminacy*, 229. Perloff defines "free prose" as characterized by short phrasing of irregular lengths and primitive syntax; she might almost have said "attic."
68. Cf. Pl.1: 206; 3: 159 and 260. P.1: 224, 3: 156 and 262. The references are to Vinteuil's septet, sonata, and Wagner (a passage of *Tristan* which the narrator compares with the sonata).
69. Amiran accepts the idea of the series from Beckett's own remarks to that effect in private letters (see *Wandering and Home*, 16–17 and 78).
70. I quote here Paola Zaccaria's use of the word "modular" as multiple and of no fixed place—that is, open to permutation. "*Fizzles* by Samuel Beckett: The Failure of the Dream of a Never-ending Verticality," in Butler and Davis eds., *Rethinking Beckett*, 106. However, the term is first applied by Jessica Prinz in her discussion of the *Foirades Fizzles* where she uses it to describe the work as a play of metonyms. "The structure is 'modular' because it stands in marked contrast to organic structures in which every element has a purposive, causal, or logical relation to the whole" (Prinz, "Foirades/Fizzles/Beckett/Johns," 509n).
71. See Zaccaria, "*Fizzles* by Samuel Beckett," 106. Also, Enoch Brater, "*Still* / Beckett: The Essential and the Incidental," *Journal of Modern Literature* 6 (1977): 16. "Because the pieces of Beckett's small planet are so impossible to place in a hierarchy, an order, and a progression, and because they are delivered to us in such confounding language, the quality of completeness must be derived from the sea of potentiality created by the interaction of the parts."

72. Gilles Deleuze, *Difference and Repetition*, trans. Paul Patton (London: Athlone Press, 1994), 125.

73. Beckett, quoted in Finney, *since how it is*, 10: "They are residual (1) Severally, even when that does not appear of which each is all that remains and (2) In relation to the whole body of previous work." Also, cf. P. J. Murphy, "Beckett and the Philosophers," in *The Cambridge Companion to Beckett*, 229–30. According to Murphy, Kant's influence on Beckett has been severely underrated. He mentions specifically, Kant's paradoxical situation of humanity as simultaneously "phenomenally determined but noumenally free."

74. Cf. Paul de Man's reading of *Remembrance of Things Past*, which reveals that while Proust leads us to a metaphoric reading by his correspondences (between the universal and the particular for example), the large part played by chance or contingency and context means that this metaphoricity is an illusion of the more frequent metonymic occasions. Paul de Man, *Allegories of Reading* (New Haven and London: Yale University Press, 1979) 57–67. See also, Charles, "Digression, régression (Arabesques)," 406, for an account of Proust's descriptions as governed by an aesthetic of profusion masquerading as progression.

75. Cf. Prinz, "Foirades/Fizzles/Beckett/Johns," 506: "The fragmented bodies of the Johns etchings cannot be re-membered either; and even if the parts were assembled, they would not constitute a whole."

76. Prose poetry is linked historically with decadent literature in France. Cf. J. A. Hiddleston, *Baudelaire and "Le Spleen de Paris"* (Oxford: Clarendon Press, 1987), 5: "*Le Spleen de Paris* with its uncertain, hybrid, and varied genre and its emphasis on fragmentation and uncertainty shows some of the formal characteristics of such masterpieces of decadent literature as *La Tentation de saint Antoine*, *A rebours*, and *Les Nourritures terrestres*." See also Richard Ellmann, "The Uses of Decadence: Wilde, Yeats, Joyce," in *The Ordering Mirror: Readers and Contexts*, ed. Phillip Lopate (New York: Fordham University Press, 1993), 116. According to Ellmann, Huysmans's Des Esseintes introduced the figure of the sampler who moves from one experience to another on the scale of sensation (his mouth organ of liqueurs) and activity (the novel reads like a catalogue of projects). In England, Ellmann names Pater's Marius as another sampler (*Marius the Epicuran*, published two years later) followed by Wilde's Dorian Gray. The *Foirades Fizzles* edition of Beckett and Johns is perhaps closest to this generic aestheticism.

77. Beckett, "Ping," *CSP*, 149.

Chapter 7. The Prose Poem and the City

1. I have not found a source that attempts to disprove this general assumption. Suzanne Bernard meticulously records the permutations of French verse to the point where it becomes prose poetry through a sustained rebellion against meter. LeRoy Breunig adds that the relative absence of the form in England at that time was due to the nature of English verse, which was traditionally more relaxed in its use of metrical restraints. Prose poetry was not revolutionary where "there was no strait jacket to pull out of" (Breunig, "Why France?" in *Prose Poem in France*, 12). Donald Wesling describes the "necessity" but "likely irrelevance" of poetic technique in the post-1790 period as the "scandal of form." The scandal is "that

form should be necessary at all in an era of stylistic pluralism" (Wesling, *New Poetries*, 19, 20). The battle against meter is, in an organic history of the prose poem, also a factor of epoch. According to Breunig writing in 1983, the tide has already turned: "Today among the younger poets the prose poem has by no means gained the ascendancy; on the contrary the *vers libre* in its many forms seems to be considerably more prevalent, and the alexandrine, no longer the enemy, has recovered its appeal along with the other regular meters, rhymed or unrhymed" ("Why France?," 19).

2. Margery Sabin, *English Romanticism and the French Tradition* (London and Cambridge: Harvard University Press, 1976), 128.

3. Marshall Berman, *All That Is Solid Melts Into Air* (London and New York: Verso, 1995), 147. I am indebted to the following comprehensive accounts of Baudelaire's work in the context of Paris: Walter Benjamin, *Charles Baudelaire: A Lyric Poet in the Era of High Capitalism* (London and New York: Verso, 1992); Christopher Prendergast, *Paris and the Nineteenth Century* (Oxford: Basil Blackwell, 1992).

4. The café and the boulevard are the subjects of Baudelaire's prose poems "The Eyes of the Poor" and "A Lost Halo," respectively.

5. F. S. Schwarzbach, "'*Terra Incognita*': An Image of the City in English Literature, 1820–1855," *Prose Studies* 5 (1982): 80.

6. Wordsworth, *Lyrical Ballads*, 160.

7. William Thesing has attempted to prove otherwise in *The London Muse: Victorian Poetic Responses to the City* (Athens: University of Georgia Press, 1982) but is, in the main, restricted to minor works. Cf. Matthew Arnold to Clough, February 1849: "Reflect too . . . how deeply *unpoetical* the age and all one's surroundings are. Not unprofound, not ungrand, not unmoving:—but *unpoetical* ." *The Letters of Matthew Arnold to Arthur Hugh Clough*, ed. Howard Foster Lowry (Oxford: Clarendon Press, 1968), 99.

8. Cf. Philippe Hamon, "Texte et architecture," *Poétique* 73 (1988): 14. Hamon describes how the constructed frame (the wall) is already inscribed by hieroglyphs, graffiti, advertisements, a coat of arms, and so on.

9. London is characterized as a fairground with its grotesques and its painted masks: "those mimic sights that ape/ The absolute presence of reality" (*Prelude* VII, 248–49). See John H. Johnston, *The Poet and the City: A Study in Urban Perspectives* (Athens: University of Georgia Press, 1984), 100: "Wordsworth invokes his experience of Nature and her component forms as a guide for the poet whose senses may be exhausted by the 'blank confusion' of the city."

10. Rosemary Lloyd translates "naît de" as "springs from," which gives the sense of the announced rise of the prose poem as the erection of a new building that has "sprung up." *The Prose Poems and La Fanfarlo* (Oxford: Oxford University Press), 30. If translated as "born from" the emphasis is on the cross-fertilization of poet with the city (or prose with poetry) that engenders the prose poem.

11. Cf. Wesling, *The New Poetries*, 191. Wesling regards the sentence as the last compositional unit remaining in the modern (post-Romantic) period after its rejection of poetic form (rhyme, meter, and so on) and therefore the basic unit of free verse and the prose poem. He implies that the prose poem is defined by its attempts to dethrone the sentence, attempts that generally fail. "In the absence of rhyme and meter the sentence is the smallest unit that contains the complete convergence of the psychological, historical, and aesthetic as well as grammatical

modes in the literary work. Between the work itself and any of its longer sentences the difference is one of degree only—a difference that disappears when the single sentence constitutes the whole poem."

12. Cf. Wall, "Geoffrey Hill's *Canaan*," 39. "Hill is not essentially an urban poet, nor is he a poet of crowds as was Baudelaire (or for that matter Eliot). Hill has his Parisian city scene in *The Mystery* (though the crowds are seen significantly from behind the bookshop window) and in 'Churchill's Funeral' but it is always solitary voices, solitary images, which lift off his pages. When a crowd appears in 'Funeral Music' it is a crowd of corpses."

13. *Oeuvres*, 372. Baudelaire's plans for future prose poems contain a project for what appears to be a poem based on Poe's tale *The Fall of the House of Usher*, where the decay and ruin of the building provides a commentary on the inevitable collapse of the accumulation of urban societies (prefiguring Roy Fisher's descriptions of the city as heaps of rubble).

14. Cf. Wordsworth, "Preface" (*Lyrical Ballads*, 160). In his preface, Wordsworth criticizes the use of events in the city as a source for narrative. The ephemerality of urban concerns is precisely what he had been attempting to combat with the *Lyrical Ballads*.

15. Matthew Arnold sees the poet and his career as lost amid the chaotic elements of modern life, especially in the city: "these are damned times—everything is against one—the height to which knowledge is come, the spread of luxury, our physical enervation, the absence of great *natures*, the unavoidable contact with millions of small ones, newspapers, cities, light profligate friends, moral desperadoes like Carlyle, our own selves, and the sickening consciousness of our difficulties." Arnold to Clough (*The Letters*, 111).

16. Baudelaire's revolutionary form is, nevertheless, still a development of the Romantic prototype as opposed to a radical subversion of its ideals and Baudelaire's proposed titles for his prose poetry collection reflect this: *Le Promeneur Solitaire* (*The Solitary Walker*), *Le Rôdeur Parisien* (*The Parisian Prowler*). Twelve of the prose poems were finally published in two periodicals under the title *Le Spleen de Paris* (*The Spleen of Paris*), yet it is significant, in terms of the relation between Baudelaire's prose poems and the history of the genre, that the Pléiade editors of its first edition in Volume 4 of the *Complete Works* (1869) dropped Baudelaire's title in favor of the defining, generic description, *Petits Poèmes en Prose* (*Little Poems in Prose*).

17. T. S. Eliot, "What Dante Means to Me," in *To Criticize the Critic*, 126. Eliot appears to be responding directly to Arnold's complaint that the age and its surroundings were deeply "*unpoetical*" (*The Letters*, 99). However, considering his own opinions on the tautology of prose poetry, Eliot's statement is more problematic. His use of the term "unpoetical" either debases the poetry that appropriates it or is not entirely unpoetic at all.

18. Burton Pike, *The Image of the City in Modern Literature* (Princeton: Princeton University Press, 1981), 77.

19. The text in *Poétique* reads "un *objet herméneutique*," but from the description that follows, I understand this to be an error and that "hermétique" was intended.

20. Hamon, "Texte et architecture," 7. The building and the text share the attributes of a hermetic object (from one side a façade, from the other, a crypt); a discriminating object (analyzing space by enclosures and contiguities); and a hierarchical object (of the text with its pre-texts ["de l'oeuvre et des hors-oeuvres"]).

21. Milan Kundera, "The Depreciated Legacy of Cervantes," in *The Art of the Novel*, trans. Linda Asher (London: Faber & Faber, 1988), 7–9.

22. Mary Ann Caws, *Reading Frames in Modern Fictions* (Princeton: Princeton University Press, 1985), 6 et passim.

23. Caws does not distinguish between types of framed episodes, "this, says the frame, is what matters" (*Reading Frames*, 29) but the differences are significant. The epiphany finally only matters to the experiencing subject: De Quincey's entire confessions (which includes the *Suspiria*) constitute an attempt to communicate the epiphany that is both the end and the starting point of his work. However, it is the set pieces, such as the death of his sister, the scene at the booksellers and so on which structurally support the edifice of his narration.

24. Johnson, on the subject of "Le Thyrse" as a model for all prose poems writes: "Instead of establishing the structure of a relationship between poetry and prose, this 'model' of the *Petits Poèmes en Prose* is an infinite *mise en abyme* of its own incapacity to serve as a model" (*Défigurations*, 65).

25. Caws, *Reading Frames*, 3. Cf. Beckett's prose poem, "Closed Space" (*CSP*, 199) where the description of the arena ends with the track which surrounds it. The track is crumbling into dust, which, at the end of the text, begins to threaten its own identity as closed place.

26. Cf. Bernard, *Le Poème en prose*, 35.

27. Albert Sonnenfeld, "L'Adieu suprême and Ultimate Composure: The Boundaries of the Prose Poem," in *Prose Poem in France*, 201.

28. Beaujour quotes Monique Parent's assertion that the prose poem finds itself associated with lyricism in order to escape the extended nature of poetic prose. It is therefore bound to the similar sudden, short outburst favored by the lyric form ("Short Epiphanies," 41). R. G. Cohn suggests an equally abstract defense for the prose poem's characteristic brevity. "When . . . Baudelaire's more garrulous pieces in the *Spleen de Paris* run on for a couple of pages, one is obscurely aware of a violation of the rules of the game" ("A Poetry-Prose Cross," 140). Cohn's argument implies that the "rules" include the time needed to read a prose poem and he places the instinct of the reader as an integral element in the arbitration.

29. The term is Ellen Moers's, quoted in Sandra M. Gilbert and Susan Gubar, *The Madwoman in the Attic* (New Haven and London: Yale University Press, 1984), 83.

30. Gilbert and Gubar distinguish between male writers' metaphorical use of the room as enclosure or imprisonment and the same image, which takes on autobiographical dimensions for female writers and readers due to the plight of the nineteenth-century woman (ibid., 83–87).

31. It is interesting then that Dowson's poem is itself heavily autobiographical. He was aware of the unfavorable opinion held by his circle of the woman with whom he was somewhat obsessed. The poem is also a frank confession of impotence. According to Barbara Johnson, in suppressing the obvious, single narrative and removing moments of heightened intensity created by rhythm and rhyme, the prose poem logically corresponds to the moment of castration. She points to the frequency of violent blows and cuts in Baudelaire's prose poetry, concluding that "castration is somehow constitutive of the prose poem" (Johnson, *The Critical Difference*, 45).

32. Cf. Gaston Bachelard, *The Poetics of Space*, trans. Maria Jolas (Boston: Beacon Press, 1969), 224. The image of the door facilitates the "correction" of the

geometrical logic of inside/outside opposition. The door introduces "images of hesitation, temptation, desire," and so on. Marjorie Perloff locates modernist ambiguity in "the space of a door," adapting a rejected title of Beckett's poem, "le temps d'une porte" [the time of a door], (Perloff, *Poetics of Indeterminacy*, 244–47).

33. Cf. Lorenz Eitner, "The Open Window and the Storm-Tossed Boat: An Essay in the Iconography of Romanticism," *The Art Bulletin* 37 (1955): 284. According to Eitner, the motif of the figure at the window became popular with (particularly French and German) painters after 1810. This image becomes, in the Romantic period, not an unavoidable detail of a domestic interior and realistic source of light but, as the sole image, "an opening into space" and is therefore associated with the angst of the Romantic artist/poet.

34. Eitner cites Baudelaire's comments in "Salon de 1845" as proof that the image is considered to be old-fashioned by this time ("The Open Window," 284 n.8). It is possible that Baudelaire is attempting to modernize the image in this prose poem.

35. Cf. Jean Starobinski, "Windows: From Rousseau to Baudelaire," trans. Richard Peaver, in *The Hudson Review* 40 (1988): 556–58. Starobinski describes the image of the window in Baudelaire's prose poem as "an eye that fascinates but does not see," it is "a setting for non-relation" heightening the feeling of solitude for which the narrator attempts to compensate by forging stories for the figures that he sees. Ultimately, however, "the distant window has served only as a mirror," as the final lines assert. Any story is subordinated to the effect of fabulation on the self-consciousness of the narrator.

36. To read Baudelaire's "Windows" with its square of black text in a white surround as well as Kafka's "Absent minded window gazing" is itself an act of looking through a window. The analogy is most obvious in Mallarmé's prose poem "Winter Shivers," where the four parenthetical references to the window in the refrain recreate the sides of the frame so that the window is seen to be encased inside the text. See Robert Greer Cohn, *Mallarmé's Prose Poems: A Critical Study* (Cambridge: Cambridge University Press, 1987), 36.

37. John Ash, "The Lecture," in *Selected Poems* (Manchester: Carcanet, 1996), 93–94.

38. John M. Grandin, "Defenestrations," in *The Kafka Debate: New Perspectives for Our Time*, ed. Angel Flores (New York: Gordian Press, 1977), 218.

39. See Donald Wesling, "Process and Closure in Tomlinson's Prose Poems," in *Charles Tomlinson: Man and Artist*, ed. Kathleen O'Gorman (Columbia: University of Missouri Press, 1988), 126. Wesling claims that Tomlinson's attraction to absences, deconstruction and the avant-garde, "is always chastened by his fact-noticing Englishness." Tomlinson, interviewed by Jordi Doce, has himself acknowledged the influence of the notebooks of Coleridge, Hopkins, and Ruskin on his work. "The Poet of the Eye," *Agenda* 33 (1996): 25. All references to *The Way of a World* are indicated by their individual titles and are taken from Charles Tomlinson, *Collected Poems* (Oxford: Oxford University Press, 1985).

40. Cf. P. Mansell Jones, *The Background to Modern French Poetry: Essays and Interviews* (Cambridge: Cambridge University Press, 1968), 99. Jones suggests that Baudelaire's ideal in his prose poems is a musical rather than (Bertrand's) pictorial form, one source probably being De Quincey's *Confessions*.

41. Tomlinson himself has said of this image, the arc that will not be completed, "there is much (necessarily) that escapes us, escapes the forms of language. And in

this I rejoice. If you could close *that* circle, if language or consciousness could completely possess their objects, there would be no more room for literary endeavour." Charles Tomlinson in *Contemporary Literature* 16 (1975), 408.

42. Cf. Johnson, *The Critical Difference*, 47–48. Johnson's deconstructionist reading of the prose poem gives voice to the previously suppressed language of poetry: "The poetic code is thus not simply a set of elements considered 'poetic' but also a process of exclusion and of negation, of active repression of whatever belongs to other codes." Johnson concludes that, in the case of Baudelaire's *Les Fleurs du Mal* and *Le Spleen de Paris*, the prose poem is not "other" or the "same" of its verse counterpart but its double, occupying "its double space as the space of its own division," which is spawned from poetry's "inability to determine its own limits." The commonly marginal status of the prose poem is reinstated into the text proper under deconstruction making a prominent feature of its lines of demarcation (attributing place, closure and so on) as a self-conscious mark of its split identity (a division which is not simply based on the correspondence of Baudelaire's two works but appears at various levels: verse/prose, text/context, verse/poetry, and so on).

43. Versions of this phrase appears in two of Tomlinson's prose poems, "Oppositions" and "Skullshapes."

44. The frame of the painting also holds associations with the window frame, see Eitner, "The Open Window and the Storm-Tossed Boat," 286. Eitner describes the Romantic "window-centered genre paintings" where there are no figures only the window itself, "neither landscape nor interior, but a curious combination of both." The viewer *becomes* the figure at the window, participating in the Romantic sense of yearning.

45. Samuel Beckett, "La Falaise," in *Celui qui ne peut se servir des mots* (Montpellier: Éditions Fata Morgana, 1975), 17. Cf. James Hansford, "Imaginative Transactions in 'La Falaise'," *Journal of Beckett Studies* 10 (1985): 81: "what the window or the frame of the canvas excludes evidently becomes an integral part in determining what is there. The window thus acts as an "emblem of separation" (79).

46. Wesling, "Process and Closure," 132. See for example, the "end to end" vision described in the opening sentence of "Poem": "The muscles which move the eyeballs, we are told, derive from a musculature which once occupied the body end to end," which is partially repeated, as a refrain, in the closing line.

47. Franz Kafka, quoted by Edwin Muir, introduction to *Amerika*, trans. Willa and Edwin Muir (Harmondsworth: Penguin Books, 1967), 9.

48. William Chapman Sharpe, *Unreal Cities: Urban Figuration in Wordsworth, Baudelaire, Whitman, Eliot, and Williams* (Baltimore and London: Johns Hopkins University Press, 1990), 2.

49. See Jacques Derrida, "The Law of Genre," trans. Avital Ronell, *Critical Inquiry* 7 (1980): 55–83. Derrida argues that a genre requires the appearance of what it excludes in order to define itself.

50. Pater and Hopkins *do* use architectural terms and concepts but usually to describe units as small as the sentence and they were not as influential as Wordsworth and Ruskin. See Ellen Eve Frank, *Literary Architecture: Essays Toward a Tradition* (Berkeley and London: University of California Press, 1979), 252.

51. See Cornelis Van de Ven, *Space in Architecture: The Evolution of a New Idea in the Theory and History of the Modern Movements* (Amsterdam: Van Gorcum Assen, 1978). By the 1890s Theodor Lipps was formulating a theory of architecture as space experience: one lives in the space created by the elimination of mass from a

geometric structure. From 1893 Adolf Hildebrand became very influential in this area.

52. Ibid., 66. Also see K. O. Garrigan, *Ruskin on Architecture* (Wisconsin and London: University of Wisconsin Press, 1973), 64. As well as avoiding the dimensions of a building beyond its façades, Ruskin found himself overwhelmed by anything of so large a size that he could not perceive it as a whole.

53. See especially, John Ruskin, "Lectures on Architecture and Painting," in *The Complete Works of John Ruskin*, eds. E. T. Cook and A. Wedderburn (London: George Allen, 1904), 12: 5–168. Also, cf. Matthew Arnold, "Lines Written in Kensington Gardens." Arnold articulates the superimposition of the city onto nature's landscape through the image of the park as a semi-independent zone that contains elements of both the countryside and the metropolis. The park is both a fragment of nature and an area of the city: it provides an oasis of self-sufficient calm but, contained inside the city, its seasonal cycle of decay and renewal seems to contract within its new urban horizon and it participates instead with the comings and goings of the everyday habits and routines of its visitors.

54. The prose poems in this collection are untitled (bar two) and will be referred to by *City* and their page number. All quotations are taken from Roy Fisher, *Poems 1955–1987* (Oxford: Oxford University Press, 1988).

55. Cf. Pike, *Image of the City*, 15: "throughout the nineteenth century we find that the isolation of the individual rather than the cohesion of urban society becomes increasingly the focus of the image of the city." Pike traces this increasing dislocation to the present day when "the word-city seems to be less a place than a negative atmosphere full of crackling static within which disembodied voices speak" (17).

56. Weatherhead regards Fisher's desired absence as a way to avoid imposing structure on his city. Both he and Tomlinson are suspicious of formal structures in art because they halt the uncontainable flux of reality (Weatherhead, *British Dissonance*, 6).

57. Pichois, Notes to *Oeuvres*, by Charles Baudelaire, 1300.

58. Cf. Sharpe, *Unreal Cities*, 15: "Only by writing the city can he [the masculine poet] make the unreal real and still its motion, possessing in the poem what eludes him in the flesh—until the forces of dissemination and difference, the double mark of Cain and Babel, indicate that even the textual city is ever elsewhere and that the site of the poem marks its loss." Here Cain represents deferral, having built the first city when driven into exile, and the cacophony of Babel is the prototype of linguistic difference.

59. In his verse poem, "Just Where to Draw the Line," Fisher describes a typical quattrocento painting where tiny cities are glimpsed in the distance of a twilight landscape and in the foreground "huge imaginary personages . . . mess up the view." *Birmingham River* (Oxford: Oxford University Press, 1994), 25.

60. Jacques Derrida, *The Truth in Painting*, trans. G. Bennington and I. McLeod (Chicago: The University of Chicago Press, 1987), 13.

61. Hamon, "Texte et architecture," 7.

62. In one of Blake's prose poems, Contemplation claims that Happiness is to be found specifically outside the city in the humble pleasures of the countryside. The narrator replies that he can never know that place, being trapped in the city of mortality where his "flesh is a prison" and his bones "the bars of death" ("Contemplation," *Poetical Sketches*, 64).

63. Bettina L. Knapp's "archetypal architecture," because it is "an expression of a psychic state" can exist outside context as a symbol despite being buried in a narrative plot. *Archetype, Architecture, and the Writer* (Bloomington: Indiana University Press, 1986), vi–x. For example, Kafka's court is abstractly imminent in the plot narrative of *The Trial* but a concrete structure in "Before the Law."

64. John Ash, "The Big House," in *The Goodbyes* (Manchester, Eng.: Carcanet, 1982), 18.

65. (Published by *La Presse*, 26 August, 1862) Scarfe renders "ni queue ni tête" as "neither beginning nor end," which somewhat loses the image of the birth of a monstrous genre.

66. Johnson, *Défigurations*, 28–29.

67. Cf. A. W. Raitt, "On *Le Spleen de Paris*," *Nineteenth-Century French Studies* 18 (1989–90): 157. Raitt revises the dates of Baudelaire's four lists of prose poem titles and argues that *Spleen* is actually a finished work and its prose poems appear in a predetermined order.

68. Michel Butor, "Le Roman et la Poésie," in *Répertoire II* (Paris: Les Éditions de Minuit, 1964), 20.

69. Ibid., 24. In a private letter to Arsène Houssaye (Christmas 1861) Baudelaire expresses concern that the prose poems, on which he has been meditating for several years, will in fact appear to be only thumbnail sketches of a projected work. He does not anticipate Butor's "unknown novel," confessing instead that they may give the impression of being plans for future verse poems. *Selected Letters of Charles Baudelaire: The Conquest of Solitude*, trans. Rosemary Lloyd (London: Weidenfeld and Nicolson, 1986), 180–81. In fact, there is a whole area of inquiry regarding the relationship between *Le Spleen de Paris* and the verse poems of *Les Fleurs du Mal*. Despite the letter to Houssaye above, Baudelaire, in later correspondence with Victor Hugo, 17 December 1863, describes *Le Spleen de Paris* as "a counterpart to the poems" (*Selected Letters,* 199–200).

70. Turgenev, despite being very much influenced by French prose poetry, appears not to view his collection in the same way as Baudelaire or Butor. His own preface, "To the Reader" advocates a reading of one prose poem per day, a method one would associate with religious meditations. Ivan Turgenev, *Poems in Prose*, trans. Evgenia Schimanskaya (London: Harrison, 1945). However, his fear that the reader would otherwise find it "boring and the book might drop from his hands" should they be read all at once, seems to accord with Baudelaire's concern that the collection should not be considered a fragmented novel where a single thread connects each prose piece fixed in a given sequence.

71. Butor's comments do highlight the relationship between the French prose poem and the epiphany. Both forms rely on a body of narrative with a perceptible teleological structure (as opposed to the beginnings/ends of texts explored by De Quincey, Hill, and Beckett). The influence continues in modern British prose poetry such as Lee Harwood's collection, *Dream Quilt*, which largely grew out of attempts to write a novel (conversation with the author, 11 October 1993). The result is a series of tableaux that require but lack the narrative contexts that would legitimize their epiphanic status. On the other hand, Gabriele D'Annunzio's *Notturno* is an example of a novel which is constructed solely of epiphanic prose pieces sketching a coherent narrative without resisting a reordering—D'Annunzio himself encourages this when he describes the separate prose pieces, which he and his narrator have written on hidden strips of paper, as analogous to the Sibyl's leaves

dispersed to the winds of fate. Gabriele D'Annunzio, *Notturno* (Milano: Oscar Mondadori, 1983), 50.

72. Cf. Blanchot, "The Athenaeum," 172 quoted in, Chapter 1, section I.

73. Berman, *All That Is Solid Melts Into Air*, 147.

74. John Woolford, *Browning the Revisionary* (New York: St. Martin's Press, 1988), 89.

75. Ibid., 91.

76. Hamon, "Texte et architecture," 16.

77. Monroe, *A Poverty of Objects*, 296.

78. Cf. Derrida, *Truth in Painting*, 12: "*Between* the outside and the inside, between the external and the internal edge line, the framer and the framed, the figure and the ground, form and content, signifier and signified and *so on* for any two-faced opposition. The trait thus divides in this place where it takes place."

Works Cited

Primary Sources

Arnold, Matthew. *The Letters of Matthew Arnold to Arthur Hugh Clough*. Edited by Howard Fraser Lowry. Oxford: Clarendon Press, 1932.

Ash, John. *The Goodbyes*. Manchester: Carcanet, 1982.

———. *Selected Poems*. Manchester: Carcanet, 1996.

Bartram, William. *Travels Through North and South Carolina, Georgia, East and West Florida, The Cheriokee* [sic] *Country* [&c]. 2nd ed. London: J. Johnson, 1794.

Baudelaire, Charles. *Baudelaire: A Self-portrait. Selected Letters Translated and Edited with a Running Commentary*. Edited by Lois Boe Hyslop and Francis E. Hyslop Jr. London: Oxford University Press, 1957.

———. *Correspondance de Baudelaire*. 2 vols. Texte établi, présénté et annoté par Claude Pichois avec la collaboration de Jean Ziegler. Paris: Éditions Gallimard, 1973.

———. *Curiosités esthétiques, L'art romantique*. Edited by Henri Lemaitre. Paris: Classiques Garnier, 1990.

———. *Un mangeur d'opium*, Avec le texte parallèle des *Confessions of an English Opium-Eater*, et des *Suspiria de Profundis*, de Thomas De Quincey. Édition critique et commentée par Michèle Stäuble-Lipman Wulf. Études Baudelairiennes VI–VII. Neuchâtel (Suisse): Les Éditions de la Baconnière, 1976.

———. *Oeuvres complètes*. 2 vols. Texte établi, présenté et annoté par Claude Pichois. Paris: Éditions Gallimard, 1975.

———. *The Prose Poems and La Fanfarlo*. Translated by Rosemary Lloyd. Oxford: Oxford University Press, 1990.

———. *The Poems in Prose and La Fanfarlo*. Edited and translated by Francis Scarfe. London: Anvil Press Poetry, 1989.

———. *Selected Letters of Charles Baudelaire: The Conquest of Solitude*. Edited and translated by Rosemary Lloyd. London: Weidenfeld & Nicolson, 1986.

Beckett, Samuel. *Celui qui ne peut se servir des mots*. Montpellier: Éditions Fata Morgana, 1975.

———. *Collected Shorter Prose 1945–1980*. London: John Calder, 1984.

---. *Disjecta: Miscellaneous Writings and a Dramatic Fragment*. Edited by Ruby Cohn. London: John Calder, 1983.

---. *How It Is*. London: John Calder, 1964.

---. *Ill Seen Ill Said*. London: John Calder, 1982.

---. *Mercier & Camier*. London: Calder & Boyars, 1974.

---. *Molloy*. Translated by Patrick Bowles in collaboration with Samuel Beckett. Paris: Olympia Press, 1955.

---. "Sounds." *Essays in Criticism* 28 (1978): 155–56.

---. "Still 3." *Essays in Criticism* 28 (1978): 156–57.

---. *Watt*. London: John Calder, 1976.

---. *Worstward Ho*. London: John Calder, 1983.

The Bijou Literary Annual. 1828.

Blackwood's Edinburgh Magazine 57 (March 1845); 57 (April 1845); 57 (June 1845). 58 (July 1845). 66 (December 1849).

Blake, William. *Poetical Sketches*. London: 1783.

Burke, Edmund. *A Philosophical Inquiry into the Origin of Our Ideas of the Sublime and Beautiful*. Edited by J. Boulton. Notre Dame and London: University of Notre Dame Press, 1958.

Chapelan, Maurice, ed. *Anthologie du poème en prose*. Paris: René Julliard, 1946.

Coburn, Kathleen, ed. *Inquiring Spirit: A New Presentation of Coleridge from His Published and Unpublished Prose Writings*. Toronto and London: University of Toronto Press, rev. ed. 1979.

Coleridge, E. H., ed. "*The Wanderings of Cain* by Samuel Taylor Coleridge." *Athenaeum*, 27 January 1894.

Coleridge, Samuel Taylor. "*The Wanderings of Cain. A Fragment.*" *The Bijou: or Annual of Literature and The Arts*. London: William Pickering, 1828, 17–23.

---. *Aids to Reflection*. Edited by John Beer. Vol. 9 of *Collected Works*, 1993.

---. *Biographia Literaria*. 2 vols. Edited by James Engell and W. Jackson Bate. Vol. 7 of *Collected Works*, 1983.

---. *Book 3rd/Cain*. British Library manuscript. Egerton 2800, fol. 1–1v.

---. *Coleridge's Miscellaneous Criticism*. Edited by Thomas Middleton Raysor. London: Constable, 1936.

---. *Collected Letters of Samuel Taylor Coleridge*. 6 vols. Edited by Earl Leslie Griggs. Oxford: Oxford University Press, 1956–71.

---. *The Collected Works of Samuel Taylor Coleridge*. 16 vols. Edited by Kathleen Coburn and Bart Winer. Bollingen Series LXXV. Princeton: Princeton University Press; London: Routledge & Kegan Paul, 1969–.

---. *Lay Sermons*. Edited by R. J. White. Vol. 6 of *Collected Works*, 1972.

---. *Lectures 1808–1819 on Literature*. 2 vols. Edited by R. A. Foakes. Vol. 5 of *Collected Works*, 1987.

---. *Logic*. Edited by J. R. de J. Jackson. Vol. 13 of *Collected Works*, 1981.

---. *Marginalia*. 2 vols. Edited by George Whalley. Vol. 12 of *Collected Works*, 1980.

---. Notebook 22. British Library. Additional manuscript 47,520, fols. 88–89.

———. *The Notebooks of Samuel Taylor Coleridge*. 4 vols. Edited by Kathleen Coburn. London: Routledge & Kegan Paul, 1962.

———. *Poetical Works*. 3 vols. London: Pickering, 1828; 1834.

———. *Poetical Works*. Edited by E. H. Coleridge. Oxford: Oxford University Press, 1912. Reprinted 1969.

———. *Shorter Works and Fragments*. 2 vols. Edited by H. J. Jackson and J. R. de J. Jackson. Vol. 11 of *Collected Works*, 1995.

D'Annunzio, Gabriele. *Notturno*. Milano: Oscar Mondadori, 1983.

De Musset, Alfred. *Oeuvres complètes en prose*. Texte établi et annoté par Maurice Allem et Paul-Courant. Paris: Gallimard, 1960.

De Quincey, Thomas. *The Collected Writings*. Edited by David Masson. Edinburgh: Adam & Charles Black, 1890.

———. *The English Mail-Coach, or the Glory of Motion*. *Blackwood's Edinburgh Magazine* 66 (July–December 1849), 485–500 and 741–755.

———. *Suspiria de Profundis: being a sequel to the Confessions of an English Opium-Eater, Blackwood's Edinburgh Magazine* 57 (March 1845) 269–85; (April 1845), 489–502; (June 1845), 739–51; 58 (July 1845) 43–55.

———. *Confessions of an English Opium-Eater and Other Writings*. Edited by Grevel Lindop. Oxford and New York: Oxford University Press, 1985, 1990.

———. *Essays from De Quincey*. Edited by J. H. Fowler. London: Adam & Charles Black, 1900.

———. *The Posthumous Works*. 2 vols. Edited by Alexander H. Japp. New York and Hildesheim: Georg Olms Verlag, 1975. Originally published by William Heinemann, 1891–93.

———. *Selections Grave and Gay, from Writings Published and Unpublished, of Thomas De Quincey, Revised and Arranged by Himself*. 14 vols. Edinburgh: James Hogg & Sons. London: R. Groombridge & Sons, 1853–60.

Descartes, René. *Selected Philosophical Writings*. Translated by J. Cottingham, R. Stoothoff, D. Murdoch. Cambridge: Cambridge University Press, 1988.

Dowson, Ernest. *The Poetical Works of Ernest Dowson*. Edited by Desmond Flower. London: Cassell, 1967.

Eliot, T. S. *Inventions of the March Hare: Poems 1909–1917*. Edited by Christopher Ricks. London: Faber & Faber, 1996.

Fisher, Roy. *Birmingham River*. Oxford: Oxford University Press, 1994.

———. *Poems 1955–1980*. Oxford: Oxford University Press, 1980.

———. *Poems 1955–1987*. Oxford: Oxford University Press 1988.

Gascoyne, David. *Collected Poems 1988*. Oxford: Oxford University Press, 1988.

Halsey, Alan. *The Art of Memory on Hay-on-Wye*. 4th edition. Textual Instability, 1996.

———. *The Text of Shelley's Death*. Herefordshire: Five Seasons Press, 1995.

Hazlitt, William. *The Complete Works of William Hazlitt*. 21 vols. Edited by P. P. Howe. London: J. M. Dent, 1931.

Hill, Geoffrey. *Collected Poems*. Harmondsworth: Penguin Books, 1986.

———. Interview with John Haffenden *Quarto* 15 (March 1981): 19–22.

———. *Mercian Hymns*. London: Andre Deutsch 1980.

———. *New and Collected Poems, 1952–1992.* Boston and New York: Houghton Mifflin, 1994.

———. *The Poetry and Voice of Geoffrey Hill.* Audiocassette. In association with the Poetry Center, New York, Caedmon, 1979.

———. *Somewhere Is Such a Kingdom, Poems 1952–1971.* Introduction by Harold Bloom. Boston: Houghton Mifflin, 1975.

———. "Under Judgment." Interview with Blake Morrison, *The New Statesman* (8 February 1980); 212–14.

Hopkins, Gerard Manley. *The Journals and Papers of Gerard Manley Hopkins.* Edited by Humphrey House and Graham Storey. London: Oxford University Press, 1959.

———. *The Letters of Gerard Manley Hopkins to Robert Bridges.* 2 vols. Edited by Claude Colleer Abbott. London: Oxford University Press, 1955.

———. *The Notebooks and Papers of Gerard Manley Hopkins.* Edited Humphrey House. London and New York: Oxford University Press, 1957.

Hume, David. *A Treatise of Human Nature.* Edited by L. A. Selby-Bigge. Oxford: Clarendon Press, 1896.

Huysmans, Joris-Karl. *Against Nature.* Translated by Robert Baldick. Harmondsworth: Penguin Books, 1959.

Jacob, Max. *The Dice Cup: Selected Prose Poems.* Edited by Michael Brownstein. New York: Sun, 1979.

Kant, Immanuel. *Critique of Pure Reason.* Translated by J. M. D. Meiklejohn. Edited by A. D. Lindsay. London: J. M. Dent, 1991. From the 2nd ed. 1787.

Keene, Dennis, ed. and trans. *The Modern Japanese Prose Poem.* Princeton: Princeton University Press, 1980.

Lowth, Robert, trans. *Isaiah.* London: J. Dodsley & T. Cadell, 1778.

Loydell, Rupert, and David Miller, eds. *A Curious Architecture: A Selection of Contemporary Prose Poems.* Devon: Stride, 1996.

Macpherson, James. *The Poems of Ossian.* Edited by William Sharp. Edinburgh: J. Grant, 1926.

Merrill, Stuart, ed. and trans. *Pastels in Prose.* New York: Harper & Brothers, 1890.

North, Christopher "Winter Rhapsody," *Blackwood's Edinburgh Magazine* 29 (February 1831) II: 287–309.

Plato. *Republic.* Translated by Paul Shorey. In *The Collected Dialogues of Plato.* Edited by Edith Hamilton and Huntington Cairns. Princeton: Princeton University Press, 1989.

Plotinus. *The Enneads.* Translated by Stephen MacKenna. London: Faber & Faber, 2nd ed. rev., 1962.

Poe, Edgar Allan. *Selections from the Critical Writings of Edgar Allan Poe.* Edited by F. C. Prescott. New York: Gordian Press, 1981.

Proust, Marcel. *A la recherche du temps perdu.* 3 vols. Texte établi et présenté par Pierre Clarac et André Ferre. Paris: Gallimard, 1954.

———. *Remembrance of Things Past.* 3 vols. Translated by C. K. Scott Moncrieff and Terence Kilmartin (vol. 3, Andreas Mayor). London: Penguin Books, 1989.

Ruskin, John. *The Complete Works of John Ruskin.* 38 vols. Edited by E. T. Cook and A. Wedderburn. London: George Allen, 1904.

Schlegel, Friedrich. *Philosophical Fragments*. Translated by Peter Firchow. Minneapolis: University of Minnesota Press, 1991.

Shelley, Percy Bysshe. *Shelley's Prose: Or the Trumpet of a Prophecy*. Edited by David Lee Clark. Albuquerque: University of New Mexico Press, 1954.

Smart, Christopher. *The Poetical Works of Christopher Smart*. Edited by Marcus Walsh. Oxford: Clarendon Press, 1987.

Sprat, Thomas. *History of the Royal Society* [1667]. Edited by Jackson I. Cope and Harold Whitmore Jones. St. Louis, Mo.: Washington University Studies, 1958.

Tomlinson, Charles. *Collected Poems*. Oxford: Oxford University Press, 1985.

———. An Interview with Charles Tomlinson by Jed Rasula and Mike Erwin. *Contemporary Literature* 16 (1975): 405–16.

Traherne, Thomas. *Centuries, Poems and Thanksgivings*. 2 vols. Edited by H. M. Margoliouth. Oxford: Clarendon Press, 1958.

Turgenev, Ivan. *Poems in Prose*. Translated by Evgenia Schimanskaya. London: Harrison, 1945.

Wilde, Oscar. *The Letters of Oscar Wilde*. Edited by Rupert Hart-Davis. London: Rupert Hart-Davis, 1962.

———. "Poems in Prose," *the Fortnightly Review* 56 (July 1894), 22–9.

———. *Poems in Prose*. Fifty copies privately printed, Paris 1905.

Wordsworth, William. *The Prelude 1799, 1805, 1850*. Edited by Jonathan Wordsworth, M. H. Abrams and Stephen Gill. London and New York: W. W. Norton, 1979.

———, and Samuel Taylor Coleridge. *Lyrical Ballads 1798*. Edited by W. J. B. Owen. 2nd ed. Oxford: Oxford University Press, 1987.

———, and Dorothy Wordsworth. *The Letters of William and Dorothy Wordsworth. I: The Early Years 1787–1805*. Edited by Ernest De Selincourt. 2nd ed. rev. by Chester L. Shaver. Oxford: Clarendon Press, 1967.

Secondary Sources

Abrams, M. H. *The Mirror and the Lamp: Romantic Theory and the Critical Tradition*. New York: W. W. Norton, 1958.

Acheson, James, and Kateryna Arthur, eds. *Beckett's Later Fiction and Drama: Texts for Company*. London: Macmillan 1987.

Adolph, Robert. *The Rise of Modern Prose Style*. Cambridge and London: MIT Press, 1968.

Amiran, Eyal. *Wandering and Home: Beckett's Metaphysical Narrative*. University Park, Pa: Pennsylvania State University Press, 1993.

Annwn, David. *Inhabited Voices: Myth and History in the Poetry of Geoffrey Hill, Seamus Heaney, and George Mackay Brown*. Frome: Bran's Head Books, 1984.

apRoberts, Ruth. *The Biblical Web*. Ann Arbor: University of Michigan Press, 1994.

Ashton, Rosemary. *The Life of Samuel Taylor Coleridge: A Critical Biography*. Oxford: Blackwell, 1996.

Astro, Alan. "Allegory of Translation in Baudelaire's *Un mangeur d'opium*," *Nineteenth-Century French Studies* 18 (1989/90): 165–71.

———. *Understanding Samuel Beckett*. Columbia: University of South Carolina, 1990.

Bachelard, Gaston. *The Poetics of Space*. Translated by Maria Jolas. Boston: Beacon Press, 1969.

Bair, Deirdre. *Samuel Beckett*. London: Jonathan Cape, 1978.

Barker, George. *The Jubjub Bird or Some Remarks on the Prose Poem and a Little Honouring of Lionel Johnson*. Warwick: Greville Press, 1985.

J. Robert Barth, S. J. *The Symbolic Imagination: Coleridge and the Romantic Tradition*. Princeton: Princeton University Press, 1977.

Barthes, Roland. *S/Z*. Translated by Richard Miller. London: Jonathan Cape, 1975.

Bartlett, Neil. "The Uses of Monotony: Repetition in the language of Oscar Wilde, Jean Genet, Edmund White, and Juan Goytisolo." The William Matthews Lecture, delivered at Birkbeck College, 17 May 1994. London: Birkbeck College, 1994.

Baxter, Edmund. *De Quincey's Art of Autobiography*. Edinburgh: Edinburgh University Press, 1990.

Beauchamp, Tom L., and Alexander Rosenberg. *Hume and the Problem of Causation*. New York and London: Oxford University Press, 1981.

Beaujour, Michael. "Short Epiphanies: Two Contextual Approaches to the French Prose Poem." In *The Prose Poem in France: Theory and Practice*, edited by Mary Ann Caws and H. Riffaterre. New York: Columbia University Press, 1983. 39–59.

Beckett, Samuel. "Proust in Pieces." Review of *Comment Proust a composé son roman*, by Professor Albert Feuillerat. *The Spectator*. 22 June 1934.

Beckett, Samuel, and Georges Duthuit. *Proust and Three Dialogues with Georges Duthuit*. London: Calder & Boyars, 1970. Originally published by John Calder, 1965.

Bedford, William. "True Sequences of Pain: 'Context' in the Critical Prose and Poetry of Geoffrey Hill." *Agenda* 30 (1992): 15–23.

Bedient, Calvin. "On Geoffrey Hill." *Critical Quarterly* 23 (1981): 17–26.

Beer, John. *Coleridge's Poetic Intelligence*. London: Macmillan, 1977.

———. *Coleridge the Visionary*. London: Chatto & Windus, 1959.

———. "The Englishness of De Quincey's Ideas." In *English and German Romanticism: Cross Currents and Controversies*, edited by James Pipkin. Heidelberg: Carl Winter Universitätsverlag, 1985. 323–47.

Beja, Morris., S. E. Gontarski, and Pierre Astier, eds. *Samuel Beckett: Humanistic Perspectives*. Columbus: Ohio State University Press, 1983.

Bent, Ian, ed. *Musical Analysis in the Nineteenth Century*. 2 vols. Cambridge: Cambridge University Press, 1994.

Bentley, G. E., Jr. *Blake Records*. Oxford: Clarendon Press, 1969.

Berlin, Adele. *The Dynamics of Biblical Parallelism*. Bloomington: Indiana University Press, 1985.

Berman, Marshall. *All That Is Solid Melts Into Air*. London and New York: Verso, 1995.

Bernard, Suzanne. *Le poème en prose de Baudelaire jusqu'à nos jours.* Paris: Librairie Nizet, 1959.

Bersani, Leo, and Ulysse Dutoit. *Arts of Impoverishment: Beckett, Rothko, Resnais.* London and Cambridge: Harvard University Press, 1993.

Beyer, Werner W. *The Enchanted Forest.* Oxford: Basil Blackwell, 1963.

Bishop, Tom, and Raymond Federman, eds. *Samuel Beckett.* Paris: Éditions de l'Herne, 1976.

Blanchot, Maurice. "The Athenaeum." Translated by D. Esch and I. Balfour. *Studies in Romanticism,* 22 (1983). Excerpted from M. Blanchot, *L'Entretien Infini* (1969).

Brater, Enoch. "*Still* / Beckett: The Essential and the Incidental." *Journal of Modern Literature* 6 (1977): 3–16.

———. ed. *Beckett at 80 / Beckett in Context.* London: Oxford University Press, 1986.

Bredbeck, Gregory W. "Narcissus in the Wilde: Textual Cathexis and the Historical Origins of Queer Camp." In Meyer ed., *The Politics and Poetics of Camp,* 51–74.

Breunig, LeRoy C. "Why France?" In *The Prose Poem in France: Theory and Practice,* edited by Mary Ann Caws and H. Rifaterre. New York: Columbia University Press, 1983. 3–20.

Brown, Calvin S., Jr. "The Musical Structure of De Quincey's *Dream Fugue.*" *Musical Quarterly* 24 (1938): 341–50.

Brown, Lee Rust. "Coleridge and the Prospect of the Whole." *Studies in Romanticism* 30 (1991): 235–53.

Brownjohn, Alan. Review of *Mercian Hymns. The New Statesman.* 6 August 1971.

Buning, Marius, and Lois Oppenheim, eds. *Beckett in the 1990s.* Selected Papers from the Second International Symposium. The Hague, April 1992. Amsterdam and Atlanta: Editions Rodopi, 1993.

Butler, Lance St. John, ed. *Critical Essays on Samuel Beckett: Critical Thought Series, 4.* Aldershot, England: Scolar Press, Brookfield, Vt: Ashgate Publications, 1993.

———, and R. J. Davis, eds. *Rethinking Beckett.* London: Macmillan, 1990.

Butor, Michel. "Le Roman et la Poésie." *Répertoire II.* Paris: Les Éditions de Minuit, 1964.

Caws, Mary Ann. *Reading Frames in Modern Fictions.* Princeton: Princeton University Press, 1985.

———, and H. Riffaterre, eds. *The Prose Poem in France, Theory and Practice.* New York: Columbia University Press, 1983.

Charles, Michel. "Digression, régression (Arabesques)." *Poétique* 40 (1979): 395–407.

Clapton, G. T. *Baudelaire et De Quincey.* Paris: Les Belles Lettres, 1931.

Clarke, Graham, ed. *Edgar Allan Poe: Critical Assessments II: Poe in the Nineteenth Century.* Mountfield, E. Sussex: Helm Information, 1991.

Clément, Bruno. "VLADIMIR: La présence d'Ivan Tourgueniev dans l'oeuvre de Samuel Beckett." In Buning and Oppenheim eds., *Beckett in the 1990s,* 67–76.

Cohn, Robert Greer. *Mallarmé's Prose Poems: A Critical Study.* Cambridge: Cambridge University Press, 1987.

Connor, Steven. *Samuel Beckett: Repetition, Theory, and Text.* Oxford: Basil Blackwell, 1988.

Cox, C. B., and Arnold P. Hinchliffe, eds. *T. S. Eliot, The Waste Land: A Casebook.* London: Macmillan, 1968.

Cox, Kenneth. "Roy Fisher." *Agenda* 29, no. 4 (1991): 31–40.

Croll, Morris. "The Baroque Style in Prose." In *Seventeenth-Century Prose*, edited by Stanley Fish. New York and Oxford: Oxford University Press, 1971. 26–52.

Culler, Jonathan. *The Pursuit of Signs: Semiotics, Literature, Deconstruction.* London and Henley: Routledge & Kegan Paul, 1981.

De Luca, V. A. *Thomas De Quincey: The Prose of Vision.* Toronto and London: University of Toronto Press, 1980.

Dearlove, Judith E. *Accommodating the Chaos: Beckett's Nonrelational Art.* Durham, N.C.: Duke University Press, 1982.

———. "'Syntax Upended in Opposite Corners': Alterations in Beckett's Linguistic Theories." In *Samuel Beckett: Humanistic Perspectives*, edited by Morris Beja, S. E. Gontarski, and Pierre Astier. Columbus: Ohio State University Press, 1983. 122–28.

Deleuze, Gilles. *Empiricism and Subjectivity: An Essay on Hume's Theory of Human Nature.* Translated by Constantin V. Boundas. New York: Columbia University Press, 1991.

———. *Difference and Repetition.* Translated by Paul Patton. London: Athlone, 1994.

Delville, Michel. *The American Prose Poem: Poetic Form and the Boundaries of Genre.* Gainesville: University Press of Florida, 1998.

de Man, Paul. *Allegories of Reading: Figural Language in Rousseau, Nietzsche, Rilke and Proust.* New Haven and London: Yale University Press, 1979.

———. "The Rhetoric of Temporality." In *Blindness and Insight.* 2nd ed. rev. London: Methuen, 1983.

Derrida, Jacques. *Dissemination.* Translated by Barbara Johnson. London: Athlone, 1981.

———. "The Law of Genre." Translated by Avital Ronell. *Critical Inquiry* 7 (1980): 55–83.

———. *The Truth in Painting.* Translated by Geoff Bennington and Ian McLeod. Chicago and London: The University of Chicago Press, 1987. Originally published as *La Vérité en Peinture*, 1978.

Devlin, D. D. *De Quincey, Wordsworth and the Art of Prose.* London: Macmillan, 1983.

Doce, Jordi. "The Poet of the Eye." Interview with Charles Tomlinson. *Agenda* 33 (1996): 22–30.

Dodsworth, Martin. "Mercian Hymns: Offa, Charlemagne and Geoffrey Hill." In *Geoffrey Hill: Essays on His Work*, edited by Peter Robinson. Milton Keynes and Philadelphia: Open University Press, 1985. 49–62.

Drain, Richard. "'The Waste Land': The Prison and the Key." In *The Waste Land in Different Voices*, edited by A. D. Moody. London: Edward Arnold, 1974. 29–45.

Driver, Tom. Interview with Samuel Beckett for Columbia University Forum (1961). Reprinted in Graver and Federman eds., *Samuel Beckett: The Critical Heritage*, 217–23.

Dussler, L. *Raphael: A Critical Catalogue.* London and New York: Phaidon, 1971.

Eco, Umberto. *The Open Work*. Translated by Anna Cancogni. London: Hutchinson Radius, 1989.

Eitner, Lorenz. "The Open Window and the Storm-Tossed Boat: An Essay in the Iconography of Romanticism." *The Art Bulletin* 37 (1955): 281–90.

Eliot, T. S. "The Borderline of Prose." *The New Statesman*. 19 May 1917, 157–59.

———. *To Criticize the Critic, and Other Writings*. London: Faber & Faber, 1978.

Ellmann, Richard. "The Uses of Decadence: Wilde, Yeats, Joyce." In *The Ordering Mirror: Readers and Contexts,* edited by Phillip Lopate. New York: Fordham University Press, 1993. 115–33.

Erdman, David V., ed. *Blake and His Bibles*. West Cornwall, Conn.: Locust Hill Press, 1990.

Esslin, Martin. "Samuel Beckett— Infinity, Eternity." In *Beckett at 80 / Beckett in Context,* edited by Enoch Brater. London: Oxford University Press, 1986. 110–23.

Faris, Wendy B. *Labyrinths of Language: Symbolic Landscape and Narrative Design in Modern Fiction*. Baltimore and London: Johns Hopkins University Press, 1988.

Finney, Brian H. *Since How It Is: A Study of Samuel Beckett's Later Fiction*. London: Covent Garden Press, 1972.

———. "*Still* to *Worstward Ho* : Beckett's Prose Fiction Since *The Lost Ones*." In *Beckett's Later Fiction and Drama: Texts for Company,* edited by James Acheson and Kateryna Arthur. London: Macmillan, 1987. 65–79.

Fisch, Harold. *Jerusalem and Albion: The Hebraic Factor in Seventeenth-Century Literature*. London: Routledge & Kegan Paul, 1964.

Fish, Stanley. *Self-Consuming Artifacts: The Experience of Seventeenth-Century Literature* Berkeley and London: University of California Press, 1972.

———. ed. *Seventeenth-Century Prose*. New York and Oxford: Oxford University Press, 1971.

Fletcher, John. "Ecrivain Bilingue." In *Samuel Beckett,* edited by Tom Bishop and Raymond Federman. Paris: Éditions de l'Herne, 1976. 212–18.

Flores, Angel, ed. *The Kafka Debate: New Perspectives for Our Time*. New York: Gordian Press, 1977.

Fowler, Alastair. Introduction to *Paradise Lost* by John Milton. London: Longman, 1991.

Frank, Ellen Eve. *Literary Architecture: Essays Toward a Tradition*. Berkeley: University of California Press, 1979.

Fredman, Stephen. *Poet's Prose: The Crisis of American Verse,* 2nd ed. Cambridge: Cambridge University Press, 1990.

Fulford, Tim. *Coleridge's Figurative Language*. London: Macmillan, 1991.

———, and Morton D. Paley, eds. *Coleridge's Visionary Languages: Essays in Honor of J. B. Beer*. Cambridge: Brewer, 1993.

Gardner, W. H. *Gerard Manley Hopkins (1844–1889): A Study of Poetic Idiosyncrasy in Relation to Poetic Tradition*. London: Secker & Warburg, 1944.

Garrigan, K. O. *Ruskin on Architecture*. Madison and London: University of Wisconsin Press, 1973.

Gervais, David. "'An Exemplary Poet': Geoffrey Hill's Wordsworth." *Agenda* 34 (1996): 88–103.

Gidal, Peter. *Understanding Beckett: A Study of Monologue and Gesture in the Works of Samuel Beckett.* London: Macmillan, 1986.

Gilbert, Sandra M., and Sandra Gubar. *The Madwoman in the Attic.* New Haven and London: Yale University Press, 1984.

Gordon, Ian A. *The Movement of English Prose.* London: Longman, 1966.

Grandin, John M. "Defenestrations." In *The Kafka Debate*, edited by Angel Flores. New York: Gordian Press, 1977. 216–22.

Graver, Lawrence, and Raymond Federman, eds. *Samuel Beckett: The Critical Heritage.* London: Routledge & Kegan Paul, 1979.

Hamilton, K. G. *The Two Harmonies: Poetry and Prose in the Seventeenth Century.* Oxford: Clarendon Press, 1963.

Hamon, Philippe. "Texte et Architecture." *Poetique* 73 (1988): 3–26.

Hansford, James. "'Imaginative Transactions' in 'La Falaise.'" *Journal of Beckett Studies* 10 (1985): 76–86.

———. "Seeing and saying in 'As the story was told'." *Journal of Beckett Studies* 8 (autumn 1982): 75–93.

Haughton, Hugh. "'How fit a title . . . ': Title and Authority in the Work of Geoffrey Hill." In *Geoffrey Hill: Essays on His Work*, edited by Peter Robinson. Milton Keynes and Philadelphia: Open University Press, 1985. 129–49.

Haxell, Nichola Anne. "The Name of the Prose: A Semiotic Study of Titling in the Pre-Baudelairian Prose Poem." *French Studies,* 44 (1990): 156–69.

Heaney, Seamus. "Englands of the Mind." In *Preoccupations: Selected Prose, 1968–1978.* London and Boston: Faber & Faber, 1980, 150–69.

Hiddleston, J. A. *Baudelaire and "Le Spleen de Paris."* Oxford: Clarendon Press, 1987.

Hill, Geoffrey. "'The Conscious Mind's Intelligible Structure': A Debate." *Agenda* 9–10 (1971/2): 14–23.

———. *The Enemy's Country: Words, Contexture, and Other Circumstances of Language.* Oxford: Clarendon Press, 1991. From the Clark Lectures, 1986.

———. *The Lords of Limit: Essays on Literature and Ideas.* London: Andre Deutsch, 1984.

———. "Redeeming the Time." *Agenda* 10–11 (1972/3): 87–111. Revised and reprinted in Hill, *Lords of Limit,* 84–104.

Hill, Leslie. *Beckett's Fiction in Different Words.* Cambridge: Cambridge University Press, 1990.

Hirsch, David H., and Nehama Aschkenasy, eds. *Biblical Patterns in Modern Literature.* Brown Judaic Studies, no.77. Presented at the First Annual Conference of the Institute for Literary Research of Bar Ilan University, Israel. May 1982. Chico, Calif.: Scholars Press, 1984.

Hodgson, John A. *Coleridge, Shelley, and Transcendental Inquiry: Rhetoric, Argument, Metapsychology.* Lincoln and London: University of Nebraska Press, 1989.

Hyde, H. Montgomery. *The Trials of Oscar Wilde.* London: William Hodge, 1949.

Jakobson, Roman. *Selected Writings.* 8 vols. Edited by Stephen Rudy. The Hague, Paris, New York: Mouton Publishers, 1971.

Jasper, David. *Coleridge as Poet and Religious Thinker.* London: Macmillan, 1985.

Johnson, Barbara. *The Critical Difference: Essays in the Contemporary Rhetoric of Reading.* Baltimore and London: Johns Hopkins University Press, 1980.

———. *Défigurations du langage poétique: la seconde révolution baudelairienne.* Paris and Montreal: Flammarion, 1979.

Johnston, John H. *The Poet and the City: A Study in Urban Perspectives.* Athens: University of Georgia Press, 1984.

Jones, P. Mansell. *The Background to Modern French Poetry: Essays and Interviews.* Cambridge: Cambridge University Press, 1968.

Jones, Roger, and Nicholas Penny. *Raphael.* New Haven and London: Yale University Press, 1983.

Juliet, Charles. *Conversations with Samuel Beckett and Bram van Velde.* Translated by Janey Tucker. Leiden: Academic Press Leiden, 1994.

Kazin, Cathrael. "'Across a Wilderness of Retrospection': A Reading of Geoffrey Hill's *Lachrimae*." *Agenda* 17 (1979): 43–57.

Keeble, N. H. Introduction to *The Pilgrim's Progress* by John Bunyan. Oxford: Oxford University Press, 1984.

Kenner, Hugh. *Flaubert, Joyce, and Beckett: The Stoic Comedians.* London: W. H. Allen, 1964.

———. "The Invisible Poet." In Cox and Hinchliffe eds., *T. S. Eliot, The Waste Land: A Casebook,* 168–99.

———. *Samuel Beckett: A Critical Study.* London: John Calder, 1962.

Kermode, Frank. *The Sense of an Ending: Studies in the Theory of Fiction.* New York: Oxford University Press, 1967.

Kessler, Edward. *Coleridge's Metaphors of Being.* Princeton: Princeton University Press, 1979.

Knapp, Bettina L. *Archetype, Architecture, and the Writer.* Bloomington: Indiana University Press, 1986.

Knottenbelt, E. M. *Passionate Intelligence: The Poetry of Geoffrey Hill.* Costerus New Series 77. Amsterdam: Rodopi, 1990.

Knowlson, James, and John Pilling. *Frescoes of the Skull: The Later Prose and Drama of Samuel Beckett.* London: John Calder, 1979.

Kugel, James. *The Idea of Biblical Poetry: Parallelism and Its History.* New Haven and London: Yale University Press, 1981.

Kundera, Milan. *The Art of the Novel.* Translated by Linda Asher. London: Faber & Faber, 1988.

Lacoue-Labarthe, Philippe, and Jean-Luc Nancy. *The Literary Absolute.* Translated by Philip Barnard and Cheryl Lester. Albany: State University of New York Press, 1988.

Levi, Peter, S. J. "Geoffrey Hill." Review of *Mercian Hymns. Agenda* 9–10 (1971/72): 99–103.

Lewis, C. S. *The Literary Impact of the Authorised Version.* The Ethel M. Wood Lecture delivered before the University of London. London: Athlone, 1950.

Lindop, Grevel. "Myth and Blood: The Poetry of Geoffrey Hill." *Critical Quarterly* 26 (1984): 147–54.

———. *The Opium-Eater: A Life of Thomas De Quincey.* London: J. M. Dent, 1981.

Lodge, David. *The Modes of Modern Writing : Metaphor, Metonymy and the Typology of Modern Literature.* London: Edward Arnold, 1977.

———. "Some *Ping* Understood." *Encounter* 30 (1968). Reprinted in Butler ed., *Critical Essays on Samuel Beckett,* 154–58.

Lopate, Phillip, ed., *The Ordering Mirror: Readers and Contexts.* New York: Fordham University Press, 1993.

Lowth, Robert. *Lectures on the Sacred Poetry of the Hebrews.* 2 vols. Translated by G. Gregory. London: J. Johnson, 1787.

Maguson, Paul. *Coleridge's Nightmare Poetry.* Charlottesville: University Press of Virginia, 1974.

Maniquis, Robert M. "The Dark Interpreter and the Palimpsest of Violence: De Quincey and the Unconscious." In *Thomas De Quincey Bicentenary Studies,* edited by Robert Lance Snyder. Norman and London: University of Oklahoma Press, 1985. 109–39.

———. "Lonely Empires: Personal and Public Visions of Thomas De Quincey." *Literary Monographs* 8 (1976): 47–127.

———. "'The Prose of Vision' by V. A. De Luca." *Studies in Romanticism* 23 (1984): 139–47.

McDonagh, Josephine. *De Quincey's Disciplines.* Oxford: Clarendon Press, 1994.

———. "Writings on the Mind: De Quincey and the Importance of the Palimpsest in Nineteenth-Century Thought." *Prose Studies* 10 (1987): 207–24.

McFarland, Thomas. "Aspects of Coleridge's Distinction Between Reason and Understanding." In *Coleridge's Visionary Languages,* edited by T. Fulford and Morton D. Paley. Cambridge: Brewer, 1993. 165–80.

———. *Romanticism and the Forms of Ruin: Wordsworth, Coleridge, and Modalities of Fragmentation.* Princeton: Princeton University Press, 1981.

———. "Patterns of Parataxis in Anglo-German Cultural Currents." In *English and German Romanticism: Cross Currents and Controversies,* edited by James Pipkin. Heidelberg: Carl Winter Universitätsverlag, 1985. 217–49.

McNees, Eleanor. *Eucharistic Poetry: The Search for Presence in the Writings of John Donne, Gerard Manley Hopkins, Dylan Thomas, and Geoffrey Hill.* London and Lewisburg, Pa.: Bucknell University Press, 1992.

Mercier, Vivian. *Beckett / Beckett.* New York and Oxford: Oxford University Press, 1979.

Meschonnic, Henri. "Translating Biblical Rhythm." In *Biblical Patterns in Modern Literature,* edited by David Hirsch and Nehama Aschkenasy. Chico, Calif.: Scholars Press, 1984. 227–40.

Metzidakis, Stamos. *Repetition and Semiotics: Interpreting Prose Poems.* Birmingham, Ala.: Summa Publications, 1986.

Meyer, Leonard B. *Emotion and Meaning in Music.* Chicago and London: University of Chicago Press, 1956.

Meyer, Moe, ed. *The Politics and Poetics of Camp.* London and New York: Routledge, 1994.

Mikhail, Edward Halim, ed. *Oscar Wilde: Interviews and Recollections.* London: Macmillan, 1979.

Miller, J. Hillis. *The Disappearance of God: Five Nineteenth-Century Writers.* Cambridge: Belknap Press of Harvard University Press; London: Oxford University Press, 1975.

———. *Tropes, Parables, and Performatives.* New York and London: Harvester Wheatsheaf, 1990.

Milne, W. S. "Decreation in Geoffrey Hill's *Lachrimae.*" *Agenda* 17 (1979): 61–71.

Mitchell, Bruce, and Fred C. Robinson. *A Guide to Old English.* 4th ed. rev. Oxford: Basil Blackwell, 1986.

Monroe, Jonathan. *A Poverty of Objects: The Prose Poem and the Politics of Genre.* Ithaca and London: Cornell University Press, 1987.

Moody, A. D. ed. *"The Waste Land" in Different Voices.* London: Edward Arnold, 1974.

Morris, David B. *The Religious Sublime: Christian Poetry and Critical Tradition in Eighteenth-Century England.* Lexington: University Press of Kentucky, 1972.

Mueller, Janel M. *The Native Tongue and the Word: Developments in English Prose Style 1380–1580.* Chicago and London: University of Chicago Press, 1984.

Muir, Edwin. Introduction to *America* by Franz Kafka. Translated by Willa and Edwin Muir. Harmondsworth: Penguin Books, 1967.

Murphy, Margueritte S. *A Tradition of Subversion: The Prose Poem in English from Wilde to Ashbery.* Amherst: University of Massachusetts Press, 1992.

Murphy, P. J. "Beckett and the Philosophers." In *The Cambridge Companion to Beckett,* edited by John Pilling. Cambridge: Cambridge University Press, 1994. 222–40.

Needham, John. "The Idiom of Geoffrey Hill's Mercian Hymns." *English* 28 (1979): 139–49.

O'Beebee, Thomas. *The Ideology of Genre: A Comparative Study of Generic Instability.* State College: Pennsylvania State University Press, 1994.

O'Gorman, Kathleen, ed. *Charles Tomlinson: Man and Artist.* Columbia: University of Missouri Press, 1988.

O'Hara, J. D. "Beckett Piece by Piece." Review of several books by or about Beckett including *Fizzles. The Nation,* 19 February 1977, 216–19.

Orsini, G. N. G. *Coleridge and German Idealism.* Carbondale and Edwardsville: Southern Illinois University Press; Amsterdam and London: Feffer & Simons Inc., 1969.

Painter, George D. *Marcel Proust, A Biography.* 2 vols. London: Penguin Books, 1990.

Pater, Walter. *The Renaissance: Studies in Art and Poetry* (the 1893 text). Edited by Donald L. Hill. London and Los Angeles: University of California Press, 1980.

Perloff, Marjorie. "Between Verse and Prose: Beckett and the New Poetry." *Critical Inquiry* 9 (1982): 415–33.

———. *The Poetics of Indeterminacy: Rimbaud to Cage.* Princeton: Princeton University Press, 1981.

———. *Poetry On and Off the Page: Essays for Emergent Occasions.* Evanston: Northwestern University Press, 1998.

Phillips, Michael. "The Reputation of Blake's *Poetical Sketches* 1783–1863." *The Review of English Studies* 26 (1975): 19–33.

Piette, Adam. *Remembering and the Sound of Words: Mallarmé, Proust, Joyce, Beckett.* Oxford: Clarendon Press, 1996.

Pike, Burton. *The Image of the City in Modern Literature.* Princeton: Princeton University Press, 1981.

Pilling, John. "Beckett after *Still*." *Romance Notes* 18 (1977): 280–87.

―――. "Fizzles." Review article for *For to End Yet Again and Other Fizzles. Journal of Beckett Studies* 2 (1977): 96–100.

―――. *Samuel Beckett.* London: Routledge & Kegan Paul, 1976.

―――. "The Significance of Beckett's *Still*." *Essays in Criticism* 28 (1978): 143–53.

―――, ed. *The Cambridge Companion to Beckett.* Cambridge: Cambridge University Press, 1994.

Pipkin, James, ed. *English and German Romanticism: Cross Currents and Controversies.* Heidelberg: Carl Winter Universitätsverlag, 1985.

Pluhar, Werner S. Introduction to *Critique of Judgment* by Immanuel Kant. Indianapolis: Hackett Publishing Company, 1987.

Pooley, Roger. *English Prose of the Seventeenth Century, 1590–1700.* London and New York: Longman, 1992.

Porter-Abbott, H. "Beginning Again: The Post-Narrative Art of *Texts for Nothing* and *How It Is*." In *The Cambridge Companion to Beckett,* edited by John Pilling. Cambridge: Cambridge University Press, 1994. 106–23.

Preston, Thomas R. "Biblical Criticism, Literature and the Eighteenth-Century Reader." In *Books and Their Readers in Eighteenth-Century England,* edited by Isabel Rivers. Leicester: Leicester University Press; New York: St. Martin's Press, 1982. 97–126.

Prickett, Stephen. *Coleridge and Wordsworth: The Poetry of Growth.* Cambridge: Cambridge University Press, 1970.

―――. *Words and The Word: Language, Poetics and Biblical Interpretation.* Cambridge: Cambridge University Press, 1986.

Prinz, Jessica. "Foirades / Fizzles / Beckett / Johns." *Contemporary Literature* 21 (1980): 480–510.

Purton, Valerie. *A Coleridge Chronology.* London: Macmillan, 1993.

Rabinovitz, Rubin. "*Fizzles* and Samuel Beckett's Earlier Fiction." *Contemporary Literature* 24 (1983): 307–21.

Raine, Kathleen. *Blake and Tradition.* 2 vols. Princeton: Princeton University Press, 1968.

Raitt, A. W. "On *Le Spleen de Paris*." *Nineteenth-Century French Studies* 18 (1989/90): 150–64.

Rasula, Jed, and Mike Erwin. "An Interview with Charles Tomlinson." *Contemporary Literature* 16 (1975): 405–16.

Reed, Arden. *Romantic Weather: The Climates of Coleridge and Baudelaire.* Hanover, N.H., and London: University Press of New England, 1983.

Reisner, Thomas A. "De Quincey's Palimpsest Reconsidered." *Modern Language Studies* 12 (1982): 93–95.

Renton, Andrew. "Disabled Figures: From the *Residua* to *Stirrings Still*." In *The Cambridge Companion to Beckett,* edited by John Pilling. Cambridge: Cambridge University Press, 1994. 167–83.

Review of *Mercian Hymns*, *TLS* (27 August, 1971), 1024.
Ricks, Christopher. *Geoffrey Hill and "The Tongue's Atrocities."* The W. D. Thomas memorial lecture delivered 15 February 1978 (Swansea: University College of Swansea, 1978).
Riffaterre, Michael. *Semiotics of Poetry.* Bloomington and London: Indiana University Press, 1978.
Rivers, Isabel, ed. *Books and Their Readers in Eighteenth-Century England.* Leicester: Leicester University Press; New York: St. Martin's Press, 1982.
Roberts, A. M. "Reflexivity and Impersonality in the Poetry of Geoffrey Hill." Ph.D. Diss., University of London, 1991.
Robinson, Peter, ed. *Geoffrey Hill: Essays on His Work.* Milton Keynes and Philadelphia: Open University Press, 1985.
Roston, Murray. *Prophet and Poet: The Bible and the Growth of Romanticism.* London: Faber & Faber, 1965.
Sabin, Margery. *English Romanticism and the French Tradition.* London and Cambridge: Harvard University Press, 1976.
Said, Edward. *Orientalism.* Harmondsworth: Penguin Books, 1985.
Scarry, E. M. "Six Ways to Kill a Blackbird or Any Other Intentional Object: Samuel Beckett's Method of Meaning." *James Joyce Quarterly* 8 (1971): 278–89.
Schulz, Max F. *The Poetic Voices of Coleridge: A Study of His Desire for Spontaneity and Passion for Order*, 2nd ed. rev. Detroit: Wayne State University Press, 1964.
Schwarzbach, F. S. "'*Terra Incognita*': An Image of the City in English Literature, 1820–1855." *Prose Studies* 5 (1982): 61–84.
Selden, Raman, ed., *The Theory of Criticism: From Plato to the Present.* London: Longman, 1989.
Shaffer, E. S. *"Kubla Khan" and the Fall of Jerusalem: The Mythological School in Biblical Criticism and Secular Literature, 1770–1880.* Cambridge: Cambridge University Press, 1975.
Sharpe, William Chapman. *Unreal Cities: Urban Figuration in Wordsworth, Baudelaire, Whitman, Eliot, and Williams.* Baltimore and London: Johns Hopkins University Press, 1990.
Silliman, Ron. *The New Sentence.* New York: Roof, 1987.
Simon, John. *The Prose Poem as a Genre in Nineteenth-Century European Literature.* London and New York: Garland, 1987.
Smith, Frederik. "Beckett and the Seventeenth-Century *Port-Royal* Logic." In *Critical Essays on Samuel Beckett,* (Aldershot, Hants, England; Scolar Press, Brookfield, VT: Ashgate Pub, 1993). 218–26.
Snyder, Robert Lance, ed. *Thomas De Quincey Bicentenary Studies.* Norman and London: University of Oklahoma Press, 1985. Papers from the annual convention of 1981 of the MLA, New York, NY.
Sonnenfeld, Albert. "L'Adieu Suprême and Ultimate Composure: The Boundaries of the Prose Poem." In *The Prose Poem in France: Theory and Practice,* edited by Mary Ann Caws and H. Riffaterre. New York: Columbia University Press, 1983. 198–211.
Spector, Sheila A. "Blake as an Eighteenth-Century Hebraist." In *Blake and His Bibles,* edited by David V. Erdman. West Cornwall, Conn.: Locust Hill Press, 1990. 179–229.

Starobinski, Jean. "Windows: From Rousseau to Baudelaire." Translated by Richard Pevear. *The Hudson Review* 40 (1988): 551–60.
Steadman, John. *The Hill and the Labyrinth.* Berkeley and London: University of California Press, 1984.
Sultana, David. *Samuel Taylor Coleridge in Malta and Italy.* Oxford: Basil Blackwell, 1969.
Suther, Marshall. *Visions of Xanadu.* New York and London: Columbia University Press, 1965.
Sutherland, James R. *English Literature of the Late Seventeenth Century.* [*The Oxford History of English Literature,* edited by Bonamy Dobrée and Norman Davis.] Oxford: Clarendon Press, 1969.
Swann, Charles. "*The Picture of Dorian Gray,* the Bible and the Unpardonable Sin." *Notes and Queries* 236 (1991): 326–27.
Symons, Arthur. *Studies in Prose and Verse.* London: J. M. Dent, 1904.
Terdiman, Richard. *Discourse/Counter Discourse: The Theory and Practice of Symbolic Resistance in Nineteenth-Century France.* Ithaca and London: Cornell University Press, 1985.
Thesing, William B. *The London Muse: Victorian Poetic Responses to the City.* Athens: University of Georgia Press, 1982.
Times Literary Supplement. No 1024. August 1971.
Todorov, Tzvetan. *Genres in Discourse.* Translated by Catherine Porter. Cambridge: Cambridge University Press, 1990.
Trieloff, Barbara. "'Babel of Silence': Beckett's Post-Trilogy Prose Articulated." In *Rethinking Beckett,* edited by Lance St. John Butler and R. J. Davis. London: Macmillan, 1990. 89–104.
Vadé, Yves. *Le Poème en prose et ses territoires.* Paris: Éditions Belin, 1996.
Ven, Cornelius van de. *Space in Architecture: The Evolution of a New Idea in the Theory and History of the Modern Movements.* Amsterdam: Van Gorcum Assen, 1978.
Vickers, Brian. *Francis Bacon and Renaissance Prose.* Cambridge: Cambridge University Press, 1968.
Villalobos, John C. "A Possible Source for William Blake's 'The Great Code of Art.'" *English Language Notes* 26 (1988): 36–40.
von Leyden, W. *Seventeenth-Century Metaphysics: An Examination of Some Main Concepts and Theories.* London: Gerald Duckworth, 1968.
Wall, Alan. "Geoffrey Hill's *Canaan.*" *Agenda* 34 (1996): 29–48.
Weatherhead, A. Kingsley. *The British Dissonance: Essays on Ten Contemporary Poets.* Columbia and London: University of Missouri Press, 1983.
Wendling, Ronald C. *Coleridge's Progress to Christianity: Experience and Authority in Religious Faith.* Lewisburg, Pa.: Bucknell University Press, 1995.
Wesling, Donald. *The New Poetries : Poetic Form Since Coleridge and Wordsworth.* Lewisburg, Pa.: Bucknell University Press, 1985.

———. "Process and Closure in Tomlinson's Prose Poems." In *Charles Tomlinson: Man and Artist,* edited by Kathleen O'Gorman. Columbia: University of Missouri Press, 1988. 125–35.
Whallon, William. *Formula, Character, and Context: Studies in Homeric, Old English, and Old Testament Poetry.* Cambridge: Harvard University Press, 1969.

———. "Hebraic Synonymy in Sir Thomas Browne." *ELH* 28 (1961): 335–52.
Wheeler, Kathleen. *The Creative Mind in Coleridge's Poetry*. London: Heinemann, 1981.
———. *German Aesthetic and Literary Criticism: The Romantic Ironists and Goethe*. Cambridge: Cambridge University Press, 1984.
Woolf, Virginia. "Impassioned Prose." *TLS* (16 September 1926). Reprinted in Virginia Woolf, *Granite and Rainbow*. London: Hogarth Press, 1958. 32–40.
Woolford, John. *Browning the Revisionary*. New York: St. Martin's Press, 1988.
Wordsworth, Jonathan. "The Five-Book *Prelude* of Early Spring 1804." *Journal of English and Germanic Philology* 76 (1977): 1–25.
Wylie, Ian. *Young Coleridge and the Philosophers of Nature*. Oxford: Clarendon Press, 1989.
Yeats, W. B. "My First Meeting with Oscar Wilde." In *Oscar Wilde: Interview and Recollections*, edited by E. W. Mikhail. London: Macmillan, 1979.
Zaccaria, Paola. "*Fizzles* by Samuel Beckett: The Failure of the Dream of a Never-Ending Verticality." In *Rethinking Beckett*, edited by Lance St. John Butler and R. J. Davis. London: Macmillan, 1990. 105–23.
Zurbrugg, Nicholas. *Beckett and Proust*. Gerrards Cross: Colin Smythe; Totowa: Barnes & Noble Books, 1988.

Index

absent work, 37–39, 47, 60, 61–65, 200; in *Confessions* (De Quincey), 71, 73, 79, 87; in *Mercian Hymns* (Hill), 135; in Romantic aesthetics, 110, 137–38, 175
Aldington, Richard, 16, 139
allegory, 39–42, 211 n.27
Annwn, David, 128
apRoberts, Ruth, 143
arabesque, 100, 107–8, 124, 165. *See also* prose poem, thyrsus
Ash, John: and Baudelaire, 192–93; "The Big House," 201; "Early views of Manchester and Paris," 201; *The Goodbyes*, 201; "The Lecture," 192

Bakhtin, Mikhail: dialogism, 13
Barker, George: "The Jubjub Bird," 16–17
baroque art, 104, 108
Barth, Robert, 42
Barthes, Roland: *L'Empire des Signes*, 15; "langue" and "parole," 40; the readerly/writerly text, 103, 105, 107
Bartram, William: *Travels through North and South Carolina*, 52, 53, 54
Baudelaire, Charles, 35, 88–89, 152, 184, 191, 192, 203; *flâneur*, 92, 182, 199, 201; in history of prose poetry, 20, 21, 23, 41, 88–90, 94, 181–85; influenced by De Quincey, 88, 91–94, 97, 183; a new prose, 90, 183, 184; translates De Quincey, 19, 21, 71–72, 83, 87–97, 100. Works: "Anywhere Out of the World," 199; "Crowds" [Les Foules], 200; "Evening Twilight" [Le Crépescule du Soir], 93; *Les Fleurs du Mal*, 88; "The Looking-Glass" [Le Miroir], 150–51; "A Lost Halo" [Perte d'auréole], 183–84; *Un mangeur d'opium*, 72, 87–91, 93, 95, 96–97, 100; "Miss Lancet" [Mademoiselle Bistouri], 188; "Notes Nouvelles sur Edgar Poe," 101; "One O'Clock in the Morning," [A une Heure du matin], 36, 92; *Les Paradis artificiels*, 88, 89; *Poems in Prose* [*Le Spleen de Paris*] 19, 20, 101, 105–6, 183, 198, 202–4; "The Port" [Le Port], 110; "The Twofold Room" [La Chambre Double], 92, 188–89; "The Useless Glazier" [Le Mauvais Vitrier], 92, 188; "The Wand" [Le Thyrse], 100, 105–6, 147, 194, 223 n.45; "Windows" [Les Fenêtres], 191–92. *See also* city, prose poem
Baxter, Edmund, 105
Beaujour, Michel, 98
Beaumont, Sir George, 49
Beckett, Samuel, 16, 23, 24, 42, 46, 161–80, 203; biblical style, 19, 22, 139, 157–60; and Hopkins, 178, 249 n.66; and Hume, 163; and Proust, 23, 168–72, 178, 180. Works: "Afar a Bird,"158; "As the Story Was Told," 174–76, 178; "He is Barehead," 195; "Closed Space," 190; *Company*, 171,

175–79; "For To End Yet Again," 173, 195; "One Evening," 176, 177–78; *The Expelled*, 181; "La Falaise," 194–95, 198; (and Jasper Johns), *Foirades/Fizzles*, 98, 161, 162, 168, 169, 180, 202; "I Gave Up Before Birth,"158, 170; "Heard in the Dark," 176; *How It Is*, 161, 162, 166–68, 175, 178; *Ill Seen Ill Said*, 171, 175–79; "Imagination Dead Imagine," 161, 167; *L'Innomable*, 161, 162; "Lessness," 157, 158, 177, 179; *Molloy*, 244 n.20 (164); "Old Earth," 168, 173; "La Peinture des Van Velde," 169; "Ping," 167; "Proust,"168, 169–70, 171; "Proust in Pieces," 169; "Sounds," 161, 171, 173–74; "Still,"158–59, 171, 172–73, 174, 175; "Still 3,"171, 173–74; "*Text IV*," 242 n.82; "*Text IX*," 159, 160; "*Text XI*," 157; "*Text XII*," 166; *Texts for Nothing*, 157; "The Two Needs," 162; *Watt*, 163–65, 179; *Worstward Ho*, 171, 175–79
Bent, Ian, 108
Berlin, Adele, 154
Bernard, Suzanne: *Le Poème en Prose*, 18, 21, 186
Bertrand, Aloysius: *Gaspard de la Nuit*, 21, 89, 98
Beyer, Werner W., 50
Bible, 50, 62–64, 138, 141; *Authorized Version*, 138, 140, 141, 148, 155, 157; "Psalm 139," 139, 141–42, 148; Old Testament, 141, 149; New Testament, 63, 145.
biblical style, 62, 138–60, 232 n.3. *See also* Lowth, Robert
Bijou Literary Annual, 49, 54, 59
Blackwood's Edinburgh Magazine, 16, 79, 80
Blake, William, 22, 138, 182; and Lowth, 237–38 n.48; parallelisms in, 148–50, 239 n.58. Works: "Contemplation," 147; "The Couch of Death," 139, 147–50, 152; "Samson," 147
Blanchot, Maurice, "The *Athenaeum*," 36, 37

brevity: in Beckett, 169; in De Quincey, 100, 114; in *Mercian Hymns* (Hill), 119; Poe's aesthetics of, 101–2; in the prose poem, 98, 99, 103
Brown, Lee Rust, 44, 46, 211 n.27
Browne, Thomas, 144; *Religio Medici*, 181
Burke, Edmund, 79
Butor, Michel, 203; *Illustrations*, 98
Byron, George Gordon Lord, 53; letter from Coleridge, 53, 54, 56, 212 n.48

causation: in Beckett, 162–79; in De Quincey, 73–74, 107; Hume's theory of, 163–66, 167, 247 n.43; Kant's theory of, 73–74; necessary connection, 43, 166–68, 169, 171, 174
Caws, Mary Ann, 185
Charles, Michel, 105
city, 23, 181–206: Gothic architecture, 185, 190, 198; London, 92, 182, 196–97; Manchester, 201; Paris, 92, 181–82, 188, 191–92, 194, 198–99, 205; windows, 191–93
Clément, Bruno, 174
closure, 37, 93, 97, 135–36; in biblical style, 150, 155, 159–60; and the city, 187, 189, 190, 191, 195, 205
Coburn, Kathleen, 55, 56
Coleridge, E. H., 52, 53
Coleridge, Edward, 53, 59
Coleridge, Samuel Taylor, 21, 32, 76, 95, 138; letter to Byron, 54, 56; and Kant's "a priori," 42–43, 65; on prose and poetry, 42, 48, 146, 236 n.40; in Malta, 45, 56, 57, 59; marginal gloss, 43, 48, 120; notebooks, 50, 51, 53, 54; Raphael, 57–58; Sara Hutchinson, 59; supernaturalism, 60, 64–65; symbol and allegory, 40–41. Works: *Aids to Reflection*, 53, 59; "Allegoric Vision," 40–41; "The Ancient Mariner," 46, 48, 51–52, 120; *Biographia Literaria*, 47; "The Blossoming of the Solitary Date Tree," 44–48, 59, 61, 65, 119; "Christabel," 54; "Kubla Khan," 45, 46, 77; *Lay Sermons*, 41, 42; MSS

Egerton 2800 (*ff*1–1v), 66, 67, 68, 69–70; *Poetical Works*, 49, 53, 54, 59, 65; *The Wanderings of Cain*, 21, 44–47, 48, 49–70, 94, 139, 153
Connor, Steven, 241 n.76
context, 41, 99–101, 103–4, 108; in Beckett, 172, 178; in De Quincey, 82–83, 106–7, 115–16, 135; in *Mercian Hymns* (Hill), 118, 119, 124–131; privileged space, 185–86, 196, 206. *See also* disjunction
Croll, Morris, 143
Curious Architecture, A (eds. Rupert Loydell and David Miller), 202, 208 n.17

D'Annunzio, Gabriele: *Notturno*, 257 n.71
Dante: *The Divine Comedy*, 63, 160
de Man, Paul, 35
De Quincey, Thomas, 21, 71–97, 98, 100–109, 159, 182: and Baudelaire, 21, 71–72, 87–97; digression, 100, 104–5, 107–8, 127, 131; dreams and visions, 77–79, 80, 83, 84–85, 87; footnotes, 82, 84, 87, 89, 115–17, 127, 131; impassioned prose, 75, 82, 90; and prose poetry, 19, 71, 97, 98. Works: *Autobiographical Sketches*, 72, 80, 84; *Confessions of an English Opium-Eater*, 72–73, 75–76, 80, 83, 114; "The Daughter of Lebanon," 79, 139; *The English Mail-Coach*, 74, 79–80, 85, 98–100, 106–9; "German Studies and Kant in Particular," 73–74; "On the Knocking at the Gate in *Macbeth*," 114–15, 116, 189; "On Novels," 80; *Selections Grave and Gay*, 72, 80; "Style", 100; *Suspiria de Profundis*, 19, 77–78, 79–87, 88–89, 93–96, 103–4, 107, 120, 175; "System of the Heavens as Revealed by Lord Rosse's Telescopes," 74, 78–79; "Sir William Hamilton," 116. *See also* Baudelaire, translates De Quincey
Death of Abel, The (Gessner), 49, 50
Deleuze, Gilles, 172–73
Delville, Michel, 113, 226 n.21

Derrida, Jacques, 14, 200; *darstellung*, 43; *Truth in Painting*, 258 n.78
Descartes, René, 162, 163
diachronic, 104–5, 106
disjunction, 60, 114–17, 119, 120–24, 169
Divine Comedy, The (Dante), 63, 160
Dowson, Ernest, 16, 117; "The Fortunate Islands,"109–10, 113; "The Visit," 189; "The Princess of Dreams," 190–91; *Decorations*, 190, 205
Drain, Richard, 128

Eliot, George: *Address to Working Men by Felix Holt*, 121–22
Eliot, T. S., 184. Works: "The Borderline of Prose,"16, 138; "Hysteria," 16, 139, 205; *The Waste Land*, 128–29, 182; "What Dante Means to Me," 184

Faris, Wendy, 104
Fish, Stanley, 143
Fisher, Roy, 16, 17, 109, 203; *flâneur*, 198, 199, 201. Works: *City*, 198–99, 201, 202, 205; *The Cut Pages*, 202; *Stopped Frames and Set Pieces*, 111–13
Fredman, Stephen: *Poet's Prose*, 14–15, 24
fugal form, 108, 114
furtherance, 22–23, 152–54, 196, 205; in Beckett, 157–60, 161, 164, 171, 173, 180

Gascoyne, David: *Collected Poems 1988*, 17
genre: cultural differences, 15–17
Gessner, Salomon: *The Death of Abel*, 49, 50; *Daphnis*, 50
Gilbert, Sandra and Susan Gubar: *The Madwoman in the Attic*, 190
Grandin, John, 193
Gubar, Susan. *See* Gilbert, Sandra

Haffenden, John, 120, 124
Halsey, Alan: *The Art of Memory on Hay-on-Wye*, 201–2, 231 n.47; *The Text of Shelley's Death*, 130, 232 n.63
Hamilton, K. G., 141

Hamon, Philippe: "Texte et Architecture," 184, 200, 205
Hayter, William, 172
Hazlitt, William, 52, 214 n.64
Heaney, Seamus: *Stations*, 119; *Station Island*, 119
Hill, Geoffrey: 24, 120, 203; hefting and tuning, 121, 123. Works: "Poetry as 'Menace' and 'Atonement'", 120; *Mercian Hymns*, 16, 118–36, 202, 204; *New and Collected Poems*, 131; "September Song" (*King Log*), 134–35
Hobbes, Thomas, 118, 121, 125
Hopkins, Gerard Manley, 122, 145–46, 149, 154–55, 178; "Redeeming the Time," 121; "Rhythm," 145
Houssaye, Arsène, 183, 202
Hume, David: causation, 166, 167, 169, 172, 177; habit, 163, 170–71, 173, 179; necessary connection, 74, 163, 166, 167, 179, 180; and Proust, 170, 171; *A Treatise of Human Nature*, 163. *See also* memory
Huysmans, Joris-Karl, 102, 104, 106, 162; *Against Nature*, 102

implied context: in De Quincey, 105–7; definition of, 22, 99, 137; in *Mercian Hymns*, 119, 127–28; in prose poems, 109–14; in the city, 183, 191

Jacob, Max, 227 n.33
Jakobson, Roman, 14, 121, 124, 152, 154; contiguity disorder, 229 n.25; poetic function, 14, 146–47, 153; referential function, 14, 146; "Linguistics and Poetics," 146
Japp, Alexander H., 80
Johns, Jasper, 98, 247 n.45
Johnson, Barbara, 203; *The Critical Difference*, 255 n.42
Jones, R. F., 144, 234 n.25
Joyce, James, 165

Kafka, Franz, 185; windows, 191, 193. Works: *Amerika* (introduction), 195; "The Street Window," 193

Kant, Immanuel, 31–32, 34, 76; a priori, 34, 42; causation, 73–74
Keene, Dennis, ed.: *The Modern Japanese Prose Poem*, 15, 202
Kenner, Hugh, 116, 129
Knottenbelt, E. M., 122, 123
Kugel, James, 22–23, 152–54; *The Idea of Biblical Poetry*, 153
Kundera, Milan, 185, 195

labyrinth: unicursal/multicursal, 104
Lacoue-Labarthe, Philippe and Jean-Luc Nancy: *The Literary Absolute*, 36–37, 61. *See also* absent work
Lamb, Charles, 182
Lindop, Grevel, 76, 79
Locke, John, 74
Lodge, David, 41
Lowes, J. L.: *The Road to Xanadu*, 51
Lowth, Robert, 140–45, 148, 150, 233 n.15: parallelism, 22, 140, 142, 144, 145; primitivism, 142, 143–45, 148; *Sacred Poetry of the Hebrews*, 140–41, 142, 145

Macbeth (Shakespeare), 114–15, 116, 189
Macleod, Fiona. *See* Sharp, William
Macpherson, James: *The Poems of Ossian*, 144–45, 148, 186; and Coleridge, 213 n.50
Mallarmé, Stéphane, 105
McFarland, Thomas, 137
memory: in Ash, 201; in Baudelaire, 93–94; in Beckett, 171, 175, 180; and forgetting, 105, 173; in Halsey, 130, 201–2, 231 n.47; in Hume, 163, 170–71, 179; personal, 124–25, 201–2; in Proust, 171–72, 180
Merrill, Stuart, ed.: *Pastels in Prose*, 187, 202, 204
Meschonnic, Henri, 232 n.3
metonymy, 41, 152, 158, 196
Metzidakis, Samos, 13–14, 151
Miller, J. Hillis, 104
Modern Japanese Prose Poem, The (ed. Dennis Keene), 202; introduction to, 15

Monroe, Jonathan, 13, 36, 38, 113; *A Poverty of Objects*, 31, 205
Mueller, Janel, 155
Murphy, Margaritte, 113, 196; *A Tradition of Subversion*, 13, 14, 16
Musset, Alfred de: *L'Anglais mangeur d'opium*, 87–88

Nancy, Jean-Luc. *See* Lacoue-Labarthe, Philippe
Needham, John, 126, 127
North, Christopher. *See* Wilson, John

O'Beebee, Thomas, 15

palimpsest, 93–96, 174; and the thyrsus, 105–6, 107–8
paradox: in the prose poem, 14, 20, 22, 32, 37, 76, 106, 198–99
parallelism. *See* Lowth, Robert
Pater, Walter, 16; *Anders-streben*, 81
Perloff, Marjorie, 243 n.5, 249 n.67
Piette, Adam, 172–73
Pike, Burton, 184
Plato, 31–33, 34, 37, 40, 165
Plotinus: *Enneads*, 33, 35
Poe, Edgar Allan, 101–2
poetic function, 146, 151–52, 154, 158, 171, 172; in parallelism, 22–23, 147, 153
Pooley, Roger, 141, 144
probability, 164, 167
prose: and poetry, 20, 46–48, 82, 138, 152, 255 n.42; in seventeenth century, 141, 143–45, 234 n.25; in eighteenth century, 144
prose poem: allegory and symbol, 41–42; anthologies, 202; in art book, 98–99; blank space around, 99, 103, 114, 128, 135; the collection, 31, 71, 94–96, 105–6, 108, 120, 174, 183, 185, 200–201, 202–6; cultural differences, 14–17; and decadent literature, 250 n.76; earliest use of the term, 16; as 'essential oil of art' (Huysmans), 102, 104; *flâneur*, 92, 182, 198, 199; fragmentation, 36, 38, 39, 66, 111; as mythical beast, 16–17; new prose, 90, 184; not poetic prose, 21, 98, 147; refrain in, 186–87, 190, 195, 205; rejected by British writers, 17; as romantic genre, 16, 36–37, 38, 41–42, 44; structural boundaries, 35, 38, 187, 200, 205–6; subversive genre, 13, 14, 20; theories of, 13–16; thyrsus image, 88, 89–90, 92, 100, 105–6, 107–8, 196; as trompe l'oeil, 168, 191, 205; and usurper of privileged space, 46, 183, 185–86, 188–91, 204, 205–6
Proust, Marcel, 171–72, 180; *Remembrance of Things Past*, 168, 169–70, 178

referential function, 146, 171, 172; in parallelism, 22–23, 146
Remacle, Adrien, "The City," 187
Remembrance of Things Past (Proust), 168, 169–70, 178
repetition, 13–14, 104; in Beckett, 157, 158–60, 164, 173, 175; in biblical style, 153, 157, 179; Deleuze, 172–73; in De Quincey, 75, 83; memory, 173, 201–2; in *Mercian Hymns* (Hill), 133–34; refrain, 187; in Romantic aesthetic, 32, 36, 37. *See also* Lowth, parallelism
Revue contemporaine, 88, 89
Richter, Johann Paul (pseud. Jean Paul), 78
Ricks, Christopher, 116, 135
Riffaterre, Michael, 113
Rimbaud, Arthur, 98
Romanticism: critical fragments, 31, 71, 99, 111; collection of fragments, 31, 35–37, 38, 61; *darstellung*, 31, 35 36, 37, 38–39, 40, 61; fragmentation, 34–37, 39, 114, 137, 175, 185; in France, 181; Ideas, 31, 34, 37, 137–38, 178; project, 38, 87
Roston, Murray, 141
Ruskin, John, 197–98; *The Seven Lamps of Architecture*, 197; *The Stones of Venice*, 197

Sabin, Margery, 181

Schlegel, Friedrich, 31, 36, 38 65; *Athenaeum* fragments, 36, 37, 38; *Critical Fragments*, 39; *Ideas*, 50. See also Blanchot, Maurice
Sharp, William (pseud. Fiona Macleod), *The Silence of Amor*, 16
Shelley, Percy Bysshe, 95
Silliman, Ron, 225 n.11, 236 n.39
Simon, John, 16, 21
Smart, Christopher, 149; *Jubilate Agno*, 148–49
Sonnenfeld, Albert, 187
Sprat, Thomas: *History of the Royal Society*, 144
subversion, genre founded on, 13–14
Sultana, David, 55, 56
symbol and allegory, 39–42
synchronic, 104–5, 106
synecdoche, 41, 180

Tait's magazine, 73, 74
Terdiman, Richard: *Discourse/Counter-Discourse*, 14
Todorov, Tzvetan, 20
Tomlinson, Charles, 17, 24, 99, 193. Works: "The Near and the Far," (*The Flood*), 205; "A Process," 195; "Oppositions," 194; "Poem," 195; "Skullshapes," 195; "Tout Entouré de Mon Regard," 193–94, 198; *The Way of a World*, 193
Traherne, Thomas: *Centuries of Meditation*, 181, 235 n.33

translation: in nineteenth-century France, 89
Trieloff, Barbara, 178
Turgenev, Ivan: *Poems in Prose*, 257 n.70

Vadé, Yves, 18, 20
Vickers, Brian, 143
Villalobos, John C., 237 n.48

"waw"/ "and" parataxis, 154–56, 240 n.68
Weil, Simone, 125
Wesling, Donald, 19, 195, 251 n.11
Wheeler, Kathleen, 39, 45
Wieland, Christoph Martin, *Oberon*, 50
Wilde, Oscar, 16, 109, 117, 142, 205. Works: "The Artist," 138, 139–40, 147, 154; "The Disciple," 109, 151; "The Doer of Good," 155; "The Master," 155–56
Wilson, John (pseud. Christopher North), "Winter Rhapsody," 16
Woolf, Virginia: "Impassioned Prose," 82
Wordsworth, William, 16, 77, 138, 154, 184, 196–97, 198; collaboration on *Cain* project, 49, 50, 51, 58; spots of time, 73, 76. Works: "Composed Upon Westminster Bridge," 197; "Ode: Intimations of Immortality," 121; Preface to *Lyrical Ballads*, 142, 182; *Prelude*, 56, 58, 182, 196–97
Wulf, Stäuble-Lipman, Michèle, 92